Government and Business

DATE DUE

AUG 2 7 2013	
DEC 1 3 2015	

Government and Business
American Political Economy in Comparative Perspective

Second Edition

Richard Lehne
Rutgers, The State University of New Jersey

CQ PRESS

A Division of Congressional Quarterly Inc., Washington, D.C.

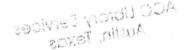

CQ Press
1255 22nd Street, NW, Suite 400
Washington, DC 20037

Phone: 202-729-1900; toll-free, 1-866-427-7737 (1-866-4CQ-PRESS)

Web: www.cqpress.com

Typeset by Circle Graphics, Columbia, MD
Cover design by Diane Buric Design Illustration
Cover photos by Getty Images and Super Stock Inc.

∞ The paper used in this publication exceeds the requirements of the American National Standard for Information Sciences—Permanence of Paper for Printed Library Materials, ANSI Z39.48-1992.

Printed and bound in the United States of America

09   08   07   06   05   1   2   3   4   5

Library of Congress Cataloging-in-Publication Data

Lehne, Richard.
    Government and business : American political economy in comparative perspective / Richard Lehne.— 2nd ed.
        p. cm.
    Includes bibliographical references and index.
    ISBN 1-933116-05-6 (alk. paper)
  1. Industrial policy. 2. Industrial policy—United States. I. Title.

    HD3611.L45 2006
    338.973—dc22   2005023464

To
Henry Lehne,
in profound admiration for his great skills
in balancing business and governance

Contents

Tables, Figures, and Boxes

Tables

Boxes

Preface

THERE IS NOTHING inevitable about the linkages between government and the economy. A nation's political and economic arrangements are not the result of irresistible forces but of myriad societal decisions that reflect its understanding of how best to achieve material well-being and secure its other political and social goals. In this book I argue that the success of a country's economy depends ultimately on the quality of its political judgments, and I maintain that the best way to analyze the American political economy is to investigate government, business, and the complex yet subtle relationships between these two institutions.

Instructors responsible for courses that explore politics and the economy face a difficult assignment. They need to assess the conduct of an especially dynamic collection of institutions in an exceptionally tumultuous age. Doctrines and conceptual formulations that not long ago seemed to convey the essence of the American experience suddenly seem terribly inadequate. Fifteen years ago instructors explained why the U.S. economy was in the doldrums; now they must account for why it has recovered so substantially. I address this subject by examining the environment that shapes government-business relations, investigating corporate activities in the political arena, and appraising public policies affecting business. The book covers politics and policy fully, yet it is sufficiently concise to be used as a core text that allows instructors to emphasize the approaches they prefer.

The cross-national comparisons to be found here acknowledge the increasingly international scope of economic activity, and they provide a framework for sophisticated discussions that can help students escape the confines of American practices and policies. I have drawn upon contemporary events to convey the excitement of relations between the government and the economy, and I have listed Web sites at the end of each chapter to guide students toward updated information and further analyses of controversial issues.

This book owes much to the students who have enrolled in the Rutgers Government and Business course in past years. They forced me to reexamine questions and reconsider answers more often than I sometimes appreciated, but the result has been constructive. They have led me to avoid jargon and make this book accessible to readers who have not majored in political science or economics.

Raymond H. Bateman and John R. Mullen have taken breaks from their distinguished careers to play a vital role in the book's development. They have demonstrated to thousands of Rutgers students that the relationship between government and business is a compelling topic that warrants the serious attention of citizens, public officials, business leaders, and scholars alike. As American society becomes more complex and the global environment more challenging, I have sought in this book to continue their efforts to promote a fuller understanding of the conditions that promote political and economic success.

Numerous guests from government and business visited with the students over the years and shared their insights and experiences: John Degnan, Richard T. Dewling, Dale J. Florio, Gov. James Florio, Steve Forbes, Bob Franks, Mark Grier, Alfred Griffith, Constance Hughes, Gov. Thomas H. Kean, Jane Kenny, Jaynee LaVecchia, Francis L. Lawrence, Gualberto Medina, Dean Paranicas, Stewart Pollock, John P. Sheridan, Baron Hans-Heinrich Freiherr von Stackelberg, Herbert H. Tate, Richard T. Thigpen, Sen. Robert Torricelli, and Gov. Christine Todd Whitman. I appreciate their generosity and have benefited from their analyses. This book would not have been possible without the efforts of scholars whose work is quoted and cited in the following pages. I have used the conclusions of their research for my own purposes, but I trust that I have not abused the integrity of their work in the process.

In crafting the second edition of this book, I have had the good fortune of working with a wonderfully talented team assembled by CQ Press: Charisse Kiino, Colleen Ganey, Erin Long, Belinda Josey, and Joanne S. Ainsworth of Ainsworth Editorial Services. I richly admired and deeply benefited from the professionalism of their work. I have benefited as well from the insightful comments and helpful suggestions of Jeffrey E. Cohen, Terrence Guay, Jonathan Hiskey, G. Zhiyong Lan, Niels Christian Siderius, and James Anderson and numerous other reviewers who mounted valiant albeit only partially successful efforts to save me from the errors of my ways.

This book is dedicated to Henry Lehne, whose intellect, generosity of spirit, and achievements in both business and government continue to be an inspiration in all that I do.

New Spotlight on an Enduring Topic

FUNDAMENTAL CHANGES ARE taking place in the relationship between government and business in the United States and around the globe as the world settles into the twenty-first century. Political developments, economic trends, and emerging values have challenged the governmental arrangements that shaped the world's economies in the post–World War II era. Although the institutions that guided the American economy have achieved remarkable success, how or even whether these institutions can adapt to the realities of a new global economy is still uncertain.

Debates about the role of government in the economy are both passionate and enduring. They are conducted in academic lecture halls as well as in the daily lives of citizens, companies, and government agencies. The enterprise implicit in these debates is actually *an exercise in social problem solving*. The goal is to design a governmental regime that will respect the country's political choices, promote its economic well-being, and enrich its cultural life.

Evidence of new thinking about the relationship between government and industry has appeared at every turn. Doctrines that were once the mainstay of government policy toward business have been subjected to new scrutiny: trade regimes have been reshaped; antitrust doctrines redefined; government regulation reformed; and industrial policies revised. The United States, policy analysts maintain, must rethink its assumptions about the responsibilities of government and business if it is to defend its political values and economic status in the years ahead.

Students of business administration contend that a fundamentally new "social compact" between business and society has been forged. Business organizations can no longer be evaluated simply in economic terms; businesses are now responsible for helping society achieve a broad range of societal objectives.

Economists have concluded that contemporary multinational, multiproduct enterprises are more self-sufficient than firms of past eras. Technological and organizational innovations have increased corporate autonomy, confounded governmental efforts to control corporate behavior, and transformed conventional ties between business and the state.

Finally, students of politics were impressed by the ability of Germany, Japan, and the nations of Southeast Asia to devise policies in the 1960s and 1970s that enhanced their political stature and economic well-being. In the United States, these decades were a period of both government activism and economic stagnation, but the revival of the country's economy in the 1990s had surprisingly little to do with government policy. The desire to draw appropriate lessons from these events has led political scientists to reexamine public policies toward business and to reconsider the nexus between the economy and the state.

It is time to take stock of contemporary relations between government and business. Government is viewed in this book not as an impediment to a nation's goals but as a tool for accomplishing those goals. It is acknowledged here, however, that tools can be used more effectively in some circumstances than in others. Governmental arrangements and corporate structures are unendingly diverse, but there are no handbooks for creating a country's economic and political system. In designing national business systems, there are no permanent solutions and no final victories.

As countries have responded to discrete problems, acting from their own traditions and resources, bonds between government and business have been forged. This book focuses on government-business relationships in the United States, but it also includes comparisons between U.S. behaviors and institutions and those in Great Britain, Germany, and Japan. Great Britain is included in the analysis because it was the world's first industrial nation, and the United States, Japan, and Germany are examined because they are the world's three leading national economies. These nations reflect different varieties of capitalism, have followed different paths of development, and present different governmental and political arrangements. Comparisons among these countries help us identify the critical features of various political and economic systems, and a comparative analysis permits us to assess the theories that have been proposed to explain how these systems function.

This book's analysis sometimes places the behaviors and institutions of our four countries beside the inchoate structures and practices of the European Union (EU). The European Union is a governmental organization composed of twenty-five European states. Through five decades EU institutions have been gradually gaining governmental authority, and they may eventually replace the individual nations as the continent's basic governing structure. European integration, however, is an uneven process. European traditions are still being defined, and EU institutions have greater impact in some policy areas than in others. In examining topics in which EU policies and practices are significant, I have included both European and national dimensions in the comparisons.

In other cases, I rest the analysis on an examination of Germany, Great Britain, Japan, and the United States.

Developing countries throughout the world are catching up with the traditional leaders, and it is important to consider how these nations address issues of business-government relations. In ten of the following chapters, boxes provide a first view of how Brazil, China, India, Mexico, or South Korea has dealt with a topic examined in the chapter. In some cases, these boxes indicate how a conventional issue has evolved in a major developing nation, and in other instances the examples demonstrate that events in the developing world sometimes take on their own unique identity.

At one period or another, each of our four industrial countries has been a star in the world's economy. Each created a business system that became a model for other nations, and each achieved a level of prosperity beyond the reach of a large majority of the world's citizens. As Thomas McCraw points out, however, each of these nations also has episodes in its history that are anything but admirable.[1] Great Britain treated some people in its empire cruelly, Japan committed atrocities against people in the lands it occupied before and during World War II, the United States permitted the enslavement of African Americans, and during the Nazi era Germany organized the mass murder of millions of its citizens and others who came under its control. Although in this book I investigate contemporary relations between the state and the economy, McCraw reminds us that these events occurred in capitalist countries. They were not the direct result of capitalism, but these countries certainly did not prevent these tragedies from happening.

In this book I examine the relationship between government and business today and consider how this association may develop in the future. I explore the environment in which relations between government and business take place, the strategies adopted by business to influence government actions, and public policies that bind business to the state.

Part I of the book contains an examination of the context in which relations between government and business are shaped. The history of government and business provides the foundation for the practices we see today. What role did government play in promoting economic development in the early years of U.S. history? How has the nature of government and business changed over the decades, and what are the implications of these changes? What features of the country's political heritage result from its formative period, and what lessons do these events offer to those seeking to design a constructive relationship between government and business for the future? What were the hallmarks of industrial development in comparable countries? These questions are addressed in chapter 1.

Countries design their governing arrangements to help them secure their political, economic, and social goals. There are as many ways of creating government-business relationships as there are countries. In chapter 2 I first examine the analytic models scholars have devised to describe the relations between business and the state, and I then consider the political and economic functions performed by the U.S. government in different eras. To appreciate more fully the magnitude of the task of designing relations between government and business, chapter 2 also includes capsule views of the British, European Union, German, and Japanese political-economic systems.

The American national government is composed of large institutions that possess their own incentives and dynamics. In chapter 3 I scrutinize the major institutions and operations of government and compare them to the government institutions in Germany, Great Britain, and Japan. I assess the assertion that governments in other countries are better able to manage government-business relations than is government in the United States. I also examine the governing institutions of the European Union.

Modern corporations possess distinct legal and organizational arrangements, and these features of firms constitute their systems of corporate governance. Corporate America has been rocked by a series of financial scandals that have called into question the governing arrangements for U.S. companies. How are corporate scandals related to systems of corporate governance? What roles are played by owners, workers, managers, and institutional investors in guiding corporations? Do American corporate leaders possess a management style that harms U.S. competitiveness in the international marketplace? How do the features of the U.S. system of corporate governance compare with those found in other countries? I consider these questions in chapter 4, and I also investigate the structures and practices that American firms devised for managing public affairs programs in the United States and in other countries.

Perhaps the most far-reaching change in the environment for conducting relations between government and industry in recent decades is the internationalization of the American economy. Today, essentially all major American firms are active in foreign markets, and most must defend domestic market share against international competitors. The growth of the global economy is said to have reduced the ability of the American government to fashion its own programs and pursue its own policy goals. In chapter 5 I assess the emergence of the global marketplace, explore the features and strategies of multinational firms, and investigate various types of capitalism.

Corporations are active in both the marketplace and the political arena. Part 2 of this book includes an investigation of companies' involvement in politics and an exploration of their strategies for affecting public policies. Government-business relations reflect a nation's system of public opinion and its structure of interest representation. Chapter 6 focuses on this advocacy environment. How trusting or how skeptical of business are Americans? What are the bases of their judgments? What changes have occurred in the advocacy environment in recent decades, and how do these changes affect the activities of labor unions and citizen groups? How has the media affected relations between business and the state?

The relationship between business and government in a democracy is an uneasy one. The position of business rests upon values that contradict the ethos of popular rule. In chapter 7 I examine the legal status of business as a political actor and review the debate about the proper role of business in politics. I also analyze the activities of business associations in the United States and compare U.S. business associations with organizations in other countries. What roles do industry groups play in the European Union, Germany, Great Britain, and Japan, and why do some analysts argue that these groups are more successful than their U.S. counterparts?

As government influence over business has become more pervasive in recent decades, business efforts to influence government decisions have multiplied. Influencing government decisions has become a growth industry that focuses on officeholders, election campaigns, and party behavior. Chapter 8 includes an analysis of business efforts to lobby Congress and participate in electoral politics. I assess the circumstances in which businesses are active, the tactics and strategies used by business interests, and the advantages and handicaps of defending producer positions. Industry also seeks to shape policy by affecting the actions of administrative agencies and the adjudication of issues by the courts. Activities directed toward these institutions are probably more numerous and may be more significant than business contacts with legislatures and chief executives.

In chapter 9 I assess business participation in politics by scrutinizing the role played by political parties in the various countries. I also draw together findings from the earlier chapters and review recent research to investigate not only why businesses win in politics but also why they may lose. I probe relations between government and business in a concrete setting by examining the rise and fall of a prominent corporation, AT&T.

In an exploration of developments in six policy areas, part 3 of this book documents the significance of the ties between government and business. The economy is a production and distribution system that affects not only producers and consumers but also communities and governments. In chapter 10 I review the history of U.S. government efforts to manage economic policy and investigate the government institutions that undertake that responsibility. I also explore the challenges posed by changing economic circumstances and survey the debates about government action in a neoliberal age.

Regulation assumes different meanings in different contexts, but there is no doubt that regulation is one of government's most influential tools in guiding business behavior. In chapter 11 the different modes of regulation are discussed and their rationale, enactment, and implementation assessed. The contest between regulation and deregulation has been a critical feature of government policy toward business in the past two decades. An investigation of developments in the telecommunications sector both explicates the features of this controversy and outlines various national styles of regulation. The growth of the global economy and the dynamism of new technologies have returned antitrust issues to a critical position in the relationship between government and business. In chapter 12 are, first, an explanation of the origins, character, and evolution of the American antitrust tradition and then, through an examination of cases from the computer industry, an analysis of current antitrust issues. Other countries approach antitrust issues on the basis of other goals and assumptions, and this chapter offers a comparison of their approaches with the American tradition.

The United States is much more involved with industrial policies than is usually recognized. Examples of the use of government authority to promote specific industries are found in the histories of the railroad, housing, computer, health care, and airline industries. In chapter 13 I investigate the history of industrial policies in the United States and in our other countries and consider the role of such policies domestically and in the increasingly competitive global economy.

The economist Paul Krugman has recently argued that it is now more important than ever before that students of politics understand the principles of international trade.[2] In chapter 14 I outline the logic of the arguments for liberal trade policies and examine the appeal of protectionism. I survey the changes that have occurred in the international trading system in recent decades and the impact these changes have had on traditional doctrines and policies. Important institutional structures and trading blocks have appeared in recent years, and the chapter concludes with an assessment of the prospects for these policy developments.

Businesses do not exist in a social vacuum. They are part of the broader society, and they are affected by a country's general policies. In chapter 15 I examine the relationship between business and social policy. What are the consequences for business of social policies? How does the country decide whether business or government is responsible for certain social programs? How is the relationship between industry and social policy likely to develop in the next decade?

The relationship between business and government inspires more heated rhetoric in the United States than in any other major country. The stature afforded business in the United States reflects the judgment that quasi-independent businesses provide the society greater benefits than firms that are tightly controlled by government. This policy judgment, however, is a complex one that reflects past events as well as current institutional developments, global trends, and societal expectations. Today's judgments about the balance between industry and government are not shared by everyone in the society, and they are certainly not permanent.

Judgments about government-business relations are continually reappraised as values change and events transpire. My goal in this book is to provide a framework that clarifies the nexus between politics and the economy. I seek less to promote doctrines than to identify issues and present analyses. My principal objective will be realized when readers begin to reach their own conclusions and make their own contributions to shaping the relationship between government and business for the decades ahead. The exercise in social problem solving continues.

NOTES

1. Thomas K. McCraw, ed., *Creating Modern Capitalism: How Entrepreneurs, Companies, and Countries Triumphed in Three Industrial Revolutions* (Cambridge, Mass.: Harvard University Press, 1997), 7.
2. Paul Krugman, *Pop Internationalism* (Cambridge, Mass.: MIT Press, 1996), 117.

Government and Business

PART I

Environment for Government-Business Relations

CHAPTER 1

Origins of Government and Business

GOVERNMENT HAS BEEN an influential factor in the American economy in every period of the nation's history. From the beginning the United States has had natural resources that other major nations lacked, a deep-rooted entrepreneurial tradition, and a large domestic market. These have given it an advantage over other industrializing nations. What has distinguished the United States from other nations, however, has been the ability of the American government to enact public policies that assisted economic growth and promoted industrial development.

The history of public policy in the United States is sometimes described as a chronicle of government responses to economic change.[1] Advocates of new manufacturing technologies, improvements in transportation, and innovations in communications all struggled against established interests defending the status quo. The results of contests between the old and the new not only altered the nation's economic practices but also transformed the country's social and political life.

A review of the nation's economic history sheds important light on the relationship between government and business today. An assessment of the activities of government in past eras helps us judge contemporary proposals for government action. An awareness of the changes that have occurred in business organization helps us appraise the corporate innovations taking place around the world today. An understanding of the evolution of American legal doctrine clarifies the legal choices now being made in the United States and other countries.

When we investigate historical occurrences, we must scrutinize past controversies carefully. Many terms and concepts used today have been around for centuries, but their meanings have changed substantially. Institutions as central to the economy as *government, business,* and *law* have been reformed from generation to generation, and an awareness of past changes in these institutions is needed to appreciate the significance of present-day events.

In this chapter I examine the role of government, the nature of industrial organization, and developments in legal doctrine in three historical periods: colonial times to 1860; the Civil War to the Great Depression of the 1930s; and the depression to the year 2005.[2] Because each country industrializes in its own way, I also explore the process of industrialization in Great Britain, Germany, and Japan.

By surveying critical features of past eras and other nations, we are better able to address the challenge of designing a constructive relationship between government and business for the years ahead.

COLONIAL TIMES TO 1860: LEGAL FOUNDATIONS OF BUSINESS

After the American Revolution, the former colonies were faced with the task of creating an economy that could survive outside the British Empire. In establishing their political and economic institutions, the founders of the new nation drew upon two distinct intellectual traditions: the market-oriented tradition associated with Adam Smith, and the active government tradition advocated by Alexander Hamilton.

The Role of Government

It is one of history's great coincidences that the Declaration of Independence and Adam Smith's *Wealth of Nations* appeared in the same year, 1776. Smith believed that a government could never be knowledgeable enough or impartial enough to manage a country's economy successfully. Because the state lacked these qualities, Smith argued that nonintervention by the state in economic matters was generally the wisest policy. This analytic tradition emphasized the advantages of freely operating markets and praised the decentralized decisions that markets permitted. Smith's viewpoint, however, was not the dominant opinion of his age. He opposed the prevailing sentiment that government should direct a nation's economic life. When the colonial leaders debated the structure of government and the economy, they accepted Smith's advice, but they also drew guidance from the activist tradition of government associated with mercantilism.

Mercantilism was the economic theory that guided British policy toward colonial America.[3] According to mercantilism, wealth was conceived as a stockpile of treasure gathered from neighbors or colonies. Government, under this policy, should control all aspects of economic activity in order to increase the wealth, unity, and power of the state.

During the colonial era British trade regulations were designed to benefit the home country. Britain limited manufacturing in the colonies, restricted the colonies to the role of producers of raw materials, and confined colonial trade to the vessels and ports of the British Empire. Until the 1750s, the colonies derived more benefits than burdens from the British mercantile system. They found British markets for their goods, received protection from the British navy for their shipping, and obtained British capital to develop their economies. The growth of the colonial economies and the increased rigor with which Britain enforced trade restrictions in the 1760s were factors that contributed to the outbreak of the American Revolution.

Two plans from the early decades of U.S. history underline the influence of mercantilist assumptions by advocating an expansive role for government in economic development. Alexander Hamilton's *Report on the Encouragement and Protection of Manufactures* in 1791 urged the national government to aid fledgling industries by providing economic assistance and tariff protection. A quarter century later, Henry Clay and John Calhoun devised a plan, christened the "American System," that would boost economic development through a combination of tariff protection and federally funded public works projects. Although the national government did not fully embrace either plan, Congress enacted numerous tariffs to promote new industries, and most of the other proposals were implemented by state governments.[4]

It was common in these years for states and municipalities to own stock in private companies that operated turnpikes, bridges, and canals.[5] The city of Baltimore supplied the money to found the Baltimore & Ohio Railroad, and it then retained stock in the company. The state of Pennsylvania owned one-third of the capital of the Bank of Pennsylvania, and the Pennsylvania Railroad was literally the railroad of the state of Pennsylvania. Government ownership of private companies aroused opposition when firms lost money, and the practice was curtailed after the Panic of 1837, when states had to appropriate funds to pay off company debts.

States and localities in these years subsidized specific industries and regulated exports, product quality, weights and measures, and agricultural harvests.[6] These programs demonstrate that both the activist and the limited government traditions were common in the early decades of the American experience.

Business Organization

Most Americans in these years were in business for themselves—they were entrepreneurs rather than employees. The United States was still a rural society, and as late as 1850, 20 million of the 23 million Americans lived in rural areas. The great majority were farmers, and most owned the farms they worked. Those who manufactured goods did so by hand at home or in small shops.[7]

Although the economy grew substantially in preindustrial America, little change occurred in the nature of the firm. Most enterprises were single-unit businesses managed by their owners and employing fewer than fifty people.[8] Before 1840 much of the stimulus for development came from Atlantic trade and favored East Coast cities. After 1840 the growth of the American market and lower per-unit production costs encouraged capitalists to turn from international trade to the domestic market. The American West benefited from this trend, and population in the new states soared.[9]

Legal Doctrine

Legal developments in this era probably had a more enduring impact on relations between government and industry than developments in the political or economic sphere. American law emphasized individual liberties and limited government action, and it provided more support for business expansion than legal systems in other countries. Befitting a new nation, the American legal system possessed an innovative spirit and a vitality that was unmatched in other lands.[10]

Three specific legal developments made essential contributions to economic development: the definition of property rights, the emergence of corporations as business entities, and government enforcement of the terms of contracts.

Economic growth requires stable commercial relationships, but the American Revolution, like most wars, had loosened the bonds of society. During the 1780s, political disorder, fears of social disintegration, and growing concern over the security of property were common in American states.[11]

Such concerns led states to adopt new constitutions that safeguarded the value of the currency, guaranteed payment of the public debt, and protected private property. These actions also contributed ideas to the drafting of the U.S. Constitution and the Bill of Rights. The Fifth Amendment to the Constitution stated, "No person shall be . . . deprived of life, liberty, or property, without due process of law; nor shall private property be taken for public use without just compensation." These guarantees reduced the risks of enterprise and encouraged entrepreneurs to undertake projects that furthered economic development.

Today, discussions of property rights might be construed as defenses of privilege and attacks on democracy. In the eighteenth century, property was viewed differently. Whereas property rights today are often seen to limit political and social rights, in the eighteenth century property rights were the foundation of political rights. In that era, the notion of property was associated with the workplace. Property provided sustenance, and people's livelihood would be threatened if government seized their property. When the possession of property became a right that government could not revoke, people were able to enjoy political freedom and promote the country's development.[12]

The second legal innovation in this era was the emergence of the corporation as a form of business organization. A corporation is a legal entity that can own property, transact business, sue others, and be sued itself. During the colonial and early national periods, corporations operated under special charters granted by state legislatures. Corporate charters were granted to organizations providing public benefits in such areas as charity, religion, or education.[13]

As the economy evolved, private firms began to sell goods and services that improved people's lives. Even though the owners sought to make a profit, their firms received corporate charters because their products offered "public benefits," such as banking services, textiles, or glass. Until the Civil War, corporate charters listed a firm's activities and identified the benefits it was supposed to provide to the public.[14]

In this period, the corporation was a more popular form of economic organization in the United States than in other countries.[15] Some historians argue that the popularity of the corporate form resulted from its "democratic" rather than its economic character. Indeed, corporate status extended economic and legal stability to all citizens, not just the few who received special favors from government. The democratic nature of the corporate form was confirmed by the enactment of general incorporation laws in the middle of the nineteenth century that normalized the incorporation process.[16]

The third major legal innovation was government enforcement of contractual obligations. Stability in economic relationships was the goal of several clauses in the U.S. Constitution. Article I, section 10, stipulated, "No state shall . . . pass any . . . law impairing the obligation of contracts."

Chief Justice John Marshall became a vigorous champion of the obligations of contracts.[17] He insisted that state governments as well as private individuals must comply with contractual provisions. *Dartmouth College v. Woodward* nominally involved control of the records and seal of the college.[18] Dartmouth was founded under a colonial charter from King George III in 1769. In 1816 a dissident group seeking to take over the assets of the college persuaded the New Hampshire legislature to enlarge the board of trustees and give it control. The New Hampshire Supreme Court approved the acts of the legislature, but John Marshall wrote for the U.S. Supreme Court that a charter was a contract and the provisions of a contract could not be altered by a state legislature. This decision reinforced the sanctity of a contract and protected corporations from legislative interference.

Whereas this ruling stressed the obligations to fulfill a contract, the decision in *Charles River Bridge v. Warren Bridge* in 1837 held that community welfare could not be ignored in assessing the meaning of a contract.[19] A corporation chartered to build and operate a toll bridge sought to invalidate a subsequent Massachusetts law that authorized the construction of a rival bridge. Even though the new legislation was said to violate the older contract, the U.S. Supreme Court upheld the law and ruled that no legislative charter could confer powers that harmed the public welfare. In this decision, the Supreme Court insisted that contracts must be interpreted and private economic activity conducted within the standards of community interest.

Legal doctrines from this era provided the foundation for the country's development. Some commentators emphasize the political dimensions of these principles, and others stress their economic motivations. In fact, such sharp distinctions were less visible in the eighteenth century than they are today. Property rights found special favor in the Constitution, but the nature of property in the eighteenth century made this almost a populist action. Corporations were permitted to become significant business entities, but corporations originally had public service obligations. Courts defended the integrity of contractual relationships, but such decisions also compelled government to honor the terms of its own agreements. In each of these instances, democratic values shaped the legal doctrines that became the foundation of relations between government and business.

As an economic document, the Constitution provided the basic framework for commercial activity. In addition to protecting property and providing a basis for enforcing contracts, it authorized the national government to impose taxes, establish a currency, borrow money, regulate commerce, and protect intellectual property, all provisions that contributed to the nation's economic success. At the same time, however, the Constitution left unresolved issues of slavery, race, gender, and the status of Indians, all topics that would do substantial harm in the decades ahead.

THE RISE OF MODERN INDUSTRY: 1860–1929

Between the Civil War and the stock market crash of 1929, the United States experienced an industrial revolution. The country was transformed from a sparsely populated agricultural society into the leading industrial and manufacturing power in the world. The Jeffersonian image of an agrarian, individualistic America receded, and an America characterized by the factory system, the closing of the frontier, robber barons, big cities, and labor conflict emerged to take its place.

Business Organization

Industrialization occurred in the United States fifty years later than in Great Britain but about fifty years before it took place in Japan.[20] The pace of economic growth had accelerated in the Civil War years because of improvements in transportation, the availability of energy sources, and increased productivity in agriculture. More important than simple growth, however, were changes that occurred in the structure of the economy.

These decades witnessed a revolution in production technologies and the development of the factory system.[21] Power-driven machinery, continuous processing, and the interchangeability of parts became the order of the day, and the American economy became noted for its high-volume and low-cost production.[22] U.S. firms at this time benefited from the large American domestic market whereas trade barriers made it difficult for firms from other nations to sell their goods internationally.[23] The new techniques of mass production reduced the role of the solitary craftsman. By 1900, 60 percent of the country's workers were employed in industry, and the typical worker now faced the dependency and regimentation characteristic of a "labor force."[24]

The size of individual businesses also increased dramatically during this era. The Civil War had given the country a model of large-scale military organization, and the country's economic institutions soon adopted comparable organizational forms.[25] Instead of a few dozen employees, companies would employ first hundreds, then thousands, and then tens of thousands of workers. The United States, in fact, was the first nation to have its economy dominated by large firms, and their size allowed U.S. manufacturers to become more efficient than their international competitors. Close relations between large firms and major universities also provided business rapid access to new and emerging technologies.

American railroads became the nation's first big businesses.[26] They were, for a time, the largest economic organizations in the world. In the late 1880s, when no manufacturer had more than 2,000 employees, the Pennsylvania Railroad employed 50,000 workers. By the time the federal government came to employ 50,000 civilian workers, some individual railroad companies already had more than 100,000 employees. Railroads also faced the era's most demanding management problems: unprecedented size, enormous capital requirements, and the technical and political problems of route planning and land acquisition.[27]

The factory system and the industrial revolution permitted sharp increases in productivity and extraordinary declines in wholesale prices. Between the end of the Civil War and 1890, one index of wholesale prices declined by more than 50 percent.[28] To reduce operating costs, many American firms assembled inside their own organization various stages of production, from gathering and transporting raw materials, through product design and mass production, to mass marketing. "Vertical integration," as it was called, increased efficiency by increasing predictability in the production, reducing profits of other firms, and permitting economies of scale—the reduction in per-unit production costs that usually accompanies increases in the number of units manufactured.

Technological innovations in this era soon resulted in more production capacity than was needed. Agreements among firms to limit production, set prices, and divide markets appeared immediately after the Civil War, but these agreements were soon outlawed by Congress. About 1880, restrictive arrangements began to be replaced by "trusts," in which companies surrendered the stock of their firms to trustees, who operated them for their mutual benefit. The Standard Oil Company was the nation's first important trust. It was broken up by the Ohio Supreme Court in 1892 but then reorganized under New Jersey law. When consolidated companies proved to be even more profitable than trusts, a wave of horizontal mergers—mergers among firms making the same product—followed in such industries as steel, copper, rubber, and tobacco. As a consequence of these horizontal mergers, individual companies at the end of the nineteenth century controlled a larger share of the market in a wider range of industries than at any other time in the nation's history.[29]

The spectacular growth in the size of American companies led to the emergence of professional managers who succeeded the entrepreneurial "captains of industry" who had founded major firms.[30] Corporations developed central managements with departments for finance, transportation, marketing, personnel, research and development, accounting, planning, and, later, advertising. The United States, in fact, pioneered university-based management education, with the first program endowed in 1883, and this too helped American firms pull ahead of competitors from other nations.[31]

In this period, fundamental changes occurred in the structure and performance of the American economy. The turbulence of the era also challenged the traditional role of government in American society.

The Role of Government

Government in the post–Civil War decades played a focused version of the promotional role it had adopted previously. In addition to imposing tariffs to protect domestic industries, Congress encouraged the development of railroads by providing massive land grants to support new construction. By the end of the century, it had given 131 million acres of land to assist private rail promoters, and the state governments had granted an additional 49 million acres.[32] The national government also appropriated public lands to promote scientific agriculture by supporting the establishment of land-grant colleges and agricultural experiment stations in each state.

In this era, government began to devise public policy responses to the new corporate economy. The replacement of the series of regional economies by a continent-wide economy sparked fierce resentment of corporate behemoths. The transformation of workers from independent entrepreneurs into salaried employees led to rancorous and sometimes violent labor-management disputes over wages, working conditions, and job security. Building a national market also resulted in the destruction of numerous local markets and the collapse of small businesses that had served these markets. The bitterness of the owners and employees of these businesses and the hostility of farmers combined to ignite a prairie revolt against corporations. The growth of national companies also alienated local elites, who lost status in their communities to the giant firms and who later provided leadership for campaigns against business. Opinion leaders came to fear not only the power of government but also the enormous economic power of private groups, and an extraordinary range of interests in virtually every sector of the economy turned to government for protection from the new corporate giants.

Meat packaging, in the years before the Civil War, had been a regional industry with local producers and local butchers serving local markets.[33] After the Civil War, Swift, Armour, and other firms established national distribution and marketing systems that threatened the positions of local producers. The National Butchers' Protective Association, dominated by local producers, advocated regional boycotts to keep meat from distant suppliers out of local markets. The association persuaded states such as Minnesota and Colorado to enact laws prohibiting the sale of meat unless the animals had been inspected by the state's officials, a requirement that effectively prevented national firms from selling products across state boundaries. Antitrust laws and statutes prohibiting price-fixing and restraint of trade were passed to address the general threat posed by giant corporations. Later, both state and national governments adopted legal standards for corporate conduct in sensitive areas such as working conditions, transportation services, and banking transactions.

Most government efforts to respond to the industrial revolution in this era were more significant as symbols than as accomplishments. Despite popular rhetoric, it was often difficult to know where the public interest in specific situations, such as the meatpacking one, stopped and where private efforts to use government authority to limit competition and secure commercial advantage began.[34] As a result of the lack of consensus, landmark pieces of legislation, such as the Interstate Commerce Act of 1887 and the Sherman Antitrust Act of 1890, resembled declarations of traditional values rather than clear statements of legislative goals. The full significance of the legislative initiatives in the era would not be realized until the nation faced the challenges of the New Deal.

Legal Doctrine

The economic transformation of the United States raised numerous legal questions.[35] Legal doctrines developed for an agrarian society were ill-suited to the problems caused by huge concentrations of industrial wealth. The issues that generated the most controversy were the role of government in regulating economic activity and the level of government responsible for regulation.

Until the end of the nineteenth century, states were the centers of regulatory activity. As one source notes, "Quite literally, state legislation was the only regulatory game in town."[36] The emergence of a national economy, however, undermined the effectiveness of state regulation. When the Fourteenth Amendment was adopted, its clauses prohibiting states from restricting the "privileges or immunities" of U.S. citizens and denying them due process of law seemed to limit state authority to regulate economic activity. When courts ruled on the Fourteenth Amendment, however, judges first upheld state regulation of economic activity and only later sustained the validity of national action.

The first major test of the Fourteenth Amendment came in the *Slaughterhouse Cases* in 1873.[37] The Republican-controlled legislature of Louisiana required as a health measure that all meat be slaughtered by a firm operated by its political friends. Other butchers sued, arguing that the legislature had abridged their "privileges and immunities" and reduced the value of their property without due process of law. The U.S. Supreme Court, however, upheld the Louisiana law and ruled that the Fourteenth Amendment clauses still allowed states to regulate economic activity.

By the end of the century, the federal judiciary began to acknowledge the dynamics of a national economy and to emphasize the significance of national rights. In 1886 the justices struck down an Illinois law that regulated railroads inside Illinois borders on the grounds that intrastate regulation could affect interstate commerce, and interstate commerce could only be regulated by Congress.[38] In 1890 the U.S. Supreme Court overturned a Minnesota law and ruled that a federal court rather than a state commission should be the final judge of the reasonableness of railroad rates.[39]

Basic changes in the structure of commerce and industry had reduced the ability of the states to regulate the country's economy, but the popularity of the laissez-faire philosophy among judges delayed the emergence of a national alternative to state regulation. Eventually the federal and state judiciaries bowed to popular preferences and accepted the social legislation designed to square legal precedent with the new economic conditions. During the period between the Civil War and 1929, the legal foundations were laid for the expansive role that the national government would assume during the New Deal.

THE EMERGENCE OF POSITIVE GOVERNMENT: 1929–2005

The stock market crash of 1929 symbolized the beginning of the Great Depression of the 1930s. Once under way, the decline rippled out into the economy in ever-widening circles until the country's market system had collapsed and national income had fallen by almost 60 percent.

Economic historians do not agree on the reasons for the depression. They mention excessive borrowing and speculation, the decline of international trade, a drop in the profitability of agriculture, inadequate investment, and damaging public policies. Regardless of the original causes, however, the economic crisis deepened, and its scope became nationwide. Care of the hungry and the unemployed exhausted the resources of states and localities and forced them to turn to Washington for assistance. By the time the depression abated, the federal government had assumed broad new responsibilities, and the political system had been permanently altered. Before the emergence of positive government was possible, however, the changes in legal doctrine that had begun in previous decades had to be completed.

Legal Doctrine

The economic emergency brought into stark focus the historic issue of the role of government in regulating the economy. Old legal doctrines had been giving way to new realities, but massive economic deprivation tested the country's patience with the slow pace of constitutional change. New Deal initiatives provoked legal confrontation.

The National Industrial Recovery Act of 1933 (NIRA) was the centerpiece of early New Deal policies.[40] It authorized the drafting of "codes" for each industry that would control the supply of goods, fix prices and wages, and regulate working conditions. The Agricultural Adjustment Act of the same year was even bolder. It sought to establish parity between industry and agriculture by raising prices for farm goods and reducing the burden of agricultural debt. It also gave government power to restrict production by limiting the acreage available for cultivation. After the slashing of wages by employers and the growth in joblessness during the 1930s aroused labor militancy, the National Labor Relations Act of 1935 threw the weight of the federal government behind union-organizing battles and outlawed anti-union practices.

The early New Deal initiatives came under surprisingly bitter attack. The constitutionality of the NIRA was challenged in *Schechter Poultry Corp. v. United States.*[41] The Schechter brothers were poultry wholesalers who openly violated the NIRA's Live Poultry Code to boost their profits. When prosecuted for selling "unfit" chickens at cut-rate prices, they argued that the NIRA statute was itself unconstitutional. The Supreme Court agreed. The justices ruled that Congress had exceeded its powers by regulating matters that were the responsibility of the states. The next year, the Supreme Court invalidated the Agricultural Adjustment Act as well. In *United States v. Butler,* the justices wrote that the act constituted "a statutory plan to regulate and control agricultural production" and held that such efforts were beyond the scope of federal authority.[42]

In other cases, state and federal judges provided more mixed reactions to New Deal initiatives.[43] Some measures were sustained, and others were found wanting. Conservative judges objected to New Deal restrictions and sometimes convinced moderate colleagues that the statutes were vague and without proper constitutional foundation. The conservatives failed, however, to identify legal principles that would permit government to act to alleviate the economic crisis.

The election landslide of 1936 confirmed the popularity of the New Deal and placed traditional judges in conflict with majority sentiment in both Congress and the executive branch. Threatened with plans to alter the composition and jurisdiction of the Supreme Court, conservative justices retreated from their earlier opposition to New Deal measures and gave their blessing to new initiatives. A 1937 decision illustrates the shift.

In *National Labor Relations Board v. Jones and Laughlin Steel Corporation,* business groups had argued that the federal government had no power to regulate factory working conditions.[44] The Supreme Court majority, however, abandoned its earlier view and ruled that the Commerce Clause did grant Congress the authority to regulate industrial relations. "When industries organize themselves on a national scale," the court wrote, ". . . how can it be maintained that their industrial relations constitute a forbidden field into which Congress may not enter?"[45] By the time prosperity returned, almost all constitutional restraints on the federal government's power to regulate the nation's economy had been discarded.

The Role of Government

Big government in the United States is mostly a product of the twentieth century.[46] At the beginning of that century, citizens could go about their lives unaware of national government decisions; today, almost every problem is a reason for government action. The ideal of limited government has been swept aside, and positive government engulfs us, despite occasional proposals to cut back some areas of government authority.

The federal government now affects every facet of corporate operations. The ways firms assemble capital are defined by federal statute, and production decisions are made with regard to public environmental and energy policies. Marketing practices, accounting rules, employee relations policies, equal opportunity procedures, and occupational health and safety standards are all within the realm of government policy.

The emergence of positive government in the twentieth century is a widely appreciated development, but the reasons for the growth of government remain controversial. An examination of federal employment and spending since 1929 reveals some reasons for the growth of government.

In 1929 the total civilian workforce of the federal government was 580,000.[47] More than half that number, more than 300,000 people, worked for the post office, and another 100,000 were civilian employees of the Defense Department. This means that in 1929 only 180,000 workers provided all the other national services a country of 120 million people required. During the 1930s the count of federal civilian workers grew from 580,000 to more than 950,000, and by the end of the 1940s it had reached 2.1 million. In the next two decades the pace of growth slowed, but by the 1970s the number of employees had climbed to 3 million. In the 1990s direct federal employment registered small declines.

In 1929 total federal, state, and local government spending equaled $10 billion, or 10 percent of the gross domestic product (GDP, the value of all goods and services produced by the nation in a specified period, usually a year), as Table 1-1 indicates. During the next decade, government spending as a share of GDP almost doubled, reaching 19 percent in 1939. Federal government expenditures increased substantially during the 1940s, and total government spending has continued to grow at a moderate pace in the decades since 1949, reaching 35 percent of GDP in 2002.

The great growth in federal employment and spending that occurred in the 1930s and 1940s coincided with the two major government crises of the twentieth century, the depression of the 1930s and World War II. The severity of the economic crisis of the 1930s led to the national programs to restructure industry, agriculture, and labor-management relations mentioned above and to emergency measures to support the unemployed and the destitute. Subsequently, permanent measures were enacted to provide Social Security pensions, unemployment compensation, and assistance for the needy and the disabled, and these programs became the foundation of the national government's expansive welfare policies.

During the depression years, the British economist John Maynard Keynes argued in *The General Theory of Employment, Interest, and Money*[48] that declines in a nation's economy could result from insufficient demand for goods and

Table 1-1   Government Expenditures and Employment, 1929–2002

Calendar year	Total government expenditures[a]	Federal government expenditures[a]	Federal civilian employment
1929	10	3	580,000
1939	19	10	950,000
1949	23	16	2,100,000
1959	27	18	2,400,000
1969	30	19	3,100,000
1979	31	21	2,900,000
1989	32	22	3,100,000
1999	34	19	2,800,000
2002	35	20	2,700,000

Sources: U.S. Advisory Commission on Intergovernmental Relations, *Significant Features of Fiscal Federalism*, December 1987; and U.S. Department of Commerce, *Statistical Abstract of the United States: 2004–2005* (Washington, D.C.: GPO, 2004).

[a] As percentage of gross domestic product.

services. To achieve higher levels of economic growth, Keynes advocated public action to stimulate economic demand by increasing government spending beyond revenues, thus incurring government deficits. New Deal policies are widely associated with Keynesian economics, even though some scholars point out that the administration of Franklin D. Roosevelt tolerated extraordinary levels of unemployment and resisted budget deficits until the eve of World War II. Regardless of the historical accuracy of the association of Keynesian economics with New Deal policies, the New Deal era did mark popular acceptance of the view that fluctuations in the economic cycle could be managed by government policy. This view represented another expansion of the role of the national government in society.

The huge military expenditures required to fight World War II finally ended the economic depression of the 1930s. The fiscal stimulus from military spending secured the economic recovery that had eluded President Roosevelt during the 1930s, and it practically wiped out unemployment. The concentration of federal employment and expenditure growth during the 1930s and 1940s demonstrates that national emergencies can lead to an expansion of government that persists after the crises have passed, but the record also indicates that other factors have contributed to the expansion in the role of government as well.

The emergence of a modern, urban-industrial economy generates problems that only positive government can address.[49] The growth of private firms has led government to become more active in regulating business practices, supervising competition, and protecting society from corporate action. The importance of this role is seen in the founding even before the New Deal of the Interstate Commerce Commission, the Federal Trade Commission, the Federal Reserve System, and the Justice Department's Antitrust Division. An urban, industrial society also implies pollution and congestion. The Environmental Protection Agency, natural resource programs, and public transportation agencies are bureaucratic responses to these factors.

Government has also grown in recent decades because it provides citizens an array of popular social services. Education, health care, Social Security, and housing have all become major public responsibilities. Some programs distribute social benefits to all citizens, and others redistribute income and benefits from one group to another.

Finally, the growth of government has been stimulated by pressures from politicians and bureaucrats. Government is composed of officials and institutions that have their own interests and ideologies. Government responses to national crises, to modernization, or to social service demands are usually bureaucratic responses. The programs enacted to address such needs sometimes take on a life of their own. They may survive because they serve the interests of officeholders rather than the goals of the broader society. In any case, once enacted, the programs of one era influence both the subsequent development of a nation's institutions and the policy choices that are available to succeeding generations.

The national government grew dramatically in the twentieth century, but its authority over private activities and institutions may have grown more rapidly than its payrolls or expenditures. As government responded to events, it shaped a new public philosophy that supports positive government. It is no longer conceivable that government could return to its pre–New Deal or even its pre–World War II scale. Positive government embodies the values and aspirations of a large majority of the American people. It is the distinctive accomplishment of the post-depression years, and it will be a critical factor in relations between government and business in the future.

Business Organization

Multinational operations, product diversification, and professional management characterized large American corporations at the dawn of the twenty-first century, and the service sector has now replaced manufacturing as the principal engine of economic growth. New technologies have revolutionized the way companies operate and made flexibility the country's greatest economic asset. Large firms, however, are only part of the U.S. economy. In 1998, 5.6 million American businesses employed 108 million workers.[50] Companies with fewer than 500 employees provided jobs for slightly more than half of all workers, and companies with more than 500 workers provided jobs for the rest. Small firms are less profitable than larger firms, but they provide 75 percent of new jobs and about half of all industrial innovations. Small businesses employ the greatest number of workers in the retail sector, whereas major companies employ the largest share of workers in manufacturing.

In the 1980s the U.S. economy faced heightened competition in the global marketplace, and it responded with a structural renewal based on innovations in information technology, communications, synthetic materials, biotechnology, and computer systems. Production techniques were modernized, research and development practices reformed, and new skills were demanded from managers and other employees. After the economy emerged from recession in 1991, the chairman of the Federal Reserve Board, Alan Greenspan, told Congress that the U.S. economy had become a "different animal."[51] In the mid- and late 1990s, the economy offered the most encouraging inflation outlook in a generation, recorded the greatest surge in productivity in twenty years, and experienced the fastest growth in gross domestic product since the boom during the administration of Ronald Reagan. In the first years of the new century, the economy experienced a mild recession as job creation weakened, business investment stagnated, government finances deteriorated, tax cuts were enacted, and spending increased for national defense and homeland security.[52] At the same time, however, productivity increases continued, inflation remained under control, consumer spending climbed, and corporate profits rose sharply.

PATHS TO INDUSTRIAL DEVELOPMENT

Each country has its own history of industrial development. Industrialization in the United States embodied its values and ideology, rested on its political framework, and reflected the specific features of its raw materials, capital, labor, and markets, and the same is true for other major countries. Industrial nations, however, also have much in common. A comparison of industrial development in the United States with the process of development in Great Britain, Germany, and Japan identifies events in other nations that were critical in shaping their institutions and policies, and it also highlights important aspects of U.S. history that might otherwise go unrecognized.

Great Britain was the world's first industrial nation.[53] Its industrialization was advanced by the country's political unity, a unified currency, and the absence of internal tariffs. At the end of the eighteenth century, agricultural productivity was increasing sharply in Great Britain, new types of machinery had emerged in the textile industry, water power and steam had replaced animals and humans as the dominant sources of energy, and government had begun to intervene less in the economy than during the heyday of mercantilism. Industrial development was largely financed by individual capitalists, their families and friends, and country banks rather than by government subsidies. In 1859 a prominent author wrote that Great Britain's economic progress depended less on national industrial policy than on the personal qualities of individual entrepreneurs.[54]

Great Britain industrialized before the nation's internal transportation system was completed, so firms served regional and foreign markets instead of a single homogeneous national market. Foreign trade accounted for 30 percent of British national income between 1860 and 1913, compared with only 5 percent in the United States.[55] "Invisible exports" such as capital, insurance, and shipping, however, were more important than manufactured goods. London was the world's financial center in the nineteenth century, but World War I destroyed its commanding position in international commerce. Small and medium-size firms dominated the British economy until World War I, but such firms lacked the resources to dominate steel, chemicals, and other heavy industries. Family control has remained such a significant feature of corporate leadership in Great Britain that one prominent historian describes the British economic system as an example of "personal capitalism."[56]

Industrialization in Germany roughly coincided with industrialization in the United States.[57] Until 1871 German identity rested on a common language rather than on the existence of a unified German state. Before Napoleon conquered central Europe at the beginning of the nineteenth century, hundreds of separate fiefdoms and principalities existed in what would become Germany. One of these states was Prussia, which modernized its administrative, economic, educational, and military systems to improve its prospects in the struggle against Napoleonic rule.[58] With Napoleon's defeat, Prussia emerged as a great European power at the Congress of Vienna in 1815. After Prussian armies defeated Austria in 1866 and France in 1870, Prussia persuaded the other German states to join it in a new German empire.

Germany's prominence in world markets resulted from its political unification in 1871, but its industrialization had roots in events that had occurred earlier in the century. Railroad development was more important in German industrialization than it had been in Great Britain or the United States. Local rail networks were built early in the nineteenth century, and these networks were then linked together to provide a national rail system that could serve national markets. The need to pool capital to finance large rail projects stimulated the development of the German banking industry, and vast demand for railway equipment provided enormous assistance to the emerging coal, iron, and machinery industries.

At the beginning of the twentieth century Germany established itself as a world leader in such classic industries as coal mining, steel production, chemicals, electrical products, and machine tools. The German economy was distinguished by its strong export orientation and its unusual commitment to employee skills. Although founding families remained influential in German companies, managers with technical skills occupied key posts in corporate hierarchies. German companies pioneered the development of corporate research laboratories and emphasized the technical training of production workers.

Germany's system of "cooperative capitalism" involved labor union representation in corporate management and public policy formation, and it also encouraged collaboration among corporations within an industry. Cartels—business organizations that can divide markets, regulate production, and set prices for member firms—were a major feature of German industry from unification in 1871 until World War II because they could prevent member firms from sacrificing the long-term interests of the industry and the economy for short-term profits. Whereas the British and American economies became more service-oriented, manufacturing industries have remained the core of the German economy. Industrialization has been a critical stage in the development of most economies, but India has leapfrogged the industrial era by moving from agriculture to high technology (see Box 1-1).

Industrial development occurred later in Japan than in Great Britain, Germany, or the United States, but once under way it took place quite rapidly.[59] In 1868 the existing Japanese government was overthrown by a coalition of regional nobles who believed that the nation had become too technologically and militarily weak to resist Western demands. A reform government was established under a member of the imperial family in an event known as the Meiji Restoration, and, after securing its position, the new government launched a modernization program with the slogan, "Rich nation, strong army."[60] The national government restructured the military, legal, and educational systems; ended feudal restrictions on domestic travel and the choice of occupations; and sought to learn as much as possible from Western administrative and technological practices.

Modern Japanese business began to emerge in the 1880s.[61] *Zaibatsu*—groups of companies owned by families that had been a part of Japan's traditional economy—evolved from trading companies of earlier centuries that were active in such areas as shipping, banking, and mining. With the encouragement of the Japanese government, the *zaibatsu* enlarged the scope of their activities and diversified into heavy industry. The government also promoted the textile industry by building model factories and selling equipment to new firms at low prices. Relationships among companies remain such an important feature of the Japanese economy that the country's business system is sometimes designated "alliance capitalism."

Japanese industry was strengthened by military spending for wars against China in 1894 and Russia in 1905, and it benefited substantially from the nation's position as a British ally during World War I. During that war, Japan seized German colonies in China and the North Pacific; its international trade doubled; the significance of industrial goods such as chemicals, dyestuffs, and machinery surged; and the *zaibatsu* continued to gain importance. With the growth of large firms, the Japanese economy acquired a dual structure: although large firms achieved high productivity and offered better working conditions, 58 percent of industrial workers in 1930 were employed by firms with four or fewer employees.[62]

Cases in Development
BOX 1-1 A SNAPSHOT OF THE INDIAN ECONOMY

A recent snapshot of the Indian economy presents an unusual puzzle. India is among the world's leaders in such modern industries as information technology, pharmaceutical production, and space research, yet it is also among the world's poorer nations. Almost two-thirds of India's workers are employed in agriculture, but agriculture accounts for less than 25 percent of the country's GDP. Almost 20 percent of workers are engaged in industries that produce textiles, chemicals, cement, and similar goods, but industrial products also contribute only about 25 percent of GDP. Accompanying the dismal state of Indian agriculture and the country's mediocre manufacturing record, however, is a service sector that has recently emerged as a dynamic participant in the global economy. With only 20 percent of the nation's workforce, the service sector produces more than half of India's GDP. How has an agricultural economy leapfrogged the industrial era to become a leader in twenty-first century industries?

India was part of the British Empire from 1858 until it achieved independence in 1947. British colonial rulers allowed British groups to manage the country's development and restricted the activities of Indian entrepreneurs. When India became independent, its new government favored policies that allowed the state to ration capital among firms, subsidize specific products, and protect favored industries. The lack of competition among firms led to inefficient operations, poor product quality, and much government ownership of industry. At the start of the 1990s, a new Indian government abandoned the interventionist philosophy of its predecessors and allowed corporations to guide more of their own affairs. Some industries were opened to foreign investment, the production of consumer goods increased, and the country's well-educated workers were able to take jobs in rapidly growing international industries, such as telecommunications, banking, and information technology. The government now faces the challenge of accommodating the country's traditional economy with the notable successes of "Shining India."

Sources: Edward Luce, "Cure for India's Rural Woes Lies in Ability to Escape the Farm," *Financial Times,* December 7, 2004, 5; "Stichwort: Indien—die grösste Demokratie der Welt," *Financial Times Deutschland,* www.ftd.de, December 14, 2004; "Country Briefings: India Economic Structure," *Economist,* July 10, 2002, www.economist.com/countries/India, ID=1223675; U.S. Central Intelligence Agency, *The World Factbook: India,* www.cia.gov/cia/publications/factbook, updated December 16, 2004; and Ananya Mukherjee Reed, *Perspectives on the Indian Corporate Economy: Exploring the Paradox of Profits* (New York: Palgrave, 2001).

The government role in the economy increased in the 1930s, and there was great growth in the steel, shipbuilding, machine-tool, and automotive industries as military spending increased in anticipation of World War II.

The nations examined here did not follow a single path to industrial development, and their governments did not embrace a single form of capitalism. The legal foundation for the U.S. democratic and commercial systems was established in the first era of the nation's history, large business organizations were created in the second era, and positive government appeared in the third era. The processes of industrialization in Great Britain, Germany, and Japan followed quite different paths of development. In Japan and Germany, in fact, the sequence of development was essentially reversed: large government bureaucracies became important before industrialization, and democratic institutions were not secured until after major business organizations were already in place.

The different sequences of national development have had enduring effects on the characteristics of the institutions and practices in the four countries. Business organizations were created in Germany and Japan after government agencies were already major societal institutions, and the new business firms depended on government for financial support and public acceptance. Corporations were created in the United States when the national government had only limited impact on the economy. Thus, it is not surprising that commentators in Germany and Japan stress the cooperation between business organizations and government whereas U.S. specialists find that relationships between businesses and public officials are characterized by suspicion and mistrust. As seen in the chapters ahead, the consequences of the alternative paths of institutional development are still evident in countless commercial practices and policy arrangements in the countries we have examined.

SUMMARY

The features of government, business, and law have changed dramatically during the successive eras of American history. Table 1-2 presents an overview of these changes. Legal doctrines developed in the country's first decades provided the foundation for its democratic and business systems. The period from the Civil War to the New Deal witnessed the emergence of a modern, industrial economy and also the turmoil associated with the disruption of traditional markets and institutions. In the years since the stock market crash of 1929, the national government has grown from a minimal institution into a major force affecting all facets of American life.

From the beginning, American history has been testimony to the continuing importance of two economic traditions, the market-oriented tradition associated with the analyses of Adam Smith and the tradition of government activism embodied in the policy proposals of Alexander Hamilton. Both intellectual traditions have persisted throughout the nation's history, although they have had different levels of importance in different eras. In the first decades of the Republic,

Table 1-2 Overview of Developments in Law, Business, and Government

Period	Legal doctrine	Business organization	Role of government
Colonial Times to Civil War	Property rights, contracts, and corporations	Agrarian economy, trading, and small firms	Creation of political framework, promotion of economy
Civil War to Great Depression	Transition from rural to industrial society	Emergence of industrial economy with large corporations	Promotion of selected industries, expansion of government regulation
Great Depression to 2005	Acceptance of regulation and activist government	Multinational firms, diversification, and information technologies	Growth of government role in sustaining welfare and economy

Source: Author.

government guided the general economy, promoted the welfare of critical industries, and involved itself in private economic decision making. The activist tradition was more restrained during the era of industrialization in the second half of the nineteenth century and the beginning of the twentieth century, when market-oriented policies dominated center stage. In the New Deal years and during World War II, the role of government expanded dramatically, to be followed in the 1980s and 1990s by renewed debate about the appropriate responsibilities of government, private institutions, and individual citizens. Throughout the nation's history, policymakers have drawn upon both the activist and the market-oriented traditions to create the mix of policies that have guided the country's economy to significant prosperity.

The place of business in a system of popular government and the role of government in the management of a successful economy are complex topics. The challenge of fashioning a constructive accord between government and business for the future requires us to supplement the historical investigation summarized here with contemporary perspectives on associations between democracy and markets.

FURTHER READINGS

The Labour History and Economic and Business History sections of the World Wide Web Virtual Library provide links to U.S. and international information centers and organizations that concentrate on labor and business history: http://www.iisg.nl/~w3vl/.

Blackford, Mansel G. *The Rise of Modern Business in Great Britain, the United States, and Japan*, 2d ed. Chapel Hill: University of North Carolina Press, 1998.

Chandler, Alfred D., Jr. *Inventing the Electronic Century: The Epic Story of the Consumer Electronics and Computer Industries.* New York: Free Press, 2001.

Hall, Kermit L. *The Magic Mirror: Law in American History.* New York: Oxford University Press, 1989.

McCraw, Thomas K., ed. *Creating Modern Capitalism: How Entrepreneurs, Companies, and Countries Triumphed in Three Industrial Revolutions.* Cambridge, Mass.: Harvard University Press, 1997.

Wells, Wyatt. *American Capitalism: 1945–2000: Continuity and Change from Mass Production to the Information Society.* Chicago: Ivan R. Dee, 2003.

NOTES

1. See Edward S. Greenberg, *Capitalism and the American Political Ideal* (Armonk, N.Y.: M. E. Sharpe, 1985), 53.
2. For other definitions of historic eras, see Robert B. Carson, *Business Issues Today: Alternative Perspectives* (New York: St. Martin's, 1984); Edwin M. Epstein, *The Corporation in American Politics* (Englewood Cliffs, N.J.: Prentice Hall, 1969); and Greenberg, *Capitalism and the American Political Ideal.*
3. Thomas C. Cochran, *200 Years of American Business* (New York: Basic Books, 1977), 173; and Frank Bourgin, *The Great Challenge: The Myth of Laissez-Faire in the Early Republic* (New York: Harper and Row, 1989), chap. 4.
4. Lawrence M. Friedman, *A History of American Law* (New York: Touchstone Books, 1973), 157–62; and James Oliver Robertson, *America's Business* (New York: Hill and Wang, 1985), 56–57, 97.
5. Friedman, *History of American Law,* 150; and Stuart Bruchey, *The Wealth of the Nation: An Economic History of the United States* (New York: Harper and Row, 1988), 36–40.
6. Subsidy of industries: Robertson, *America's Business,* 125; regulation of imports: Friedman, *History of American Law,* 158–69, 447.
7. Friedman, *History of American Law,* 12–13, 58, 103.
8. Alfred D. Chandler Jr., *The Visible Hand: The Managerial Revolution in American Business* (Cambridge, Mass.: Harvard University Press, Belknap Press, 1977), 14.
9. Cochran, *200 Years of American Business,* 20–25; Robertson, *America's Business,* 67–68.
10. Cochran, *200 Years of American Business,* 30–32.
11. Bruchey, *Wealth of the Nation,* 16.
12. Robertson, *America's Business,* 57, 198.
13. Ibid., 72; and Ronald E. Seavoy, "The Public Service Origins of the American Business Corporation," *Business History Review* 52, no. 1 (Spring 1978): 30–60.
14. Ibid.; Friedman, *History of American Law,* 167–68; and Robertson, *America's Business,* 71.
15. Ibid., 70.
16. Oscar Handlin and Mary F. Handlin, "Origins of the American Business Corporation," *Journal of Economic History* 5, no. 1 (May 1945): 1–23; Cochran, *200 Years of American Business,* 76.
17. This section relies on Cochran, *200 Years of American Business,* 63.
18. 4 Wheat. 518, 4 L. Ed. 629 (1819).
19. 11 Pet. 420.
20. Mansel G. Blackford, *The Rise of Modern Business in Great Britain, the United States, and Japan* (Chapel Hill: University of North Carolina Press, 1988); Cochran, *200 Years of American Business;* and Louis Galambos and Joseph Pratt, *The Rise of the Corporate Commonwealth: United States Business and Public Policy in the 20th Century* (New York: Basic Books, 1988).
21. Chandler, *Visible Hand,* chap. 8.
22. Bruchey, *Wealth of the Nation,* 117.
23. Richard R. Nelson, "U.S. Technological Leadership: Where Did It Come From and Where Did It Go?" *Research Policy* 19 (1990): 117–32.
24. Robertson, *America's Business,* 175.

25. Ibid., 135.

26. Chandler, *Visible Hand,* chaps. 3–5.

27. Ibid., 3–10, 56; Robertson, *America's Business,* 125–26; and Thomas K. McCraw, *Prophets of Regulation* (Cambridge, Mass.: Harvard University Press, 1984), 64–67.

28. The Warren and Person index fell from 193 to 82 between 1864 and 1890. Cochran, *200 Years of American Business,* 72.

29. Ibid., 127–57; Blackford, *Rise of Modern Business,* 55; and Bruchey, *Wealth of the Nation,* 120–33.

30. Chandler, *Visible Hand,* chap. 12.

31. Blackford, *Rise of Modern Business,* 57; Cochran, *200 Years of American Business,* 56, 158; Galambos and Pratt, *Rise of the Corporate Commonwealth,* 80–91; and Robertson, *America's Business,* 126.

32. Blackford, *Rise of Modern Business,* 191.

33. Bruchey, *Wealth of the Nation,* 122–23.

34. Galambos and Pratt, *Rise of the Corporate Commonwealth,* 56–57.

35. Kermit L. Hall, *Magic Mirror: Law in American History* (New York: Oxford University Press, 1989), 227.

36. Advisory Commission on Intergovernmental Relations, *The Condition of Contemporary Federalism: Conflicting Theories and Collapsing Constraints* (Washington, D.C: Commission, 1981), 57–58; Hall, *Magic Mirror,* 234.

37. Ibid., 233–34; ACIR, *Condition of Contemporary Federalism,* 45–55.

38. *Wabash, St. Louis, and Pacific Railway Co. v. Illinois,* 188 U.S. 557.

39. 134 U.S. 458 (1890); see also *Smyth v. Ames,* 169 U.S. 466 (1898).

40. ACIR, *Condition of Cont`emporary Federalism,* 79.

41. 295 U.S. 495 (1935); Hall, *Magic Mirror,* 280.

42. 297 U.S. 1 (1936).

43. Hall, *Magic Mirror,* 279–81.

44. 301 U.S. 58 (1937).

45. As quoted in Hall, *Magic Mirror,* 282.

46. This section relies on Robert Higgs, *Crisis and Leviathan: Critical Episodes in the Growth of American Government* (New York: Oxford University Press, 1987); Stephen Skowronek, *Building a New American State: The Expansion of National Administrative Capacities, 1877–1920* (New York: Cambridge University Press, 1982); David Lowery and William D. Berry, "The Growth of Government in the United States: An Empirical Assessment of Competing Explanations," *American Journal of Political Science* 27, no. 4 (November 1983): 665–94; and Greenberg, *Capitalism and the American Political Ideal.*

47. U.S. Bureau of the Census, *Historical Statistics of the United States, 1789–1945* (Washington, D.C.: GPO, 1945); U.S. Bureau of the Census, *Historical Statistics of the United States: Colonial Times to 1970* (Washington, D.C.: GPO, 1975); and U.S. Bureau of the Census, *Statistical Abstract of the United States* (Washington, D.C.: GPO, various years).

48. John Maynard Keynes, *The General Theory of Employment, Interest, and Money* (New York: Harcourt, Brace, 1936).

49. John F. Walker and Harold G. Vatter, *The Rise of Big Government in the United States* (Armonk, N.Y.: M. E. Sharpe, 1997).

50. U.S. Small Business Administration, *The Small Business Economy: A Report to the President, 2001* (Washington, D.C.: GPO, 2004).

51. Michael Prowse, "A Potential World-beater," *Financial Times,* February 8, 1993, 11.

52. Organisation for Economic Co-operation and Development, *Economic Outlook 75* (Paris: OECD, 2004), 41–42.

53. This section draws from Mansel G. Blackford, *The Rise of Modern Business: Great Britain, the United States and Japan,* 2nd ed. (Chapel Hill: University of North Carolina Press, 1998); Peter Botticelli, "British Capitalism and the Three Industrial Revolutions," in *Creating Modern Capitalism: How Entrepreneurs, Companies, and Countries Triumphed in Three Industrial Revolutions,* ed. Thomas K. McCraw (Cambridge, Mass.: Harvard University Press, 1997), 51–93; and Frank Dobbin, *Forging Industrial Policy: The United*

States, Britain, and France in the Railway Age (New York: Cambridge University Press, 1994).

54. Cited in Botticelli, "British Capitalism," 67.

55. Blackford, *Rise of Modern Business,* 1st ed., chap. 3.

56. Alfred D. Chandler Jr., *Scale and Scope: The Dynamics of Industrial Capitalism* (Cambridge, Mass.: Harvard University Press, Belknap Press, 1990).

57. Jeffrey Fear, "German Capitalism," in McCraw, *Creating Modern Capitalism,* 135–82; and H. Giersch, K. H. Paque, and H. Schmieding, *The Fading Miracle: Four Decades of Market Economy in Germany* (New York: Cambridge University Press, 1992).

58. Frederick B. Artz, *Reaction and Revolution, 1814–1832* (New York: Harper and Bros., 1934), 136–42.

59. This section draws from Jeffrey R. Bernstein, "Japanese Capitalism," in McCraw, *Creating Modern Capitalism;* and Blackford, *Rise of Modern Business,* 2nd ed., esp. chap. 5.

60. For an analysis of the consequences of this ideology, see Richard J. Samuels, *"Rich Nation, Strong Army": National Security and the Technological Transformation of Japan* (Ithaca, N.Y.: Cornell University Press, 1994).

61. Bernstein, "Japanese Capitalism," 450–54.

62. Ibid., 458.

CHAPTER 2

Creating Government-Business Relations

COUNTRIES CREATE THEIR own political and economic systems.[1] Their governing arrangements are not the product of irresistible forces but of myriad societal decisions. Some of these decisions are made at specific times, and others emerge from traditions whose origins are too remote to discover. There are as many ways of organizing political and economic systems as there are countries. Each nation seeks governing arrangements that help it both to achieve material well-being and to secure its other political and social goals, but national success is never foreordained.

The ways countries structure the relationships between politics and economics are so fundamental to the countries' identities that they often become the basis for classifying total societies. Socialist nations believe that a country's economic and social needs are best served when government owns major industries and provides a comprehensive array of social services. Communist governments restrict private ownership of property and authorize public agencies to allocate the nation's resources to meet its needs. Capitalist countries divide politics and economics into distinct spheres, thus ensuring societal diversity and denying any institution complete domination.

In the United States, Japan, and the major nations of western Europe, privately owned firms are responsible for most employment and production decisions, governments define the framework within which corporate activity takes place, and markets play a key role in allocating resources. These countries have accepted the presence of large corporations in their economies because they believe such firms contribute to their material well-being, but this judgment has often been contested by influential dissenters.[2] Important intellectual traditions have insisted that large corporations do not improve society but make societies less equitable, less efficient, and less accountable to public preferences than they could be. Even prominent critics of corporations, however, have begun to acknowledge that corporations do make positive contributions to society. In *People Before Profit,* the noted social critic Charles Derber appeals for major changes in the existing corporate system, but he then concedes:[3]

I recognize that large global corporations deliver essential and often magical goods and services, and that millions of people around the world depend on them for jobs. Critics of the corporation have often lost credibility by demonizing companies or failing to acknowledge the contributions that corporations have made to our lives. . . . I am firmly persuaded that many in the business world would like to help create a more humane order.

The challenge for major industrial nations then is to design governing arrangements that deliver the greatest prosperity for their citizens from the activities of private corporations while still championing their basic political rights and social principles.

This chapter is an investigation of how countries structure their state-economy relations. First, I identify the different functions governments may perform in an economy by drawing upon the account of U.S. development in Chapter 1. I then outline the analytic models scholars use to describe the relationship between a nation's political and economic systems. Then I shift from the abstract to the concrete and conclude the chapter by presenting capsule views of how Germany, Great Britain, and Japan now organize their political-economic systems.

THE ROLE OF GOVERNMENT

Government inevitably plays a vital role in a nation's economy. Governments enforce the laws, protect natural resources, purchase goods and services, and provide national defense. The question thus becomes, what type of role should government play in a specific country in particular circumstances? Chapter 1 includes numerous examples of government action in the U.S. economy in various historical eras. These events reveal four distinct functions governments commonly perform.

The Framework State

Politics and markets are frequently viewed as alternative mechanisms for guiding societies. In fact, however, they are inevitably intertwined.[4] A society establishes a set of political institutions that embody its values. These institutions in turn construct the legal framework in which the country's economy operates and its markets function, and this framework, too, reflects the nation's political judgments. Since a nation's political values permeate its economic institutions, markets can never be completely divorced from politics.

The U.S. Constitution created a set of institutional rules that acknowledged the prominence of state governments at the end of the eighteenth century. At the same time, the Constitution limited the capacity of the national government by dividing its authority among institutions whose agreement was required before government could act. This system was intended to allow a broad measure of individual liberty and inhibit the national government from abusing citizens' rights, and it did. The structure also made it difficult for the national government to manage the nation's economy.

As noted in Chapter 1, the country's new political institutions made a series of legal decisions that affected how markets would function: private ownership of property was guaranteed in the Constitution; the Supreme Court ruled that government would enforce contractual agreements; and corporations were allowed to emerge as major vehicles of economic activity. These decisions stabilized marketplace activity and affirmed values that shaped both politics and society.

The major task of the *framework state* is to create the institutional structure in which political and economic activity occurs. Government in a framework state is sometimes portrayed as playing a minimal role, but the challenge of designing a nation's political and economic institutions is formidable and never ending. The decade of the 1990s witnessed the tribulations of the new states that had made up Eastern Europe and the former Soviet Union as they struggled to create political and economic structures to replace their earlier systems. At the beginning of the twenty-first century, Congress, the judiciary, and regulatory agencies in the United States were deciding under what conditions some firms could market long-distance telephone service, broadband access, and Web phone service at the expense of competing companies. Although some governments respond to each societal issue by inventing new public policies, other societies pursue their objectives by designing private institutions that then define specific political and economic practices.

The Promotional State

The principal responsibility of government in the *promotional state* is to use its authority to enhance the nation's economy. Early American leaders believed that market structures alone would not be sufficient to promote economic well-being. The mercantilism of British trade policy had been part of their historical experience, and the new government became a positive instrument of economic policy.[5] American leaders regarded the state as an arsenal of practices and policies that could be used *selectively* to aid the new republic's economy. Although government did not control all facets of economic activity, state and local governments frequently used their resources in the early decades to aid specific sectors of the economy, and in the middle of the nineteenth century, the national government boosted the economy by providing massive subsidies for railroads, agriculture, and community development.

Today, governments on every front use their resources to promote the economic well-being of their regions. In the 1990s state governments fashioned an active economic role for themselves by sustaining mature industries, assisting high-technology initiatives, and encouraging international commerce,[6] and now hardly a month passes without some state or local government authorizing huge expenditures on behalf of a sports team on the grounds that it will aid the local economy. The national government also protects traditional sectors such as automobiles and steel, subsidizes new projects and industries such as biotechnology and the Internet, and adopts macroeconomic strategies that have a positive impact on specific industries like housing. Government sponsorship of commercial activities has become so pervasive that the present era is sometimes described as a "neomercantilist" age.

The Regulatory State

The basic assignment of government in the *regulatory state* is to mitigate the undesirable consequences of market activity without losing the benefits of a competitive economy. Thus, government regulates the products and production processes of private firms and issues rules governing collective bargaining, equal opportunity, and human resource policies. The industrial revolution in the United States had transformed the nation's social and economic patterns, but numerous groups wanted government to preserve various elements of the old economic order. Government responded with the enactment of creative statutes that regulated the most objectionable features of the new competition without halting its development. The national government outlawed unfair market practices and regulated the operations of controversial industries. Antitrust laws prohibited monopolies, and regulations imposed government standards in sensitive areas where markets functioned poorly, such as workplace safety and the employment of children.[7]

Inadequate marketplace competition is the formal rationale for most activities of the regulatory state, but much regulation cannot be justified so decorously. Many instances of government regulation are prompted by groups favoring outcomes that competitive markets would not provide. A group believing that society would be better off with more symphony orchestras and fewer professional football teams, for example, might advocate regulations to achieve this objective. The local butchers mentioned in Chapter 1 sought to exclude national firms from local markets so that they could maintain their commercial position, and they succeeded for a time in obtaining government regulations to do this.

The regulatory state is intended to provide the benefits of marketplace competition when markets are not fully competitive. Sometimes, however, the regulatory state is captured by groups that use government authority to produce the policy results they favor.

The Social Service State

The *social service state* focuses on the distribution of wealth and income among people in a society.[8] For Marx, property arrangements and, specifically, ownership of the means of production were the most important features of a society. Every society could be divided into a small capitalist class that owned the means of production and a larger subject class who worked for the capitalists. Workers created value through their labor, and capitalists accumulated capital and enlarged their fortunes by seizing the surplus produced by workers. Capitalism would finally end, Marx believed, when the gap between wealth and poverty grew so large that workers became conscious of their subjugation and recognized their common interest in overthrowing the capitalist system. The revolutionary victory of the workers would lead to a classless society where the fruits of production would be distributed to citizens according to need. Under Marxism, the means of production would be collectively owned, and government would make economic decisions in the name of the workers.

Although distributional questions are central to Marxist analysis, Marxists certainly possess no monopoly of concern about the distribution of wealth and income in a society. Socialists, social democrats, social reformers, and conservatives all attach special importance to distributional issues, although their notions of equity range from egalitarian to merit-based. The United States, and most other majority industrial nations, now direct about half of their outlays to social service purposes, such as health care, retirement costs, and assistance to low-income groups. As a rule, the social service state rejects the apportionment of wealth and income produced by marketplace activity and uses government authority to achieve a different standard of equity. Continuing debates about tax rates, health care, Social Security, and the plight of the disadvantaged underline the centrality of social service issues in the responsibilities of modern governments.

It would be a mistake to associate pure forms of the social service state, the regulatory state, the promotional state, or the framework state with a single era or a specific government. Governments pick and choose among these functions to fashion the mixture of activities they think corresponds to their needs and traditions. They devise one set of political-economic practices to meet the problems of one era and then strike a new policy balance to fit the altered circumstances of the next era.

American government in the early national period was both liberal, in that it believed that unregulated markets would provide substantial economic benefits, and promotional, in that it used government authority to enhance the success of specific industries. The regulatory function of government was already evident in the early decades of the country's history, but the significance of government regulation expanded enormously in the period between the Civil War and the New Deal. Since the New Deal era, government regulations have multiplied, and increasing public resources have been devoted to providing social services. Despite this, the United States still stresses market decision making and uses government authority to regulate and promote the economy.

Innovative combinations of government functions and imaginative changes in policy constantly emerge from struggles that take place within a country's political system. Business influence in determining the mixture of government functions a country selects in a particular era reflects the place of business in the broader political process.

MODELS OF BUSINESS AND GOVERNMENT

Most Americans evaluate political issues concretely. They are more concerned about immediate problems than about the ideological implications of potential policies. The relationship between governments and business is rarely addressed directly in the United States. It is usually fought out, instead, on the margins of such topics as working conditions, environmental costs, campaign contributions, and health care costs. Implicit in such disputes is an intense rivalry over the influence of business and nonbusiness groups in society. Various scholars address this rivalry by presenting models that express their understanding of what the relationship among government, business, and nonbusiness groups in the society is or should be.[9]

The Business Dominance Model

An enduring American intellectual tradition maintains that political power in society is concentrated in the hands of social and economic elites. At the beginning of the twentieth century, Charles A. Beard argued in *An Economic Interpretation of the Constitution* that the convention that drafted the U.S. Constitution was an assembly of the rich and the well-connected who represented the interests of financiers, merchants, and slave owners rather than the goals and aspirations of ordinary citizens.[10] In modern times, C. Wright Mills described an American society whose policies were dominated by a "power elite" composed of a network of social, economic, and military elites.[11] As Gabriel Kolko writes, business leaders are often thought to be the decisive figures in shaping the nation's policies: "The real questions are (1) Do a small *group* of very wealthy men have the power to guide industry and thereby much of the total economy, towards ends that they decide are compatible with their own interests? (2) Do they own and control major corporations? The answers must *inevitably* be affirmative."[12]

The *business dominance model* of the relations between business, government, and society sees political authority as an extension of economic power. According to Charles E. Lindblom's analysis, business has a "privileged position" that allows it to translate its economic power into political domination in three ways.[13] First, business benefits from a supportive climate of public opinion in the United States, and it advances its interests by linking its policy goals with popular symbols such as liberty, democracy, and patriotism. Through the manipulation of opinion, business enhances its legitimacy and suppresses such issues as corporate welfare and the abuse of corporate power. Second, corporations participate in the political process through interest groups, lobbying, campaign contributions, and other direct and indirect methods of swaying government decisions.

Because of their abundant resources, businesses are uniquely able to define the government's agenda, determine the range of policy options, and dictate the content of public policies. The third way business exercises political influence is through its role in the economy. Firms make decisions about production, investment, and employment, and these decisions affect both citizens' living standards and public revenues. If corporations oppose a government's policies, they can retaliate by reducing their economic activity. Levels of investment, employment, and production will fall; living standards will decline; public revenues will drop; and the resulting public wrath will jeopardize the electoral prospects of public officials.

In *Golden Rule,* Thomas Ferguson continues Lindblom's analysis by arguing that election contests and party politics in the United States are dominated by elite investors.[14] "Major investors," usually business elites, invest in politics in order to "control the state."[15] Ferguson regards political parties as nothing more than blocs of investors who coalesce to advance the prospects of candidates who represent their interests. The dominance of politics by major investors is confirmed, according to Ferguson, by the fact that agreement on a topic by major investors precludes discussion of that issue by parties or candidates regardless of the sentiments of voters.

The Pluralist Model

Pluralists maintain that American society is composed of numerous power centers that compete with each other to shape public policy. Neither business nor any other single group, they insist, dominates the policy process. The Constitution created an open government system that diffuses political power between the federal and state governments, through several branches of the federal government, among numerous agencies with their own goals and incentives, and among officials holding office under varying conditions. Countless groups continuously struggle to persuade officials of the validity of their policy views, and when a group fails to find support in one department or agency, it turns to another administrative office or political party for backing. Under the *pluralist model,* government recognizes the range of policy opinions expressed by groups in the society and then devises a policy response that balances the various viewpoints as effectively as possible.

In recent decades, David Vogel has been the best-known proponent of the pluralist model of government-business relations in his books *Fluctuating Fortunes: The Political Power of Business in America* and *Kindred Strangers: The Uneasy Relationship between Politics and Business in America.*[16] Vogel explains his view of the political power of business: "My contention is not that individual companies, trade associations and inter-industry coalitions do not wield significant political power; of course they do. . . . [But b]usiness is not unique. There is nothing about the nature, scope or magnitude of the power wielded by business that cannot be accounted for within the framework of a sophisticated model of interest-group politics."[17]

In contrast to Lindblom's view that business has a "privileged position" in the political process, Vogel and other pluralists insist that many other groups bring substantial advantages to contests over public policy. Senior citizen organizations have millions of members with high rates of electoral participation; education and health groups champion causes that are popular with the American people; and the messages of environmental groups cannot be dismissed as selfish and profit-oriented. Corporations lack these political advantages.

Furthermore, the business class does not have monolithic policy goals. Exporters have policy positions different from those of importers, semiconductor manufacturers are affected by policies different from those of lumber companies, and franchisers have interests different from those of industries with heavy capital needs. Companies also compete with each other in the marketplace. Local telephone companies compete with traditional long-distance firms, cable companies, television broadcasters, Internet firms, and cellular businesses, and policies that benefit one part of an industry may harm or even sound the death knell for another group of firms. In addition, companies are consumers of goods as well as producers. Soft drink companies are hurt by policies that increase the price growers receive for sugar; airlines face cost increases when gasoline prices rise; and employers pay most of the bill when health care costs increase. Because of their diverse policy goals, businesses are often political antagonists, and thus some businesses inevitably lose a political struggle when other businesses win. Given the varied circumstances where businesses suffer policy defeats, the pluralists insist they cannot be dominant.

The Market Capitalism Model

The *market capitalism model* of relations between business and the state embraces the assumptions of market-oriented economists about how an economy works. (Variations of this model are sometimes described as "neo-classical" or "neo-liberal.") The model assumes that corporations operate for the benefit of their shareholders and that corporate managers act to maximize shareholder value. Only by providing shareholders a greater return on their investment than is available elsewhere can managers guarantee that their firms will have access to the capital needed for corporate operations.

The market capitalism model also assumes that individuals and firms purchase the products that give them the greatest satisfaction for their money and that they purchase these goods in perfectly competitive markets. A perfectly competitive market is a market in which no single producer or consumer is powerful enough to affect prices or other terms of sale. Manufacturers who sell goods in competitive markets attract customers by producing the best possible product at the lowest possible price. To do this, they search out new technologies and devise ever more efficient production techniques. Since consumers, by definition, purchase the goods that give them the greatest benefit for the least cost, the choices of individual consumers represent the policies that provide the greatest benefit to the society. In theory, reliance on markets produces an efficiently functioning economy that allocates resources among competing producers and purposes in an optimal way.

The market capitalism model makes a powerful political statement. Since, according to this model, properly functioning markets chart the optimal policy course for society, any government action that departs from market judgments renders the economy less efficient and deprives the society of resources. The principal task of government under the market capitalism model is to guarantee that markets function properly. If companies have power to fix prices or limit competition, if consumers lack the information needed to select the best products, if market exchanges affect people who are not party to the transaction, or if the structure of an industry blocks new firms from entering business, a market failure has occurred, and government should act to correct it. In keeping with the model, governments can also provide national defense, establish a currency, and discharge other responsibilities that markets alone cannot undertake.

The opponents of market capitalism argue that some social values are not expressed through marketplace exchanges, and they maintain that adding up individual preferences is an inadequate method for determining social policy. Some goods, the critics contend, have more long-term social value than current exchanges recognize, and some people, they remind us, lack the resources to express their preferences through the marketplace. Proponents of the market capitalism model frequently have more influence in the economic arena than in the political sphere, whereas the opponents of this model usually believe that their policy goals receive a more sympathetic hearing from public officials than from economists and businesspeople.

The Stakeholder Model

The *stakeholder model* sees companies as the hub of relations among societal groups that have a stake in corporate decisions. From this perspective, when managers shape corporate policy they should consider the welfare of each stakeholder affected by corporate actions. Thus, the stakeholder model rejects both the market capitalism assumption that the interests of stockholders alone should guide corporate decisions and the pluralist view that a comprehensive array of societal groups has a say in the public policies that govern firms. The stakeholder perspective expects corporate policies to emerge from the interplay of business associations, organized groups, and political agencies. In a departure from the market capitalism, business dominance, and pluralist models, however, the stakeholder model expects government to play an active role in forging policy agreements that goes beyond the brokering of group preferences.

Many European nations structure their policy processes according to a particular type of stakeholder model called *corporatism*.[18] A corporatist model of governance understands the two major stakeholders in a modern society to be labor unions and business associations. In a pure corporatist system, a single organization speaks for the business community, and another organization expresses the interests of labor. Corporatist structures emphasize cooperation and restrain conflict. When critical economic problems emerge, government officials call together the representatives of business and labor to develop a policy on which labor, capital, and government can agree. This program then becomes the nation's policy response to the crisis. According to corporatist logic, political systems that best integrate labor and management into the policy process have the greatest chance of successfully meeting the global challenges of an international economy.

A second type of stakeholder model emerges from a survey of the chief executive officers (CEOs) of 220 major U.S. firms.[19] In this survey, the managers were asked to list the groups to whom they had the greatest responsibility when they made decisions, and the managers responded that their principal stakeholders were customers, stockholders, employees, governments, and the communities in which they were located. Chiseled in stone in the lobby of the Johnson & Johnson headquarters in New Jersey is that firm's answer to the same stakeholder question. The Johnson & Johnson credo holds that its first responsibility is to its customers, the second is to the employees, and the third is to the communities in which the company and its employees live and work. The final responsibility, according to the company's credo, is to the stockholders, who should earn a fair return only if the company has fulfilled its responsibilities to the other stakeholders.

These four models demonstrate that the choices involved in designing a country's political and economic systems are not easy ones. The alternatives are not a simple dichotomy between governments and markets but a complex array of options that combine government and market-oriented arrangements in an infinite variety of ways. Although all four models combine normative and descriptive features, the business dominance and pluralist models seek to describe existing societal relations, whereas the market capitalist and stakeholder perspectives advocate what their champions believe to be beneficial for the society. The subtlety of the relationships between government and business is best recognized by examining political-economic arrangements in real situations. Box 2-1 is a description of how relations between government and business have endured during Mexico's development process.

GOVERNMENT AND BUSINESS: INTERNATIONAL PERSPECTIVES

Germany, Japan, Great Britain, and the United States are all influential nations with market-oriented economies in which private firms play a major but not unlimited role. Despite broad similarities, the four countries organize relation-

Cases in Development
BOX 2-1 MANAGING DEVELOPMENT IN MEXICO

Mexico has become a more democratic and market-driven country during the last decade. The election victory of Vicente Fox of the National Action Party in 2000 marked the electoral defeat of the Institutional Revolutionary Party and delivered the first transfer of political power to an opposition party in seventy years. Fox had attracted younger, better-educated, largely urban voters from Mexico's northern states with promises of delivering the benefits of economic growth to the people.

Industrialization took root in Mexico during World War II when the government subsidized industries whose products could substitute for goods imported from abroad. In the 1970s, public ownership of industry increased, and state intervention in corporate activities escalated, but government revenues from oil sales declined, improvements in productivity disappeared, trade deficits soared, and the country was forced to devalue its currency. Carlos Salinas, president from 1988 to 1994, reversed the economic policies of his predecessors. He rejected protection of industries in favor of policies that lowered trade barriers and promoted exports, but the trade deficit climbed once again, and the peso was again devalued. In 1995 the Clinton administration arranged a $47 billion loan to Mexico to prevent economic collapse, but the Mexican government was still forced to rescue banks and industries from recessionary circumstances. The North American Free Trade Agreement (NAFTA) came into effect at this time, and the Mexican economy rebounded, recording 5.5 percent annual growth between 1996 and 2000.

As Mexico faced its 2006 presidential election, Fox's fate was uncertain. His public approval ratings fell as the legislature delayed his reform agenda, and his party lost seats in the 2003 congressional election. As Mexico sought to upgrade the skill level and wages of its workforce, economists feared that it was losing its competitive advantage to China and other lower-cost manufacturers. Despite producing price and monetary stability, Fox had not yet improved social conditions and overcome the inequalities that plagued the nation.

Sources: This discussion is based on Russell Crandall, Guadalupe Paz, and Riordan Roett, eds., *Mexico's Democracy at Work: Political and Economic Dynamics* (Boulder, Colo.: Lynne Rienner, 2004); Kevin J. Middlebrook and Eduardo Zepeda, eds., *Confronting Development: Assessing Mexico's Economic and Social Policy Challenges* (Stanford, Calif.: Stanford University Press, 2003); and Carol Wise and Riordan Roett, eds., *Post-Stabilization Politics in Latin America: Competition, Transition, Collapse* (Washington, D.C.: Brookings Institution Press, 2003).

ships between government and business in strikingly different ways. John Zysman has investigated the economic processes of various countries and identified the institutions that provide economic leadership in each.[20] For Zysman, the United States is a country with a *company-led* economy, in which private corporations organize the economy and government intervention is limited. Japan has a *state-led* economy, in which the structure of the financial system itself is an instrument of government intervention in the marketplace. Economic leadership in Germany is *negotiated,* with major decisions resulting from specific deals between finance, labor, government, and industry. Zysman describes Britain as a country without a coherent approach to managing its economy: government occasionally seeks to take the economic initiative, but companies retain their autonomy, and unions are not constituted to negotiate economic policy with government and business. Closer examination of the traditions and institutions in Germany, Japan, and Great Britain enhances Zysman's characterizations.

Table 2-1 presents background information on our four countries and the European Union. The population of the United States is slightly larger than the population of Germany, Great Britain, and Japan combined.

The term *gross domestic product* is used here as a measure of the size of a country's economy. GDP per capita reports the amount produced in a country divided by its population; it is a measure of the country's wealth. The per capita GDP figure is adjusted to reflect national differences in the cost of living, so the totals reflect the value of comparable goods the inhabitants of each country can purchase. Government spending as a percentage of GDP is an indication of the prominence of government in a country's economy, but spending, of course, is not a perfect measure of government influence.

Table 2-1   Major Industrial Countries

	Population (in millions)	Gross domestic product (in billions)	Gross domestic product per capita	Government spending as a percentage of GDP
Germany	82	$1,986	$25,917	49%
Great Britain	60	1,565	27,976	44
Japan	127	3,988	26,954	38
United States	290	10,383	36,121	36
European Union	378	9,459	23,228	49

Sources: Data in first three columns: *Statistical Abstract of the United States: 2004–2005* (Washington, D.C.: GPO, 2004); data in last column: *OECD Economic Outlook,* December 2004.

Note: Years for data: population, 2003; gross domestic product, 2002; gross domestic product per capita, 2001; government spending as percentage of GDP, 2003.

Great Britain

Britain was the world's first industrial nation and the first model of a modern capitalist system. Merchants, bankers, and consumers were more influential in Britain than were manufacturers, and the country's business system developed a distinctly international orientation. Britain was also the first nation to experience widespread industrial decline, as the institutions that had been responsible for the nation's industrial and imperial successes in the eighteenth and nineteenth centuries failed to adapt to evolving economic conditions.[21] Modern corporations were slow to emerge in Britain, government remained distant from industrial development, and labor unions emphasized distributional conflicts rather than concern for the common economic goals. Through the 1950s, government lacked both the eyes to follow events in industry and the tools to intervene in specific situations.

In subsequent decades, Great Britain built the institutional capacity to sustain economic policies, but the government still failed to cure the economic stagnation.[22] The Treasury was responsible for taxation, public expenditures, and exchange rate policy, whereas individual departments championed the interests of specific industries, but the government lacked a coherent strategy to support its policy initiatives. The government frequently intervened in the marketplace to assist specific industries, but its assistance responded more fully to the claims of political influence than to the substantive requirements of economic growth.

After their electoral victory in 1979, Prime Minister Margaret Thatcher and the Conservative Party guided Great Britain away from episodic interventions in specific industries and sought instead to build an "enterprise" culture.[23] Economic policy shifted from stimulating employment to stabilizing the money supply and fighting inflation. Nationalized industries were sold, and industrial activity was deregulated to promote competition. The Thatcher era increased short-term unemployment and aggravated social tensions, but it also improved productivity, revived investment, increased corporate profits, and gave new life to persistently weak industries. When the Labour Party returned to power in 1997, Great Britain enjoyed one of Europe's stronger economies, and Labour Party Prime Minister Tony Blair emphasized his government's commitment to continue the policies of the Thatcher regime. Seeking to demonstrate its competence in managing the nation's economy, the Labour government rejected proposals to renationalize industry, emphasized monetary stability over full employment, and limited increases in universal social benefits. Despite internal dissent, the Labour Party went on to be elected by a large margin to a second term in 2001 and again, by a smaller margin, in 2005.[24]

Germany

The recovery of the German economy after World War II is often described as an "economic miracle."[25] German economic policies in the 1950s and 1960s were market oriented, and the country profited from the expansion then occurring in the international economy. With the oil price hikes, inflationary pressures, and rising unemployment of the 1970s and 1980s, the country's economic policies became more interventionist.[26] Nevertheless, the postwar record of the German "social market" economy remains impressive, and by the early 1990s Germany was one of the world's leading trading nations.

The country's economic success is usually attributed to four factors. First, the German government is based on a series of institutional relationships that emphasize consensus and political stability. The country's parliamentary system, the influence of the bureaucracy, and the pattern of coalition governments have yielded a predictable policy environment that stresses rational decision making and encourages economic growth.

A second factor that has contributed to economic success is a harmonious system of labor-management relations. Postwar German unions have focused on worker participation in corporate governance and accepted the importance of economic productivity. Employee representation on corporate boards of directors and the presence of workers' councils in factories have reduced tensions during periods of decline.

Third, banking institutions hold a stronger hand in Germany than in other major countries.[27] Banks own stock in major corporations and are also permitted to vote the stock they hold for their customers. As a consequence, banks are directly represented on corporate boards of directors; representatives of the three largest banks chair the boards of fifteen of the country's largest companies.[28] For this reason, banks are able to provide an informed, yet somewhat detached, view of the long-term interests of companies and industries. Finally, the success of the German economy has depended on a vigorous export program. Exports not only deliver a healthy trade surplus to the nation's economy, but they also provide marketplace discipline for German companies.[29]

In the 1990s commentators began to debate whether the German business system had lost its industrial competitiveness.[30] The reunification of Germany and the integration of East Germany into West German economic and political systems had been slower, more costly, and more contentious than anticipated. At the same time, Germany's already high labor costs rose in comparison to costs in other industrial nations as it became more tightly integrated into the European and global economies. The increasing authority of the European Union has limited the ability of the German government to deal with economic stagnation and stubbornly high unemployment.

The European Union

The European Union (EU) is an organization of twenty-five European nations whose population now tops 450 million. The Union was created to reduce conflict and increase cooperation among European nations, to make European values and viewpoints more influential in the world, and to secure the benefits of a unified economy for European firms, states, and citizens. In the past quarter century, EU institutions have gradually assumed some of the governmental responsibilities of its member states, and eventually a United States of Europe may supersede the existing nation-states. Europeans are seeking to create a continent-wide political and economic structure that will secure for them the prosperity and influence in the world that a continental system allowed to the United States.

Economically, the European Union has sought to lower internal trade barriers, promote a common currency, and create European economic standards. It allows citizens of member states to cross national borders at will, has defined community-wide standards for such products as cell phones and automobiles, and champions European approaches to banking, agriculture, trade, and innovation policy. The member states, however, harbor histories of conflict, diverse governmental and cultural traditions, divergent geopolitical ambitions, different income levels, and dissimilar economic interests. Because of these differences, the European Union has difficulty formulating and enforcing common programs, as was illustrated in 2004 when various countries failed to fulfill their obligations to limit the budget deficit to 3 percent of national expenditures. Although the progress toward European integration has been impressive, no one expects project Europe to be completed any time soon.

Japan

In much of the post–World War II era, the Japanese economy was one of the world's success stories, but Japanese economic achievements were not solely a post–World War II phenomenon. In the decades before World War II, Japan had built a large, efficient industrial sector that was supported by an active government and an influential bureaucracy.[31] Postwar reconstruction was guided by a similar coalition of industrial leaders, bureaucratic elites, and political figures who forged a public consensus based on the primacy of economic growth.

In the 1950s and 1960s the Ministry of Finance (MOF) and the Ministry of International Trade and Industry (MITI) worked with business panels to draft elaborate plans for economic development.[32] Through a process of "administrative guidance," the agencies gave firms and industries economic direction.[33] The Japanese economy was mostly closed to foreign competition in these years, and the ministries used their role in international trade to provide product protection to cooperative industries. The ministries' professional stature and their control of scarce capital, foreign exchange, and technology ensured business support for their program. In these years, the MOF and the MITI probably constituted the capitalist world's most powerful economic bureaucracy, and the parliament was the weakest legislature in major industrial democracies.

Japanese economic planning was more important as a mechanism of coordination between government and industry than as a compendium of specific decisions. Collaboration and negotiation were so intense that some argued it was an error to regard government and industry as distinct institutions. Businesspeople and bureaucrats had joint jurisdiction over markets and productive resources, and both the state and private groups worked to enhance the authority of the other.[34] As a result, public policy and private economic activity achieved a level of coordination unmatched in other industrial economies.[35]

In the 1970s and 1980s the Japanese economy matured, and the country emerged to play a prominent international role. Policy attention shifted from macroeconomic policies to mercantilist efforts to foster the welfare of specific commercial sectors. In industry after industry, Japan captured first place in the global marketplace, and the country's promotional policies contributed to this achievement.[36]

Despite the country's wealth and the successes of its largest corporations, national economic performance deteriorated in Japan in the 1990s.[37] Contradictions between the international and domestic sectors of the economy became more severe, and the alignment among the political, economic, and social institutions that had brought Japan prosperity after World War II was strained. At the beginning of the twenty-first century, government leaders remained unable to devise policies to overcome the earlier excesses in the financial and real estate markets and recapture the prosperity and political stability the nation had enjoyed in previous decades.

Government leaders who create or subsequently alter a country's political and economic arrangements must choose between imperfect alternatives. Capitalism appears in various national forms, and each decision involves a trade-off among core values. The division of authority between separate but mutually dependent economic and political realms requires mechanisms to resolve continuing public-private conflicts. Relations between government and business are an expression of a country's moral and political sentiments, but if any specific value is championed too vigorously, the flexibility and dynamism of both the economy and the political processes could be jeopardized. Both public and private sectors should strengthen the other, but if either sector is too powerful, it could frustrate the accomplishments of the other.

SUMMARY

Given the design complexities of government, it should be no surprise that scholars who investigate relations between government and business differ about what they observe. In the United States, privately owned firms have been allowed to play a prominent role in the economy because such firms are seen to provide the society more benefits than costs.[38] Government not only seeks to promote the success of economic activity, but it also reserves the right to veto marketplace decisions when those decisions produce social or economic distress. Some scholars understand the United States to be an example of the business dominance model of government-business relations, whereas others see it as a fundamentally pluralist system that allows a voice to various groups and organizations.

Japan has usually been regarded as a political-economic system, wherein business plays a preeminent role, but some authorities conclude that respected government ministries employ an array of regulatory measures to lead business organizations to accept their understanding of economic policy. The German business system is commonly described as a "social market" economy, in that corporatist traditions assemble the representatives of labor, industry, and government to negotiate policies that maintain a market-oriented economy and distribute public resources in social benefits. Under Prime Minister Thatcher in the 1980s and early 1990s, Great Britain moved toward a framework state with a market capitalist system in which government-owned enterprises were privatized, industries deregulated, and stakeholder and corporatist decision-making arrangements dismantled. Since 1997, the Labour Party has maintained much of Prime Minister Thatcher's program.

Conflicts between business and nonbusiness groups are a recurrent feature of political life in major industrial nations. Groups disagree about the priority to be given to maintaining an efficient economy or redistributing the society's rewards and opportunities as they struggle to win support for their policy objectives. The outcome of these conflicts is determined in part by the structures of the nations' political institutions, which are examined in the following chapter.

FURTHER READINGS

The Web site of Paul M. Johnson at Auburn University contains "A Glossary of Political Economy Terms": http://www.auburn.edu/~johnspm/glossind.html. The World Wide Web Virtual Library for EuroIntegration contains links to EU institutions and organizations concerned about the European Union: http://www.eiop.or.at/euroint/.

Beason, Dick, and Dennis Patterson. *The Japan That Never Was: Explaining the Rise and Decline of a Misunderstood Country.* Albany: State University of New York Press, 2004.

Dennis, Mike, and Eva Kolinsky, eds. *United and Divided: Germany Since 1990.* New York: Berghahn Books, 2004.

Lindblom, Charles E. *The Market System: What It Is, How It Works, and What to Make of It.* New Haven, Conn.: Yale University Press, 2001.

Ludlam, Steve, and Martin J. Smith, eds. *Governing as New Labour: Policy and Politics under Blair.* New York: Palgrave Macmillan, 2004.

Roy, William G., *Socializing Capital: The Rise of the Large Industrial Corporation in America* Princeton: Princeton University Press, 1997.

NOTES

1. This discussion is drawn from Marshall B. Clinard, *Corporate Corruption: The Abuse of Power* (New York: Praeger, 1990), 1–3; Stephen L. Elkin, *City and Regime in the American Republic* (Chicago: University of Chicago Press, 1987), 11; and Wyn Grant, *Business and Politics in Britain* (London: Macmillan Education, 1987), 1–2.

2. Charles E. Lindblom, *The Market System: What It Is, How It Works, and What to Make of It* (New Haven: Yale University Press, 2001); Harrison C. White, "Where Do Markets Come From?" *American Journal of Sociology* 87 (1981): 517–47; and William G. Roy, *Socializing Capital: The Rise of the Large Industrial Corporation in America* (Princeton: Princeton University Press, 1997).

3. Charles Derber, *People Before Profit: The New Globalization in an Age of Terror, Big Money, and Economic Crisis* (New York: Picador, 2002), 16–17.

4. John Zysman, *Governments, Markets, and Growth: Financial Systems and the Politics of Industrial Change* (Ithaca, N.Y.: Cornell University Press, 1983), 17–18; and Frank Dobbin, *Forging Industrial Policy: The United Sates, Britain, and France in the Railway Age* (New York: Cambridge University Press, 1994).

5. Frank Bourgin, *The Great Challenge: The Myth of Laissez-Faire in the Early Republic* (New York: Harper and Row, 1989), chap. 4.

6. Peter Eisinger, *The Rise of the Entrepreneurial State* (Madison: University of Wisconsin Press, 1988); R. Scott Fosler, ed., *The New Economic Role of American States* (New York: Oxford University Press, 1988); and David Osborne, *Laboratories of Democracy* (Boston: Harvard Business School Press, 1988).

7. See, for example, Peter Asch and Rosalind S. Seneca, *Government and the Marketplace* (Chicago: Dryden Press, 1989), chaps. 3–5; and Tyler Cowen, ed., *The Theory of Market Failure: A Critical Examination* (Fairfax, Va.: George Mason University Press, 1988).

8. For example, John Kenneth Galbraith, *The Age of Uncertainty* (Boston: Houghton Mifflin, 1977).

9. For a similar structure, see George A. Steiner and John F. Steiner, *Business, Government, and Society: A Managerial Perspective*, 8th ed. (New York: McGraw-Hill, 1997), 6–15.

10. Charles A. Beard, *An Economic Interpretation of the Constitution* (New York: Macmillan, 1913).

11. C. Wright Mills, *The Power Elite* (New York: Oxford University Press, 1965). See also Edward Digby Baltzell, *The Protestant Establishment* (New York: Random House, 1984), and William G. Domhoff, *Who Rules America?* (Englewood Cliffs, N.J.: Prentice Hall, 1967).

12. Gabriel Kolko, *Railroads and Regulation: 1877–1916* (New York: Nelson, 1965), 169.

13. Charles E. Lindblom, *Politics and Markets: The World's Political-Economic Systems* (New York: Basic Books, 1977); and David Marsh, "Interest Group Activity and Structural Power: Lindblom's *Politics and Markets*," and David Marsh and Gareth Locksley, "Capital in Britain: Its Structural Power and Influence over Policy," in *Capital and Politics in Western Europe*, ed. David Marsh (London: Frank Cass, 1983), 3–13, 36–60. For an analysis of Lindblom's "three pillars of business power," see Neil J. Mitchell, *The Conspicuous Corporation: Business, Public Policy, and Representative Democracy* (Ann Arbor: University of Michigan Press, 1997), chaps. 3–5.

14. Thomas Ferguson, *Golden Rule: The Investment Theory of Party Competition and the Logic of Money-Driven Political Systems* (Chicago: University of Chicago Press, 1995), esp. chap. 1.

15. Ibid., 22.

16. David Vogel, *Fluctuating Fortunes: The Political Power of Business in America* (New York: Basic Books, 1989); and Vogel, *Kindred Strangers: The Uneasy Relationship between Politics and Business in America* (Princeton: Princeton University Press, 1996).

17. Vogel, *Kindred Strangers,* 265.

18. P. C. Schmitter and G. Lehmbruch, eds., *Trends towards Corporatist Intermediation* (London: Sage Publications, 1979); and W. Streeck, "Neo-corporatist Industrial Relations and the Economic Crisis in Germany," in *Order and Conflict in Contemporary Capitalism,* ed. J. H. Goldthorpe (Oxford: Oxford University Press, Clarendon Press, 1984).

19. Linda D. Lerner and Gerald E. Fryxell, "CEO Stakeholder Attitudes and Corporate Social Activity in the Fortune 500," *Business and Society,* April 1994.

20. Zysman, *Governments, Markets, and Growth,* 92–94.

21. Ibid., 175–206; and Geoffrey Shepherd, "United Kingdom: A Resistance to Change," in *Managing Industrial Change in Western Europe,* ed. François Duchêne and Geoffrey Shepherd (London: Frances Pinter, 1987), 145–77.

22. Wyn Grant, *The Political Economy of Industrial Policy* (London: Butterworths, 1982), esp. 125, 146–47; and Scott Newton and Dilwyn Porter, *Modernization Frustrated: The Politics of Industrial Decline in Britain since 1900* (London: Unwin Hyman, 1988), esp. x, 185.

23. See Newton and Porter, *Modernization Frustrated,* 84–112; and Jeffrey B. Freyman, "Industrial Policy: Patterns of Convergence and Divergence," in *Political Economy: Public Policies in the United States and Britain,* ed. Jerold L. Waltman and Donley T. Studlar (Jackson: University Press of Mississippi, 1987), 44–68.

24. Steve Ludlam and Martin J. Smith, eds., *Governing as New Labour: Policy and Politics under Blair* (New York: Palgrave Macmillan, 2004).

25. This section is drawn from Ernst-Juergen Horn, "Germany: A Market-led Process," in Duchéne and Shepherd, *Managing Industrial Change,* 41–75; Jeffrey A. Hart, "West German Industrial Policy," in *The Politics of Industrial Policy,* ed. Claude E. Barfield and William A. Schambra (Washington, D.C.: American Enterprise Institute, 1986), 161–86; and Andrew P. Black, "Industrial Policy in W. Germany: Policy in Search of a Goal?" in *European Industrial Policy,* ed. Graham Hall (London: Croom Helm, 1986), 84–127.

26. Juergen B. Donges, "Industrial Policies in West Germany's Not so Market-oriented Economy," *World Economy* 3, no. 2 (1980): 185–204.

27. Andrew Shonfield, *Modern Capitalism* (New York: Oxford University Press, 1965). For an alternative view, see Wyn Grant, William Paterson, and Colin Whitson, *Government and the Chemical Industry: A Comparative Study of Britain and West Germany* (Oxford: Oxford University Press, Clarendon Press, 1988), 84–97.

28. Zysman, *Governments, Markets, and Growth,* 264.

29. See the discussion of "fulcrum" industries in Christopher S. Allen and Jeremiah M. Riemer, "The Industrial Policy Controversy in West Germany: Organized Adjustment and the Emergence of Meso-Corporatism," in *The Politics of Economic Adjustment: Pluralism, Corporatism, and Privatization,* ed. Richard E. Foglesong and Joel D. Wolfe (New York: Greenwood Press, 1989), 45–64.

30. Wolfgang Münchau, "A Country Losing Competitiveness: Germany Faces Hard Choices after Today's Jobless Rise," *London Financial Times,* February 8, 1996, 8; and Martin Wolf, "German Handicap," *London Financial Times,* March 31, 1999, 16.

31. Charles J. McMillan, *The Japanese Industrial System,* 2nd ed. (Berlin: Walter de Gruyter, 1989).

32. Chalmers Johnson, *MITI and the Japanese Miracle* (Stanford, Calif.: Stanford University Press, 1982); and Chalmers Johnson, "The Institutional Foundation of Japanese Industrial Policy," in Barfield and Schambra, *Politics of Industrial Policy,* 187–205.

33. James Horne, "The Economy and the Political System," in J. A. A. Stockwin, Alan Rix, Aurelia George, James Horne, Daiichi Itō, and Martin Collick, *Dynamic and Immobilist Politics in Japan* (Honolulu: University of Hawaii Press, 1988), 141–70.

34. See Richard J. Samuels, *The Business of the Japanese State: Energy Markets in Comparative and Historical Perspective* (Ithaca, N.Y.: Cornell University Press, 1987), esp. 8–9, 260, 286.

35. George C. Eads and Kozo Yamamura, "The Future of Industrial Policy," in *The Political Economy of Japan: The Domestic Transformation,* ed. Kozo Yamamura and Yasukichi Yasuba (Stanford, Calif.: Stanford University Press, 1987), 423–68.

36. Clyde V. Prestowitz, *Trading Places: How We Are Giving Our Future to Japan and How to Reclaim It* (New York: Basic Books, 1988).

37. T. J. Pempel, *Regime Shift: Comparative Dynamics of the Japanese Political Economy* (Ithaca, N.Y.: Cornell University Press, 1998).

38. Herbert McClosky and John Zaller, *The American Ethos: Public Attitudes toward Capitalism and Democracy* (Cambridge, Mass.: Harvard University Press, 1984), chaps. 1 and 9, esp. p. 7.

CHAPTER 3

The Stakes in Government Systems

ON THE WALLS of the historic city council chamber in Siena, Italy, are magnificent frescoes by the fourteenth-century painter Ambrogio Lorenzetti entitled *Consequences of Good and Bad Government.*[1] When bad policy decisions are made, according to the frescoes, death and destruction are everywhere in the city. With a horned tyrant in command, soldiers massacre the residents, and children are murdered as they play. Citizens suffer from epidemics and famines, nothing grows in the fields, and little productive activity occurs. When government makes good policy decisions, peace, justice, wisdom, and harmony triumph. The buildings in these frescoes are spotless and appealing, roads are well-maintained, and vineyards, fields, and small lakes dot the landscape. With good policy judgments, citizens engage in all forms of productive labor, and abundance prevails.

Why do some nations become rich while others are mired in poverty? Centuries after Lorenzetti there is still reason to believe that the success of a country's economy depends ultimately on the quality of its political decisions.[2] In *The Political Economy of Poverty, Equity and Growth,* Deepak Lal and H. Myint maintain that a country's wealth is a product of its investment record, but investment success depends on an environment shaped by government policy.[3] Only if a nation's governing institutions provide necessary public services, maintain a competent bureaucracy, ensure stable fiscal and monetary policies, and establish an effective legal system is investment success likely.[4] Because countries need governing arrangements that correspond to their needs and traditions, successful policymaking institutions will assume a range of different features.

The quality of government decisions is critical to business and other sectors of society. If a government's policies in health care, defense, education, or any other area impose costs without delivering commensurate benefits, the society is the poorer. This chapter begins with a survey of government decisions that are particularly important to business. The structure of a country's governing institutions both defines the procedures by which its policies are made and influences who will have a central role in the policy process and who will not. John E. Chubb and Paul E. Peterson have written that the "problem of governance in the United States is mainly one of creating institutions . . . that can pursue policies of sufficient coherence, consistency, foresight, and stability that the national welfare is not sacrificed for narrow or temporary gains."[5] In the second part of this chapter, I review the structure of the American political system and ask whether or not these features encourage the productive policymaking a prosperous economy requires. Government institutions in other countries are sometimes said to function more capably than the U.S. system. In the third section of the chapter, I examine government arrangements in Great Britain, Germany, Japan, and the European Union to consider whether features of these systems might improve the effectiveness of U.S. government.

GOVERNMENT ACTIVITIES

No single agency is the focal point of contacts between government and business in the United States. Instead, myriad departments and agencies are important to business. Table 3-1 provides a list of the organizations and programs that concern business most. Numerous other commissions and bureaus hold life-and-death control over specific industries.

U.S. business, in principle, holds government at arm's length. It fears that government involvement will lead to government domination. In fact, relations between government and industry are less adversarial than rhetoric suggests. The actions of government and business are more often cooperative than combative. Government offers numerous services that are not only valuable to business but sometimes indispensable. The more effectively government performs its tasks, the greater the likelihood that business will make a positive contribution to the society.

Infrastructure

Firms operate in a specific societal setting, and only government can maintain the social systems on which their operations depend. Discussions of infrastructure traditionally emphasize transportation and utilities. If these systems break down even temporarily, as when storms hit, many businesses cannot operate.

Recent analyses have understood the concept of infrastructure more broadly, encompassing, for example, software, venture capital, and data networks. Companies benefit from high-quality educational systems, advanced medical facilities, supportive child-care programs, and renowned cultural institutions, and governments seek to promote such institutions. Firms are more successful when they have access to progressive financial services, the latest research innovations, and well-developed systems for Internet commerce, and governments now undertake initiatives in each of these "infrastructure" areas.

Financial Assistance

Government promotes economic development by providing subsidies, loans, loan guarantees, and tax preferences. Direct subsidies go to farmers for irrigation

Table 3-1   Activities of Departments and Agencies

Government agency	Activities
Department of Agriculture	Price supports, the forest service, food inspection programs
Department of Commerce	Trade programs, tourism, technical and statistical services
Department of Defense	Massive procurement expenditures, research projects
Department of Education	Student aid programs, vocational education
Department of Energy	Energy sales, energy technology, nuclear energy
Department of Health and Human Services	Health care financing, Food and Drug Administration, health research
Department of Homeland Security	Protection of infrastructure, safeguarding of transportation
Department of Housing and Urban Development	Housing finance and construction
Department of the Interior	Public lands, minerals, mining
Department of Justice	Antitrust, commercial litigation
Department of Labor	Occupational safety, pension supervision
Department of Transportation	Construction, auto, rail, air, maritime safety
Department of the Treasury	Tax policy, regulation of financial institutions, public debt
Environmental Protection Agency	Numerous air, water, solid waste, toxic substance regulations
Export-Import Bank	Financing and insurance for exports
Federal Communications Commission	Regulation of competition in telecommunications, broadcasting, cable industries
Federal Reserve Board	Regulation of money supply, interest rates, banks
Federal Trade Commission	Regulation of commercial practices
General Services Administration	Government procurement and construction
National Labor Relations Board	Administration of labor laws

Source: Author.

projects and market information, to Amtrak for railroad travel, to the maritime industry for shipping operations, and to petroleum companies for depleting their stock of oil. Loans are provided by the Small Business Administration to expand small businesses, by the Economic Development Administration to aid firms in distressed areas, and by the Export-Import Bank to assist export sales; loan guarantees have been used to benefit the housing industry, satellite broadcasters, and college students. Tax breaks promote job training, the life insurance industry, the construction of sports stadiums, and the sale of gasohol. Some industries would not exist if public financial assistance were withheld.

Research and Development

Government also promotes economic development by supporting research and development activities. The prominence of American biotechnology is largely due to massive research expenditures by the National Institutes of Health. The national government maintains hundreds of laboratories to conduct research in technical areas and funds universities, medical institutes, and corporations to help support their research agendas. It encourages technical progress through the patent system and helps inventors capture the rewards of their innovations. State governments also provide tax breaks for research activities and appropriate funds for university research.

Government Procurement

Approximately 25 percent of the national government's budget is used to purchase products and services from private companies. When government procurement is mentioned, we think first of the defense budget and space expenditures. Most of these expenditures go to purchase exotic products, but large portions of these budgets also go to buy such ordinary products as motor vehicles, medical supplies, building materials, and communications equipment. The Federal Supply Service buys products for civilian agencies, and it is an important purchaser of food, health care, alarm systems, office supplies, consultant services, and all the other products of a complex economy. State and local governments have diverse procurement policies, but their purchases probably exceed in volume those of the national government. In recent years, many government functions—such as managing arenas, issuing driver's licenses, and operating prisons—have been privatized or contracted out, and this trend has created further opportunities for the private sector.

Government Regulation

Government regulation is a pervasive fact of contemporary life. A seemingly endless list of national agencies restricts what companies can do: the Federal Trade Commission, the Food and Drug Administration, the Consumer Product Safety Commission, the Occupational Safety and Health Administration, the Equal Employment Opportunity Commission, the Federal Communications Commission, the Environmental Protection Agency, and on and on. There is an even longer list of state agencies that spell out the rules that businesses must follow in the various states.

Although regulation is invoked by politicians to symbolize conflict between government and industry, companies themselves often seek regulation and exploit the commercial advantages that regulation offers. The Telecommunications Act of 1996 was delayed for years while companies fought over the conditions under which local telephone firms, long-distance carriers, broadcasters, cable companies, software firms, and publishers could protect their own markets and gain advantage in new markets. Government regulations require drivers to purchase automobile insurance, dictate the installation of pollution-control devices manufactured by a few firms, authorize some companies rather than others to provide a service, and establish product standards that drive some corporations, but not others, out of business. When regulatory systems fail, as they did in the late 1990s with Enron and WorldCom, it is the employees and investors as well as the business community that bear most of the burden.

Market Stability

Businesses and economists focus on transactions that occur in the marketplace.[6] Markets, however, should be viewed both behaviorally and institutionally. Marketplace behavior is guided by rules that are themselves social and political creations, and businesses rely on government to organize marketplace activity.

Most businesses say they favor competition, but few want unbridled competition. Most corporations seek to limit the riskiness of their investments. They prefer stable markets with predictable outcomes. They favor a live-and-let-live style of competition that offers rewards for competent operations rather than winner-take-all struggles that deliver enormous profits for knockout victories.[7] As the prosecution of Microsoft demonstrated, government actions help structure marketplace competition. Government determines whether banks can take over brokerage firms, whether doctors can run medical laboratories, whether television stations may own newspapers, and whether American Airlines may forge an international alliance with British Air. Although businesses compete in the marketplace, they depend on government to defend the stability and predictability of that competition.

Economic and Foreign Policy

Economic and foreign policies affect business even though they are not normally regarded as part of the relationship between government and business. Government actions influence inflation rates, the cost and availability of credit, the level of business activity, and the condition of the stock market. Foreign policy events are important to business because they can either open foreign markets or poison international relations. U.S. negotiations over the admission of China to the World Trade Organization guaranteed competitive opportunities for some industries but left the commercial fate of others uncertain.

Government decisions in these domains and a host of more complex programmatic areas can have a critical impact on firms and industries. If well conceived, government actions can help create a flourishing economy, but if a country's policies fail to address problems adequately they can squander resources and derail economic opportunity. What is it about the U.S. policy system that has led many to question its capacity to manage the country's problems?

PATTERNS OF AMERICAN GOVERNANCE

The U.S. government is composed of a set of institutions that were created two centuries ago to guide the affairs of 3 million people living in simple conditions along the Atlantic coast. The Founders of the new government sought to prevent the emergence of domestic tyrants who might act as despotically as British monarchs. To do this, they created a federal system that assigned separate powers to the states and the national government and then diffused the powers of the national government among loosely linked executive, legislative, and judicial institutions. The Founders sought to maintain political equilibrium by depending on the ambitions of the officeholders in each institution to prevent others from gaining excessive power. These early decisions have served the country well, but whether the historic institutions have the capacity to govern a complex society in an increasingly interdependent world is a question worth exploring. Those who doubt the capacity of the U.S. government to sustain prosperity and mitigate the nation's problems concentrate on three issues.

Separation of Powers

Governmental systems can be assessed by comparing the authority of government with the power of other groups in the society.[8] A government is said to be *strong* when it has the political and administrative authority to make decisions and carry out policies to deal with the country's problems; it is described as *weak* when it lacks those capacities. In these terms, the United States is regarded as a weak system of government. The decision to disperse authority among government institutions has increased the costs of coordinating disparate agencies, and the operations of the policy process may now be so complex that critical problems are poorly addressed. The difficulties Congress and the president have had in agreeing on the proper structure for the nation's intelligence agencies, homeland security issues, energy needs, and the cost and availability of health care may have allowed these problems to worsen.

Expansion of government authority has enhanced the role of the presidency. The president symbolizes American government and coordinates its far-flung activities.[9] The Executive Office of the President encompasses the Office of Management and Budget, the National Security Council, the Council of Economic Advisers, the Council on Environmental Quality, and the U.S. Trade Representative. Despite the organizational apparatus, the president grapples with leadership problems no other government head must endure.[10] The president faces an independently elected Congress often controlled by the opposition party. The U.S. judiciary is more deeply involved in policy issues than is the judicial system of any other country, and it too is independent of presidential control. The president cannot depend on the support of party colleagues, interest group leaders, or the Federal Reserve System and is, in fact, only one player in a complex system.

Congress is also conscious of its own institutional prerogatives. Journalists and academics have likened Congress to an obstacle course.[11] Sponsors of legislative measures must avoid obstructions presented by the substantive, appropriations, and rules committees in both chambers before their proposals are even considered on the floor or in a conference committee. The decision process has been further fragmented by the decline in the importance of seniority and the proliferation of congressional staff. With the decentralization of power, Congress now speaks with many voices on each issue.

Executive departments and agencies have also grown in influence with the emergence of positive government. Theoretically, executive departments carry out congressional decisions, but, in fact, it is not possible for Congress to instruct agencies in every circumstance. Agencies must and do exercise discretion in determining how to interpret statutory provisions and what to do when statutes are silent on an issue. Although such discretion is nominally exercised on the basis of professional objectivity, departments and agencies inevitably develop their own viewpoints and interests. When policy issues arise, the executive branch is likely to express two or three positions rather than one. Trade with China, for example, is perceived by the State Department as a foreign policy topic,[12] by the Treasury as a matter of international economic policy, by the Defense Department as a national security issue, and by the U.S. Trade Representative as a commercial topic. Such diverse perspectives impede U.S. ability to develop coherent strategies to deal with such critical issues.

Furthermore, both the president and Congress have enhanced their powers to control the actions of the bureaucracy.[13] In recent years, the presidency has increasingly screened administrative appointments to ensure loyalty to the president, and policy initiatives have been more frequently based on White House than departmental perspectives. At the other end of Pennsylvania Avenue, legislation is now regularly accompanied by committee reports with detailed instructions on how the new laws are to be administered, and Congress has increased its capacity to review and "oversee" the actions of executive agencies. Ironically, the increased capacity of Congress and the president to deal with policy issues has complicated the problems of building agreement, increased the challenges of coordination, and compounded the constitutional tendency toward inertia.

Subgovernments

A separation-of-powers system leads groups with related policy goals to establish links with each other to get things done. The links among institutions in one policy area are said to constitute a "subgovernment."[14] Subgovernments focus on specific areas, such as broadcast regulation, weapons procurement, or housing construction. They are composed of legislators on subcommittees responsible for the issue area, bureau chiefs who administer the programs, representatives of interest groups affected by the policy, and semi-autonomous policy analysts with specialized expertise in the area. Subgovernments are inspired by enduring policy interests and remain relatively stable. Although they may have less influence on prominent issues, subgovernments usually dominate the less dramatic topics that define most of what government does. (The term *iron triangle* emphasizes cooperation among congressional subcommittees, bureau chiefs, and interest groups, and the phrase *issue network* refers to more inclusive and fluid groups of policy activists that respond to changes in the society.)

Consultants and analysts often urge corporations to contact subgovernment insiders when trying to influence government decisions.[15] Success in such efforts depends on building relationships with congressional staffers rather than members, permanent civil servants in the departments and agencies rather than political executives, and long-time professionals in interest groups rather than outsiders who are assigned to an organization for a limited term.

Subgovernment decision making is characterized by substantial policy expertise and little political accountability. When a policy conflict arises, members of the subgovernment seek to resolve it themselves and resist the participation of outsiders. Subgovernment decisions are characteristically incremental, reflecting limited departures from established policy. They normally escape the notice of elected officials and remain the province of subgovernment specialists. Thus, it is not surprising that subgovernment bargains usually reflect the interests of sector participants rather than the concerns of the broader public.

Instability

A description of government that stresses political deadlock and a lack of accountability captures only part of the reality.[16] There are also occasions when political leaders stampede into action and tolerate no delays in putting their position on the record. Television has become the primary medium of political communication, but opinions generated by the media are less informed and less intensely felt than opinions that result from direct experiences.[17] It is not unusual for a topic to dominate the media for a few weeks or months, rise high in the surveys of public concern, and then fade from the public's mind.

When the media lead the nation from crisis to crisis, the governing institutions are unable to preserve political continuity. Televised meetings and published records have made elected officials more subject to interest group scrutiny and less able to resist momentarily popular but fundamentally ill-conceived policies. Officials can never be certain what side of an issue will be popular during the next election cycle or how a controversial vote may be represented to the public. Political instability is accentuated by the rapid turnover among top administration officials who typically come to Washington, serve for two or three years, and then return to their previous careers. Changes in the leadership of the executive branch occur so frequently that the United States is said to have a government led by "strangers" and "talented amateurs."[18]

Political instability begets policy instability. The U.S. government often proclaims a grand policy initiative, which, once the hoopla passes, recedes into obscurity as other issues attract attention. Under President Jimmy Carter, Congress created an ambitious program to manufacture synthetic fuels to replace imported oil. A few billion dollars later, interest flagged, and Congress cut off funding before the program had had time to achieve its legislative goals.[19] U.S. policy has been said to display a "pattern of repeated initiatives and wobbly follow-up."[20]

Chubb and Peterson argue, "Americans have always been better at representing than governing."[21] The American system of government disperses power broadly and allows many groups access to the policy process. Since many organizations are able to block decisions if their issues are not given attention, solutions to problems often resemble a catalog of items for specific interests with little coherence or attention to the national welfare. For example, to gather the votes needed to respond to a World Trade Organization ruling that invalidated $5 billion in subsidies for U.S. exporters, congressional leaders designed legislation in 2004 that showered $137 billion in new tax breaks on firms in every corner of the economy.[22]

Is it appropriate to conclude from this discussion that the structure of government itself has become a barrier to the decisions the country needs to sustain prosperity and address its problems? There is certainly evidence for this view, but before answering this question it is necessary to consider whether other institutional arrangements would make better policy decisions and whether the structure of the U.S. government has qualities that offset fragmentation, limited accountability, and unstable policies. An investigation of the capabilities governments need to make sound decisions and an examination of decision-making arrangements in other countries help frame these issues.

GOVERNMENT INSTITUTIONS IN COMPARATIVE PERSPECTIVE

Did the U.S. government do a poor job of managing energy policy when it allowed gasoline usage to climb, supplies to be jeopardized, and competition in the petroleum industry to decline? Governmental arrangements affect how a country understands policy events and how it responds to them.[23] In contrast to the United States, which has a presidential system and a separately elected Congress, Great Britain, Germany, and Japan are all parliamentary democracies. In these countries parties guide the parliament in selecting the prime minister. Although each of these nations was once renowned for its economic success, each has faced major crises in recent decades. Did each country's system of government help it address its economic problems, or was the system of government part of the problem? In order to assess the arrangements for making policy decisions, I will begin by specifying the qualities necessary for good policymaking.

R. Kent Weaver and Bert A. Rockman have investigated governing arrangements in various countries, and they define ten criteria to assess a country's policy processes.[24] They ask whether a country's governing institutions can perform the following tasks:

1. Target resources to areas where they will do the most good
2. Devise new policies when old policies have failed
3. Set priorities among conflicting policy demands
4. Coordinate efforts to achieve conflicting objectives
5. Impose losses on powerful groups
6. Represent the interests of unorganized groups in the policy process
7. Ensure effective implementation of policies
8. Ensure stable policies
9. Manage domestic political conflicts so that they do not become destructive
10. Make and maintain international agreements

Having specified these qualities, Weaver and Rockman then examine how individual countries make decisions in particular policy areas.

Great Britain

Critics of decisions made by the American government often regard the British parliamentary system as a model government. The British system is labeled a Westminster democracy, and it is characterized by two strong, programmatic parties that alternate in controlling Parliament; a prime minister chosen by Parliament; a vigorous cabinet; and an influential, nonpartisan civil service.[25] The cabinet is the primary institution of government. Ministers are individually responsible for the affairs of their departments and collectively responsible for the decisions of the government. The prime minister is a member of Parliament, is normally a party leader, and represents the authority of government. The prime minister plays a key role in government but has not necessarily dominated collegial decisions. Parliament legitimizes the policies fashioned by the bureaucracy and proposed by the cabinet, but it has little independent law-making influence.

Great Britain's adversarial democracy is based on strong, disciplined parties, and its electoral system overrepresents large parties and marginalizes third parties.[26] The governing party sets the political climate, controls the bureaucracy, and pays the price when its policies fail. When in office, both the Conservative and the Labour parties have lost popularity and suffered by-election defeats, and party control normally shifts after every two or three elections. Until recently, the government's economic policy goals have oscillated between achieving equity by regulating the market under Labour and overcoming economic decline by freeing the market and subsidizing producers under the Conservatives.

The senior civil servants are often regarded as the strength of the British system. They are depicted as talented but cautious careerists who sustain the government from election to election. They are typically trained as generalists rather than as specialists, and they promote a policy style that emphasizes consultation and avoids challenging well-entrenched interests.[27] The twentieth century witnessed frequent bouts of government activism in the economy, but until recently these outbursts were prompted by the collapse of prominent industries or surges of nationalism rather than by a coherent economic strategy.[28]

Margaret Thatcher was chosen prime minister in 1979 when the British economy was hobbled by a series of strikes during an especially cold winter, and the incumbent Labour Party government appeared unable to solve the crisis.[29] Thatcher presented herself as a strong leader whose goal was to restore the fading global competitiveness of the British economy, and in large measure she succeeded. She emphasized low inflation and a stable currency even at the expense of high unemployment. Prime Minister Thatcher used her cabinet and large majority in Parliament to restrict the power of labor unions, deregulate major industries, and sell off nationalized companies such as British Telecom and British Gas. The number of shareholders in Britain tripled during her tenure as she stressed "people's capitalism," an "enterprise culture," and the responsibility of firms for their own prosperity and survival. After dominating British politics for more than a decade, Thatcher resigned as prime minister in November 1990 and was succeeded by a member of her cabinet, who continued the economic policies she had championed.

When the Labour Party recaptured control of the government after the 1997 election and Tony Blair became prime minister, one commentator concluded, "The economic principles of Thatcherism had become conventional wisdom, and the Thatcher reforms in the civil service, business, industry, and the unions were generally accepted."[30] Even though it had been founded by labor unions, the Labour Party under Blair "distanced itself from the unions, its traditional backers, and developed links with the private sector."[31] Once in office, Blair strengthened the prime minister's office, devised a proactive media profile, and relied on the cabinet and Parliament as little as possible.[32] By adopting what his critics describe as a "presidential" approach, Prime Minister Blair has been able to implement his economic and international policies despite significant opposition from his own party. The policy process in Brazil, in contrast, limits the ability of the president to enact the administration program, as is described in Box 3-1.

Germany

Since 1949, Germany has adapted to extraordinary domestic and international developments without fundamental changes in its political institutions.[33] The foundation of this stability was Germany's remarkable economic recovery in the decades after World War II. Since economic deprivation had contributed to the collapse of the Weimar Republic and the emergence of the National Socialist regime in the 1930s, economic stability and growth have remained high priorities. The preferred

Cases in Development
BOX 3-1 POLICY PROCESS IN BRAZIL

As the largest, most populous nation in South America, Brazil has become the continent's foremost economic power. Since achieving independence from Portugal in 1822, however, Brazil has followed a political path that has limited its ability to realize its potential. Having survived long periods of rule by colonial masters, traditional oligarchs, and military governments, Brazil's experience with democracy has been limited.

The country's political system favors the executive branch, but the president, nonetheless, has difficulty building stable coalitions to support government programs. Brazil's federal system and its policy process permit multiple veto points, and the highly fragmented party system allows minor parties with little popular support to exercise significant legislative influence. The country has one of the largest public sectors in Latin America, and the broad diffusion of administrative authority limits the ability of the executive to implement even those programs that are passed by the legislature.

Luiz Inácio Lula da Silva was elected Brazil's president in 2002 with 61 percent of the popular vote. A leftist union leader, da Silva was the candidate of the Workers' Party, which had consistently advocated social justice in Brazil and denounced globalization in the world economy. Having lost three previous elections, da Silva moderated the historic positions of the Workers' Party during the 2002 campaign and endorsed the market system and the private sector. These policy shifts were opposed by elements of the Workers' Party and others in the governing coalition, but the da Silva government has stuck to its position. As Brazil heads toward a new presidential election in 2006, the economy has been performing well and the government's approval rating exceeds 60 percent. Divisions within the governing coalition, however, and cohesion among opposition parties may block legislative action on revenue needs, political corruption, deficiencies in education, and antipoverty programs as the election nears.

Sources: This discussion is based on Nicola Phillips, *The Southern Cone Model: The Political Economy of Regional Capitalist Development in Latin America* (New York: Routledge, 2004); Riordan Roett, "Brazil's Protracted Transition to Democracy and Market," in *Post-Stabilization Politics in Latin America: Competition, Transition, Collapse,* ed. Carol Wise and Riordan Roett (Washington, D.C.: Brookings Institution Press, 2003), 199–218; and "Lula at Half-time," "To Lula's Credit," and "Make or Break," *Economist,* November 6, 2004, 40; September 4, 2004, 13; and February 20, 2003, http://www.economist.com.

strategy for economic growth has been a vigorous export program, and this strategy has been supported by a "productivity coalition" composed of business, unions, and semipublic institutions.[34]

Germany has a parliamentary system wherein political parties select the chancellor and dominate the policy process. The chancellor is elected for a four-year term and has the right to appoint and dismiss cabinet ministers. The effective power of the chancellor is limited, however, by the influence of party organizations, the decisions of the Federal Constitutional Court, and the latitude given individual ministers in running their own departments. During almost all of the past fifty years, as well, the government has been controlled by party coalitions rather than by a single party, and this too has strengthened the forces of moderation. State governments are also influential players in national politics because of their direct representation in one house of the national parliament, their role in implementing national policies, and the importance of state party organizations on the national scene. Although this governing process has stabilized German politics, the autonomy of various institutions limits the capacity of government to respond to crises.[35]

The German policy process is a corporatist partnership between the government, labor unions, and business associations. The policy style relies on devising consensual solutions to problems rather than allowing a majority to impose its own will. Opposition to the productivity coalition and its economic sentiments appeared in Germany in the 1970s, as a variety of popular movements articulated postmaterialistic concerns about the environment, nuclear energy, and human rights.[36] These movements had a visible impact on societal values and government policy, but the nation's traditional governing practices remained in place.

In the 1990s the country faced the challenge of integrating the territory and residents of the former German Democratic Republic into a reunified Germany, but this task has been more difficult than anticipated. Rather than fading away, the economic and social cleavages between the old and the new German states have become more pronounced in public discourse and more prominent in political debate. At the beginning of the twenty-first century, the expansion of the European Union made Germany's position as the largest contributor to the EU budget ever more burdensome, and the globalization of the economy made it easier for manufacturers to seek out low-cost countries for new investment and avoid Germany's expensive industrial structures. In 2004 one of Germany's most prominent research foundations released a report concluding that the days of the once stellar German economic performance were past and the country now ranked last in employment and economic growth among twenty-one industrial nations.[37] The institutional constraints in the German policy process have now made it difficult to build the necessary consensus needed to rejuvenate the country's flagging economy.[38]

Japan

Japan has the world's second largest economy and, until a decade ago, one of the world's most extolled. The country had devised a successful model of state-led development that had produced a high level of economic growth and permitted Japan's emergence as a major figure in global commerce. Unfortunately, as one scholar writes, in the 1990s the "parts of the once fine-tuned machine no longer meshed so smoothly."[39] As the recession begins its second decade, it is necessary to ask why has the Japanese economy failed to recapture its earlier vitality?

Beginning in the 1950s Japan experienced a long period of political stability and economic prosperity.[40] Political leaders had fused a market ideology with traditional values to overcome the political turmoil then gripping the country, and a consensus was forged on the importance of economic growth and international competitiveness.[41] Government and society were then seen to "form mutually reinforcing parts of a whole."[42] Government played a highly interventionist role in the economy, and its key task was to create a framework that unified private interests and government agencies on critical issues.

The image of stability in Japanese politics emerged from three factors. First, the ruling Liberal Democratic Party (LDP) has dominated the government for fifty years. Second, the permanent bureaucracy was the most influential institution of government. This was especially true of the economic ministries that were created before World War II, gained vast powers during wartime, survived the postwar years mostly intact, and largely charted their own policy course in subsequent decades. Finally, major business interests were well organized to participate in the policy process, and they maintained close ties with important bureaucrats and political leaders.

The system of government dominated by a coalition of the LDP, bureaucratic elites, and industry figures was often caricatured as the "1955 System" or "Japan, Inc.," and it pursued an economic policy based on economic concentration, export promotion, and the prevention of foreign penetration of the domestic economy.[43] The LDP, the bureaucracy, and organized business have remained the most prominent features of the political landscape, but for more than a dozen years they have failed to deliver the prosperity that typified the earlier high-growth era. In the last decade, deflation, low business investment, weak consumer spending, and an unstable financial system have plagued the nation's economy, but the policy process has failed to produce the requisite reforms.[44] Japan's modern industries are now the principal advocates of policies to revitalize the economy, but these corporations have lost political influence in the last decade because of changes in campaign finance practices and the internationalization of the economy.[45] In contrast, the traditional sectors of the economy, such as agriculture, construction, and retailing, have relied on the government to sustain their marketplace viability. These industries have continued to fund LDP candidates and support the ministries that protect their economic position. The traditional sectors have retained their political influence and have stood solidly against the proposed reforms.

The enactment of the structural reforms needed to revive the economy requires overpowering the influence of elected LDP politicians and the ministries allied with the traditional sectors of the economy. The Japanese system of government, however, assigns the prime minister and the cabinet a secondary place in the policy process. As Aurelia George Mulgan emphasizes, "Japan's political system is structured to undermine the power of the executive . . . [so that it] lacks power as an engine of reform. . . . As a result, solutions to economic problems continue to be delayed and postponed."[46] The primacy of economic growth was once enough to facilitate agreement on policy matters in Japan, and accepted practice encouraged compensation to be paid to the losers in policy disputes. Now, however, the stagnant economy means that the resources needed to placate protected industries must be taken from more productive sectors of the economy. Satisfying the needs of traditional industries prevents the revitalization of the balance of the economy. The fragmentation of the LDP, the political influence of the traditional industries, and their alliances with associated ministries mean that the prospects for reform remain dim.

The European Union

The European Union is an evolving confederation that has its origins in three international organizations founded in the 1950s by Belgium, France, the German Federal Republic (then West Germany), Italy, Luxembourg, and the Netherlands: the European Economic Community, the European Coal and Steel Community, and the European Atomic Energy Community.[47] Denmark, Great Britain, and Ireland were admitted to the European Community in 1973; Greece, Portugal, and Spain joined between 1981 and 1986; and the membership reached fifteen when Austria, Finland, and Sweden were added in 1995. In 2004 ten other countries with about 75 million residents also became members: Cyprus, the Czech Republic, Estonia, Hungary, Latvia, Lithuania, Malta, Poland, Slovakia, and Slovenia.

The members of the European Union, as the principal organization is now called, have pooled their sovereignty to undertake joint actions, including a common agriculture policy, the creation of a single European market, a unified position on international trade issues, and the introduction of a single European currency, the euro.[48] Although the association began as an effort to promote regional economic integration, it has gradually assumed the additional responsibilities of facilitating the movement of people and information among the member states and developing European foreign and security policies. The European Union is commonly characterized today as an intergovernmental or supranational body, but it is slowly acquiring the status of a sovereign nation.

The European Union has three major governing institutions, and each is based on a different political principle. The Council of Ministers is composed of delegates of the member governments, and it represents their national interests. The Commission is an executive body made up of full-time officials appointed by the member governments for fixed terms and headed by one official, who is designated Commission president. Each commissioner is responsible for specific functional areas and is supposed to act in the interests of the European Union rather than those of the commissioner's home country. The Commission initiates legislative proposals, implements EU policies, and is the Union's "motor of integration." The members of the European Parliament are popularly elected by voters in the member countries. This assembly is gradually achieving formal law-making authority, but the use of the term *parliament* here is still a symbol of unification rather than a description of the institution's current role.

Two other organizations are also integral parts of the European Union. The heads of the member states meet at least twice a year as the European Council to discuss common interests and make decisions about the EU's development. The European Court of Justice is composed of judges, nominated by the member states, who interpret EU statutes and treaties with an authority that resembles the role of the U.S. Supreme Court.

The European Union is an evolving organization, and the influence of its institutions is affected by European events and politics in the member states. EU decisions have traditionally emerged from a dialogue between the Commission and the Council of Ministers, representing the national governments, during which the parliament was consulted. The member states have gradually increased the effectiveness and authority of EU decision making, and the European Parliament has had some success in enhancing its role, but the admission of ten new members has placed additional burdens on its governing institutions, and reforms are needed. The European Union cannot yet be regarded as a sovereign state, and it would face an immediate crisis if it disregarded the fundamental positions of its strongest members.

The Impact of Government Institutions

The review of governing institutions confirms that various arrangements can be employed to manage a country's problems. Governing practices in the United States disperse power broadly, anticipate widespread interest group access and conflict, posit congressional approval of policies, and expect conflicts during implementation. According to Weaver and Rockman's analysis, the United States does a poor job of targeting resources, setting priorities, coordinating conflicting objectives, implementing policies, and ensuring policy stability. Still, the U.S. process frequently produces innovative policies, manages domestic political conflict reasonably well, can impose substantial losses on powerful groups, and represents the poor and the unorganized comparatively well.

In Great Britain, political power has been concentrated in the cabinet and the governing party in the House of Commons, and the prime minister has recently become an increasingly pivotal figure. This structure enables the government to target resources, implement innovative policies, impose losses on the resourceful, and coordinate efforts to achieve conflicting policy objectives. At the same time the British system does not manage domestic conflict well, and its policies are subject to abrupt reversal when the governing party loses to the opposition.

German institutions encourage stability. A coalition rather than a single party normally controls the government, and the federal system usually allows opposition parties to influence national policymaking and implementation through control of state governments. Labor unions and employer groups have privileged access to the policy process in Germany, and policies typically target resources and coordinate conflicting policy objectives effectively. German policies, however, are usually incremental rather than fundamental, are unable to resolve differences among the principal policy actors, and rarely impose substantial losses on the powerful.

Until the 1990s the Japanese political system concentrated authority in key bureaucratic agencies, the LDP, and business organizations, and its policy process delivered innovative policies, coherent policy objectives, and the successful implementation of public policies. In the last dozen years, however, Japan has failed to adapt to changing circumstances. In the face of an alliance among traditional industries, LDP politicians, and the protective ministries, Japan has been unable to restrain politically influential groups and enact the policies needed to rejuvenate its stagnant economy.

The experience of these countries demonstrates that the characteristics of a nation's policies are linked both logically and empirically to the features of its governing institutions. What is more difficult, however, is managing the relationship between a country's governing institutions and its needs at any particular time. Does a country need policy stability or innovation? Is it more important to target resources where they will do the most good or manage domestic political conflict? Policymaking is impeded by political instability and the fragmentation of government authority, but, at the same time, fragmentation probably facilitates the adoption of innovative policies and facilitates the management of political conflict. Germany and Japan recorded great economic successes in the 1970s and 1980s, but both have been slow to reform their institutions to address new circumstances. Does the reluctance to adapt governing systems to new problems reflect the prudent conviction that traditional practices will soon regain their previous effectiveness, or is it evidence that the groups that prospered in the past are now so influential that they can block changes that might jeopardize their privileged status? Both businesses and the society at large are still affected by the consequences of good and bad government decisions.

SUMMARY

U.S. businesses complain that government is an unreliable partner, but both business and government rely on the effective performance of the other to meet their goals. Government depends on businesses to create jobs, generate revenues, promote innovation, and provide goods and services, whereas businesses need government to provide specific opportunities for firms and industries and to maintain conditions in which economic activity can flourish.

Commentators often contend that the structure of the U.S. government is an impediment to successful policymaking. With institutional arrangements from the eighteenth century, the U.S. government is characterized today by a fragmentation of authority, the domination of decisions by "subgovernment" organizations, and an instability of programs and policy. As a result, it is said, the U.S. government often fails to address critical policy issues in a timely fashion and often produces policy responses that do little more than balance the claims of insider groups. Although experts differ, the institutional features of the U.S. policy process probably produce both positive and negative consequences. The fragmentation of authority may impede timely action to address important issues, but fragmentation of authority probably makes the system more open to minority concerns and innovative proposals. Government authority is usually more concentrated in parliamentary systems, but arrangements in Germany and Japan have produced policy deadlocks, and Britain has witnessed disruptive policy reversals.

The United States relies less on government to guide its society and manage its economy and trusts more in the interaction between the public and private sectors. If the institutional cooperation necessary for policy success is to be maintained, businesses and government both need to act in a manner that respects public standards and expectations.

FURTHER READINGS

The White House Web site provides links to the Executive Office of the President and other executive offices: http://www.whitehouse.gov. The home page of the Library of Congress is a basic source for congressional hearings, reports, legislation, and links to other congressional home pages: http://www.thomas.loc.gov. Vanderbilt Library provides links to U.S. government information sources: http://www.library.vanderbilt.edu/central/staff/fdtf.html.

The official Web site of the European Union provides statistics, press releases, policies, and links to government institutions: http://www.europa.eu.int. Links to online editions of newspapers and publications are available at http://www.world-newspapers.com. Access Germany, Japan, or the United Kingdom. The British government Web site provides information for citizens and residents as links on Newsheadlines and Directories: http://www.direct.gov.uk. For the English version of the German government Web site, go to http://www.bundesregierung.de/en.

Information about the Japanese government is accessible at http://www.kantei.go.jp/foreign/index-e.html.

Cameron, Fraser, ed. *The Future of Europe: Integration and Enlargement.* New York: Routledge, 2004.

Mulgan, Aurelia George. *Japan's Failed Revolution: Koizumi and the Politics of Economic Reform.* Canberra, Australia: Asia Pacific Press, 2002.

Reutter, Werner, ed. *Germany on the Road to "Normalcy": Policies and Politics of the Red-Green Federal Government (1998–2002).* New York: Palgrave Macmillan, 2004.

Seldon, Anthony, ed., *The Blair Effect: The Blair Government, 1997–2001.* London: Little, Brown, 2001.

Weaver, R. Kent, and Bert A. Rockman, eds. *Do Institutions Matter? Government Capabilities in the United States and Abroad.* Washington, D.C.: Brookings Institution, 1993.

NOTES

1. For a more complete description see, Chiara Frugoni, *Pietro and Ambrogio Lorenzetti* (Florence, Italy: Scala Books, 1988).
2. For discussions of this point, see Friedrich List, *The Natural System of Political Economy 1837,* trans. and ed. W. O. Henderson (Totowa, N.J.: Frank Cass, 1983); Martin Wolf, "The Poverty of Nations," *Financial Times,* August 20, 1996, 10; and Anders Aslund, "Russia's Collapse," *Foreign Affairs* 78 (September/October 1999): 64.
3. Deepak Lal and H. Myint, *The Political Economy of Poverty, Equity and Growth: A Comparative Study* (New York: Oxford University Press, Clarendon Press, 1996).
4. R. Kent Weaver and Bert A. Rockman, eds., *Do Institutions Matter? Government Capabilities in the United States and Abroad* (Washington, D.C.: Brookings Institution, 1993), 37–40.
5. John E. Chubb and Paul E. Peterson, eds., *Can the Government Govern?* (Washington, D.C.: Brookings Institution, 1989), 4.
6. John R. Bowman, *Capitalist Collective Action: Competition, Cooperation, and Conflict in the Coal Industry* (Cambridge: Cambridge University Press, 1989), 30, 221–22.
7. Ibid., 30.
8. Stephen Krasner, "The United States Commercial and Monetary Policy," in *Between Power and Plenty: Foreign Economic Policies of Advanced Industrial States,* ed. Peter J. Katzenstein (Madison: University of Wisconsin Press, 1978), 57.
9. This section benefits from John E. Chubb and Paul E. Peterson, "American Political Institutions and the Problem of Governance," in Chubb and Peterson, *Can the Government Govern?* 1–43.
10. Fred Greenstein, ed., *Leadership in the Modern Presidency* (Cambridge, Mass.: Harvard University Press, 1988).
11. See sources cited in Steven S. Smith, "New Patterns of Decisionmaking in Congress," in *The New Direction in American Politics,* ed. John E. Chubb and Paul E. Peterson (Washington, D.C.: Brookings Institution, 1985), 203–33.
12. Clyde V. Prestowitz, *Trading Places: How We Are Giving Our Future to Japan and How to Reclaim It* (New York: Basic Books, 1988), 423–26.
13. See Terry M. Moe, "The Politics of Bureaucratic Structure," in Chubb and Peterson, *Can the Government Govern?* 267–329.
14. J. Leiper Freeman and Judith Parris Stevens, "A Theoretical and Conceptual Reexamination of Subsystem Politics," *Public Policy and Administration* 2, no. 1 (1987): 9–24.
15. Frank Shipper and Marianne M. Jennings, *Business Strategy for the Political Arena* (Westport, Conn.: Quorum Books, 1984), chap. 1.
16. This argument is prompted by James Q. Wilson, "American Politics, Then and Now," *Commentary* 67, no. 2 (February 1979): 39–46.

17. Benjamin Ginsberg, *The Captive Public: How Mass Opinion Promotes State Power* (New York: Basic Books, 1986), chap. 3.

18. Hugh Heclo, *A Government of Strangers: Executive Politics in Washington* (Washington, D.C.: Brookings Institution, 1977); and Raymond Vernon and Debora L. Spar, *Beyond Globalism: Remaking American Foreign Economic Policy* (New York: Free Press, 1989).

19. Eric M. Uslaner, *Shale Barrel Politics: Energy and Legislative Leadership* (Stanford, Calif.: Stanford University Press, 1989).

20. Vernon and Spar, *Beyond Globalism*, 7.

21. Chubb and Peterson, *Can the Government Govern?* 7.

22. Edmund L. Andrews, "How Tax Bill Gave Business More and More," *New York Times,* October 13, 2004, A1.

23. This analysis was prompted by John Zysman, *Governments, Markets, and Growth: Financial Systems and the Politics of Industrial Change* (Ithaca, N.Y.: Cornell University Press, 1983); and Jeffrey A. Hart, "The Effects of State-Social Arrangements on International Competitiveness: Steel, Autos, and Semiconductors in the U.S., Japan, and Western Europe" (paper presented at the annual meeting of the American Political Science Association, August 30–September 2, 1990); see also Hart, *Rival Capitalists: International Competitiveness in the United States, Japan, and Western Europe* (Ithaca, N.Y.: Cornell University Press, 1992).

24. R. Kent Weaver and Bert A. Rockman, "Assessing the Effects of Institutions," in Weaver and Rockman, *Do Institutions Matter?* 6.

25. A. G. Jordan and J. J. Richardson, *Government and Pressure Groups in Britain* (Oxford: Oxford University Press, Clarendon Press, 1987); Walter Williams, *Washington, Westminster and Whitehall* (Cambridge: Cambridge University Press, 1988); and Geoffrey Marshall, ed., *Ministerial Responsibility* (Oxford: Oxford University Press, 1989).

26. This section draws from Martin Harrop, "The United Kingdom," in *Power and Policy in Liberal Democracies,* ed. Martin Harrop (New York: Cambridge University Press, 1992), 71–94.

27. Grant Jordan and Jeremy Richardson, "The British Policy Style or the Logic of Negotiation?" in *Policy Styles in Western Europe,* ed. Jeremy Richardson (London: Allen and Unwin, 1982), 80–110.

28. Wyn Grant, *Government and Industry: A Comparative Analysis of the US, Canada and the UK* (London: Edward Elgar, 1989), 86–87.

29. See Earl A. Reitan, *Tory Radicalism: Margaret Thatcher, John Major, and the Transformation of Modern Britain, 1979–1997* (Lanham, Md.: Rowman and Littlefield, 1997).

30. Ibid., 194.

31. Charles Pattie, "Re-electing New Labour," in *Governing as New Labour: Policy and Politics under Blair,* ed. Steve Ludlam and Martin J. Smith (New York: Palgrave Macmillan, 2004), 18.

32. Anthony Seldon, ed., *The Blair Effect: The Blair Government 1997–2001* (London: Little, Brown, 2001), chaps. 1–3.

33. This section draws from Peter J. Katzenstein, "Stability and Change in the Emerging Third Republic," in *Industry and Politics in West Germany: Toward the Third Republic,* ed. Peter J. Katzenstein (Ithaca, N.Y.: Cornell University Press, 1989), 307–53; Gordon Smith, "Structures of Government" and "Political Leadership," in *Developments in West German Politics,* ed. Gordon Smith, William E. Paterson, and Peter H. Merkl (Durham, N.C.: Duke University Press, 1989), 24–39, 60–76; and M. Donald Hancock, *West Germany: The Politics of Democratic Corporatism* (Chatham, N.J.: Chatham House, 1989).

34. Katzenstein, "Stability and Change," 312–13. See also Kenneth Dyson, "West Germany: The Search for a Rational Consensus," in Richardson, *Policy Styles in Western Europe,* 17–46.

35. Smith, "Structures of Government."

36. Jost Halfmann, "Social Change and Political Mobilization in West Germany," in Katzenstein, *Industry and Politics in West Germany,* 51–86.

37. "Standortranking: Rote Laterne für Deutschland," Bettelsmann Stiftung, www.n-tv.de, "Wirtschaft und Börse," accessed October 8, 2004.

38. Sabine Kropp, "Gerhard Schröder as 'Coordination Chancellor': Impact of Institutions and Arenas on the Style of Governance," in *Germany on the Road to 'Normalcy': Policies and Politics of the Red-Green Federal Government (1998–2002),* ed. Werner Reutter (New York: Palgrave Macmillan, 2004), 67–88.

39. T. J. Pempel, *Regime Shift: Comparative Dynamics of the Japanese Political Economy* (Ithaca, N.Y.: Cornell University Press, 1988), 12.

40. Kent Calder, *Crisis and Compensation: Public Policy and Political Stability in Japan, 1949–1986* (Princeton: Princeton University Press, 1988), chaps. 4 and 11; Karel van Wolferen, *The Enigma of Japanese Power* (New York: Vintage Books, 1989); Takeshi Ishida and Ellis S. Krauss, *Democracy in Japan* (Pittsburgh: University of Pittsburgh Press, 1989), chaps. 3, 6, and 14; and Pempel, *Regime Shift,* introduction, chap. 6, and conclusion.

41. Michio Muramatsu and Ellis S. Krauss, "The Conservative Policy Line and the Development of Patterned Pluralism," in *The Political Economy of Japan: The Domestic Transformation,* ed. Kozo Yamamura and Yasukichi Yasuba (Stanford, Calif.: Stanford University Press, 1987), 516–54.

42. Daniel I. Okimoto, "Japan, the Societal State," in *Inside the Japanese System,* ed. Daniel I. Okimoto and Thomas P. Rohlen (Stanford, Calif.: Stanford University Press, 1988), 211–15.

43. Pempel, *Regime Shift,* 51–53.

44. See the imaginative contribution by Aurelia George Mulgan, *Japan's Failed Revolution: Koizumi and the Politics of Economic Reform* (Canberra, Australia: Asia Pacific Press, 2002), 240. Also Roger W. Bower, *Japan's Dysfunctional Democracy: The Liberal Democratic Party and Structural Corruption* (Armonk, N.Y.: M. E. Sharpe, 2003); and Dick Beason and Dennis Patterson, *The Japan That Never Was: Explaining the Rise and Decline of a Misunderstood Country* (Albany: State University of New York Press, 2004).

45. Mulgan, *Japan's Failed Revolution,* 230.

46. Ibid.

47. See, for example, David M. Wood and Birol A. Yesilade, *The Emerging European Union* (White Plains, N.Y.: Longman, 1996).

48. Jeffrey Frieden, Daniel Gros, and Erik Jones, eds., *The New Political Economy of the EMU* (Lanham, Md.: Rowman and Littlefield, 1998).

CHAPTER 4

Corporate Governance and Public Space Responsibility

EXECUTIVES OF THE Enron company triggered the largest bankruptcy in the nation's history when they covered up the firm's deteriorating financial situation, looted its assets, and left employees and investors to deal with the rubble.[1] The Enron collapse then kicked off a series of scandals that gnawed away at public confidence in corporate America. Officials in the telecom giant WorldCom-MCI confessed to having falsified $11 billion in financial records and perpetrating the largest accounting fraud on record. Senior managers of Adelphia, a cable system operator, were convicted of plundering that company's assets and misleading regulators; the chief financial officers of Healthsouth, an operator of rehabilitation centers, pleaded guilty to fraudulent accounting; and executives from a raft of other firms were hauled before judges to confess their own criminal misconduct.

Some analysts attributed the cavalcade of corruption to an unusual incidence of "infectious greed,"[2] but such a theory fails to explain why the outbreak of misconduct occurred when it did. Rather than seek the roots of misconduct in the flaws of individuals, it is more helpful to search for the causes of criminality in the rules that govern corporate behavior.

Modern corporations are nineteenth-century inventions,[3] but they are now required to obey both contemporary criminal statutes as well as special rules that structure corporate governance. Professional managers are hired to apply economic principles to a firm's operations so it can earn an acceptable profit, but as a by-product of deploying a firm's assets, corporate managers also make decisions about products, employment, and investment that shape the society and influence its policies.[4] A system of corporate governance spells out first who makes decisions for corporations and how those decision makers are selected.[5] Second, it defines how corporate officials are held accountable for their actions and required to behave as they should. Finally, corporate governance also concerns economic efficiency, seeking to align incentives so that managers strive to produce the best results possible from their firm's resources. If corporate governance systems don't work properly, a nation's economy will operate at a sub-par level, and its companies could violate legal standards and community values.

There is nothing inevitable about who dominates a company's political and economic affairs. In this chapter I first examine corporate governing structures in the United States and investigate the Enron scandal from the perspective of corporate governance. I then scrutinize the patterns of corporate governance in other countries and assess the features of their systems. Government decisions are an increasingly influential factor in shaping corporate conduct, but firms do not accept public judgments passively.[6] Most large companies now have units to monitor government and express their policy views to public officials. Here I explore the structure of corporate public affairs programs and consider the issues these agencies raise.

WHO CONTROLS CORPORATIONS IN THE UNITED STATES?

The celebrated World War II film *Twelve O'Clock High* is often used to illustrate important lessons about organizational leadership and accountability.[7] The affable leader of a bomber group that has experienced heavy casualties is removed from command when he presents a series of facile excuses for the unit's poor performance. He is replaced by Gregory Peck, who faces up to the organization's problems, rallies the troops, clarifies priorities, and accepts personal responsibility for improving the company's record—and immediately everything gets back on track.

Who takes charge when a company's management has settled for substandard performance? How are CEOs held responsible for poor business judgments, defective corporate strategies, disregard of community standards, or huge financial losses? Corporations retain substantial legal autonomy in the United States because many think they contribute to the nation's wealth and provide citizens economic and social opportunity. Still, corporate leaders are not infallible, and the chief executives of General Motors, IBM, American Express, and Kodak have relinquished their posts when their firms did not measure up. How is corporate accountability achieved in a global age? The basic laws governing corporate organization in the United States remain state laws rather than federal statutes.[8] These laws usually require major companies to have boards of directors that are elected by the shareholders and responsible to them.

Shareholders

Shareholders are the legal owners of business corporations, and when many people own a company's stock, it is said to be "publicly held."[9] Shareholders have purchased a "share" of the company's assets and future profits, and they have the legal right to guide its activities. Diffuse stock ownership, however, means that individuals usually own only a microscopic portion of a company's stock.

Therefore there is little incentive for these owners to take time to learn the details of the company's operations. Shareholders meet once a year to review the firm's performance and to elect members of a board of directors, but since individual shareholders know almost nothing about the firm's projects and strategies, they usually accept the management's reports and recommendations.

Boards of directors are intended to represent the interests of the shareholders.[10] Boards establish a firm's policies and select senior managers who are then responsible for carrying out those policies. The typical board meets monthly or quarterly and has fourteen members. "Inside" boards are dominated by the company's top executives, whereas "outside" boards draw their members from external organizations, such as law firms, banks, universities, foundations, and other corporations. An outside or independent director of a major corporation typically receives an annual retainer of about $100,000, fees of $3,000 for attending each meeting, stock options, and retirement credits. Outside, or nonemployee, directors are supposed to be independent of management, and the New York Stock Exchange requires boards to have audit committees composed of nonemployee directors. In addition, most boards have compensation and nominating committees composed primarily of outside directors.[11]

Outside directors sometimes exercise power during periods of crisis or management transition, as occurred at General Motors and IBM in the 1990s, but normally boards of directors do little more than ratify proposals of the incumbent managers.[12] Outside directors should be independent of management so they can make an impartial assessment of executive performance, but they are usually recruited by the very managers they are evaluating.[13] As one scholar concludes: "directors in large mainstream corporations normally tend to play a passive role, as invited guests, characteristically tied to the inside hosts by some sort of personal or business relationship."[14] Because part-time board members know less about the company's activities than the full-time managers, they usually have little impact on corporate policy. In 2003 and 2004, directors of the Walt Disney corporation and the New York Stock Exchange had private ties to the organizations' CEOs, and these associations were said to have led the directors to compensate the CEOs too lavishly and overlook emerging problems in the organizations' operations.[15] Boards of directors are symbols of corporate power, but they appear to be "pawns" of management.[16]

Management

The diffusion of stock ownership and the weaknesses of boards of directors have created a power gap in modern corporations. In a renowned study Adolf A. Berle and Gardiner C. Means argue that corporate managers have filled the gap by extending their responsibility for a firm's operations to de facto control of its policies.[17] Management today is usually regarded as the dominant force in guiding a company's destiny. With their knowledge of company affairs and control of critical procedures, managers can become a self-perpetuating elite who place their personal interests above those of the shareholders or the firm.

U.S. companies are usually dominated by their chief executive officer, regardless of exact titles. The CEO is usually both a member of the board and the firm's public representative. Managers sometimes have different interests from those of shareholders, and they may use their position to place their views ahead of those of the shareholders. Shareholders may want to have a larger portion of profits distributed as dividends, whereas managers seek to retain profits for use in the firm's operations. Shareholders may favor investments in pioneering areas, whereas managers favor investments in less risky projects. Shareholders may object to high salaries, annual bonuses, generous fringe benefits, lucrative stock deals, and "golden parachute" severance payments, whereas managers may contend that these benefits are necessary to retain talented executives.

Managers were thought in the 1980s to focus on expanding their firm's revenues and size, but they seemed less concerned with profits.[18] In the 1990s the total compensation of senior executives came to be based less on their salary and more on corporate profitability and the price of a company's stock. Whereas the salary of the chief executive was traditionally dismissed as an insignificant percentage of the firm's earnings, the total amounts paid to some CEOs today are no longer such small change.[19] The country's highest-paid chief executive in 2003 was Barry Diller of InterActiveCorp, whose direct compensation and exercised stock options totaled $156 million, and Reuben Mark, the chairman and CEO of Colgate Palmolive, was not far behind with $141 million.[20] Most of the remuneration of executives in this range comes from exercising stock options, but Steve Jobs, CEO of Apple Computer, received the highest pure salary and bonuses in 2003, $75 million. Although high CEO pay is sometimes associated with great company performance, the CEO of Global Crossing, Ltd., the imploded telecom firm, received $20 million in 2003, and Bill Gates received only $865,000 in direct compensation for his contributions to Microsoft's achievements.

Employees

The interests of U.S. employees in corporate actions are legally expressed through labor unions and bargaining. The National Labor Relations Act guarantees employees the right to join unions and bargain collectively with employers. Management and labor representatives are required by law to bargain in good faith over wages and working conditions. The large majority of American workers, however, are not members of unions. Most employees believe their interests overlap, to some degree, the interests of their employers. Because companies need competent workers, such employees conclude they are better off relying on company practices and legal guarantees than in seeking the assistance of labor unions.

Traditionally, employees in the United States exercise some influence in a firm's operations, but they lack a formal role in corporate governance. Direct representation by workers on company boards of directors is rare, and employee advisory councils seldom have an official role. Employee ownership of company stock gained a new hearing in the 1980s as a means of accommodating the competing demands of shareholders and employees, and its popularity grew in the 1990s as a feature of retirement plans. Such investment plans, however, are risky ventures for employees who already have their careers invested in their company's fate, and employee investments in an employer's stock may end up serving the interests of management more than it benefits employees.[21] American unions have shown little enthusiasm for alternatives to collective bargaining as means of exercising employee influence, but the next decade may witness the emergence of new mechanisms to expand employee influence in corporate decision making.

Financial Institutions

When you ask who controls corporate America, one indisputable response is large financial institutions. At the start of the new century, according to one estimate, pension funds, mutual funds, insurance companies, and other financial institutions controlled two-thirds of the stock of major corporations.[22] Traditionally, financial institutions have been passive investors, supporting a company's management or sitting on the sidelines, but those days are passing quickly. Financial institutions are now beginning to act more like company owners than simple investors.

The amount of money controlled by pension funds, mutual funds, and insurance companies is so huge that these institutions cannot sell their stock holdings without driving down share prices and incurring losses. When dissatisfied with company performance, large institutional investors now lobby corporations to change their policies and alter their governance systems.[23] Fred Buenrostro, the chief executive officer of the California Public Employees' Retirement System, and his counterparts in Massachusetts, New Jersey, New York, and Wisconsin participated in efforts in the 1980s to pressure companies to cease doing business in South Africa because of its apartheid policies, and they then urged Exxon to change its environmental procedures after a disastrous oil spill in Alaska. More recently, activist funds have concentrated on corporate governance issues. Several funds compelled Honeywell Corporation to alter its policies for electing directors, led Xerox to add more independent directors to its board, persuaded Lockheed to change its rules to resist takeovers, and urged TRW and Occidental Petroleum to establish stockholder advisory committees.

At the dawn of the twenty-first century, the world's largest private pension fund was Teachers Insurance and Annuity Association–College Retirement Equities Fund (TIAA-CREF), which managed almost $300 billion in assets on behalf of 1.8 million educators and others affiliated with educational institutions.[24] CREF regards itself as an "advocate for improved corporate governance and performance," and seeks "a balance between the rights of shareholders—the owners of the corporation—and the need of management and the board to direct the corporation's affairs free from distracting short-term pressures." CREF believes in working with companies rather than against them, but it has recently battled Disney, Heinz, and W. R. Grace over the independence from management of members of their boards. Its current agenda also includes executive compensation, shareholder rights, social responsibility, and international standards for corporate conduct.

The trend toward investment-fund activism draws sharply mixed reviews. Most corporate executives are wary of investment-fund managers. They resent outsiders telling them how to run businesses they think the funds know little about. They charge that fund managers focus on short-term rather than long-term results and contend that the funds' willingness to sell out companies to fast-buck manipulators aggravated the takeover mania of previous decades.[25] Others respond that investment funds are in a better position to watch over the interests of stockholders than any other institution. In an era of dispersed stock ownership and weak boards of directors, investment funds can identify chief executives who treat public companies as personal fiefdoms and blow the whistle on management proposals that benefit executives at the expense of companies.[26]

Enron and Corporate Governance

Enron was created in 1985 from a merger of natural-gas companies located in Houston and Omaha.[27] Previously these companies had concentrated on exploration, production, and transportation of natural gas, but the new entity took advantage of the deregulation of the natural gas market to reposition itself in the energy trading business. When the profitability of energy trading soared, Enron abandoned the energy production business. Furthermore, Enron concentrated its efforts in the most complex, exotic, and rewarding area of energy trading, the trading of energy derivatives. A derivative is a financial instrument whose value is determined or derived from the value of another product or financial instrument. Rather than selling natural gas or crude oil, commodities that had concrete value, Enron traded, for example, the right to buy or sell various energy products at some time in the future. Derivative trading was inherently speculative, could be extremely complicated, was largely unregulated, and could deliver extraordinary profits.

Companies in the energy business frequently create partnerships to undertake major projects, such as the construction of pipelines and refineries, and such entities were permitted to borrow money, own assets, and manage business operations. The activities of energy partnerships were not required to be included in a firm's balance sheet so long as the firm owned no more than 50 percent of a partnership and its existence was noted, however obliquely, in the firm's financial statements. Enron created numerous partnerships and other "special purpose entities" that engaged in a mixed bag of corporate endeavors, and they had the effect of covering up the firm's financial transactions, concealing risk, disguising liabilities, generating dubious profits, and enriching company executives. Enron's off-balance-sheet transactions were so successful in misleading the financial community that almost all Wall Street analysts recommended purchasing the firm's stock as it sped into bankruptcy.[28] After Enron declared bankruptcy in December 2001, the court examiner discovered $25 billion in unrecognized company debt; thousands of workers lost their jobs, and countless employee retirement plans simply imploded. Who should be held responsible for the Enron scandal?

Numerous company executives were charged with criminal offenses for their part in Enron's collapse, but the U.S. Congress focused its attention on the company's auditors. Auditors are responsible for verifying the accuracy of an organization's financial records, but Congress concluded that corporate auditors were not doing their jobs. Auditing for Enron was done by Arthur Andersen, then one of the nation's "Big Five" accounting firms, but accounting firms had also become business consultants.[29] Andersen had received $25 million in 2000 for auditing Enron's financial records, and it had also received $27 million for performing consulting tasks. It appeared that Andersen was not aggressive in scrutinizing Enron's financial statements because it wanted to increase its consulting revenues. Andersen was convicted of obstructing justice in the Enron case and soon went out of business in what was described as "the most significant death of an accounting firm ever." Congress responded to the Enron scandal by enacting the Public Company Accounting Reform and Investor Act of 2002, known as the Sarbanes-Oxley Act.[30] The legislation, sponsored by Sen. Paul S. Sarbanes, D-Md., and Rep. Michael G. Oxley, R-Ohio, established a regulatory oversight board for accountants, prevented accounting firms from performing both auditing and consulting services for the same clients, and required corporate chief executives and chief financial officers to certify the accuracy of their firm's financial reports.

Others argued, however, that the source of Enron-style misconduct was not the auditing practices but the compensation packages given senior executives. John Coffee concludes, "The blunt truth is that recent accounting scandals . . . are by-products of a system of corporate governance that has indeed made corporate managers . . . extremely responsive to the (stock) market."[31] During the 1990s, the compensation of senior executives shifted from being based primarily on cash payments to resting on the price of the company's stock. The granting of stock options to senior executives was intended to align the interests of managers with those of stockholders, and remuneration based on stock values encouraged managers to seek ways to increase the price of their company's stock. Unfortunately, changes in security regulations at this time allowed company officials to sell their stock as soon as they received it. Rather than building long-term value for the stockholders' benefit, executives were encouraged to make optimistic forecasts to inflate the price of the stock, manipulate financial records to validate their aggressive predictions, and then sell their own shares as soon as the stock price peaked. From this perspective, you could never hire enough auditors to discover the balance sheet misrepresentations senior executives could concoct if they had an enormous personal stake in driving up the price of the company's stock.

The U.S. system of corporate governance anticipates that company officials will make mistakes and behave improperly, but it expects boards of directors to monitor management performance. Why didn't the Enron board close down the deceptive financial reporting and insist on a full accounting of corporate activities? Enron's model of governance reflected the tradition of "managerial capitalism," in which the chief executive chairs the board of directors and controls company operations.[32] The Enron board lacked the resources to investigate management behavior, and the board's nonexecutive members were either privately beholden to Enron management or too busy with other activities to oversee Enron affairs. The only way to prevent a recurrence of the corporate scandals of the late 1990s and early 2000s, Paul W. MacAvoy and Ira M. Millstein argue, is to separate the leadership of the board of directors from the firm's senior management and to provide the board with the information, resources, and independence needed to scrutinize the activities of company officials.[33]

A nation's system of corporate governance should contribute to the success of its economy. U.S. corporations are dominated by the top executives who manage their firms' activities on a daily basis. The theoretical control of a company by shareholders is rarely exercised, because stock ownership is broadly dispersed and boards of directors are typically uninvolved in the firm's operations. The growing proportion of stock owned by pension and investment funds has made fund managers a potential force in guiding corporations in the decades ahead, but they will need to observe management conduct more closely.

Chief executive officers need the flexibility to direct a company's activities, but they must also be held accountable. Without strong boards and attentive shareholders, the U.S. system of corporate governance relies on government regulation, litigation, and public scrutiny to sustain appropriate conduct, and it depends on equity markets and potential takeovers to punish firms for inadequate performance. Have other countries done a better job of providing corporate flexibility and accountability without relying on the cumbersome procedures that accompany corporate governance in the United States?

CORPORATE GOVERNANCE IN COMPARATIVE PERSPECTIVE

Countries everywhere have reconsidered their systems of corporate governance in the wake of the Enron scandals, but styles of corporate governance remain aligned with each country's traditions and practices. Companies were first incorporated in Great Britain in the middle of the nineteenth century.[34] Acts of Parliament now require large British corporations to have boards of directors elected by the shareholders to supervise the business; the board then delegates its power to management. In practice, directors are approved by the incumbent board and ratified by the stockholders. Family ownership of corporations remains important in Great Britain, and most UK firms are controlled by board members and the senior management.[35] Pension funds, insurance companies, and other financial institutions are the largest investors, but they rarely vote on shareholder resolutions and are not usually players in corporate operations. Banks play a larger role in corporate management in Britain than in the United States, but stock markets in Britain are far less influential.

Boards of directors average sixteen members, and they convene ten or twelve times a year. In most cases, boards select both a chair and a chief executive, who is often called the managing director. Great Britain relies on shareholders and boards of directors to ensure management accountability, but commentators contend that the system functions erratically. Jonathan P. Charkham insists, "The accountability of management to the board . . . is by common consent the bedrock of the system. The plain fact is that in many companies it scarcely works at all."[36] Reform commissions appointed in response to the Enron debacle have stressed the need for more stringent auditing practices, advocated the selection of more nonexecutive board members, and championed the separation of the chief executive's position from the post of chair of the board.[37]

In Great Britain, the corporate governance debate has concentrated on whether companies have performed as well financially as they should. Because companies are usually dominated by insiders, commentators contend that British managers do a poor job and deliver smaller returns than they should. Mergers, acquisitions, and takeovers have become more common in Great Britain in recent years, and critics insist that these changes prove that boards have not required managers to deploy the firm's assets as profitably as they could.

German corporate and political institutions are especially successful at generating stability and uniting economic actors in pursuit of corporate goals.[38] In this "stakeholder" system, employees, banks, public officials, and shareholders are represented on company boards; companies are embedded in a network of organizational relationships; and hostile takeovers are virtually unknown.

The ownership of stock in German firms is far more concentrated than in the American companies. Of the 171 largest German industrial firms, 86 percent have a shareholder who holds at least 25 percent of the firm's stock.[39] German banks, corporations, and family trusts are substantial shareholders, and they are usually represented in the governance structure. The existence of large blocks of stock provides an incentive for major shareholders to monitor management performance, and complex webs of intercorporate holdings help control corporate conduct.[40]

German companies have both supervisory boards and management boards. The supervisory board's main task is to appoint the management board. Shareholders select half the members of the supervisory board, and the company's employees select the other half. The chair is always a shareholder representative, one employee member must come from the salaried (often clerical) employees, and another employee representative must come from the executive ranks. The management board, which is responsible for the firm's operations, normally convenes weekly, is a genuine decision-making body, and is expected to operate collegially. The board may elect a chair from among its members, but the law does not assign any specific powers to the post. The chair is commonly called the board's "spokesperson," but the chair's role varies greatly by personality and circumstance. Management board members frequently have well-defined areas of administrative responsibility, but they are expected to act on the board as members of a group, not as representatives of a specific corporate interest.

German law also requires firms to establish councils in individual plants, whose members are selected by employees. The approval of these councils is needed before companies can alter operations in ways that significantly affect workers. National labor unions are the sole bargaining agents on issues of salary and working conditions. Factory councils do not have the right to strike or negotiate, but they have substantial influence on matters outside the union's domain.

Whereas American managers are criticized for emphasizing short-term perspectives, the German corporate structure displays the disadvantages of long-term relationships.[41] To maintain solidarity, the German system allows many groups to veto corporate policies, but these vetoes restrict management's ability to launch new programs and devise innovative administrative arrangements. German firms are at their best when making incremental changes to existing products and practices, but their record in commercializing revolutionary technologies has been less impressive. Movements to reform company procedures appeared in Germany at the start of the new century, but continued acceptance of traditional practices still circumscribes the innovativeness of the economy.

Before World War II, many Japanese companies belonged to one of four groups of corporations, or *zaibatsu,* that together controlled 32 percent of the country's investment and 50 percent of bank deposits.[42] These groups were broken up in the postwar years but were succeeded by similar groups called *keiretsu.* In vertical *keiretsu,* a manufacturer is associated with suppliers and subcontractors to create an efficient network for the production and distribution of products. A horizontal *keiretsu* resembles a U.S. conglomerate in which firms in different industries are associated with a bank and a trading company. Companies in a *keiretsu* commonly own stock in each, discuss economic prospects, share risks, and favor each other in commercial dealings. Three characteristics of Japanese firms influence their conduct. First, stock ownership and stock markets have less influence on a company's operations than in the United States. About 30 percent of a company's stock is owned by other firms in the group, and much of the rest is owned by other banks and corporations with which a company is affiliated. Because much stock ownership is based on stable business relationships, management worries little about hostile takeovers and can concentrate, instead, on product development and market share. Second, major Japanese corporations are normally headed by powerful chief executives who act with the nominal assistance of large boards of directors. Most board members are lifelong employees whose selection was approved by top managers. A firm's entrepreneurial decisions are rarely limited by fears of litigation or takeovers, and its main bank usually becomes an influential adviser in times of trouble. Third, major Japanese firms have a strong commitment to their current employees, although "lifetime" employment is no longer as secure as it once was. Employees are considered an essential asset of the firm, and the task of management is to mediate between shareholders and employees. Large Japanese firms typically have fewer employees than comparable American companies, so they can maintain a homogeneous workforce and protect employees during recession. The economic stagnation that has curbed Japanese growth in the past decade has led reformers to question whether the nation's traditional practices have become outmoded in a global age.

There are substantial variations in the ways national systems of corporate governance guarantee adherence to standards of conduct and ensure adequate economic performance. The United States relies on government regulations and capital markets to supervise the conduct of firms, and it tolerates corporate instability and inefficient regulation. Corporate managers in Germany and Japan are embedded in institutional networks that reinforce traditional economic practices, but this stability comes at the expense of outsiders and of losing out on the full benefits of marketplace competition. Great Britain relies on senior managers and large shareholders to lead companies, but its system offers little defense against chief executives who seek excessive compensation for themselves while settling for mediocre performance from their firm.

Despite the variations, we should not lose sight of the commonalities in these national governance systems. The legal foundations of the modern joint stock company define how firms in each country are governed and financed, and recent reform proposals suggest that pressures for standardization are increasing.[43] Corporate governance in China has its own set of issues, as demonstrated in Box 4-1.

CORPORATE PUBLIC AFFAIRS PROGRAMS

The growth of government has been one of the most profound developments in the corporate environment. Although businesses do compete in the marketplace to sell their products, they also gain commercial advantage in the political arena. Businesses employ political tactics to secure favorable operating rules, expand sales, reduce costs, and impede the success of competitors. One of the sectors of the economy most affected by government policies is the pharmaceutical industry; for example, government affects the operations of Merck & Company, a major prescription drug manufacturer, at every level.

Cases in Development
BOX 4-1 CORPORATE GOVERNANCE AS PRACTICED IN MAINLAND CHINA

Corporate governance as conducted in major industrialized states does not fit the circumstances in mainland China. The People's Republic of China is still a Communist nation, and most companies are owned and operated by the government. It was not until 1997 that China officially sanctioned private property and private enterprise, and the country still insists that state-owned enterprises remain the dominant force in the nation's economy.

The 1975 and 1978 constitutions recognized only state or collective ownership of property, and most economic activities were then performed by government ministries. In the mid-1990s these functions were transferred from the government ministries to state-owned enterprises, and former ministers and officials were then assigned to manage the new enterprises. The traditional government agencies were transformed into regulatory authorities, and the state-owned enterprises became companies whose shares might be traded on the Chinese stock exchanges that had opened in 1990 and 1991.

Approximately 1,200 companies are now listed on the Shanghai and Shenzhen exchanges, but two-thirds of the shares in these companies are not traded. The government owns almost all the untraded stock, and it remains the majority shareholder in most enterprises.

Most company managers have come from government service, and they still regard their political standing to be more important than their company position. As majority shareholder, the government's broad political interests certainly differ from the narrow economic interests of the other stockholders. The managers' future careers are determined by the government, so they may well reflect the government's concerns and disregard the long-term interests of the minority shareholders. Because the independence of corporate decisions from government wishes is uncertain, the value of investments in Chinese companies remains problematic.

Sources: Anthony Neoh, "Corporate Governance in Mainland China," in *Corporate Governance and Capital Flows in a Global Economy,* ed. Peter K. Cornelius and Bruce Kogut (New York: Oxford University Press, 2003), 431–42; Jill Solomon and Aris Solomon, *Corporate Governance and Accountability* (Hoboken, N.J.: Wiley, 2004), 164–65; and John Burton and Mure Dickie, " 'Model of Corporate Governance' Fights for Survival," *Financial Times,* December 2, 2004, 16.

At the supranational level, the World Health Organization (WHO) lobbies on behalf of developing nations, and it is acquiring quasi-regulatory powers over the approval of pharmaceutical products. The WHO's decisions are not binding, but countries that lack technical capacity to make scientific rulings often accept the WHO's judgments about new drug products. Almost all national governments outside the United States regulate drug prices and thus control the revenues companies can earn. The U.S. government affects research-oriented pharmaceutical companies by supporting research, specifying the terms of patents, approving new drugs, and shaping tax policy. Recent controversies about importing prescription drugs from Canada and Mexico underline the importance of state governments in specifying the conditions under which individuals and public programs purchase pharmaceutical products.

How do companies respond to the impact of government on their operations? Most CEOs lament government influence but accept it as a fact of life.[44] Because governments affect a company's bottom line, most CEOs believe that they should seek to influence the policies that affect their firms' operations. Furthermore, three of every four CEOs believe that they should speak out on issues affecting the broader public interest. A small portion of CEOs disagree, maintaining that their expertise is in running companies rather than in debating public policies. These corporate leaders argue that they have no mandate to become involved in policy debates, and they fear that "politicizing" companies will have more negative than positive consequences.

Virtually all large firms, however, have accepted the notion that they must participate in the policy process, but not all companies have the same needs.[45] Corporate public affairs programs differ by industry and company.[46] Public affairs programs are more fully developed in industries that have a history of federal regulation or in which government is an important purchaser of products, such as utilities, transportation, petroleum, and defense weapons; these programs are now regarded as profit centers like any other part of the corporation.[47] Firms have begun to look to public affairs departments not only to defend against government initiatives but also to help them use government authority to improve their operations and gain advantage over competitors.

Corporate public affairs programs typically have the following four elements:[48]

1. Issues management—identifies issues, evaluates impact, and formulates responses
2. Government relations—maintains representatives in Washington and state capitals to explain views on pending proposals
3. Public communications—provides information about the company and its views to the public, external groups, and key shareholders
4. Community affairs—includes charitable support, employee involvement programs, and community activities

These public affairs functions are placed in a corporate context in Figure 4-1, which is an organization chart of a public affairs program of a typical firm, a health care company. Issues management (sometimes called public policy management), government relations, and social responsibility are examined in greater detail in this section.

Issues Management

Issues management is a shorthand phrase for a slightly longer idea. It refers not to a strategy for managing issues but is, more modestly, an approach to managing a company's response to public issues. It is "the process by which the corporation can identify, evaluate and respond to those social and political issues which may impact significantly on it."[49] According to one survey, 91 percent of *Fortune* 500 firms have issues management programs, and 74 percent of the leaders of these firms regard the programs as very important or extremely important.[50]

Issues management systems resulted from the frustrations executives experienced when changes in government policy caught them by surprise. By then, they argued, it was too late to have much effect on the course of events.[51] The earlier

Figure 4-1   Merck & Company Public Affairs Department

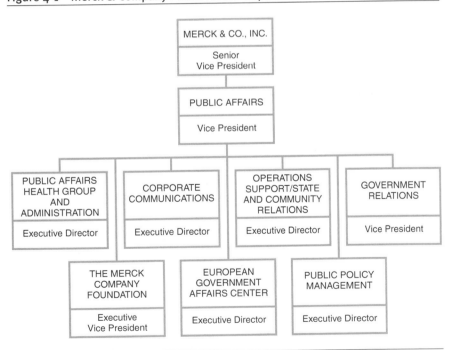

Source: Adapted from material provided by Merck & Company.

companies focused on an issue, the more likely they were to achieve their objectives. A typical issues management system is composed of six activities:[52]

- Monitoring trends and identifying issues
- Assessing the impact of issues on firm
- Prioritizing issues
- Developing the company's position
- Designing the company's strategy to achieve its goal
- Implementing strategy

The first step in an issues management process is to identify emerging issues. Some analysts scan the sociopolitical environment to detect trends that might affect their companies in the years ahead. Rising energy prices might generate citizen demand for improved public transportation systems, and changes in marriage and child-rearing practices could influence housing needs. Other issue analysts search out issues that are more immediate and concrete.[53] Corporate agents responsible for legislative affairs often visit top aides of the senators and representatives on committees that handle company issues to learn what topics might concern the legislators in the months ahead. Among the policy issues identified by analysts are *operational* issues that directly affect how the company conducts its business. Manufacturers are concerned about the regulation of chemicals used in production processes, and broadcasters worry about proposals to provide free air time to political candidates. Issue managers also focus on *corporate* issues that affect a company's general welfare. In addition, some companies are concerned about broader *social* issues that affect them only indirectly, such as the budget deficit, quality of education, or welfare reform.

Issue analysts can easily identify scores or even hundreds of issues that could be significant to a company.[54] The standards used most often to prioritize issues are the impact on the company and the probability that the issue will arise. Actual priorities are usually set either by the chief executive, by a diverse group of executives, or by the public affairs staff itself. The top executives at Monsanto, the life sciences and chemical company, identified five issue areas critical to its stature as a global company specializing in high-value-added products: international trade, biotechnology regulation, intellectual property, agricultural policy, and hazardous waste disposal.[55]

Developing a company's position on an issue is not as easy as it sounds. Most corporations today are multiproduct, multinational enterprises, and different units of firms have different positions on specific issues. In addition, companies compete with other firms, and their market strategies can complicate their reaction to government initiatives. The divisions of General Motors that sell large cars view government regulations mandating increases in fuel efficiency more critically than do the divisions producing smaller cars. In contrast, firms that already sell a large proportion of fuel-efficient cars may support government proposals in this area.

Given these complications, some managements prefer to be *bystanders* in the policy process.[56] Others accept the continuing significance of government decisions and are frequent *participants* in the policy process. Still other firms are policy *activists* that try to get a jump on their competitors by anticipating changes in the public arena and taking the initiative themselves to promote revisions in public policies. Once issues have been identified and prioritized and the firm's position has been determined, government relations representatives develop a strategy to achieve the company's goal.

Government Relations

The job of attending to government relations has been described as "*the* principal new responsibility added to top corporate management's traditional functional concerns."[57] Most major firms have now assembled full-time government relations staffs and established executive committees to guide their external relations. The chief executives of the largest corporations typically devote up to half their time to dealing with extracorporate concerns, and government is the most important of these concerns.[58] CEOs no longer ignore external factors and focus simply on internal operations, regardless of their individual preferences. The CEO of a major utility described the importance he attaches to government relations in these terms: "There is very little policy that I will accept that does not have some input from public affairs. I spend half my time on external affairs even though I am trying to run a business. . . . Government relations and issues management are probably the only way a business will survive in the future in the political arena."[59]

The personal involvement of a company's chief executive is sometimes the only way to convince policymakers that the issue is important. One member of Congress from Ohio commented, "If an executive vice president wants to see me, fine if I have time. If I don't, he can see my staff. If it's really important to the company, you expect the CEO to get involved."[60] One survey of 200 CEOs reported that 56 percent had spent more than ten days in Washington in the past year, and 39 percent had spent more than twenty days there.[61]

Federal relations usually occupies the center of a company's government relations program. This office is responsible for monitoring the activities of legislative and executive officials and reporting on existing programs and future initiatives.[62] Federal relations executives are expected to design strategies to help the firm achieve its federal policy goals and participate in implementing those strategies. Permanent Washington representatives help a firm maintain contacts with officials working on key issues, understand the nuances of ongoing events, anticipate crises, and bring cohesion to the government relations activities of different parts of the company.[63]

Government relations programs have expanded most in recent years in the areas of state government and international affairs. The decline in policy activism in Washington often stimulates an array of state policy initiatives. The failure of Washington officials to prevent corporate financial scandals at Enron, WorldCom-MCI, and other firms prompted state attorneys general in Connecticut, Massachusetts, and New York to prosecute wrongdoing themselves, and opposition to stem-cell research in Washington led California to create its own program to support the research.[64] The internationalization of business has also led to the emergence of international public affairs strategies. Historically, companies wanted to assess the risk of investing in particular nonindustrialized countries.[65] The concentration of business activity in major industrial countries has shifted the focus of analysis. International enterprises now engage in negotiations and lobbying with stable foreign countries. Companies active in countries such as Germany and the United Kingdom now utilize the same techniques they employ in domestic government relations programs to promote their interests abroad.

Some firms also sponsor political activities. If a company sponsors a political action committee (PAC), it is usually administered in the government relations office and regarded as an activity that helps company representatives develop contacts with federal and state officials.

Social Responsibility

The most effective way for businesses to achieve their goals, some business figures argue, is to behave as good corporate citizens.[66] Business, they submit, must be socially responsible and look beyond the immediate demands of the marketplace.[67] The phrase *social responsibility* is used to describe a range of business practices, but only some are motivated by a desire to improve the welfare of society. Most corporate actions presented as examples of social responsibility are forms of enlightened self-interest, and they are intended to serve the interests of a company's shareholders and employees. In Figure 4-2, I identify different perspectives on social responsibility by examining the basis of the company's social role and the focus of management concern.[68]

Corporate philanthropy and community service are often marketing devices.[69] McDonald's regards community relations and its Ronald McDonald Houses, which provide free or low-cost accommodations to families visiting children's hospitals, as part of its marketing program. "Twenty years ago," noted its marketing chief, "we decided we wanted an image beyond food, based on strong virtues. We put up a value structure that's difficult to penetrate. It makes us dependable in a world of strange new things."[70] The dominant New Jersey telephone company worked to improve that state's education system because many

Figure 4-2   **Perspectives on Social Responsibility**

FOCUS OF MANAGEMENT CONCERN

		Market Activities	Nonmarket Activities
BASIS OF COMPANY ROLE	Shareholders and Employees	Enlightened Self-interest	Political Legitimacy
	Larger Society	Marketplace Efficiency	Social Improvement

Source: Author.

future employees would be graduates of state schools and because improvements in education would benefit the economy, which, in turn, would benefit the communications industry.[71]

Some scholars argue that the doctrine of social responsibility has significant political implications.[72] From this perspective, actions presented as examples of social responsibility promote public acceptance of corporate actions and increase the political legitimacy of corporate power. The doctrine of social responsibility originated at the beginning of the twentieth century, shortly after the emergence of national corporations had disrupted traditional patterns of economic and social life. Corporate support for popular causes at that time increased the political legitimacy of corporations and dampened enthusiasm for government regulation. Classic economic thought holds that firms best serve the interests of the larger society by ignoring social causes and stressing marketplace efficiency.[73] A company's highest social responsibility, according to this view, is to offer consumers the best possible goods at the lowest price. By responding to consumer preferences, a firm provides jobs for employees, fair returns for investors, and products for the society. Expenditures unrelated to products impose hidden costs on consumers, employees, and investors, and they give corporations influence over social institutions that should remain independent. From this perspective, a company's social responsibilities are expressed through its products, not through charitable causes.

Business efforts to demonstrate social responsibility have had only limited impact. The magnitude of purely altruistic corporate action is small. Corporate charitable contributions equal about 1 percent of profits, and this figure includes expenditures that are at least partially motivated by marketing concerns. Opinion surveys provide little evidence that the general public recognizes corporate support of charitable and community services. Elite groups probably appreciate corporate contributions more fully, but they are also more cynical. Socially responsible conduct provides business few general rewards, but the disregard of community standards might generate animosities.

SUMMARY

Corporations are fundamental institutions in major industrial nations. In the United States, firms are dominated by the management and especially the CEO, whereas boards of directors, employees, and individual shareholders have only a marginal role. Pension funds, mutual funds, and other financial institutions now control most stock in major companies, and their influence on company policies could well expand in the future. The Enron and other recent financial scandals emphasize the power CEOs exercise in major companies, highlight the temptations inherent in the increased use of stock options, and draw attention to the weakness of boards of directors and other institutions that should restrain corporate misconduct. Without effective boards and attentive shareholders to hold management accountable, corporate governance in the United States depends on regulation, litigation, and public scrutiny, costly and inefficient mechanisms all. Systems of corporate governance in Germany and Japan embed companies in networks of institutional relationships that reinforce traditional patterns and practices. These systems promote stability and limit the chances of management misconduct, but they also limit the ability of managers to take full advantage of the commercial and technological opportunities before them. In Great Britain, large stockholders and senior managers direct major firms, but they have little incentive to demand improved economic performance from their companies.

The emergence of public affairs as a management function reflects the increased importance of government in the political environment of corporations. Corporate public affairs programs include an issues management capacity that prioritizes issues, a government relations unit that maintains communications with elected and appointed officials, and a community affairs office that expresses the firm's understanding of its social responsibilities. These offices were originally established in reaction to government initiatives, but they now help firms expand the effectiveness of their operations and gain competitive advantage in the marketplace. As business operations more frequently cross national borders, the international significance of corporate public affairs programs and corporate governance systems will also increase.

FURTHER READINGS

Information about the efforts of the California Public Employees' Retirement System to improve corporate governance can be found at http://www.calpersgovernance.org. To access a discussion of recent activities, click on Shareholder Action, and to access the ten companies selected for attention each year, click on CalPERS Focus List. For TIAA-CREF's corporate governance policy, see http://www.tiaa-cref.org/libra/governance/index.html. The Merck & Company home page provides information about the company, including its philanthropy report: http://www.merck.com/overview/philanthropy. General Motors's Web site offers information about its public affairs activities: http://www.gm.com/company/community_involvement/index.htm.

Charkham, Jonathan P. *Keeping Good Company: A Study of Corporate Governance in Five Countries.* New York: Oxford University Press, Clarendon Press, 1994.

Cornelius, Peter K., and Bruce Kogut, eds. *Corporate Governance and Capital Flows in a Global Economy.* New York: Oxford University Press, 2003.

Learmount, Simon. *Corporate Governance: What Can Be Learned from Japan?* New York: Oxford University Press, 2002.

Roe, Mark J. *Political Determinants of Corporate Governance: Political Context, Corporate Impact.* New York: Oxford University Press, 2003.

Solomon, Jill, and Aris Solomon. *Corporate Governance and Accountability.* Chichester, West Sussex: Wiley, 2004.

NOTES

1. "Corporate Scandals: A User's Guide," *New York Times,* May 11, 2003, sec. 4, p. 2.
2. Frank Partnoy, *Infectious Greed: How Deceit and Risk Corrupted the Financial Markets* (New York: Times Books/Holt, 2003).
3. Thomas K. McCraw, "The Evolution of the Corporation," in *The U.S. Business Corporation: An Institution in Transition,* ed. John R. Meyer and James M. Gustafson (Cambridge, Mass.: Ballinger Publishing, 1988), 1–20.
4. Edward S. Mason, "Introduction," in *The Corporation in Modern Society,* ed. Mason (New York: Atheneum, 1974).
5. Peter R. Cornelius and Bruce Kogut, "Introduction: Corporate Governance and Capital Flows in a Global Economy," in *Corporate Governance and Capital Flows in a Global Economy,* ed. Cornelius and Kogut (New York: Oxford University Press, 2003), 2, 19–20.
6. Mike H. Ryan, Carl L. Swanson, and Rogene A. Buchholz, *Corporate Strategy, Public Policy, and the Fortune 500: How America's Major Corporations Influence Government* (New York: Basil Blackwell, 1987).
7. Dana Wechsler Linden and Nancy Totenier, "Good-bye to Berle & Means," *Forbes,* January 3, 1994, 100–103.
8. This section draws from Jonathan P. Charkham, *Keeping Good Company: A Study of Corporate Governance in Five Countries* (New York: Oxford University Press, Clarendon Press, 1994), esp. chap. 5.
9. Some argue that family ownership of firms remains important. See Philip H. Burch, *The Managerial Revolution Reassessed* (Lexington, Mass.: Lexington Books, 1972).
10. Winthrop Knowlton and Ira M. Millstein, "Can the Board of Directors Help the American Corporation Earn the Immortality It Holds So Dear?" in Meyer and Gustafson, *U.S. Business Corporation;* Business Roundtable, "The Role and Composition of the Board of Directors of the Large Publicly Owned Corporation: Statement of the Business Roundtable," *Business Lawyer,* July 1978, 296–312; and C. P. Alderfer, "The Invisible Director on Corporate Boards," *Harvard Business Review* 64, no. 6 (November 1986): 38–46.
11. Charkham, *Keeping Good Company,* 191–93; and Doron P. Levin, "G.M. Plans to Shift Power to Outside Directors," *New York Times,* March 29, 1994, D6.
12. Levin, "G.M. Plans to Shift Power."
13. Arch Patton and John C. Baker, "Why Directors Won't Rock the Boat," *Harvard Business Review* 65, no. 6 (November 1987): 10–18; and Colin B. Carter and Jay W. Lorsch, *Back to the Drawing Broad: Designing Corporate Boards for a Complex World* (Boston: Harvard Business School Press, 2004).

14. Edward S. Herman, *Corporate Control, Corporate Power* (New York: Cambridge University Press, 1981), 48.

15. Peter Elkind and Joan L. Levinstein, "The Fall of the House of Grasso," *Fortune (Europe),* November 1, 2004, 68; and Rebecca Winters, "The Mouse's Miserable Mikes," *Time,* November 1, 2004, 105.

16. Jay W. Lorsch, with Elizabeth MacIver, *Pawns or Potentates: The Reality of America's Corporate Boards* (Boston: Harvard Business School Press, 1989); and Charles A. and Robert W. Anthony, *The New Corporate Directors* (New York: Wiley, 1986).

17. Adolf A. Berle and Gardiner C. Means, *The Modern Corporation and Private Property* (New York: Macmillan, 1932).

18. John C. Coffee, "What Caused Enron? A Capsule of Social and Economic History of the 1990s," in Cornelius and Kogut, *Corporate Governance and Capital Flows in a Global Economy,* 31–32.

19. The phrase "small change" comes from Patrick McGurn, as quoted in Richard Waters, "Irrational rewards," *Financial Times,* March 31, 1999, 19. This article is the source of information in this paragraph on stock options.

20. Information on compensation in this paragraph comes from http://www.companypay.com, accessed February 17, 2005.

21. Krene Lynch Fannon, *Working within Two Kinds of Capitalism: Corporate Governance and Employee Stakeholding: US and EC Perspectives* (Portland, Ore.: Hart, 2003), chap. 5.

22. Ira Millstein, reported in Sarah Bartless, "Big Funds Pressing for Voice in Management of Companies," *New York Times,* February 23, 1990, A1, D5.

23. Lauren Talner, *The Origins of Shareholder Activism* (Washington, D.C.: Investor Responsibility Research Center, 1983).

24. On CREF procedures, Daniel Bögler, "Corporate governance raises fewer hackles," *Financial Times,* April 22, 1999, 4. Quotations are from Teachers Insurance and Annuity Association–College Retirement Equities Fund, "TIAA-CREF Policy Statement on Corporate Governance" (New York: TIAA-CREF, 1997), 1. See the latest edition of the policy statement by going to http://www.tiaa-cred.org and clicking on Governance.

25. This paragraph relies on Martin Dickson, "Investors Wake Up to Their Power," *Financial Times* (London), December 3, 1990, 16.

26. For activities of the State of Wisconsin Investment Board, see Emory Thomas, "Cold War on Hot Stock Options," http://www.msnbc.com/news/287955.asp, accessed July 9, 1999.

27. See B. Cruver, *The Unshredded Truth from an Enron Insider: Enron, Anatomy of Greed* (London: Arrow Books, 2002); Loren Fox, *Enron: The Rise and Fall* (Hoboken, N.J.: Wiley, 2003); and Peter C. Fusaro and R. M. Miller, *What Went Wrong at Enron: Everyone's Guide to the Largest Bankruptcy in US History* (Hoboken, N.J.: Wiley, 2002). These two paragraphs reflect Partnoy, *Infectious Greed,* chap. 10.

28. Partnoy, *Infectious Greed,* 332, 339.

29. This and the next four sentences draw mainly from Jill Solomon and Aris Solomon, *Corporate Governance and Accountability* (Hoboken, N.J.: Wiley, 2004), 36–39, quotation on 38.

30. Stephen Labaton, "Will Reforms with Few Teeth Be Able to Bite?" *New York Times,* September 22, 2002, sec. 3, p. 4; and the U.S. House of Representatives, Committee on Financial Services, hearing on "Sarbanes-Oxley: Two Years of Market and Investor Recovery," July 22, 2004.

31. Coffee, "What Caused Enron?," 29–33, quotation on 29–30.

32. Paul W. MacAvoy and Ira M. Millstein, *The Recurrent Crisis in Corporate Governance* (New York: Palgrave Macmillan, 2003), 71–76; and Solomon and Solomon, *Corporate Governance and Accountability,* chap. 2.

33. MacAvoy and Millstein, *The Recurrent Crisis in Corporate Governance,* 4.

34. This section is based on Charkham, *Keeping Good Company,* chap. 6.

35. M. Goergen and L. Renneboog, "Strong Managers and Passive Institutional Investors in the United Kingdom," in *The Control of Corporate Europe,* ed. Farbrizio Barca and Marco Becht (New York: Oxford University Press, 2001), 259.

36. Charkham, *Keeping Good Company,* 335.
37. Solomon and Solomon, *Corporate Governance and Accountability,* chap. 3.
38. This section draws from David Goodhard, "There's Still Life in the Old Model," *Financial Times,* April 12, 1994, 13; and Charkham, *Keeping Good Company,* chap. 2.
39. Goodhard, "There's Still Life in the Old Model," 13.
40. Julian Franks and Colin Mayer, "Ownership and Control of German Corporations," *Review of Financial Studies* 14 (Winter 2001): 943–77; and Marco Becht and Ekkehart Böohmer, "Ownership and Voting Power in Germany," in Barca and Becht, *Control of Corporate Europe,* 128–53.
41. In addition to ibid., see Herbert Giersch, Karl-Heinz Paque, and Holger Schmieding, *The Fading Miracle: Four Decades of Market Economy in Germany* (New York: Cambridge University Press, 1992), chap. 5.
42. Charkham, *Keeping Good Company,* chap. 3; Merton J. Peck, "The Large Japanese Corporation," in Meyer and Gustafson, *U.S. Business Corporation,* 21–42; and Masakiko Aoki, "The Japanese Firm in Transition," in *The Political Economy of Japan: The Domestic Transformation,* ed. Kozo Yamamura and Tasukichi Yasuba (Stanford, Calif.: Stanford University Press, 1987), 263–88.
43. John Griffin, "National Capitalisms? Toward a Comparison of Tenuous States from a Modern Perspective of Ownership Politics" (paper presented at the annual meeting of the American Political Science Association, Washington, D.C., August 28–31, 1997); and "Institutional Change as a Collective Learning Process? A U.S.–German Comparison of Corporate Governance Reform" (paper presented at the annual meeting of the American Political Science Association, Chicago, August 31–September 3, 1995).
44. David G. Moore, *Politics and the Corporate Chief Executive* (New York: Conference Board, 1980), chap. 3.
45. Kirk Victor, "Being Here," *National Journal,* August 6, 1988, 2021–25.
46. Seymour Lusterman, *Managing Federal Government Relations* (New York: Conference Board, 1981).
47. David Vogel, *Fluctuating Fortunes: Political Power of Business in America* (New York: Basic Books, 1989), 287.
48. This list draws from P. N. Andrews, "The Sticky Wicket of Evaluating Public Affairs: Thoughts about a Framework," *Public Affairs Review* 6 (1985): 94–105.
49. Jon Johnson, "Issues Management—What Are the Issues?" *Business Quarterly* 48, no. 3 (Fall 1983): 22.
50. Robert L. Heath and Richard Alan Nelson, *Issues Management: Corporate Public Policymaking in an Information Society* (Beverly Hills, Calif.: Sage Publications, 1986), 21.
51. Joseph T. Nolan, "Political Surfing When Issues Break," *Harvard Business Review* 63, no. 1 (January 1985): 72–81.
52. These elements are discussed differently in various works. See, for example, Johnson, "Issues Management," 23; and Heath and Nelson, *Issues Management,* 20.
53. James K. Brown, *Guidelines for Managing Corporate Issues Programs* (New York: Conference Board, 1981), chap. 4.
54. Ibid., 13–16.
55. Stephen E. Littlejohn, "Competition and Cooperation: New Trends in Issue Identification and Management at Monsanto and Gulf," in *Business Strategy and Public Policy,* ed. Alfred A. Marcus, Allen M. Kaufman, and David R. Beam (New York: Quorum Books, 1987), 22.
56. These distinctions are suggested by Ryan, Swanson, and Buchholz, *Corporate Strategy, Public Policy, and the Fortune 500,* 95.
57. Richard G. Darman and Lawrence E. Lynn, "The Business-Government Problem: Inherent Difficulties and Emerging Solutions," in *Business and Public Policy,* ed. John T. Dunlop (Cambridge, Mass.: Harvard Graduate School of Business Administration, 1980), 49.
58. George A. Steiner, *The New CEO* (New York: Macmillan, 1983), 26.
59. "A Chief Executive's View of Public Affairs," Rutgers University presentation, February 16, 1984.

60. Quoted in John M. Barry, "CEOs Make the Best Lobbyists," *Dun's Business Month,* February 2, 1986, 28.

61. Ibid., 32.

62. Lusterman, *Managing Federal Government Relations,* 6.

63. Kirk Victor, "Being Here," *National Journal,* August 6, 1988, 2021–25.

64. Seymour Lusterman, *Managing Business-State Government Relations* (New York: Conference Board, 1983).

65. Thomas L. Brewer, ed., *Political Risks in International Business: New Directions for Research, Management, and Public Policy* (New York: Praeger, 1985); Stephen J. Kobrin, *Managing Political Risk Assessment* (Berkeley: University of California Press, 1982).

66. See, for example, Committee for Economic Development, *Social Responsibilities of Business Corporations* (New York: CED, 1971); and Robert K. Ackerman, *The Social Challenge to Business* (Cambridge, Mass.: Harvard University Press, 1975).

67. Jerry W. Anderson, *Corporate Social Responsibility: Guidelines for Top Management* (New York: Quorum Books, 1989), 9.

68. This typology was suggested by Daryl G. Hatano, "Should Corporations Exercise Their Freedom of Speech Rights?" *American Business Law Journal* 22, no. 2 (Summer 1984): 165–87.

69. Louis W. Fry, Gerald D. Klein, and Roger E. Meiners, "Corporate Contributions: Altruistic or For-Profit?" *Academy of Management Journal* 25, no. 1 (1982): 94–106.

70. "McDonald's Combines a Dead Man's Advice with Lively Strategy," *Wall Street Journal,* December 12, 1987, 1, 12.

71. "Chief Executive's View of Public Affairs."

72. Neil J. Mitchell, *The Generous Corporation: A Political Analysis of Economic Power* (New Haven: Yale University Press, 1989), esp. 56, 62, 141.

73. Theodore Levitt, "The Dangers of Social Responsibility," *Harvard Business Review* 36, no. 5 (September 1958): 41–50; Milton Friedman, *Capitalism and Freedom* (Chicago: University of Chicago Press, 1962), 132–33; and Milton Friedman, "The Social Responsibility of Business Is to Increase Its Profits," *New York Times Magazine,* September 13, 1970, 122–26.

CHAPTER 5

Globalization of Business Activity

THE WORLD BANK reports that global economic growth made 2004 the most prosperous year in human history.[1] Although the United States did rather well, it was the developing nations that led the economic parade with a growth rate of better than 6 percent. All the world's developing regions expanded their economies in the half decade ending in 2004, but "spectacular" reductions in poverty appeared in East and South Asia. Even setting aside the dynamic economies of China, India, and Russia, the rest of the developing world still recorded a growth rate in 2004 of almost 5 percent. The reason for this good fortune, some commentators insist, was the increasing globalization of the world's economy.[2] The developing nations that embraced international trade, foreign investment, and an increased presence of multinational firms recorded greater declines in poverty than did countries that vetoed pro-globalization policies.

At the time the World Bank report was released, however, a top American Federation of Labor and Congress of Industrial Organizations (AFL-CIO) official delivered a strikingly different assessment of the impact of globalization.[3] From the AFL-CIO perspective, globalization was spreading joblessness throughout the world and increasing disparities in income. Globalization had created a world in which the rich became richer and working families everywhere suffered reduced living standards. Increased transnational economic activity restricted health insurance, lowered wage levels, cut pension benefits, and limited investments in good jobs. Globalization has fashioned "a new world order in which employers roam the world in search of cheaper and cheaper labor, pitting workers against workers in a relentless race to the bottom."

These contradictory interpretations of globalization result in part from the basket of diverse images associated with the term *globalization.* When the members of the World Trade Organization gathered in Seattle a few years ago to set the group's agenda for the new millennium, they were met by 40,000 protesters who linked the emerging global economy to just about every concern then unpopular. For groups unhappy with immigration policies, genetically modified food, American movies, the defects of democracy, lax environmental standards, or human rights abuses in China, the global economy was the culprit. Even though the internationalization of business has brought considerable prosperity to numerous nations, influential groups in many countries regard globalization as a "trap" and consider it to be the source of their own domestic problems.[4] In this chapter I investigate what globalization actually is and consider why it has become a prominent symbol in contemporary politics.

Today's global economy is driven by the actions of multinational corporations (MNCs).[5] Explored here are the emergence of multinational enterprises, their strategies in the industrialized world, and their impact on the countries where they are headquartered and where they are active. The United States was a significant player in the world economy throughout the twentieth century, and it remains an influential force in the early years of the new century. Although U.S. producers have long been active in global markets, international firms now affect economic conditions within the United States as well. A British company has bought Holiday Inns, Japanese firms acquired Firestone and CBS Records, and German corporations took over the A&P, Chrysler, and a major cell phone operator. Each country's economic institutions define its style of capitalism and determine how its firms fit into the emerging global framework. The chapter concludes with an assessment of national styles of capitalism and their relationship to globalization.

THE EMERGENCE OF THE GLOBAL MARKETPLACE

In his best-selling book *The Lexus and the Olive Tree,* Thomas Friedman, a columnist for the *New York Times,* contends that globalization now "shapes virtually everyone's domestic politics and international relations."[6] Friedman associates globalization with an impressive array of important world events, but he fails to define what globalization actually is. Friedman and other analysts find little value in forcing the multiple facets of globalization into a single framework, but without clarity the concept becomes difficult to apply.[7] Globalization originated as an economic concept involving the behavior of firms, and it will be used in that sense here.[8] Globalization is an increase in cross-border commercial activity. Globalization, therefore, involves the establishment of cross-border production systems, distribution networks, financial markets, and product development centers. Globalization was made possible by both technological advances and international agreements. Enhanced technology has increased the mobility of people, goods, and capital across national borders, and it has created communications networks that permit people everywhere to share messages instantaneously.[9] As individual corporations rationalize their use of resources globally, they increase their productivity and improve their position in the marketplace. When some firms benefit from new conditions, competitive pressures prompt other corporations to follow suit.

The post–World War II regime of economic renewal was framed in a series of treaties negotiated in Bretton Woods, New Hampshire, in July 1944, and these agreements championed increased international economic activity as the best means to promote economic welfare.[10] Since many nations lacked the resources to revive their economies after wartime destruction, the Bretton Woods treaties created the World Bank to provide long-term loans for reconstruction and development. Fluctuating rates of exchange among currencies were a common barrier to international trade because firms could not be certain how much they would receive from the sale of their products. To limit this risk, the Bretton Woods treaties created the International Monetary Fund to stabilize exchange rates among currencies. The Bretton Woods negotiations also led to an executive agreement establishing the General Agreement on Tariffs and Trade (GATT), whose signatories pledged to reduce international tariffs and comply with a code of fair trade practices.

The current global era is characterized by an increased volume of cross-border economic activity, but this is not the first time the world has experienced a surge in international activity.[11] In the period from 1870 to 1913, the volume of trade, the amount of capital, and the number of workers crossing national borders rivaled, relative to the size of the world economy, what we see today. The devastation of World War I and the turmoil of the Great Depression of the 1930s brought this era of globalization to an end.

The current era of globalization, however, does not simply reprise past levels of cross-border activity. The new globalization differs from the older version in that it reflects a deeper level of economic integration. This is seen in the changing nature of international trade. International commerce traditionally involved the sale of commodities and the exchange of finished goods that were manufactured in one country and sold in another. An increasing share of international trade today involves the exchange of intermediate goods, often between divisions within the same company. IBM, for example, may ship disk drives from Taiwan to France, where they are combined with components from other locations to yield finished products. This change in the nature of trade reflects the emergence of multinational production systems and more interdependent operations.

The modern financial landscape also differs from the earlier era.[12] During the previous era of globalization, only a limited number of countries, led by Great Britain, invested in foreign countries, and these funds were concentrated in long-term investments in public infrastructure projects in developing countries. Today numerous countries make international loans, and these loans are concentrated in industrial rather than emerging nations. Contemporary investment activity normally occurs in knowledge-intensive industries through joint ventures, alliances, and franchise arrangements. In addition, international finance has witnessed a tremendous increase in the flow of capital into short-term bonds, commercial paper, equities, and derivatives and an extraordinary surge in currency transactions.

The older era of globalization rested largely on improvements in transportation, whereas the current era is based on enhanced communication services.[13] Advances in information technologies permit the transmission of vast amounts of data, text, pictures, and speech faster, farther, and more cheaply than most people could have imagined. From this perspective, the new globalization encompasses both an increased volume of cross-border economic activity and a qualitative change in the nature of that activity. National economies today are more profoundly affected by international economic activity than they were during the older era of globalization, and international economic decisions now affect countries' internal practices more directly than in the past.

Contemporary discussions of globalization also involve issues that reach beyond corporate operations, but the relationship between globalization and these issues is more problematic. The United States has certainly lost manufacturing jobs in recent years as globalization has become more pronounced, but it is a mistake to presume that all events in a global age are the product of globalization. In recent decades, the world, not just the United States, has experienced a formidable increase in manufacturing productivity.[14] The world's production of manufactured goods increased by 30 percent between 1995 and 2002, but world employment in manufacturing fell by 11 percent. As the United States developed a postindustrial economy, fewer workers were needed to produce far more goods. One source reports, for example, that U.S. steel production increased in the last decade from 75 to 102 million tons, but the number of workers employed in the steel industry actually fell from 289,000 to 74,000.[15] Even if a ten-foot wall had been built around the United States after World War II, the proportion of workers employed in manufacturing would still have declined in past decades and would still be declining today. This does not mean that outsourcing and international fabrication of products for the U.S. market does not occur. Of course they do. But it does mean that globalization is only one of the developments now occurring in the world economy.

Globalization is understood in some quarters to be a political rather than an economic project.[16] Some who believe that limited government will promote economic growth and individual freedom champion globalization as a technique for advancing these goals.[17] For them, globalization implies the self-regulation of markets and the deregulation of national economies. The activities of governments in the global marketplace, however, contradict the image of free and neutral exchanges among autonomous economic actors. Global markets are the product of political decisions intended to promote national advantage, and they have become forums that witness national subsidies for aircraft firms such as Airbus Industries, the manipulation of trade laws to benefit steel manufacturers, the invocation of antitrust laws to protect software enterprises, adjustments in the value of currencies to advance nationalistic policies, and so much more. Although globalization may have limited the utility of some tools governments use to implement their policies, there is little evidence that the withering away of the state will be the result of global trends. As Paul N. Doremus and his colleagues point out, "states charter MNCs and shape the operating environment in which they flourish. States retain the political authority to steer their activities."[18]

Globalization is thought by still other analysts to increase the leverage of major corporations in the political arena. This view is difficult to assess, as Graham K. Wilson indicates, because major corporations are usually perceived as politically influential actors in every arena and we lack an accepted metric for differentiating their power in specific circumstances.[19] Companies are said to gain political power because globalization has made it easier for them to shift facilities and employment to another country if a government enacts policies that increase their costs.[20] We do know that employment costs are only one factor in a firm's location decisions, and it is likely to be decisive only when the gap between high and low wage levels remains substantial over a considerable period of time. Sizable variations in income levels among American states have persisted for more than a century, and large numbers of employers still maintain their facilities in high-cost regions where governments are often unfriendly.[21]

Diverse factors shape globalization, but neither the extent nor the nature of globalization is inevitable. The period from 1870 to 1913 indicates that seemingly irreversible global trends can be halted and even rolled back.[22] Furthermore, globalization is not entirely global. Some industries and some countries are more "global" than others. The pharmaceutical, computer, and semiconductor industries are truly international, but resource- and labor-intensive sectors are still largely national. The dominant share of international economic activity is also concentrated in the three dozen countries of the Organisation for Economic Cooperation and Development (OECD), and many nations stand at the border of the global economy looking in. Even countries deeply involved in the global economy, however, maintain their distinct national identities. In most years, the United States is the world's largest exporting nation, but exports still account for only about 11 percent of the U.S. gross domestic product. As Paul R. Krugman insists, a nation's prosperity depends more on its performance in the domestic marketplace than in the global economy.[23] South Korea's efforts to deal with the challenges of globalization are examined in Box 5-1.

MULTINATIONAL CORPORATIONS IN THE GLOBAL ECONOMY

Of the one hundred largest economic organizations in the world, half are national governments and half are multinational corporations. For decades MNCs have been entering new markets through mergers, takeovers, partnerships, joint ventures, and direct investments, and they are now the world's dominant vehicle for conducting global business.

Literally, a multinational corporation is simply a company that operates in more than one nation.[24] By some definitions, a firm must have manufacturing facilities or service locations in more than one country or conduct a specific proportion of its business outside the country in which it is headquartered in order to qualify as an MNC. In fact, being a multinational firm is as much an evolutionary process as a specific condition. Typically, corporations begin to export

Cases in Development
BOX 5-1 SOUTH KOREAN RESPONSES TO GLOBALIZATION

By the mid-1990s, South Korea had created a strong economy. Its state-led development policy had reduced unemployment to 2 percent, increased per capita income from $200 per year in 1960 to $10,000 per year, created the world's most efficient steel industry, and made the country the world's largest producer of DRAM microchips. The South Korean government believed that globalization was shifting manufacturing away from the mass production of standardized goods based on energy- and labor-intensive processes toward more flexible manufacturing based on capital- and knowledge-intensive procedures, and the country needed to adapt. The administration sought to bring the country's labor practices up to international standards so as to confirm South Korea's emergence as an advanced nation and prepare for its entry into the World Trade Organization and the Organisation for Economic Cooperation and Development. The Korean president proposed to reduce government intervention in the economy and reorganize the agencies that administered economic policy.

Little progress had been made on these proposals when South Korea was hit by the Asian financial crisis of 1997–98. The crisis began in July 1997 with the collapse of Thailand's currency, and it then spread to Indonesia and other nations in the region. When it reached Korea, the economic panic highlighted problems that had previously been acknowledged but remained unaddressed. The decades of economic growth had increased income inequality and concentrated economic power in the hands of a few large Korean conglomerates. The conglomerates were unable to repay their loans, companies of all sizes went bankrupt, banks were unable to deal with the pile of bad loans, and fearful international lenders demanded that South Korea pay them what was owed. The country's currency lost its value, and the government turned for assistance to the International Monetary Fund (IMF). The IMF organized a $58 billion bailout, and South Korea agreed to financial reforms, more open trade, and radical restructuring that required major corporations to limit their expansion. A new president endorsed the IMF bailout, and the national legislature enacted a reform package that had been blocked by interest groups before the financial crisis hit. The new government saw the Asian financial crisis as an opportunity to win agreement to implement long overdue reforms in the Korean economy. South Korean scholars debate whether globalization constituted a threat to South Korea's economy or whether it was an opportunity to carry out necessary policies.

Sources: Based on Young Whan Kihl, *Transforming Korean Politics: Democracy, Reform, and Culture* (Armonk, N.Y.: M. E. Sharpe, 2005), chap. 5; and Charles Harvie and Hyun-Hoon Lee, *Korea's Economic Miracle: Fading or Reviving?* (New York: Palgrave Macmillan, 2005), chap. 4.

products from their home country and then create overseas marketing organizations to boost sales. Later the firms license foreign companies to make certain products and eventually build their own manufacturing plants in other countries. Gradually, companies internationalize their workforce, management structure, and ownership; eventually they organize their total operations on an international basis. Even though major companies now stand at different points in this evolution, most are increasingly internationalized.

When MNCs became prominent in the 1950s and 1960s, they were perceived as a new form of colonialism.[25] MNCs typically came from the United States and focused their operations in so-called third world nations. MNCs were regarded as instruments—or, at least, symbols—of Western domination, and the United Nations established an agency to monitor their operations. Although multinationals provided nonindustrial nations access to capital, technology, management skills, and export markets, they were also criticized for deepening the economic dependence of these countries, importing inappropriate technologies, interfering with domestic politics, and destroying traditional cultures.[26]

Whatever the validity of these views, the world of multinational operations has changed. The lion's share of transnational business activity today occurs in industrial countries that have sophisticated governments. Industrial nations, and especially the United States, are now the targets of MNCs as well as their homes. Today, developing nations protest being ignored by MNCs as frequently as they complain that they are exploited by them.[27] Other changes in MNCs are revealed by an examination of Table 5-1.

Multinational firms are no longer an exclusively American phenomenon. Of the 500 largest firms by revenues in 2003, only 189, or 38 percent, were based in the United States, and 35 were headquartered in Great Britain.[28] The number of the largest companies located in Japan fell from 149 in 1994 to 82 in 2003, and the number at home in Germany declined from 44 to 34 in the same period. In 2003, moreover, 15 of the largest corporations were based in China, 11 came from South Korea, and 4 resided in India.

Multinational Strategies and Tactics

General Electric, number 9 on the *Fortune* list, confirmed its status as a global enterprise in 2004 by obtaining $72 billion of its $152 billion in revenues outside the United States. Its international activities include manufacturing for local and export markets, import and sale of goods produced in other regions, leasing of aircraft, and provision of financial services for various regional economies.[29] In 2005, Sony Corporation, the Japanese entertainment conglomerate, displayed its multinational credentials by naming Sir Howard Sringer, the British-born chief of its U.S. unit, to be its first non-Japanese CEO.[30] Deutsche Bank, whose name testifies to its prominent status in Germany, was accused in 2005 of being

Table 5-1 The World's Largest Corporations, 2003

Corporation	Home country	Sales in millions of $
Wal-Mart Stores	United States	263,009
British Petroleum Amoco	Britain	232,571
Exxon Mobil	United States	222,883
Royal Dutch Shell Group	Britain/Netherlands	201,728
General Motors	United States	195,324
Ford Motor	United States	164,505
Daimler Chrysler	Germany	156,602
Toyota Motor	Japan	153,111
General Electric	United States	134,187
Total	France	118,441
Allianz	Germany	114,950
Chevron Texaco	United States	112,937
AXA	France	111,912
Conoco Phillips	United States	99,468
Volkswagen	Germany	98,637
Nippon Telegraph & Telephone	Japan	98,229
ING Group	Netherlands	95,893
Citigroup	United States	94,713
IBM	United States	89,131
American International Group	United States	81,303

Source: "Global 500 World's Largest Corporations," *Fortune,* July 26, 2004, 163. Used with permission.

"un-German" for announcing plans to lay off German workers at the same time that it reported that profits had risen 87 percent.[31]

Multinational companies differ. Their international activities are intended to benefit from the following forms of competitive advantage:

1. Location-specific production advantages based on differences in costs
2. Extra-national production efficiencies based on large volume
3. Access to important national markets
4. Production locations in countries with advantages in skills and technology
5. Global distribution policies with cost and cross-product advantages[32]

Firms pursuing a *domestic* market strategy concentrate on defending their home market against foreign competition. They turn to the international arena to find production locations where the costs of production are cheaper than at home. They hope to gain a marketplace advantage by manufacturing their products in these "export platforms" and then shipping them home for sale at a better price than competitors can offer. Companies following a *national* strategy establish semi-autonomous subsidiaries in large countries to gain access to national markets that might otherwise be closed to them, thus capturing advantages from economies of scale. They may also believe that partially independent corporate structures inspire more creativity and dedication from their employees than divisions tightly controlled by a foreign headquarters. Finally, a company's international activities may be part of a plan to build a *global* production and distribution strategy and establish a multiproduct identity in various geographic markets. Firms pursuing a truly global strategy will decide where to buy raw materials and components, where to obtain capital, whom to hire, what to sell, and where to manufacture products on the basis of worldwide operating considerations.

Government Relations

The distinctive features of multinational firms are that they are active in multiple countries and maintain relations with numerous governments. As they pursue their strategies, MNCs must comply with the laws of the home country where they are headquartered as well as the requirements of the host countries where they are active. The dual identity of MNCs makes both home-country and host-country governments suspicious and renders conflict between governments and multinationals almost inevitable.

Most home-country governments regard multinationals as vehicles to promote their political and economic interests. Firms are their modern-day gladiators. Home-country governments usually seek to expand the international role of firms headquartered in their countries, help them win access to lucrative foreign markets, and defend them against hostile action by other governments.

The U.S. government has been less diligent in promoting the interests of its MNCs than other major governments. Although U.S. foreign policy sometimes operates on behalf of American business interests, U.S. economic concerns have normally been subordinated to foreign-policy objectives.[33] For decades, for example, the pattern of U.S. policy toward Germany and Japan was to secure political objectives by surrendering economic advantages, and today U.S. policy toward China is guided by a desire to shape that country's place in the international community.[34] In addition, U.S. administrations may seek to achieve their political objectives by restricting the actions of the foreign subsidiaries of American MNCs, and they often attempt to change other countries' human rights, political, labor, environmental, and emigration policies by penalizing American companies whose foreign subsidiaries are active in those countries.[35]

Host-country governments welcome MNCs because of their potential to enhance their nations' economies, but they also resent MNCs because of the subordination of their countries' welfare to the interests of the MNCs and the policies of home-country governments. They fear MNCs' ability to shift factories, products, and employment from country to country, and they worry that

MNCs will gather up economic rewards in their countries and leave without help-ing to solve their social and political problems.[36]

Conflicts between MNCs and host countries proceeded in the 1970s under the threat of nationalization of MNC assets by the host country. In recent decades, however, industrial nations have avoided extreme actions and managed relations with MNCs within a framework of bargaining and negotiation.[37]

Most major countries walk a fine line between welcoming MNCs and demanding that their national interests be respected.[38] Foreign multinationals have traditionally found that certain sectors of a host country's economy—such as defense, telecommunications, and broadcasting—are closed to them.[39] Host-country governments often review the plans of MNCs when they enter the country and establish performance requirements for incoming firms in such areas as investment, product development, employment, and ownership by host-country nationals.

MNCs, in turn, are not defenseless in their negotiations with host govern-ments. They control the capital, technology, and access to export markets that host governments want. MNCs also play one country against others while seeking investment subsidies, research and development (R&D) funding, job training, infrastructure projects, favorable pricing rules for their products, and favored treat-ment under national procurement programs.

Multinational Investment and the United States

Multinational firms are accused both of damaging their home country's economy by exporting jobs and factories and hurting the host country by exploiting its markets and weakening its production capacity. Any assessment of the impact of MNCs should be done cautiously because multinational strategies differ dramat-ically and negotiations between MNCs and host governments vary from case to case. The effects of the outward investment by MNCs on a home country and of the inward investment by MNCs on a host country are discussed in this section, using the United States as an example.

The AFL-CIO official mentioned earlier believed that transnational economic activity and, especially, investment by U.S. firms in other countries make it tougher for U.S. workers to defend the salaries and benefits they now receive. Others, who maintain that investments by U.S. firms in foreign countries help the American economy, argue that outward investment by MNCs occurs because U.S. firms can earn higher profits abroad than at home. The subsequent spending of these increased profits in the United States then stimulates the growth of the U.S. econ-omy more than if the MNC had only invested at home. The failure of U.S. firms to invest outside the United States would close off profitable investment oppor-tunities, raise overall production costs, increase prices to American consumers, lower aggregate sales, slow the growth of the U.S. economy, and thus reduce the number of jobs available to American workers.[40]

Even though outward investment may have a net positive effect on the U.S. economy, there is no doubt that some workers and communities are "dislocated" by outward investment. Plants are closed, workers are fired, and communities are devastated as MNCs move investments from the home country into the global economy. Organized labor is one of the groups most harmed by the outward investment practices of MNCs.[41] Outward investment typically occurs in manufacturing industries, where unions are strong, and it places national labor groups in competition with one another. Although multinational union bargaining is a logical response to this situation, it has been slow to emerge because of the nationalistic structure of the labor movement, the diversity of national labor laws, and ideological divisions among unions.

The American government "encourages" foreign investment in the United States.[42] An interagency Committee on Foreign Investment in the United States can screen foreign investments that threaten the nation's security, but the committee seldom meets. Japan, in comparison, requires every foreign investor to submit a detailed investment proposal and secure approval before proceeding. Foreign investments in Japan can be prohibited on national security grounds or because they might have adverse effects on Japanese companies. Among the most ardent defenders of foreign direct investment in the United States are state and local governments.[43] Forty states have established offices to woo international investors. Governors and mayors travel widely and look to foreign investment as a means of stimulating employment, increasing tax revenues, gaining new technology, and obtaining development capital.

Foreign investment in the United States totals $3 trillion. More than 80 percent of these investments are *portfolio* investments in government securities, corporate stocks and bonds, and bank deposits. The portfolio investor is a passive investor who plays no role in managing assets. The balance of the investments are *direct* investments in companies, banks, and real estate in which the investor can make decisions about how those assets will be used. Recent increases in foreign investment in the United States have been large, but the total value of direct foreign holdings in the United States remains at a modest level by international standards.[44] Total foreign holdings in most other countries are a larger share of GDP than in the United States. The value of British holdings in the United States recently equaled 2.1 percent of U.S. GDP, but the value of U.S. holdings in Great Britain was 5.7 percent of British GDP.

Transnational investments in the United States or other host countries affect the host-country economies in either of two ways.[45] First, international investors can enter a region and *stimulate* the local economy. A MNC can introduce new techniques, increase demand for local goods and services, generate new employment, and be a tough competitor that prods indigenous companies to improve their operations. Alternatively, transnational investors can come into a region and *displace* local economic activity. They can aggravate the weaknesses of the region by shifting high-value-added functions to their home country and reducing the skill level of the remaining workers. They can steer business away from innovative local firms in favor of suppliers from their own country.

Werner Meyer-Larsen argues that major German companies have adopted a strategy of challenging corporate America by investing in U.S. firms.[46] Daimler-Benz's agreement to merge with Chrysler, he argues, is evidence of a campaign being conducted by Deutsche Bank, Volkswagen, Bertelsmann, Siemens, and other major German corporations to gain control of American companies. This strategy builds upon earlier actions by German firms to locate production facilities in the United States, as represented by Daimler-Benz's decision to manufacture Mercedes automobiles in Tuscaloosa, Alabama, and BMW's choice of Spartanburg, South Carolina, as its manufacturing site. Will such investments by German firms attract new suppliers to Tuscaloosa and Spartanburg, improve the skills of local workers, and generate additional business for Charleston and other ports, or will the German firms ultimately transfer the highest-value-added functions to Munich or Stuttgart, ship the most sophisticated parts from Germany to the United States, and leave only low-paid jobs for American workers? Only in retrospect is it possible to determine whether specific investments have actually stimulated or displaced local economies.

The critics of foreign direct investment in the United States argue that MNCs are more likely to displace local economic activity than to stimulate it.[47] They point out that most foreign outlays are used to acquire existing businesses rather than to establish new ones.[48] Whereas 3 million Americans work for foreign firms, by one estimate, these enterprises created only 90,000 new jobs in a recent seven-year period.[49] The critics maintain that MNCs have reduced the skill level of American jobs and transformed successful firms into hollow shells for assembling products that were conceived and designed elsewhere, and they insist that the United States must restrict multinational investors whose actions displace U.S. economic activity, destroy local firms, and diminish American jobs.[50]

The best policy response both to the outward investment by U.S. firms and foreign investment in the United States is to make the U.S. economy as productive as possible. Foreign MNCs generally assign sophisticated tasks to countries with highly trained workers, exceptional suppliers, and a well-developed infrastructure, and U.S. firms invest outside the United States when they obtain better returns than are available in the U.S. economy.[51] When challenges such as the "offshoring" of service jobs emerge, it is important to rest the debate on reliable data and acknowledge that some workers and firms will be dislocated regardless of the eventual benefits to the total economy.[52] Critical job skills, an attractive location for high-value services, and a fair playing field remain a sound strategy.

In the era of globalism, nations seek to aid home-based MNCs in their competition with firms from other nations, but the national identity of the

MNC is eroding. It is increasingly difficult to determine exactly what it means to say a firm is an American or a German multinational.[53] The author of a prominent article on MNCs posed the question, in fact, in his article "Who Is Us?"[54] All of a company's directors and most of its owners and managers may be American citizens, and yet the company may still place most of its facilities, employ most of its workers, and conduct most of its research outside U.S. borders. In the future, it may be no more meaningful to say a firm is an American company than it is today to view an enterprise as a Delaware or a New Jersey corporation. Even though we live in a globalizing world, the politics that define a nation's economy are still predominantly national politics. National governments strive to devise policies and institutional arrangements that will give their firms a competitive advantage both at home and in the global arena.

CARVING UP THE GLOBAL PIE: VARIETIES OF CAPITALISM

The principal question facing national models of capitalism in a globalizing age is whether their traditional institutions and practices can still deliver the prosperity their citizens have come to expect. Although each nation creates its own variety of capitalism, economic relations in the United Kingdom and the United States are frequently contrasted with those in Germany and Japan. The United Kingdom and the United States are said to have "liberal market economies" that rely on market-oriented mechanisms to guide economic activity, whereas the German and Japanese systems are described as "coordinated market economies" that emphasize institutional arrangements to direct economic practice.[55] From the mid-1960s to the mid-1980s the coordinated market economies in Germany and Japan flourished while the performance of the liberal market economies lagged behind. In the 1980s the Anglo-American competitors began to restore their position, and by the early 1990s Germany and Japan recognized that their version of capitalism no longer delivered the level of economic performance found elsewhere.

National economies are embedded in international markets and production processes, but scholars disagree about the extent to which globalization may supplant national sovereignty and restrict political diversity. Andrew Shonfield leads one group of researchers, who argue that the institutional features of a nation's capitalist system determine the success of the country's economy and its quality of life.[56] These analysts emphasize the significance of the organizational arrangements of capitalist systems and the societal context of the institutions. Other scholars maintain that the ability of governments to define national practices and policies has already been largely eroded by globalization and all that is left for national governments in a global age, as Colin Crouch and Wolfgang Streeck write, is to hide from "their voters the dirty secret that it is no longer they who determine their country's economic policies."[57] Whether events finally prove the globalists or the nationalists correct, capitalist systems will continue for some time to reflect divergent national circumstances.

The United States

In 2004 the *World Competitiveness Yearbook*, compiled by the Institute for Management Development in Switzerland, ranked the United States the world's most competitive economy.[58] The organization's ranking of 50 nations was based on more than 300 criteria grouped into four factors: economic performance, government efficiency, business efficiency, and infrastructure. Focusing on the ability of nations to create and maintain an environment in which firms can compete, Singapore was ranked second, followed by Canada and Australia. Germany was ranked twenty-first, Great Britain twenty-second, and Japan, which had been ranked first until 1994, was twenty-third.

Two decades earlier, the picture had looked very different. Americans were then told that the United States had entered a period of irreversible economic decline: the dollar was finished as the world's currency of choice, the country's technological lead had disappeared forever, and future generations of Americans would never again experience an increased standard of living. The Yale historian Paul Kennedy, author of the best-selling *The Rise and Fall of the Great Powers,* then appraised the nation's geopolitical future in these terms: "The only answer to the question increasingly debated by the public of whether the United States can preserve its existing [international] position is 'no.'"[59] Kennedy's analysis coincided with the prominence of non-American goods in the global marketplace and the view that the glory days of the U.S. economy were over. Long before the 1990s ended, these experts insisted, the United States would be relegated to third place among world economic powers, behind Germany and Japan.[60]

Why were these dire predictions wrong? First, they exaggerated the severity of the U.S. decline. Most theorists predicting decline compared the position of the United States in 1990 with its position in the late 1940s.[61] These comparisons had ignored the fact that the devastation of the world's other economies in World War II made the United States appear more dominant than it actually was. The largest part of the decline in the U.S. share of world production since the late 1940s reflected the ebbing away of temporary postwar conditions.

The forecasts of decline were also off the mark because they ignored the historic strengths of the American economy. In the years before World War II, the United States had consolidated its nineteenth-century lead in mass production industries, and its educational advances and large consumer market had spurred invention and innovation. The country emerged from World War II with a massive corporate R&D sector, a strong university research base, and unprecedented investment in science and technology, and the country combined these advantages to dominate the "high-tech" industries of the postwar era.[62] As a result of its cultural traditions and institutional arrangements, U.S. capitalism has displayed an unusual degree of organizational flexibility, financial efficiency, entrepreneurship, and innovation.

In the 1980s the value of some of these historic advantages had eroded. The increased volume of international trade had reduced the benefits American firms derived from being located in the world's largest consumer market. Although U.S. companies had pioneered techniques of mass production to serve this market, mass production principles had been largely superseded by Japanese-style flexible manufacturing. A cross-national investigation of key manufacturing industries in the 1980s reported that the United States had lost its monopoly of efficient production techniques and best industry practices.[63] The global diffusion of commercial technology meant that companies everywhere could now compete with U.S. firms as technological equals.[64]

U.S. companies eventually woke up to the reality of foreign competition and domestic decline, and the historic benefits of the American system of capitalism gradually reappeared. As a liberal market economy, U.S. firms faced the competitive discipline of the marketplace. Demonstrating flexibility and responsiveness, U.S. firms in the 1990s reviewed their strategies, restructured their operations, and redesigned their procedures. The overvaluation of the U.S. dollar moderated, and the availability of capital slowly improved. During the second half of the 1990s, American workers learned to use the computers that had been sitting on their desks, the Internet penetrated the corporate world, and extraordinary innovations in information technologies appeared at every turn. As a result, the United States enjoyed surprising economic growth, and the economy reported improvements in manufacturing and service-sector productivity that had not been seen in decades.[65] And to much surprise, the federal government in 1999 reported its first budget surplus in thirty years.

There is no reason for complacency about the U.S. economy and many grounds to recall Paul Kennedy's admonition that it "simply has not been given to any one society to remain permanently ahead of all the others."[66] During the George W. Bush administration, the budget deficit reached historic heights, the merchandise trade deficits grew to amounts not previously imagined, corporate spending for basic research declined, and the nation still recorded low, occasionally even negative, savings and investment rates. Although corporate America has repaired and revitalized its production systems, it has not recaptured the comparative advantage it once had in such industries as motor vehicles and consumer electronics. Even more alarming is the evidence of deterioration in the political and social arena. Substance abuse, medical costs, litigation, incarceration rates, and functional illiteracy are costly problems that place substantial burdens on a competitive society. In international comparison, American high school drop-out rates are high, and levels of achievement are low. The T-shirt slogan "Underachiever—and Proud of It" is curiously emblematic of the problems the United States continues to inflict on itself.

Germany and Japan

In the 1970s and 1980s the advantages of the coordinated market economies found in Germany and Japan were widely celebrated by journalists and academics. For most of these years Japan was the world's model for economic success as its management methods and capitalist arrangements produced results that surpassed its American and European rivals. Japanese firms conducted business in corporate networks that emphasized the value of long-term relationships over short-term performance. Dubbed "alliance capitalism," these networks shared technical information, production assistance, and strategic advice.[67] Because network members such as lenders, suppliers, affiliates, and strategic customers hold large blocks of stock in Japanese firms, there is little need for the firms to respond to ordinary shareholders. Personal relations among Japanese managers are a central feature in a system that prioritizes commitments to executives, employees, lead banks, regulators, affiliated corporations, suppliers, and important customers and de-emphasizes the importance of high profits and capital markets.

A frequent explanation for Japan's economic success was its peculiar combination of institutional stability and operational flexibility.[68] The alliance of the Liberal Democratic Party (LDP), business figures, and bureaucratic elites facilitated the flow of information and unified the state and the civil society. Strong state institutions nurtured the system's adaptability by stressing the benefits of technocratic competence, emphasizing national unity on economic goals, and insulating economic policy from political pressures.[69]

In the 1990s, however, changes in the country's socioeconomic structure forced the LDP to transform its electoral base, the gap between successful global firms and domestic companies dependent on protectionist barriers widened, and the prestige of the bureaucracy declined. The Japanese system had emphasized production and market share as corporate goals and had accepted high levels of corporate debt. When the economy flourished in the 1980s, large debts were little problem, but when the government was unable to maintain economic growth in the 1990s, the costs of borrowing for many companies became unsustainable, and financial institutions were then forced to acknowledge vast uncollectible loans. As a result of these developments, the ability of Japan's developmental state to fashion effective responses to national crises vanished. In 1998 only 2 of the world's top 100 companies by market capitalization were Japanese, whereas in 1989 fully 43 of the top 100 firms were owned by Japanese interests.[70] Japan's economic plight is confirmed by the wave of corporate restructuring announcements, the first acquisitions of Japanese companies by international buyers, and the continuing absence of a consensus on the policies needed to restore growth.[71]

The German capitalist system presents an institutional framework within which governments, corporate representatives, and labor unions negotiate responses to changing market conditions.[72] Not known for radical innovations, industries organized under this model excel at balancing the interests of traditional groups and implementing improved production technologies. As Doremus and associates note, banks are the key providers of capital in the German system, core members of the supervisory boards, and sources of guidance and support in times of crisis. Its champions argue that West Germany's coordinated market system gave it the world's most successful economy at the end of the 1980s.[73] The country accounted for a larger share of world exports than Japan, even though it had half the population, and for about the same share as the United States, whose population was four times the German total. German wages were higher than Japanese or American wages, wage inequality was lower, and the system protected the position of established groups such as unions, farmers, civil servants, and small business.

By the mid-1990s, however, the weaknesses of the German model had become more apparent.[74] Commentators insist that the German economy is unusually rigid, permits little competition among German firms, and is characterized by significant weakness outside its core industries. As a result of protecting established groups, the nation incurred enormous public-sector deficits in financing the reunification with its eastern states with disappointing results. The country's high wage rates cut into its international trade surplus, and its persistently high social expenditures, living costs, and unemployment rates eroded the social cohesion its institutional arrangements were designed to ensure.[75] Germany has traditionally relied on political intervention to alter market behavior, but in recent years, it lacked a strategy to accommodate its high-cost production system with its leadership aspirations in the European Union and the global economy.[76]

Great Britain and the European Union

Most EU members have styles of capitalism that stress institutional coordination, whereas the Anglo-American model of capitalism gives market-oriented activities greater prominence. The conservative era of Prime Minister Thatcher mirrored this disposition by minimizing taxes, restraining government, relying on private companies to make production decisions, and accepting social inequality as an inevitable by-product of economic development.[77] The Thatcher government succeeded in reducing inflation, increasing manufacturing productivity, revitalizing British management, and expanding both home and stock ownership, but its accomplishments came at the price of increased social tensions. Great Britain has continued to support its liberal market economy by favoring deregulated labor and financial markets, supporting low levels of business coordination, and seeking to make Britain the "Enterprise Centre of Europe."

The European Union is an inchoate system of government resting atop twenty-five member nations. The Union's governing institutions administer a single market for most products, services, employees, and flows of capital. It has fashioned an agricultural sector that is dominated by public subsidies and government programs, and it has become the single voice in trade negotiations. A European Central Bank has been established in Frankfurt, and a common European currency, the euro, replaced national currencies in most of its countries.

The European Union is now creating its own model of capitalism.[78] British traditions reflect a liberal market philosophy, Germany has created coordinated market mechanisms, France has proposed policies urging more aggressive government intervention, and newer member states from Eastern Europe are still struggling to fashion their own economic identity after decades of Soviet domination. A single market, a common currency, and a unified position in trade negotiations will make it difficult for national styles of capitalism to endure unchanged, but it is reasonable to assume that the member states will strive to fashion a European model of capitalism that lets them maintain as far as possible the economic advantages they derive from their existing arrangements.[79] Many European companies have long been shielded from takeovers, guaranteed high prices for their goods, spared domestic competition, and given priority in public procurement, but they are now beginning to face a more challenging environment. A rash of mergers and takeovers suggests that the stronger, larger European companies with skilled employees and advanced technologies will emerge as eventual winners in the new system.

Multinational firms are a new way of structuring competition and increasing economic efficiency, but tensions between multinational enterprises and a political order composed of nation-states are inevitable. As Raymond Vernon points out, however, neither national governments nor multinational corporations are likely to become obsolete.[80] The world is now experiencing a lag in institutional development.[81] The internationalization of business has outpaced the development of the political institutions needed to regulate the new global economy. Similar to the American experience at the end of the nineteenth century, economic events have undermined the capacity of one set of political institutions to regulate economic activity, but the emergence of new institutions to take their place has not yet occurred.

A logical response to the globalization of business is to create an international regime to regulate MNCs on a global basis, but most governments are not yet prepared to cede sovereignty over important national activities.[82] The successes in international regulation have appeared in functional areas where all parties gain from collective action, such as in the international regulation of telecommunications and air transport.[83] A structure for the regulation of MNCs will probably emerge, but it will be preceded by a long period of frustration and experimentation.

SUMMARY

Globalization, the increase in cross-border commercial activity, has resulted from developments in technology and the policy decisions of national governments.

There have been earlier eras of globalization, such as the period from 1870 to 1913, but the current era is distinguished by a deeper level of economic integration than has appeared in the past. Globalization has far-reaching implications for national economies and political systems, but only some scholars fully embrace the assertions that globalization has led to the disappearance of U.S. manufacturing jobs, the withering away of the state, and the political hegemony of multinational corporations. Many factors will contribute to the future of the global economy, but past events demonstrate that apparently unstoppable global trends can sometimes be halted and even reversed.

The global economy is driven today by multinational corporations, and most of their activity in concentrated in major industrial states. Companies are profit-seeking entities, and they have entered the international arena to win production efficiencies, gain marketing advantages, and obtain access to scarce skills and technologies. The countries where multinational firms are headquartered usually support their endeavors, but the host governments, although believing the MNCs can enhance their economies, also fear that they will displace existing economic activity and aggravate the problems the nations hoped they would solve.

National economies are embedded in global markets and production processes, but the evolving relationship between the global economy and diverse national economic systems is unclear. Some argue that global economic systems will aid liberal market economies at the expense of coordinated market economies, whereas other scholars investigate whether national diversity itself can survive the emergence of global capitalism.

FURTHER READINGS

Fortune magazine assembles an informative listing of domestic and global firms, and these are available at http://www.pathfinder.com/fortune. Corporate Watch is an organization that investigates the consequences of corporate power in a global age: http://www.corpwatch.org/trac/globalization/corp/index.html. The Novartis Foundation for Sustainable Development discusses the responsibilities of multinational corporations in the global economy: http://www.foundation.novartis.com.

Derber, Charles. *People before Profit: The New Globalization in an Age of Terror, Big Money, and Economic Crisis.* New York: Picador, 2002.

Doremus, Paul N., William W. Keller, Louis W. Pauly, and Simon Reich. *The Myth of the Global Corporation.* Princeton: Princeton University Press, 1998.

Hall, Peter A., and David Soskice, eds. *Varieties of Capitalism: The Institutional Foundations of Comparative Advantage.* New York: Oxford University Press, 2001.

Wolf, Martin. *Why Globalization Works.* New Haven: Yale University Press, 2004.

Yamamura, Kozo, and Wolfgang Streeck, eds. *The End of Diversity? Prospects for German and Japanese Capitalism.* Ithaca, N.Y.: Cornell University Press, 2003.

NOTES

1. As reported in David Brooks, "Good News about Poverty," *New York Times,* November 27, 2004, A15.
2. Martin Wolf, *Why Globalization Works* (New Haven: Yale University Press, 2004).
3. Richard L. Trumka, "Remarks, Forum on the Working Poor, Villanova University," October 25, 2004, and "Global Economy." Both available at www.aflcio.org/issuespolitics/globaleconomy/.
4. Hans-Peter Martin and Harald Schumann, *The Global Trap: Globalization and the Assault on Prosperity and Democracy* (New York: St. Martin's, 1997).
5. John H. Dunning, "The Organisation of International Economic Interdependence: An Historical Excursion," in *Structural Change, Economic Interdependence and World Development,* vol. 4, *Economic Interdependence,* ed. John H. Dunning and Mikoto Usui (New York: St. Martin's, 1987), 15–16.
6. Thomas L. Friedman, *The Lexus and the Olive Tree* (New York: Farrar, Straus, and Giroux, 1999), xvi, xviii.
7. Fredric Jameson and Masao Miyoshi, eds., *The Cultures of Globalization* (Durham, N.C.: Duke University Press, 1998), xi–xii.
8. This discussion follows Wolfgang H. Reinicke, *Global Public Policy: Governing without Government?* (Washington, D.C.: Brookings Institution Press, 1998), chap. 1.
9. John M. Stopford and Louis Turner, *Britain and the Multinationals* (New York: Wiley, 1985), 25–39; and Raymond Vernon and Debora L. Spar, *Beyond Globalism: Remaking American Foreign Economic Policy* (New York: Free Press, 1989), 111.
10. Theodore Geiger, *The Future of the International System: The United States and the World Political Economy* (Boston: Unwin Hyman, 1988), chap. 2.
11. See Reinicke, *Global Public Policy,* 18–48.
12. Ibid., 29, 30, 45.
13. Friedman, *Lexus and Olive Tree,* xvii–xviii. See also Viktor Mayer-Schönberger and Deborah Hurley, "Globalization of Communication," in *Governance in a Globalizing World,* ed. Joseph S. Nye and John D. Donahue (Washington, D.C.: Brookings Institution Press, 2000), 135–51.
14. The principal sources for this paragraph are Charles L. Schultze, "Offshoring, Import Competition, and the Jobless Recovery" (Brookings Policy Brief 136 Brookings Institution, Washington, D.C., 2004), http://www.brookings.edu, and Institute for Management Development (IMD)—World Competitiveness Center, "Executive Summary," in *IMD Yearbook 2004,* http://www02.imd.ch/wcc, accessed November 22, 2004.
15. IMD-World Competitiveness Center, *IMD Yearbook 2004.*
16. See Robert W. Cox, "A Perspective on Globalization," and Stephen Gill, "Globalization, Democratization, and the Politics of Indifference," in *Globalization: Critical Reflections,* ed. James H. Mittelman (Boulder, Colo.: Lynne Rienner, 1996), 21–30 and 205–28.
17. See Manfred B. Steger, *Globalism: The New Market Ideology* (New York: Rowman and Littlefield, 2002), 47–54.
18. Paul N. Doremus, William W. Keller, Louis W. Pauly, and Simon Reich, *The Myth of the Global Corporation* (Princeton: Princeton University Press, 1998), 3–4.
19. Graham K. Wilson, *Business and Politics: A Comparative Introduction,* 3rd ed. (New York: Chatham House, 2003), 172.
20. See, for example, William Greider, *One World, Ready or Not: The Manic Logic of Global Capitalism* (New York: Simon and Schuster, 1997); Richard J. Barnet and John Cavanagh, *Global Dreams: Imperial Corporations and the New World Order* (New York: Simon and Schuster, 1994); and David C. Korten, *When Corporations Rule the World* (West Hartford, Conn.: Kumanian Press, 1995).
21. Steven K. Vogel, *Freer Markets, More Rules: Regulatory Reform in Advanced Industrial States* (Ithaca, N.Y.: Cornell University Press, 1996), chap. 7.
22. Paul R. Krugman, "Growing World Trade: Causes and Consequences" (Brookings Papers on Economic Activity, 1, Brookings Institution, Washington, D.C., 1995).

23. See, for example, Paul R. Krugman, *Pop Internationalism* (Cambridge, Mass.: MIT Press, 1996).
24. For a discussion of definitions of multinational enterprises, see Alan M. Rugman, Donald J. Lecraw, and Laurence D. Booth, *International Business: Firm and Environment* (New York: McGraw-Hill, 1985).
25. Raymond Vernon, *Sovereignty at Bay: The Multinational Spread of U.S. Enterprises* (New York: Basic Books, 1971), and Vernon, *Storm over the Multinationals* (Cambridge, Mass.: Harvard University Press, 1977). See also Rhys Jenkins, *Transnational Corporations and Uneven Development* (New York: Methuen, 1988).
26. For an accessible discussion of these points, see Graham K. Wilson, *Business and Politics: A Comparative Introduction,* 2nd ed. (Chatham, N.J.: Chatham House, 1990), chap. 9.
27. United Nations Centre on Transnational Corporations, "Executive Summary," in *Transnational Corporations in World Development: Trends and Prospects* (New York: United Nations, 1988).
28. Paola Hjelt, "2003: The Fortune Global 500," *Fortune,* July 26, 2004, 161–65.
29. General Electric, *Annual Report, 2004* (Fairfield, Conn.: General Electric, 2005), 58.
30. Lorne Manly and Andrew Ross Sorkin, "At Sony, Diplomacy Trumps Technology," *New York Times,* March 8, 2005, http://www.nytimes.com.
31. Louise Cooper, "Deutsche Bank Faces Critics at Home," BBC News, March 18, 2005, http://www.newsvote.bbc.co.uk.
32. Jack N. Behrman, "International Industrial Integration through Multinational Enterprises," in Dunning and Usui, *Structural Change, Economic Interdependence and World Development,* 65.
33. William Appleman Williams, *The Rise of the Modern American Empire: A Study of the Growth and Shaping of Social Consciousness in a Marketplace Society* (New York: Random House, 1969).
34. See, for example, Clyde V. Prestowitz, *Trading Places: How We Are Giving Our Future to Japan and How to Reclaim It* (New York: Basic Books, 1988), chap. 8.
35. Vic Razis, *The American Connection: The Influence of United States Business on South Africa* (London: Frances Pinter, 1986).
36. Fernando Henrique Cardoso and Enzo Faletto, *Dependency and Development in Latin America* (Berkeley: University of California Press, 1979); and Douglas C. Bennett and Kenneth E. Sharpe, *Transnational Corporations versus the State: The Political Economy of the Mexican Automobile Industry* (Princeton: Princeton University Press, 1985).
37. Vernon, *Sovereignty at Bay;* and Thomas A. Poynter, *Multinational Enterprises and Government Intervention* (London: Croom Helm, 1985).
38. Stopford and Turner, *Britain and the Multinationals,* 229–31. Some nations narrowly restrict the activities of MNCs. See, for example, Dennis J. Encarnation, *Dislodging Multinationals: India's Strategy in Comparative Perspective* (Ithaca, N.Y.: Cornell University Press, 1989).
39. A. E. Safarian, "Introductory Comments and Summary Report on Part III," in Dunning and Usui, *Structural Change, Economic Interdependence and World Development,* 177–92.
40. Peter Enderwick, *Multinational Business and Labour* (New York: St. Martin's, 1985), 158–59; and Stopford and Turner, *Britain and the Multinationals,* 186–88.
41. Enderwick, *Multinational Business and Labour,* esp. chap. 6; and C. K. Prahalad and Yves L. Doz, *The Multinational Mission* (New York: Free Press, 1987).
42. This paragraph is drawn from Linda M. Spencer, *American Assets: An Examination of Foreign Investment in the United States* (Arlington, Va.: Congressional Economic Leadership Institute, 1988), 19–23, 29, 35.
43. This paragraph is based on ibid., 35.
44. This paragraph follows *Economic Report of the President, 1990* (Washington, D.C.: GPO, 1990), 124–25.
45. John Cantwell, "The Reorganization of European Industries after Integration: Selected Evidence on the Role of Multinational Enterprise Activities," in *Multinationals and the European Community,* ed. John Dunning and Peter Robson (Oxford: Basil Blackwell, 1988), 25–49.
46. Werner Meyer-Larsen, *Germany, Inc.: The New German Juggernaut and Its Challenge to World Business* (New York: Wiley, 2000).

47. Norman J. Glickman and Douglas P. Woodward, *The New Competitors: How Foreign Investors Are Changing the U.S. Economy* (New York: Basic Books, 1989); and Martin Tolchin and Susan Tolchin, *Buying Into America: How Foreign Investment Is Changing the Face of the Nation* (New York: Random House, 1988).

48. Spencer, *American Assets,* 10–11.

49. Glickman and Woodward, *New Competitors,* 149–52.

50. See "EC Tightens Up on 'Screwdriver' Plants," *Japan Economic Institute Report,* March 18, 1988, 5.

51. "Benefits from foreign flows," *Financial Times* (London), December 28, 1990, 8.

52. Lael Brainard and Robert E. Litan, " 'Offshoring' Service Jobs: Bane or Boon and What to Do?" (Brookings Policy Brief 132, Brookings Institution, Washington, D.C., 2004), http://www.brookings.edu.

53. See, for example, Wyn Grant, William Paterson, and Colin Whitson, *Government and the Chemical Industry: A Comparative Study of Britain and West Germany* (Oxford: Oxford University Press, Clarendon Press, 1988), 317.

54. Robert B. Reich, "Who Is Us?" *Harvard Business Review* 68, no. 1 (January–February 1990): 53–65.

55. These terms appear in Peter A. Hall and David Soskice, eds., *Varieties of Capitalism: The Institutional Foundations of Comparative Advantage* (New York: Oxford University Press, 2001); and Kozo Yamamura and Wolfgang Streeck, eds., *The End of Diversity? Prospects for German and Japanese Capitalism* (Ithaca, N.Y.: Cornell University Press, 2003).

56. Andrew Shonfield, *Modern Capitalism* (Oxford: Oxford University Press, 1964).

57. Colin Crouch and Wolfgang Streeck, "Introduction: The Future of Capitalist Diversity," in *Political Economy of Modern Capitalism: Mapping Convergence and Diversity,* ed. Crouch and Streeck (London: Sage Publications, 1997), esp. 1–4, 8–10.

58. Frances Williams, "Lean and Mean, but Is It Fair?" *Financial Times,* September 4, 1994, 4; and IMD-World Competitiveness Center, *IMD Yearbook 2004,* http://www02.imd.ch/wcc, accessed November 22, 2004.

59. Paul Kennedy, *The Rise and Fall of the Great Powers: Economic Change and Military Conflict from 1500 to 2000* (New York: Random House, 1987), 515, 533 (quotation on 515).

60. Lester C. Thurow, *Head to Head: The Coming Economic Battle among Japan, Europe, and America* (New York: Morrow, 1992).

61. See, for example, Geiger, *Future of the International System,* 19–30.

62. Richard R. Nelson, "U.S. Technological Leadership: Where Did It Come From and Where Did It Go?" *Research Policy* 19, no. 2 (April 1990): 117–32, esp. 119–22.

63. Michael L. Dertouzos and others, *Made in America: Regaining the Productive Edge* (Cambridge, Mass.: MIT Press, 1989), 26.

64. Tony Jackson, "The Myth behind the Miracle," *Financial Times,* November 22, 1995, 15.

65. Paul E. Erdman, "America: Back on Top," *CBS MarketWatch,* November 24, 1999.

66. Kennedy, *Rise and Fall of Great Powers,* 533.

67. M. L. Gerlach, *Alliance Capitalism: The Social Organization of Japanese Business* (Berkeley: University of California Press, 1992).

68. Ronald Dore, "Asian Crisis and the Future of the Japanese Model," *Cambridge Journal of Economics* 22, no. 6 (November 1998); and Bill Emmott, *The Sun Also Sets: The Limits to Japan's Economic Power* (New York: Times Books, 1989).

69. Chung-in Moon and Sang-young Rhyu, "Between Flexibility and Rigidity: Understanding Economic Hard Times in Japan and South Korea" (paper presented at the annual meeting of the American Political Science Association, Atlanta, September 2–5, 1999).

70. This paragraph relies on "High Output, Low Profits," *Financial Times,* June 2, 1999, 15.

71. Gillian Tett, "Milestone on Japan's Slow Road to Reform," *Financial Times,* June 10, 1999, 17.

72. Doremus, Keller, Pauly, and Reich, *Myth of the Global Corporation,* 32–35.

73. See Wolfgang Streeck, "German Capitalism: Does It Exist? Can It Survive?" in Crouch and Streeck, *Political Economy of Modern Capitalism,* 33–54.

74. Yamamura and Streeck, *The End of Diversity?* "Introduction," esp. 11–15; also "Germany: Special Report," *Financial Times,* December 8, 2004.

75. Kenneth Dyson, "Economic Policy," in *Developments in West German Politics,* ed. Gordon Smith, William E. Paterson, and Peter H. Merkl (Durham, N.C.: Duke University Press, 1989), 148–67; also Yamamura and Streeck, *End of Diversity?* 13.

76. For alternative views, see Meyer-Larsen, *Germany, Inc.;* and Karen Adelberger, "Semi-Sovereign Leadership: The State's Role in German Biotechnology and Venture Capital Growth" (paper presented at the annual meeting of the American Political Science Association, Atlanta, September 2–5, 1999).

77. Andrew Graham, "The UK 1979–95: Myths and Realities of Conservative Capitalism," in Crouch and Streeck, *Political Economy of Modern Capitalism,* 117–32, esp. 119 and 121.

78. Hugo Dixon, "Europe's New Frontier," *Financial Times,* April 21, 1999, 9.

79. See Orfeo Fioretos, "The Domestic Sources of Multilateral Preferences: Varieties of Capitalism in the European Community," in Yamamura and Streeck, *The End of Diversity?* 213–44.

80. Raymond Vernon, *In the Hurricane's Eye: The Troubled Prospects of Multinational Enterprises* (Cambridge, Mass.: Harvard University Press, 2005).

81. Paul Streeten, "Interdependence: A North-South Perspective," in Dunning and Usui, *Structural Change, Economic Interdependence and World Development,* 19–29.

82. Raymond Vernon, "Codes on Transnationals: Ingredients for an Effective International Regime," in Dunning and Usui, *Structural Change, Economic Interdependence and World Development,* 227–40, esp. 238.

83. James G. Savage, *The Politics of International Telecommunications Regulation* (Boulder, Colo.: Westview Press, 1989); and Ramon de Murias, *The Economic Regulation of International Air Transport* (Jefferson, N.C.: McFarland, 1989).

PART II

Corporate Activities in the Political Arena

CHAPTER 6

The Advocacy Environment: Public Opinion, Unions, and Groups

JAMES FENIMORE COOPER, the nineteenth-century novelist and essayist, viewed shaping public opinion in a democracy and staging a military coup as comparable ways of seizing political power.[1] Today public opinion can still focus attention on specific issues and determine who wins or loses political battles. As the world's largest retailer, Wal-Mart was said by its critics to treat its employees badly and import so many products from China that it was partially responsible for the surging U.S. trade deficit.[2] Confronted by hostile protesters, Wal-Mart finally announced a nationwide advertising campaign to rebuild its tattered image. Somewhat earlier, the president of the Motion Picture Association of America appeared before the National Press Club in Washington to argue that Hollywood did, in fact, share America's values and that it was aware of congressional and public concern about indecency in the media.[3] Microsoft stood back for years as its critics convinced the public and the political establishment that it was a rogue corporation.[4] Only when faced with legal ruin and political defeat did Microsoft finally respond with a seven-day-a-week program of print and broadcast advertising, petition drives, letter-writing campaigns, and contributions to think tanks and research groups to contend that its products made an indispensable contribution to the country's prosperity.

Public opinion is only one component of the advocacy environment in which political conflicts between supporters and opponents of business are fought out. Labor unions are the classic opponents of business in the workplace and the political arena, and the labor movement's effectiveness in promoting its viewpoints can determine the fate of numerous policy proposals. Both business and labor are also part of a broader constellation of interest groups representing most segments of American society, and the interaction among these groups, public opinion, and government officials shapes the public policies that govern the country's political and economic systems. In recent years a regiment of nongovernmental organizations (NGOs) has also emerged in the global arena to provide public services and champion political causes, and these groups too have created a vital place for themselves in the policy process that affects business operations.

In this chapter I ask what the advocacy environment for government-business relations looks like. I examine public attitudes toward business, review changes that have occurred in those attitudes, and investigate the factors that led to the shifts in attitude. I also appraise the labor movement's participation in the policy process. In recent decades, the number of groups seeking to influence public policy in the United States and internationally has increased dramatically, and some new groups have emerged as the most effective rivals of business organizations. After examining the evolving interest group environment, I draw back to consider the broader trends that may affect public reactions to the place of business in society.

PUBLIC ATTITUDES TOWARD BUSINESS

Businesspeople believe that the media, especially television, routinely portray them as crooks and swindlers who ravage communities and exploit workers.[5] They complain that the media emphasize the faults of American industry without acknowledging its achievements. Tune in any drama or detective show, watch any movie, and the chances are that a businessperson is the culprit.[6] Although the media often suggest that success in business has nothing to do with competence or creativity, it is wrong to believe that all portraits of businesspeople are negative or that the critical portraits are an invention of the television age.

Popular Images of Business

One analysis of the images of business in literature finds that negative portrayals of businesspeople have characterized American life from the start.[7] This study insists that the "American writer mounted direct attacks on capitalism as an economic system during and shortly after the War of Independence" and continued those attacks in subsequent generations.

Literary criticisms of business originally stressed moral and cultural themes. William Dean Howells's *The Rise of Silas Lapham* (1885) is usually regarded as the first American business novel.[8] It is an account of Silas Lapham, a young Vermont man who recognized the commercial value of materials discovered on the family farm and began to manufacture paint. Needing additional capital, Lapham took on a partner, but he then forced the partner out of the business and seized his partner's share of the profits. In an effort to make amends, Lapham lent money to the former partner, but Lapham encountered financial setbacks, his new home was destroyed by fire, and he fell into bankruptcy. The novel concludes by suggesting that bankruptcy was a cleansing experience that expiated Lapham's earlier sins.

The theme that business success rested on tainted money was soon joined by the literary image of businesspeople as shallow and uncultured. In *Winesburg, Ohio*

(1919), Sherwood Anderson's businesspeople were narrow and insensitive residents of a small town who denied cultural freedom to artists. The protagonist of Sinclair Lewis's *Babbitt* (1923) was a businessperson who contributed nothing of value to his community, used commercial standards to evaluate social institutions, and craved products simply because they were nationally advertised.

Explicitly political criticisms of business first appeared in novels about the ruthless tactics of the giant new corporations at the beginning of the twentieth century. Frank Norris's chronicle of railroad development in California, *The Octopus* (1901), focused on battles between farmers and railroad companies, but the charges his characters made against railroads could have been leveled against large corporations in general:

> They own us, these task-masters of ours; they own our homes, they own our legislatures. We cannot escape from them. There is no redress. We are told we can defeat them by the ballot-box. They own the ballot-box. We are told that we must look to the courts for redress; they own the courts. We know them for what they are—ruffians in politics, ruffians in finance, ruffians in law, ruffians in trade, bribers, swindlers, and tricksters. . . .
>
> They swindle a nation of a hundred million and call it Financiering; they levy a blackmail and call it Commerce; they corrupt a legislature and call it Politics; they bribe a judge and call it Law; they hire blacklegs to carry out their plans and call it Organization; they prostitute the honour of a State and call it Competition.[9]

While Norris's embattled heroes were wealthy farmers and community leaders, the country's first major proletarian novel was Upton Sinclair's *The Jungle* (1906), which featured a Lithuanian immigrant family who settled in Chicago and found work in the brutal stockyards area. The immigrants gradually recognized that the workers were slaves to their machines and were treated no better than the animals they slaughtered. The personal jealousies of capitalism destroyed the humanity of all who worked in the system, and salvation, according to the novel, could only be found through socialism.

At the start of the twentieth century, many business leaders also recognized that the new corporate giants lacked public legitimacy.[10] Corporate representatives had been denounced during the wave of mergers in 1895–96, and companies were then blamed for society's ills and the economy's depressions. Fearing their position was vulnerable to attack by an enraged citizenry, corporations launched public relations campaigns to enhance their image. Companies sponsored welfare programs to benefit their employees and demonstrate their compassion, they profiled their founders to offset the impression of impersonal size and monopolistic power, and they published images of their factories to emphasize their humble origins and commitment to community development. Despite the public relations efforts, however, big business did not win public acceptance until it boosted its stature by providing military equipment during World War II.

Negative portrayals of businesspeople have pervaded American culture, but they are not universal. The popular Horatio Alger novels of the nineteenth century taught that business virtues provided handsome rewards, and business figures were often associated with attractive personal qualities such as inventiveness and hard work.[11] Occasionally businesspeople have even been cast as cultural heroes. Recall that James Stewart's character in Frank Capra's classic movie *It's a Wonderful Life* (1946) was a savings-and-loan company executive. In the 1990s Bill Gates, Steve Jobs, and other corporate officials in the information technology sector were introduced as pioneers of a new economy, and they remain folk heroes for significant segments of the society.[12]

Public Confidence in Business Leaders

In the 1950s and early 1960s public opinion surveys reported that citizens trusted the leaders of business and the country's other major institutions.[13] More than 60 percent of citizens told interviewers they had great confidence in the people running universities, medical institutions, and the military. Almost half said that they had a great deal of confidence in people heading ten different social institutions, including religious organizations, the press, the Supreme Court, labor unions, Congress, and the executive branch. As late as 1966, 55 percent of those interviewed responded that they had a great deal of confidence in the leaders of major companies (see Table 6-1).

Public confidence in the nation's leaders plummeted between 1966 and 1974. The collapse included both private and government institutions. By 1976 only 9 percent of respondents reported great confidence in the leaders of Congress,

Table 6-1 Public Confidence in the Leaders of Institutions, 1966–2004

Question: As far as people in charge of running _____ are concerned, would you say you have a great deal of confidence, only some confidence, or hardly any confidence at all in them?

	Percentage responding "a great deal of confidence"								
	1966	*1971*	*1976*	*1981*	*1986*	*1991*	*1997*	*2000*	*2004*
Major companies	55	39	16	21	16	15	18	28	12
Congress	42	24	9	15	21	9	11	15	13
Labor unions	22	16	10	11	11	10	9	15	15
Average of ten institutions	48	33	20	23	23	23	21	30	28

Source: Louis Harris and Associates, various years.

down from 42 percent ten years earlier. Only 16 percent indicated great confidence in the managers of major companies, down from 55 percent, and the drop involved business in general and every segment of the business community.[14] The proportion of people reporting great confidence in the leaders of ten institutions fell from 48 percent in 1966 to 20 percent in 1976.

Public confidence in the nation's leaders was destroyed by two events: the Vietnam War and the Watergate scandal. Both were national traumas, and they undermined confidence in the leaders of all institutions. The public lost faith in the leaders of religion, education, the media, labor, and business as profoundly as in the leaders of the executive, legislative, and judicial branches of the national government. At the end of the 1990s, there were modest signs of recovery of confidence in the stewards of some of the nation's most important institutions, particularly the military and major companies. Public confidence in business leaders plummeted once again, however, with the dramatic revelations of financial scandals at Enron, WorldCom, and other firms in 2000–2 and the reappearance of unemployment as a popular concern.

Attitudes toward Business

Judgments about the leaders of institutions should be distinguished from opinions about the institutions themselves and from attitudes toward the broader political and economic systems. Responding that the individuals running institutions are untrustworthy, the public still retains deep confidence in the nation's political system and its entrepreneurial economy. In contrast to the uniformly negative assessments of business leaders and the conspicuously positive views of the political and economic systems, citizens make complex judgments about business itself.

By a large margin, citizens after World War II regarded good times for business as good news for the public. As reported in Table 6-2, when asked if they believed that what was good for business was bad or good for the average person, 57 percent in 1981 and 61 percent in 1987 answered that what benefited business was good for the average person. The responses became less positive in the 1990s. In 1991 the proportion answering that favorable business events were positive for the public fell to 53 percent and then continued to drop to 42 percent in 1996 and 40 percent in 2002. The decline in probusiness sentiments may reflect the deepening perception of large businesses as global institutions increasingly less concerned about American workers. Most respondents who no longer regarded good times for business as good for citizens, however, did not embrace antibusiness attitudes but instead developed mixed feelings. They concluded that what was good for business was sometimes good for the average person and sometimes bad.

In addition to concluding that the interests of business and the public at least sometimes coincide, most citizens between 1963 and 1991 also believed that large companies make a vital contribution to the nation's well-being. As reported in Table 6-3, 85 percent of respondents in 1963 agreed with the statement, "Large

Table 6-2   Citizen and Business Interests, 1981–2002

Question: Some people think what's good for business is bad for the average person. . . . Others think what's good for business is also good for the average person. . . . What do you think—what's good for business is bad for the average person, or what's good for business is also good for the average person?

	Percentage responding				
	1981	*1987*	*1991*	*1996*	*2002*
What's good for business is good for the average person	57	61	53	42	40
What's good for business is bad for the average person	20	17	20	20	21
Mixed feelings (volunteered)	18	19	22	30	33
Don't know	5	4	5	8	6

Source: NOP-World/*Roper Reports, 2002-3.* Used with permission.

companies are essential for the nation's growth and expansion." In the 1970s and 1980s public attitudes on this item remained remarkably positive. In 1991 the proportion with this opinion fell, but even then 70 percent still believed that large companies played an essential role in the country's economy.

Other public attitudes toward large companies were more cynical. In 1963, 64 percent of the sample shared the premise, "The profits of large companies help make things better for everyone." Support for this assertion fell sharply through the 1970s, and in 1991 only 36 percent accepted the view that corporate profits benefited everyone.

Two other statements in Table 6-3 also address the issue of corporate power. The first declares, "There's too much power concentrated in the hands of a few large companies for the good of the nation." In 1963, 54 percent shared the anxiety about concentrations of corporate power. These fears spread in the late 1960s and 1970s, being expressed by 80 percent of those interviewed in 1979 and moderating only slightly in subsequent years. Table 6-3 offers a solution to worries about the power of corporations: "For the good of the country, many of our largest companies ought to be broken up into smaller companies." In 1963, 39 percent agreed that the largest companies should be broken up. The portion adopting this sentiment increased strongly during the Vietnam and Watergate years, reached 57 percent in the mid- to late 1970s, and then moderated slightly through 1991.

The public, to summarize, has a more positive view of business institutions than of people running them. By a 2 to 1 margin, citizens believe that what is good for business is good rather than bad for the average person, and seven out of ten respondents agree that large companies make a vital contribution to the coun-

Table 6-3 **Assessments of Large Companies, 1963–1991**

	Percentage agreeing with statement							
	1963	*1967*	*1971*	*1975*	*1979*	*1983*	*1987*	*1991*
*Large compa*nies are essential for the nation's growth and expansion	85	85	83	80	80	81	87	70
The profits of large companies help make things better for everyone	64	63	51	41	37	41	43	36
There's too much power concentrated in the hands of a few large companies for the good of the nation	54	54	66	78	80	75	72	74
For the good of the country, many of our largest companies ought to be broken up into smaller companies	39	36	47	57	57	54	50	48

Source: Opinion Research Corporation, "Attitudes toward Large Companies," 1991.

try's growth and expansion. By the early 1990s, however, the public had become more critical of corporate power and less tolerant of corporate profits.

Basis for Attitudes toward Business

Although the levels of support and criticism of business are important, it is even more meaningful to understand the reasons for these views. Historically, public assessments of business reflect changes in the state of the economy.[15] The 1880s were a period of prosperity and positive attitudes toward business. Probusiness sentiments grew as Americans moved beyond the disruption of the industrial revolution and concluded that the best way to material progress was through private rather than government action. As might be expected, public confidence in business fell precipitously in the 1930s with the collapse of the nation's economy. Public confidence was firmly reestablished during World War II and probably reached its height in the early 1960s.

A statistical analysis of the relationship between the state of the economy and public confidence in business leaders confirms the historical record. A comparison of opinion data on confidence in corporate leaders with measures of unemployment and inflation for the years 1966–80 demonstrate that low unemployment and, to a lesser extent, low inflation were associated with high confidence in the people running major companies.[16]

Public attitudes toward business are also a product of citizen appraisals of corporate performance in specific areas. Table 6-4 contains a list of ten societal tasks many believe are responsibilities of business along with citizen assessments of how well businesses fulfilled these responsibilities between 1978 and 2000.

Business gets high marks throughout this period on items involving products and services.[17] Almost nine of ten respondents in each year believed that business fulfilled its responsibilities fully or fairly well in developing new products and services. Producing good-quality products and services and making products that are safe to use are the responsibilities citizens think are most important. Eight of ten people interviewed in 1996 and 2000 answered that business performed well in these areas, and the proportion assessing business conduct positively on these two items has increased notably since 1978.

Business receives fewer accolades but still majority endorsement for its employment-related performance. In 1978 about 70 percent of the sample concluded that business had discharged its responsibilities fully or fairly well in hiring minorities, providing jobs, and paying good salaries and benefits. By 1996 and 2000 the positive ratings had declined in each category with the exception of the

Table 6-4   Responsibilities of Business, 1978–2000

Question: Now here's a list of things people have said are or should be responsibilities of business in this country. . . . [F]or each one tell me whether you think business fulfills its responsibilities fully, fairly well, not too well, or not at all?

Responsibility	Percentage responding business fulfills responsibility fully/fairly well			
	1978	1988	1996	2000
Developing new products and services	88	88	87	88
Producing good-quality products and services	66	77	84	87
Making products that are safe to use	65	76	77	77
Hiring minorities	74	73	67	68
Providing jobs for people	71	72	65	79
Paying good salaries and benefits to employees	69	66	59	60
Paying their fair share of taxes	40	45	50	56
Charging reasonable prices for goods and services	33	34	54	55
Cleaning up their own air and water pollution	40	36	43	49
Advertising honestly	33	42	42	48
Mean of ten scores	58	61	63	67

Source: NOP-World/*Roper Reports, 2001-1.* Used with permission.

Cases in Development
BOX 6-1 LOBBYING TRIES PUBLIC OPINION

Major Washington lobbying projects are increasingly taking on the trappings of election campaigns, the *National Journal* reports. Not only are campaign consultants moving into the lobbying business with substantial success, but traditional lobbyists are turning more frequently to polling, grassroots mobilization, media purchases, and public relations to execute their strategies. The trend toward integrating public relations with lobbying services appeared almost a decade ago when the fabled Washington lobbying firm of Cassidy & Associates purchased a public relations company, and the trend was confirmed over the past year when other major lobbying operations such as Patton Boggs and Blank Rome hired more public relations personnel. The Washington lobbying business is increasingly competitive, and these firms hoped they could provide their clients better service by expanding their public relations expertise and, thus, gain an edge on their competitors.

Sources: Bara Vaida, "Lobbying and Law Firms" and "Lobbyists Embrace PR," *National Journal,* September 11, 2004.

unusually positive response to the general question of providing jobs in 2000, the year of surging U.S. employment.

According to the survey, business does less well in fulfilling its responsibilities in social areas, but its conduct is improving. In 1996 and 2000 half the respondents believed that business paid its fair share of taxes and held prices to reasonable levels. In the same years, more than 40 percent of those interviewed concluded that business did a responsible or fairly responsible job of cleaning up its own air and water pollution and advertised honestly.

These citizen attitudes are one part of the advocacy environment that shapes relations between government and industry. Various techniques are now employed to mobilize public opinion and guide lobbying strategies, as is reported in Box 6-1. Labor unions and nonbusiness groups are also active players in policy controversies affecting business, and we now examine these organizations and the resources they bring to the political arena.

LABOR UNIONS

Labor unions, Gary Marks has written, were one of "the great innovations of modern times."[18] They were a response to the emergence of the factory system and the transformation of workers from independent artisans to salaried employees. In unions, workers could combine to influence company decisions involving wages and hours and gain a measure of control over their working lives.

Early union activities encountered legal barriers based on English common-law principles. Common-law precedents prohibited commercial conspiracies in "restraint of trade" and "to injure others," and these principles were applied to labor organizations.[19] The earliest legal judgment in the United States involving unions occurred in 1806 and found a Philadelphia association to be an illegal conspiracy and its actions "coercive and arbitrary." The constant threat of prosecution hampered union organizing efforts and provoked occasional violent reactions from workers.

An 1842 decision reinterpreted common-law precedents and ruled that unions were presumed to be legal unless outlawed by statute or actually intended to harm others. This decision gave American unions legal recognition that their counterparts in Britain did not achieve until 1875, but it did not resolve questions about labor unions' legal status. Unions were frequently prosecuted as monopolies under the Sherman Antitrust Act of 1890 until they were protected by the Clayton Act of 1914 and the Norris-LaGuardia Act of 1932.

The American Federation of Labor was founded in 1886 as an association of twenty-five unions embracing skilled workers, such as carpenters, bakers, miners, and printers. The AFL's concern for craft workers conflicted with the rapid growth of mass production industries that employed a less skilled labor force. Relations between unions representing skilled trades and those serving industrial workers became so strained that the AFL expelled the industrial unions in the mid-1930s, and these unions then founded the Congress of Industrial Organizations. Despite tensions between the traditional leadership of craft unions and the liberal policies of industrial unions, the AFL and CIO reunited after World War II.

Unions were originally drawn to the political arena in the 1870s and 1880s by the need to define their legal rights and defend themselves against judicial actions. Once in the political arena, labor pursued a moderate strategy, stressing worker benefits rather than founding a political party. Unions supported the creation of a federal Department of Labor under President Woodrow Wilson in 1914, and they sought to persuade government to improve employment conditions by mandating minimum standards for wages, retirement benefits, and health care.

Organized labor achieved unparalleled institutional advances under the New Deal in the 1930s, as President Franklin D. Roosevelt transformed the antiunion Democratic Party into a champion of workers. The National Labor Relations Act of 1935 defined a system of collective bargaining that allowed representatives of workers to negotiate with management over the terms and conditions of employment while still leaving strategic policy to managerial control.[20] Under the National Labor Relations Board (NLRB) system, labor unions experienced an unprecedented surge in membership, with the union membership as a share of nonfarm workers rising from 12.7 percent in 1930 to 22.5 percent in 1940 and 31.6 percent in 1950, as reported in Figure 6-1.

Figure 6-1 Union Membership, 1930–2004

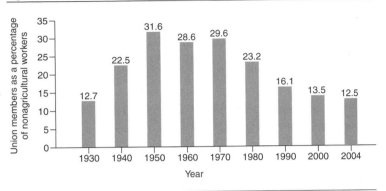

Sources: 1930–80: Leo Troy and Neil Sheflin, *Union Sourcebook* (West Orange, N.J.: Industrial Relations Date and Information Services, 1985); 1990: National Directory Series, Bureau of Labor Statistics, Department of Labor (ftp://146.142.4.23/pub/special.requests/collbarg/unmen.txt), as reported in Taylor E. Dark, *The Unions and the Democrats: An Enduring Alliance* (Ithaca, N.Y.: Cornell University Press, 1999), 15; and 2000 and 2004: U.S. Department of Labor, Bureau of Labor Statistics, "Union Members Summary," http://stats.bls.gov/news.release/union2.nr0.htm, 27 January 2005.

Labor unions are now said to have shifted their principal efforts from economic markets to political ones.[21] Taylor Dark has written that "by the 1990s it seemed . . . easier (for union leaders) to obtain benefits by procuring new legislation from Congress than by achieving a breakthrough in collective bargaining with employers. Union leaders now naturally turn to politics as a rich source of benefits that can help secure their organizational status."[22] The key benefits they seek are protection for union organizing and bargaining campaigns, jobs for members, and government grants for internal projects.

To the extent that the labor movement is feared or appreciated, it has influence. The AFL-CIO, however, is not a union but a federation that cannot command its constituent unions to obey its directives.[23] The federation provides services to individual unions and represents common interests, but it has little control over the member organizations. The AFL-CIO encourages political involvement and supports policies and candidates when its members are unified, but the federation's role is limited by the diverse interests of the unions. Not the federation, but individual unions such as the Service Employees International Union; the American Federation of State, County and Municipal Employees; and the International Association of Machinists are the locus of union political activity.

Some unions seek to use government to improve working conditions and to champion political causes, but union and employee circumstances vary considerably. Auto workers who have generations of experience with the same manufacturer, restaurant employees who work for a single season, and state and local government employees with civil service status all have different political interests. Some union members make their living through defense expenditures, whereas other unions campaign for increases in social service expenditures. In the best of times, the influence of labor in politics is limited by the diversity of union interests.

In recent decades, labor's political influence has been eroded by changes in union membership.[24] Although absolute union membership has risen slightly from 13 million in the mid-1950s,[25] membership as a proportion of the nonagricultural workforce has declined sharply, as displayed in Figure 6-1. After reaching a peak of 33 percent in the mid-1950s, union membership as a proportion of the non-agricultural workforce declined dramatically to only 12.5 percent in 2004.[26] In that year, government workers were unionized at a much higher rate than workers in the private sector, 36 percent versus 8 percent. The most heavily unionized occupations in the public sector were teachers, police officers, and firefighters, and the highest unionization rates among private-sector industries appeared in transportation and utilities, construction, and manufacturing.

Many factors account for the downward trend in union membership.[27] The decline of the manufacturing economy has reduced employment in traditional bastions of union strength, and the migration of jobs from the Northeast to the South and West has increased the importance of states where laws hindering union activity are common. Increasing competitive pressures have led employers to multiply efforts to resist unions. Employee need for union representation has also been reduced by the enactment of government programs to maintain workplace safety, mandate equal opportunity, and protect family and medical leave. Unions themselves have not done an effective job of attracting new members, preferring instead to respond to the needs of their current membership. Traditional American hostility to unionism has recurred in recent years, but union membership has also been declining in most industrial nations.

At the beginning of the twenty-first century, organized labor occupies an ambiguous position in the United States. The fact that fewer than one private sector worker in twelve was a union member in 2004, combined with union defeats in the political arena, suggests a movement in decline. Evidence for this view comes from survey research that asked citizens, "In your opinion, which of the following will be the biggest threat to the country in the future—big business, big labor, or big government?" When citizens responded in 1957, as reported in Table 6-5, 15 percent regarded business as the biggest threat, 14 percent chose government, and 41 percent said labor unions. By 2003, 57 percent believed government to be the country's greatest threat and 29 percent named business, but only 10 percent identified labor as the object of their concern. The impression of political marginality was reinforced by an analysis of network coverage of policy issues that concluded that the opinions of labor unions were "systematically ignored."[28]

Table 6-5   Biggest Threat to Nation, 1957–2003

Question: In your opinion, which of the following will be the biggest threat to the country in the future—big business, big labor, or big government?

| | | | | *Percentage selecting each alternative* | | | | |
	1957	1968	1977	1981	1985	1995	1999	2003
Business	15	12	23	22	22	25	24	29
Labor	41	26	26	22	19	9	8	10
Government	14	46	39	46	50	64	65	57
No opinion	30	16	12	10	9	3	3	5

Source: George Gallup Jr., *The Gallup Poll: Public Opinion 1985* (Wilmington, Del.: Scholarly Resources, 1986), and subsequent editions.

Evidence of a resurgence of union political influence, however, is identified by Taylor Dark and traced to events that began in 1995.[29] In that year the AFL-CIO experienced an internal uprising that led to the election of John J. Sweeney as federation president. Sweeney had campaigned on a platform of aggressive organizing efforts and extensive political involvement, and his victory signaled a shift in power from the federation's traditional craft unions to the more liberal public employee unions. Dark regards Sweeney's selection as the first victory for the social democratic wing of the labor movement.[30] Labor leaders, he insists, benefited from the Clinton administration's pro-union appointments to the Labor Department and the National Labor Relations Board and its support for union legislative goals in areas other than international trade. He believes that union leaders will be influential in Democratic presidential primaries, their financial resources will command respect from elected officials, and they will receive privileged access to promote their positions on policy issues. Whether the resurgence of union political influence becomes a reality, however, or the decline in membership persists, both labor and business institutions remain prominent features of an increasingly complex interest group universe.

INTEREST GROUP UNIVERSE

A vibrant system of interest group activity constitutes a pluralist vision of how democracy should work. When a significant issue arises, groups appear to debate the concern. Group activity represents citizen opinions to government, and competition among various interests, in which no single group is dominant, then yields public policies broadly responsive to public preferences.

Most scholars who have studied the Washington lobbying process, however, have concluded that it usually produces biased results. Rather than a socially equitable balancing of varied interests, some groups routinely win, it seems, whereas others systematically lose. E. E. Schattschneider aptly summarizes the conclusions of traditional interest group scholarship: "The flaw in the pluralist heaven is that the heavenly chorus sings with a strong upper-class accent."[31]

A long line of researchers has confirmed Schattschneider's observation that the interest group universe overrepresents the business community. E. Pendleton Herring's register of Washington organizations in 1927 was dominated by economic interests, Donald C. Blaisdell's updated version of the list verified the predominance of business interests in 1941, and David B. Truman's account of Washington after World War II corroborated the preponderance of economic groups.[32] Based on data from 1981, Kay Schlozman and John T. Tierney reported that business associations and corporations accounted for 71 percent of groups then represented in Washington, and they believed that business dominance of the interest group community was increasing.[33] Business and occupational interests are easier to organize than citizen groups, and they are simpler to mobilize when legislative issues emerge.

In recent years, several conspicuous developments have transformed the Washington interest group universe. First, Burdett A. Loomis and Allan J. Cigler find an explosion in the number of groups.[34] They report that the number of interest groups surpassed 22,000 in 2001, an increase of more than 50 percent since 1980 and 400 percent since 1955. Even though the number of groups has leveled off, Washington observers still report that the halls of Congress are so jammed with lobbyists that legislators have trouble moving from room to room.[35]

Not only are more groups represented in Washington than in past eras, but most researchers believe that previously underrepresented segments of the population have now found a voice.[36] Jack L. Walker's analysis of Washington organizations, for example, repeats that the interest group universe grew by 75 percent between 1960 and 1985 but that the number of citizen groups increased in the same period by 180 percent.[37] Although most scholars agree that business interests are still overrepresented, women, consumers, environmentalists, senior citizens, and advocates of rights, conscience, and ideology must now be counted among the groups with an unmistakable Washington presence.[38]

Policy analysts have concluded that the issue domains in which public policies are formed have also become more diverse. Policymaking was once thought to occur in subgovernments, or "iron triangles," composed of business interests, congressional committees, and bureaucratic agencies, but analysts now examine policy choices that transpire in diverse and quarrelsome policy networks, often including citizen and nonprofit groups. Many new groups are staff-led organizations no longer dependent on grassroots members for continuity and expertise, and this permits these groups to play a continuing role in the policy process.[39] Heinz and his associates report that business representatives are still the principal participants in policy networks, but they also document the increased representation of noneconomic groups.[40]

Jeffrey Berry's analysis of interest group activities in Congress sharpens the findings of earlier researchers and carries their conclusions one step further.[41] Berry agrees that the interest group universe in Washington has become more diverse, but he insists that the most important change is the increased representation of a particular type of citizen group. Berry believes that American politics has shifted its policy agenda from material to quality-of-life issues, from questions of how to divide the economic pie to concerns about how to balance economic growth with environmentalism, consumer protection, and personal well-being. The new interest group force in Congress is liberal citizen groups that stress a postmaterialistic agenda of culture, lifestyle, status, morality, and personal rights. Berry's analysis concludes that these citizen groups have become "a particular nemesis for business lobbies" because of their effectiveness in promoting an agenda opposed by business and their ability to hold their own when issues come up for a vote. Whereas business suffered only infrequent defeats in the past, Berry's data indicate that on recent congressional measures liberal citizen groups were almost as likely as business interests to be victorious. Although business remains the most powerful interest, Berry argues that it has lost influence in Congress and that its political advantages are decreasing.

Berry maintains that business is separated from the liberal citizen groups by a "different vision of America." Whereas business believes in economic expansion and opportunity, postmaterialistic groups believe that the country's noneconomic goals should take precedence.[42] Although Berry reports that postmaterialistic issues are gaining importance in Congress, both labor and management still benefit from a successful economy. As a result, companies and unions are sometimes allied on legislative measures that create jobs and promote prosperity, and a survey of Washington lobbyists found that corporate representatives believe labor unions are less antagonistic to business than citizen groups.[43]

Another change in the interest group universe in recent decades is the prominence in the global arena of NGOs, such as Greenpeace, Global Exchange, and Oxfam International.[44] From one perspective all interest groups are NGOs, but the expression *NGO* is usually used more narrowly. The World Bank reserves the designation for groups or institutions that are independent of government and have humanitarian objectives.[45] NGOs may include environmental, human rights, ethnic, antipoverty, or religious organizations, and some restrict the term further to apply only to those associations whose activities are international. Some NGOs are operating bodies that provide services to the needy, and others are advocacy groups that promote changes in policy.

NGOs have emerged at a critical point in world development when business activities have become increasingly global but other institutions have been slow to internationalize.[46] NGOs are often regarded as a bridge between governments and citizens, but neither governments nor the associations of the civil society are yet organized to act internationally. Citizens are divided by national borders and accustomed to express their preferences through state-based organizations, such as political parties, but political parties have made little cross-national headway. Democratic governments usually respond to their electoral or institutional constituencies, but they normally pay only scant heed to opinions that arise outside of their borders. NGOs try to overcome these difficulties by advocating the preference of the civil society and working with influential institutions to overcome problems even if they are not formally authorized to act in specific situations.

Jonathan P. Doh argues that the "rapid growth in the power and visibility of NGOs" has "radically transformed" relations between government and business.[47] NGOs are important in raising issues, mobilizing pubic opinion, lobbying both corporations and governments to accept their policy proposals, and serving as intermediaries between government and business to devise policy solutions acceptable to both sides. Influential NGOs, such as Doctors Without Borders, were instrumental in persuading pharmaceutical companies to lower prices on HIV drugs for poorer countries, and the antiglobalization NGOs claimed victory in blocking the adoption of the Multilateral Agreement on Investment that would have strengthened safeguards for cross-border investments.[48]

SUMMARY

The United States is a diverse country, and its advocacy environment is both dynamic and evolving. The reliance on television as the primary means of political communication leads the country from crisis to crisis, and the weakness of the party system reduces the nation's political stability. As a result, public opinion displays uncommon fluidity within political and economic systems that are themselves remarkably stable. The persistence of both positive and negative appraisals of business contributes to a singular pattern of American politics in which industries are often under attack but the basic structure of economic activity is left intact. Berry's examination of television coverage of congressional issues emphasizes the weakness of businesses in the media:

> Business, with its immense resources, is no match for citizen groups when it comes to media coverage. . . . Journalists especially like to emphasize conflict, and thus stories about competing interest groups are often framed as good guys versus bad guys. This works to the disadvantage of business groups, who are often the heavies fighting public spirited citizens who have organized to fight to protect their communities.[49]

Politicians, too, often advance their policy goals and enhance their standing by demonizing business. Because of the importance of public opinion in American politics, business remains vulnerable to attack by citizens, the media, and government officials, but its fundamental role remains secure as long as it delivers the economic benefits the public expects.

The American political system's adaptability is enhanced by its encouragement of group formation and interest articulation. No government approval is required, and few groups have an exclusive franchise to organize a specific activity.[50] The new communications technologies enable activists with limited resources to found an association, and established organizations that are unresponsive to changing values can be elbowed aside by the upstarts. Government officials also find the advocates of change knocking at their doors, and they too must be attentive, or they may be overrun by emerging social movements.

Americans hold complex, yet surprisingly ambivalent attitudes toward big business. Most citizens regard corporations as the mainstay of the nation's consumer society.[51] By a large margin, they perceive their interests to be fully or partially compatible with the interests of business rather than in conflict with them. Large companies are seen to make essential contributions to the growth and expansion of the economy and to act responsibly in providing products and employment. At the same time, the public harbors deep reservations about large companies. Business, especially big business, is distrusted because it is powerful and because it is regarded as selfish and self-centered. Many believe that companies place profits before the public interest, pollute the environment in pursuit of profits, and act without adequate regard for the community.

The U.S. interest group environment is unusually dynamic, and the outcomes of policy contests remain unpredictable. Labor union membership as a proportion of the nonfarm workforce reached its peak in the mid-1950s, but in 2004 less than 8 percent of employees in the private economy were union members. The decline in union membership has been accompanied by an erosion of labor influence in politics, and evidence of a resurgence of union power is problematic. Most researchers conclude that business interests are overrepresented in the policy process, and businesses can argue that they are the champions of economic growth and individual opportunity. Both domestically and internationally, however, groups advocating postmaterialistic values have scored impressive victories in the policy process, and there is every reason to believe that they will have continued success in the years ahead.

FURTHER READINGS

The Web sites of the Gallup and Roper organizations contain the results of numerous polls and links to other public opinion Web sites: http://www.gallup.com, and http://www.ropercenter.uconn.edu/links.html. The AFL-CIO Web site describes the federation's political agenda, press releases, reports on legislative action, and campaign activities: http://www.aflcio.org. The home page of the United Automobile Workers union provides similar information: http://www.uaw.org.

Asher, Herbert B., Eric S. Heberlig, Randall B. Ripley, and Karen Snyder, *American Labor Unions in the Electoral Arena*. Lanham, Md.: Rowman and Littlefield, 2001.

Baumgartner, Frank R., and Beth L. Leech. *Basic Interests: The Importance of Groups in Politics and in Political Science.* Princeton: Princeton University Press, 1998.

Berry, Jeffrey M. *The New Liberalism: The Rising Power of Citizen Groups.* Washington, D.C.: Brookings Institution Press, 1999.

Dark, Taylor E. *The Unions and the Democrats: An Enduring Alliance.* Ithaca, N.Y.: Cornell University Press, 1999.

Marchand, Roland. *Creating the Corporate Soul: The Rise of Public Relations and Corporate Imagery in American Big Business.* Berkeley: University of California Press, 1998.

NOTES

1. Cooper described public opinion in a democracy as "the lever by which all things are moved." See James Fenimore Cooper, *The American Democrat* (New York: Knopf, 1931), 197.

2. Dan Roberts, "Wal-Mart Attempts to Improve Its Image," *Financial Times,* January 14, 2005, 19.

3. William L. Watts, "Lobbyist: Hollywood Shares Values," CBS MarketWatch.com, November 11, 2004, http://www.cbs.marketwatch.com.

4. John M. Broder, "Microsoft Tries Another Court: Public Opinion," *New York Times,* June 12, 2000, 1.

5. Martha Bayles, "Tycoons on the Tube," *Wall Street Journal,* November 18, 1985, 28; and "Business Thinks TV Distorts Its Image," *Business Week,* October 18, 1982, 26.

6. Nigel Andrews, "The Cinema Bites Back at Big Corporations," *Financial Times,* January 3, 2005, 8; S. Robert Lichter, Linda S. Lichter, and Stanley Rothman, *Watching America* (New York: Prentice Hall, 1991); and L. J. Theberge, ed., *Crooks, Conmen, and Clowns: Businessmen in TV Entertainment* (Washington, D.C.: Media Institute, 1981).

7. Emily Stipes Watts, *The Businessman in American Literature* (Athens: University of Georgia Press, 1982), 2–5, 6.

8. Ibid., 55–59.

9. Frank Norris, *The Octopus: A Story of California* (New York: Bantam Books, 1958), 369.

10. This paragraph relies on Roland Marchand, *Creating the Corporate Soul: The Rise of Public Relations and Corporate Imagery in American Big Business* (Berkeley: University of California Press, 1998), esp. 7, 21, 41.

11. Watts, *Businessman in American Literature,* chap. 13; and Wilson C. McWilliams and Henry A. Plotkin, "The Historic Reputation of American Business," *Journal of Contemporary Business* 5 (Autumn 1976): 3–18.

12. For some examples of this overwhelming literature, see Gary Rivlin, *The Plot to Get Bill Gates: An Irreverent Investigation of the World's Richest Man . . . and the People Who Hate Him* (New York: Times Books, 1999); David A. Kaplan, *The Silicon Boys and Their Valley of Dreams* (New York: William Morrow, 1999); Joshua Quittner and Michelle Slatalla, *Speeding the Net: The Inside Story of Netscape and How It Challenged Microsoft* (New York: Atlantic Monthly Press, 1998); and Tim Jackson, *Inside Intel: Andy Grove and the Rise of the World's Most Powerful Chip Company* (New York: Dutton, 1997).

13. This discussion draws from the principal work on this topic, Seymour Martin Lipset and William Schneider, *The Confidence Gap: Business, Labor, and Government in the Public Mind* (New York: Free Press, 1983).

14. Ibid., 37.

15. Ibid., 369–71; and Louis Galambos and Joseph Pratt, *The Rise of the Corporate Commonwealth: United States Business and Public Policy in the 20th Century* (New York: Basic Books, 1988), 70.

16. Lipset and Schneider, *Confidence Gap,* 62–63. The correlation between confidence in people running major companies and the percentage of civilian unemployment was −.72, and the correlation between confidence and the increase in the consumer price index was −.38.

17. This discussion is based on data contained in NOP-World/*Roper Reports 89–1,* 112–15.

18. These paragraphs are drawn from Gary Marks, *Unions in Politics: Britain, Germany, and the United States in the Nineteenth and Early Twentieth Centuries* (Princeton: Princeton University Press, 1989), 9–10.

19. Ibid., 68–69.
20. Thomas A. Kochan, Harry C. Katz, and Robert B. McKersie, *The Transformation of American Industrial Relations* (New York: Basic Books, 1986).
21. Taylor E. Dark, *The Unions and the Democrats: An Enduring Alliance* (Ithaca, N.Y.: Cornell University Press, 1999).
22. Ibid., 34.
23. Harry Holloway, "Interest Groups in the Postpartisan Era: The Political Machine of the AFL-CIO," *Political Science Quarterly* 94, no. 1 (Spring 1979): 117–33.
24. Michael Goldfield, *The Decline of Organized Labor in the United States* (Chicago: University of Chicago Press, 1987); Kim Moody, *An Injury to All: The Decline of American Unionism* (New York: Verso, 1988); and Seymour Martin Lipset, "Unions in Decline," *Public Opinion* 9, no. 3 (September/October 1986): 52–54.
25. AFL-CIO, *Executive Council Report, 1995* (Washington, D.C.: AFL-CIO, 1995), 223, as reported in Dark, *Unions and the Democrats,* 18.
26. U.S. Department of Labor, Bureau of Labor Statistics, "Union Members Summary," http://www.stats.bls.gov/news.release/union2.nro.htm, January 27, 2005.
27. This paragraph draws from Dark, *Unions and the Democrats,* 20; and Jeffrey E. Cohen, *Politics and Economic Policy in the United States* (Boston: Houghton Mifflin, 1997), 117–20.
28. Jeffrey M. Berry, *The New Liberalism: The Rising Power of Citizen Groups* (Washington, D.C.: Brookings Institution Press, 1999), 129.
29. This paragraph is based on Dark, *Unions and the Democrats.*
30. Ibid., 183.
31. E. E. Schattschneider, *The Semisovereign People* (Hinsdale, Ill.: Dryden Press, 1975), 34–35.
32. E. Pendleton Herring, *Group Representation before Congress* (Washington, D.C.: Brookings Institution, 1929); Donald C. Blaisdell, *Economic Power and Political Pressures* (Washington, D.C.: GPO, 1941); David B. Truman, *The Governmental Process: Political Interests and Public Opinion* (New York: Knopf, 1951).
33. Kay Schlozman and John T. Tierney, *Organized Interests and American Democracy* (New York: Harper and Row, 1986), 67–73.
34. Burdett A. Loomis and Allan J. Cigler, "Introduction: The Changing Nature of Interest Group Politics," in *Interest Group Politics,* 6th ed., ed. Cigler and Loomis (Washington, D.C.: CQ Press, 2002), 12. See also Jeffrey M. Berry, *The Interest Group Society,* 2nd ed. (Glenview, Ill.: Scott, Foresman, 1989), chap. 2.
35. Jeffrey H. Birnbaum and Alan S. Murray, *Showdown at Gucci Gulch: Lawmakers, Lobbyists, and the Unlikely Triumph of Tax Reform* (New York: Random House, 1987).
36. For the most persuasive current analysis of the group literature, see Frank R. Baumgartner and Beth L. Leech, *Basic Interests: The Importance of Groups in Politics and in Political Science* (Princeton: Princeton University Press, 1998), chap. 6.
37. Jack L. Walker, "The Origins and Maintenance of Interest Groups in America," *American Political Science Review* 77 (1983): 390–406; and Walker, *Mobilizing Interest Groups in America* (Ann Arbor: University of Michigan Press, 1991).
38. See, for example, such classics as Jo Freeman, *The Politics of Women's Liberation* (New York: David McKay, 1975); Anne W. Costain, *Inviting Women's Rebellion* (Baltimore: Johns Hopkins University Press, 1992); Henry J. Pratt, *The Gray Lobby* (Chicago: University of Chicago Press, 1976); David Vogel, *Trading Up* (Cambridge, Mass.: Harvard University Press, 1995); and Thomas R. Rochon, *Mobilizing for Peace: The Antinuclear Movements in Western Europe* (Princeton: Princeton University Press, 1988).
39. Robert H. Salisbury, "Interest Representation: The Dominance of Institutions," *American Political Science Review* 78 (March 1984): 64–76.
40. John P. Heinz, Edward O. Laumann, Robert L. Nelson, and Robert H. Salisbury, *The Hollow Core: Private Interests in National Policy Making* (Cambridge, Mass.: Harvard University Press, 1993), chap. 2.
41. The following paragraphs are drawn from Berry, *New Liberalism,* 4, 15, 61, 75–76, 84, 86.
42. See Ronald Inglehart, *Culture Shift in Advanced Industrial Society* (Princeton: Princeton University Press, 1990).

43. Schlozman and Tierney, *Organized Interests and American Democracy,* 284.
44. M. Keck and K. Kikkink, *Activists beyond Borders: Advocacy Networks in International Politics* (Ithaca, N.Y.: Cornell University Press, 1998).
45. Justin Greenwood, *Interest Representation in the European Union* (New York: Palgrave Macmillan, 2003), 279.
46. Gerald Keim, "Nongovernmental Organizations and Business-Government Relations: Importance of Institutions," in *Globalization and NGOs: Transforming Business, Government, and Society,* ed. Jonathan P. Doh and Hildy Teegen (Westport, Conn.: Praeger, 2003), 19–34.
47. Jonathan P. Doh, "Nongovernmental Organizations, Corporate Strategy, and Public Policy: NGOs as Agents of Change," in Doh and Teegen, *Globalization and NGOs,* 3.
48. Jacqueline Deslauriers and Barbara Kotschwar, "After Seattle: How NGOs Are Transforming the Global Trade and Finance Agenda," in Doh and Teegen, *Globalization and NGOs,* 42–43; and Hildy Teegen and Jonathan P. Doh, "Conclusion: Globalization and the Future of NGO Influence," in Doh and Teegen, *Globalization and NGOs,* 219.
49. Berry, *New Liberalism,* 3, 129.
50. Virginia Gray and David Lowery, *The Population Ecology of Interest Representation* (Ann Arbor: University of Michigan Press, 1996).
51. James Oliver Robertson, *America's Business* (New York: Hill and Wang, 1985), 193.

CHAPTER 7

Corporations and Business Associations in the Political Arena

THE HEADQUARTERS BUILDING of the U.S. Chamber of Commerce is located across Lafayette Park from the White House. It is a ponderous structure from the 1920s on what was once the site of a mansion occupied by Daniel Webster. From the front windows of the Chamber building, guests look past the statue of Andrew Jackson in Lafayette Park toward the front, pillared entrance to the White House.

A plaque in the Chamber's foyer insists that the Chamber of Commerce is dedicated to promoting the "national economic welfare." The problem, of course, is that there are different opinions about that welfare. Fundamentally different understandings of the national welfare are espoused by the National Resources Defense Council, the Consumers Union, the Family Research Council, the Service Employees International Union, and the National Organization for Women.

No topic provokes more sharply divergent opinions than the role business should play in politics. Some commentators contend that business is an illegitimate force that distorts the political process and protects the interests of a small ruling class, whereas other observers see business struggling to maintain a dwindling position in a postmaterialistic society. In this chapter I examine the debate about the role of business in the American political process and assess the opposing sides.

Business viewpoints are expressed in the political process in various ways. As noted in Chapter 4, large American companies have established public affairs departments to monitor government events and express their positions on policy issues. To supplement the activities of these departments, companies have also created numerous organizations, such as the Chamber of Commerce, to communicate their interests to government officials.

Systems of business representation differ by country. The U.S. system of business organizations and corporate public affairs offices contrasts with the more orderly networks of business associations found in other countries. Here I ask whether the U.S. system of business representation helps the country define its common interests or obstructs the pursuit of those interests.

BUSINESS INVOLVEMENT IN POLITICS

Business advocates argue that a vibrant private sector has served the country extraordinarily well. Further restrictions on business, they contend, will jeopardize the product innovations and employment opportunities the society expects. The political agenda of the business community promotes economic growth and preserves the country's basic political and economic values. Opponents of business respond that the society can be made more equitable, the performance of the economy can be enhanced, corporate decisions can be made more socially responsible, and the country's noneconomic goals can be better realized by expanding the scope of government.[1]

Although public debate contrasts the imagery of perfectly competitive markets with the symbolism of perfectly functioning government, reality offers the alternatives of imperfect markets and imperfect government.[2] In fact, markets frequently yield results that are suboptimal for a society and inconsistent with expected standards of conduct; government action is often arbitrary, inefficient, inequitable, and intolerant of diversity. When given the real choice between imperfect markets and imperfect government, the United States has compromised. Government is supposed to expand its role in economic decision making and, at the same time, the business community is permitted to use its political resources to influence government policy.

As a consequence, corporate political action is both a customary feature of the American political scene and a perennially troubling phenomenon. The juncture of economic and political power is disturbing because it threatens to overwhelm alternative views and distort the country's policy judgments. Business involvement in politics is regarded by some as a sinister activity that advances private interests at society's expense, but it is seen by others as a salutary force that safeguards democracy. Both viewpoints should be considered.

Business Political Involvement Seen as Desirable

Those who believe that industry involvement in politics is both legitimate and desirable identify three advantages business activity provides the political system. Defenders of business participation stress that business has provided a standard of living most people admire.[3] A successfully functioning economy and an effectively operating business sector require a supportive policy environment. Inappropriate policies can damage the country's economy and hinder business efforts to provide the goods and services, employment opportunities, and returns on investment the public expects. Only business participation in politics will guarantee that the policy prerequisites for an effective economy find a place on the political agenda. A prohibition of business involvement in politics would, in effect, torpedo the policies needed to support a successful economy.

Defenders of corporate political activity also argue that business participation in politics is necessary to maintain the pluralistic democracy.[4] American democracy is based on the existence of multiple power centers within a diverse society, but the expanding influence of government in American life jeopardizes the autonomy of other social institutions. Economic institutions are among the most powerful nongovernmental institutions in the society. Private business organizations are potential allies for other nongovernmental groups struggling against government domination. If business institutions were prevented from participating in politics, the ability of any group to stand against a domineering government would be diminished.

Finally, those who see industry involvement as legitimate contend that business organizations help safeguard individual liberties. Legally, corporations are artificial persons that have some of the same constitutional rights as regular citizens. When corporations defend their rights to freedom of speech, freedom of association, or due process, they are also strengthening the claims that individual citizens make to these same rights. If business were barred from the political arena, there would be one less group struggling against government encroachment on constitutional rights.

Business Political Involvement Seen as Undemocratic

From the other perspective, private corporations are not instruments of democracy but barriers to democracy. "The large private corporation fits oddly into democratic theory and vision," Charles E. Lindblom observed. "Indeed, it does not fit."[5]

According to this view, there is no justification for business entities to participate in politics. Corporate political resources are used to overpower other groups and subvert the policy process. Corporations engage in politics to enhance their economic position and that of their owners. Their political gains come at the expense of the general society and especially the less fortunate. The fundamental impact of corporate involvement in politics is to accentuate already existing inequities, and any benefits to society from corporate political activities are incidental and insignificant.

Furthermore, the political activities of modern corporations are not directed by their owners but by hired managers. In a democracy, individuals rather than concentrations of wealth are supposed to exercise political influence. Corporate managers, however, have acquired the ability to exert political influence without any legitimate basis for having such influence. To the extent that firms are vehicles for pursuing the political goals of individuals, the country would be better served if those individuals participated in politics directly.

Finally, business involvement in politics no longer safeguards societal diversity or checks abuse of government power by officeholders. Incumbent officeholders have learned to exploit the resources businesses devote to political action for their own purposes. Incumbents in Congress, for example, capture the vast majority of campaign contributions from business sources, and they use these resources to prevent the emergence of meaningful challenges to their electoral position. Corporate involvement in politics suppresses rather than promotes social diversity.

Compromise

The political arena has responded to the issue of business participation in politics by accepting the premises of both sides. Corporations are seen both as making essential contributions to sustaining the nation's quality of life and as exacerbating the nation's social inequalities (see Chapter 6).

Corporate political activity occurs within a constitutional and statutory framework that authorizes some actions and prohibits others.[6] In constitutional terms, corporations are "artificial" persons. They receive the same constitutional rights as "natural" persons unless there is a compelling reason for denying them these rights.

Freedom of speech on policy issues is a constitutional right that is protected for both corporations and "natural" persons. According to the U.S. Constitution, corporations are free to use their funds to advocate positions on public issues, to influence public opinion on ballot questions, and to present corporate views to public officials. These activities are constitutionally protected forms of "speech."

Elections of candidates for public office are a different matter. Here the need to prevent the "appearance of corruption" is enough to justify government regulation. Contributions by both corporations and individuals in candidate campaigns may be restricted. The federal government regulates the contributions and expenditures of presidential and congressional candidates, and the states regulate their candidate elections in their own ways. The federal government, and most state governments, limit or occasionally ban corporate financial contributions to candidate campaigns. Other states, in contrast, do not restrict corporate donations at all.

American political-economic arrangements constitute a system of *imperfect alternatives*. Instead of choosing either government or markets to make economic decisions, the country has created a private economy that is both fostered and superseded by government. Government combines the diverse and sometimes contradictory functions of the framework, promotional, regulatory, and distributional states. Aware of the strengths and defects of both government and business, the nation shaped a political process in which various forces struggle continuously to win approval for their positions.

The choice between governments and markets as the primary vehicle for economic decision making is more complicated in the political arena than in theory. The alternatives are not a simple dichotomy between governments and markets but a complex array of options that combine institutional and market-oriented arrangements in an infinite variety of ways. The actual functions of government and activities of industry possess a political subtlety that is best realized by examining concrete situations. An examination of the principal characteristics of the business associations in the United States and in other countries illustrates this complexity.

BUSINESS ASSOCIATIONS IN THE UNITED STATES

Business associations in the United States serve three purposes.[7] Some groups provide *management services* that help member firms improve their operations. Associations distribute information on product innovations, train workers, sponsor insurance programs, advise on managerial tasks such as labor relations, undertake advertising campaigns, and gather industry statistics. Most firms could not provide these services alone, or could do so only at greater cost.

Some associations establish *product standards* that ensure product quality and facilitate use. In the past, business associations also organized cartels that controlled production levels, fixed prices, and allocated markets. Such anticompetitive practices are now illegal in the United States in most circumstances.[8]

Third, business associations conduct *government relations* activities. Groups monitor events in Congress and the executive branch and disseminate information about new programs. They also develop policy positions on issues affecting their members, represent views of members to government officials, and encourage firms to become politically active.

There is in the United States a multiplicity of business associations, which are independent of each other and, often, are competitors. There are leadership associations with broadly based memberships, trade associations that represent members in specific industries or sectors, and specialized business groups that serve specific constituencies. Some leading associations, the year each was founded, the number of members, and the size of each group's staff and budget are shown in Table 7-1.

Leadership Associations

The country's most prominent general business associations are the National Association of Manufacturers, the Chamber of Commerce, the National Federation of Independent Business, and the Business Roundtable.[9] The National Association of Manufacturers (NAM) is the nation's senior general business group. Even though most of its members have fewer than 500 employees, it accounts for about 75 percent of the nation's manufacturing production and employment. The NAM originally focused on labor relations and was a vehicle for attacks on New Deal policies. Its anti-union, anti–New Deal heritage gave the organization an obstructionist image that has been difficult to shed.

NAM membership peaked in 1957 at 22,000 companies and then began to decline.[10] To slow the membership loss and participate more effectively in national affairs, the association moved its headquarters from New York to Washington. The organization now sponsors policy groups and represents the views of its members on national and international topics. It seeks to develop positive positions on

Table 7–1   American Business Associations

Organization	Year founded	Member firms	Staff size	Budget millions of $
Leadership Associations				
National Association of Manufacturers	1895	14,000	180	5
Chamber of Commerce of the United States	1912	219,200	1,200	70
Business Roundtable	1972	150	21	23
National Federation of Independent Business	1943	600,000	225	65
The Business Council	1933	299[a]	3	1
Committee for Economic Development	1942	225[a]	24	4
Trade Associations				
American Chemical Council	1872	195	300	110
American Bankers Association	1875	8,000	410	62
National Association of Broadcasters	1922	7,500	165	27
American Trucking Association	1933	4,500	298	50
Air Transport Association of America	1936	28	120	45
Specialized Business Associations				
American Business Women's Association	1949	70,000[a]	40	2
International Alliance	1980	10,000[a]	2	[b]
National Association of Women Business Owners	1974	8,000[a]	10	2
Latino Business Association	1976	1,200[a]	10	[b]

Sources: C. Maurer and T. E. Sheets, eds., *Encyclopedia of Associations, 39th ed.*, vol. 1, pts. 1–3 (Farmington Hills, Mich.: Gale Research, 2003); author interviews.

[a] Members are individuals rather than firms.

[b] Less than $1 million.

economic and industrial issues, but the diversity of its membership limits its ability to advance forceful positions on controversial topics.[11]

The U.S. Chamber of Commerce is the largest and most representative business association in the country. It was founded in 1912 at the suggestion of President William Howard Taft to provide a sounding board for all segments of the economy, not just manufacturing. The Chamber now has 219,200 corporate members plus several thousand memberships from state and local chambers and trade associations. The great majority of its members are small firms with fewer than one hundred employees, but large firms participate extensively in Chamber affairs.

In the early 1960s the Chamber stressed its opposition to communism, big government, and welfare expenditures.[12] In recent decades, its positions have become more moderate, and its claim to be the principal representative of U.S. business has been more widely accepted. The Chamber has dozens of committees and councils that develop policy positions on a range of business issues. Its representatives testify before congressional committees, lobby government leaders, and organize litigation to support business positions.

The distinctive features of the Chamber are its elaborate communications apparatus, its extensive grassroots membership, and its influential staff. The Chamber produces daily and weekly television programs, and it publishes a monthly magazine, *uschamber.com,* and weekly updates. The Chamber has used its computer facilities and its network of local chambers to organize district action committees whose members communicate Chamber positions to officials in Congress and the executive branch.

The Chamber's need to consult its members on policy questions restricts its ability to respond to fast-moving issues. Despite this, the Chamber's continuing relationships with corporations and associations, the skill of its staff in promoting its positions, and the Chamber's well-organized grassroots network have won it a conspicuous place among the country's most influential business associations.

The National Federation of Independent Business (NFIB) is the largest group in the country representing the views of small business. About half of its 600,000 members are retailers, and the rest come from agriculture, construction, finance, manufacturing, professional services, and wholesaling.[13] The distinctive activity of the NFIB is that it regularly polls its members on business issues and then reports their views to Congress and the executive branch. It has an aggressive lobbying program with important grassroots support.[14] Its local network and the symbolic appeal of small business make the NFIB an important ally of the general business associations and a significant force in partisan disputes.

The Business Roundtable was established in 1972 from a merger of two small groups concerned about construction costs and labor law.[15] What distinguishes the Roundtable from the NAM and the Chamber of Commerce is that it is made up of the chief executive officers of 150 major corporations. Membership is by invitation. The chief executives agree to participate directly in Roundtable meetings, chair task forces on specific policy questions, and take part in the organization's lobbying program.

The Roundtable focuses on broad policy questions and avoids single-industry issues. Its Washington activities are guided by a steering committee composed of the Washington representatives of twenty-five member companies. The group has developed a pragmatic, accommodationist approach to policy issues and a preference for working behind the scenes. It rarely testifies before congressional committees, and its nonpublic approach allows the group flexibility in making compromises during the legislative process. The Roundtable has an uneasy relationship with other business groups. It represents the views of major corporations that are often less antagonistic to labor unions and government regulation than are small and medium-size firms. The Roundtable is criticized by NAM and Chamber lobbyists for being too quick to compromise free enterprise principles to reach short-term accommodations.[16] In a recent battle over federal spending, the Chamber of Commerce and the NAM resisted tax-hike proposals, whereas the Roundtable stressed the need for increased revenues.[17]

Two other general business associations have played a notable, albeit more limited, role in representing business to government. The Business Council was established at the beginning of the New Deal to provide a forum wherein government officials and business leaders could exchange views on economic and industrial policy issues. As a quasi-official body, the council was originally a part of the Commerce Department, but it declared its independence in 1961 when a Commerce secretary tried to control the group's meeting agenda.

The Business Council is composed of almost three hundred company heads, many of whom are also members of the Business Roundtable. Unlike the Roundtable, however, the council does not lobby or take formal positions. It convenes a few times each year to discuss issues. Administrations use the meetings to build political support for their programs or for an upcoming election, and business leaders attend to promote their firms' causes and display their credentials for future projects.

The Committee for Economic Development (CED) was organized in 1942 to help the country avoid economic hardship after World War II. True to its origins, the CED remains a research and information organization. Since its creation, the CED has published hundreds of monographs on such topics as hardcore unemployment, the social responsibility of business, urban education, international trade, and the like. The organization does not engage in lobbying, but its reports influence the course of policy debates.

Trade Associations

The resources and influence of trade associations representing specific industries are, in the aggregate, many times larger than those of the more prominent leadership associations. Whereas the decade of the 1980s was a period of stability for the general business organizations, it was a time of growth for the trade groups. The number of trade, business, and commercial associations grew from 3,100 in 1980 to 3,800 in 1989, an increase of 23 percent.[18]

Many trade associations are small operations with a narrow scope, such as the Frozen Potato Products Institute or the Fresh Garlic Association. Others, however, are prominent organizations, such as the American Bankers Association or the American Petroleum Institute, that have staffs and budgets that rival or exceed in size those of the broader associations. Some associations, such as the Air Transport Association of America, are composed of a handful of national or international corporations, whereas other groups, such as the American Trucking Association, include thousands of local businesses (see Table 7-1).

One snapshot of the activities of trade associations is obtained by examining the organization chart of one of the country's largest trade groups, the American Bankers Association (ABA), as displayed in Figure 7-1.[19] The ABA was founded in 1875, and its major purpose is to enhance the role of commercial banks in providing financial services. It has a staff of 410 and an annual budget of $62 million. It is directed by a large board and a five-person executive committee.

ABA member banks possess 95 percent of the banking industry's assets. Seven thousand of the ABA's 8,000 members, however, are small community banks. Only a few score are money-center institutions with familiar names. The ABA focuses its services on smaller banks. One-third of ABA staff make up the Membership and Administrative Services group, which plans conventions, manages publications, and responds to information requests. The Banking Organizations section works with members to ensure that the association is responsive to specialized member concerns. The ABA trains bank employees through its American Institute of Banking and promotes executive development through its educational services program. The Banking Professions group disseminates information about new products, services, and developments in banking occupations. Government relations activities are fundamental to the ABA's members, but they consume only a fraction of the organization's staff and resources.

A similar view of the activities of trade groups comes from recent surveys of associations in manufacturing industries.[20] Eighty-five percent of these trade associations assemble data on their industry's operations, three out of four support public information programs, and about half manage education and training programs for industry employees. Somewhat less than half engage in product-related tasks, such as establishing technical standards, developing sales and marketing programs, and encouraging product research and safety. More important, the surveys also report that "the extent to which associations have placed their emphasis on government relations has grown significantly over the last several years."[21] Associations typically create government affairs committees, lobby regulatory agencies and Congress on behalf of their members, and hold government affairs conferences.

Specialized Business Associations

Countless other organizations serve the specialized needs of individual businesses or businesspeople. The American Business Women's Association has promoted opportunities for women in business since 1949 by offering education, leadership, and networking recognition. The National Association of Women Business Owners provides a forum for women who own and operate businesses to share experiences, and it represents the particular interests of women business owners before government bodies. The Latino Business Association provides a voice for a cross-section

Figure 7-1 American Bankers Association Staff Organizational Chart

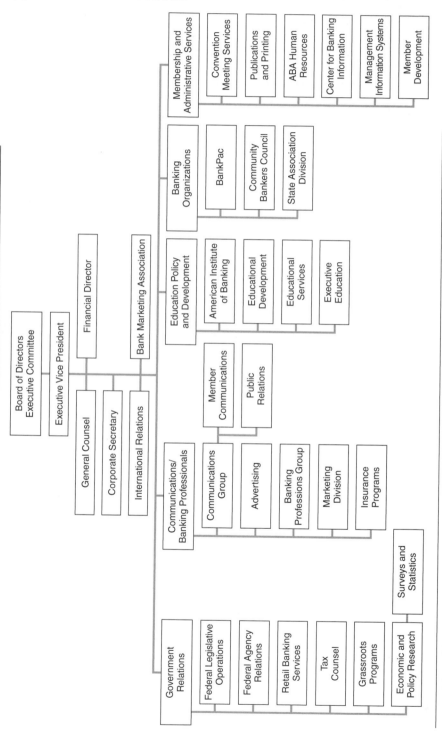

Source: Adapted from American Bankers Association data, November 1989.

of financial, manufacturing, and professional Hispanic businesses and assists Latino business owners in developing their enterprises.

Despite the extensive array of leadership associations, specialized groups, and trade associations, U.S. companies and businesspeople often break away from established business groups when they think their interests are not being forcefully represented. The head of the John Hancock Financial Services Corporation testified before a Senate committee in favor of a bill that would allow non-banking companies to operate banks.[22] The bill had been written by the Financial Services Council—a consortium that included John Hancock, American Express, Ford, Merrill Lynch, and Sears, Roebuck—which had been formed because the companies' primary trade associations, the American Bankers Association, the Securities Industry Association, and the American Council of Life Insurance, opposed the bill. The trade associations represented the fears of their small members that they would be run out of business by increased competition from large companies. Acknowledging the opposition of the established associations, the John Hancock representative said, "[S]ometimes it makes us wonder why we are paying dues to an organization that lobbies against us." Once the legislation was enacted, nineteen of the country's major financial-service companies were forced to create a new Financial Services Forum, a lobbying organization whose purposes overlapped the activities of existing financial service associations.[23]

Even with the variety of business groups, firms frequently abandon traditional associations and form ad hoc coalitions or go it alone when important issues arise. Each major firm has its own marketplace characteristics and its own relations with suppliers, distributors, employees, and government. The nation's traditions emphasize the autonomy of individual firms, and the legal heritage stresses competition among firms rather than cooperation.[24] Thus, U.S. business groups can never depend on the allegiance of their members.

The perpetual need to secure the support of their members compels associations to emphasize the benefits they provide individual firms. They also seek to demonstrate that they are doing more than other business groups to advance member goals. For this reason, U.S. business associations are reluctant to endorse policies opposed by member firms even if the policies would benefit the national economy or specific industries. Some of the conflicts that occur among trade groups in the alcohol beverage industry are described in Box 7-1. Business associations in other countries are stronger than U.S. groups and better able to participate in complex policy debates.[25] Other differences become clear when American business associations are compared with groups in other countries.

BUSINESS ASSOCIATIONS: A COMPARATIVE PERSPECTIVE

Business associations can serve the interests of individual firms, promote the health of specific industries, or advance the goals of the society. These three orientations

Cases in Development
BOX 7-1 HAPPY HOUR?

Representatives of the alcoholic beverages industry are haunted by a common nightmare. They fear the public will one day wake up as disgruntled with the brewers, distillers, and vintners as they are with tobacco companies and gun makers. Anti-alcohol groups, they agonize, will then launch an intense legislation and litigation campaign to destroy their place in society.

Alcohol industry trade associations have a reputation for historic rivalries and squabbling memberships. For years, hard liquor has lost market share to wine and beer, and the Distilled Spirits Council of the United States blames the decline on unfair taxes and restrictive market access. Beer and wine carry a lighter tax burden, the distillers claim, and television networks welcome beer advertising but reject liquor ads. The trade associations for beer and wine have battled the distillers' initiatives to equalize taxes and alter advertising policies, and the resulting animosities persist.

The wine industry is sharply divided about Internet sales and direct wine shipments to consumers across state borders. The Wine Institute represents the principal California wineries and small, family-owned operations that see direct sale to consumers through catalogs and over the Internet as a way to increase sales and lower costs. The Wine and Spirits Wholesalers of America champions the interests of firms that distribute wines to liquor stores, and they worry about declines in member income.

The beer industry has profited from the strong economy of recent years and is well represented in Washington. The Beer Institute is dominated by Anheuser-Busch, Miller Brewing, and other brewing giants. The Brewers Association of America represents the growing number of independent breweries, and the National Beer Wholesalers Association the beer distributors. The beer industry's key trade groups have often clashed over policy issues, but the associations have recently changed leaders, and the new presidents insist that they are now determined to bury nasty feuds and unify their industry.

When the alcohol groups have been united, they have scored impressive victories. They helped block a White House plan to raise alcohol taxes, beat back a proposal to limit the tax-deductibility of alcohol advertising, killed a plan to purchase antidrinking ads, and joined with the National Restaurant Association and the National Association of Beverage Retailers to oppose a congressional measure to lower the national drunk-driving standard.

The beer groups and the other alcohol trade associations believe they can preempt the "neo-prohibitionists" who oppose alcohol by emphasizing

(continued)

the industry's commitment to responsible drinking and by arguing that moderate alcohol consumption is part of a healthy lifestyle. The anti-alcohol groups, however, have no intention of going away, and whether the public will buy the industry public relations message remains to be seen.

Source: Louis Jacobson and Shawn Zeller, "Happy Hour," *National Journal* 32, no. 7 (February 12, 2000): 468–73.

are reflected in different models of business interest representation: individualism, associationalism, and corporatism.[26]

From the perspective of business associations, *individualism* is a system of interest representation in which companies act alone or with other firms to pursue their particular interests. Individualistic business associations are dependent on member support, are independent of government, and have nonhierarchical organizational arrangements.

Associationalism is a system of interest representation in which the focus shifts from firms to industries.[27] Companies here assume that their success depends on the health of their industry. Under this model, industry associations acquire an independent status that allows them to champion policies that promote the long-term interests of the industry even when these policies harm specific companies. Such associations, which develop financial and organizational independence from the particularistic demands of member companies, resemble an industry's governing body. The government may endorse these associations and help them win the approval of member firms for their policy proposals.

In a *corporatist* system, companies are organized into a limited number of functionally defined business associations that have the legal sponsorship of the state. Membership in such associations is sometimes compulsory, and the groups may be authorized by the state to speak for the industry in the public arena. These organizations have a semipublic status, are related to each other hierarchically, and may perform public functions. The boundary between the public and private realms in these circumstances is sometimes blurred. Whereas individualistic business groups express the preferences of companies to government, business organizations under a corporatist model constitute a structure through which government decisions are communicated to companies.

The individualistic structure of business representation in the United States allows companies to pursue their own interests as they see them, and it provides no compelling mechanism to promote the broader interests of an industry or the society. Companies may act alone, as part of an association, or as members of an ad hoc coalition when they believe it is to their benefit to do so. No single business voice emerges in the U.S. system, and business representatives often advocate contradictory positions. Firms in Germany, Japan, and Great Britain have created business associations whose characteristics differ in fundamental ways from those of U.S. groups.

Structure of National Associations

Business groups in Germany and Japan are large, hierarchical, and inclusive organizations that have both associational and corporatist characteristics. There is one general business organization in each country for political and economic questions, and other groups concentrate on labor-management issues and regional business questions. These associations are listed in Table 7-2.

National business associations in these countries, in contrast to the American practice, are usually "peak" organizations, meaning that most members are other business associations rather than individual companies. The Federation of German Industry, the first association listed in Table 7-2, is that country's principal business organization.[28] It is made up of thirty-five associations that repre-

Table 7-2   National Business Associations

Association	Structure
Federal Republic of Germany	
Federation of German Industry	Peak
Confederation of German Employers' Associations	Peak
Diet of German Industry and Commerce	Peak
Japan	
Japan Business Federation	Mixed
Japan Chamber of Commerce and Industry	Peak
Japan Association of Corporate Executives	Direct
Great Britain	
Confederation of British Industry	Mixed
Institute of Directors	Direct
The British Chambers of Commerce	Peak
European Union	
Union of Industrial and Employers' Confederations of Europe	Peak
European Round Table of Industrialists	Direct
EU Committee of American Chamber of Commerce	Direct
United States	
National Association of Manufacturers	Direct
Chamber of Commerce of the United States	Mixed
Business Roundtable	Direct

Source: Author.

sent such particular industries as chemicals, aerospace, textiles, and machinery.[29] These industry associations are in turn composed of more narrowly defined product associations whose members are individual companies. A total of 550 specific associations are represented in the Federation of German Industry, and the membership of the individual associations includes 95 percent of all industrial firms. The Federation helps develop business positions on major economic and political issues and is the principal representative of business viewpoints. The component industry associations deal with issues that concern their members and also seek to settle conflicts with other associations.

The Confederation of German Employers' Associations is also a peak association composed of business groups, but it concentrates on labor-management matters. Although not the actual bargaining agent for employers in collective bargaining situations, it does play a strong hand in devising employer strategies and establishing parameters for bargaining. It also seeks to shape legislation defining legal relationships between employers and employees or affecting corporate personnel costs.[30] Employer associations devoted to labor relations are less common in the United States than in other countries, but such groups do appear in U.S. industries with small employers and dominant unions, such as coal mining, hotels, or trucking.[31]

The Diet of German Industry and Commerce is a different type of business association.[32] The Diet is an obligatory, quasi-public organization composed of eighty-one local chambers of industry and commerce. Businesses are required by law to be dues-paying members of the local chamber. The local chambers are legally responsible for representing the economic interests of a region to the federal, state, local, and European governments, and they administer job-training programs and assemble financial and technical information from their region.

The Japan Business Federation is a comprehensive business organization that was formed in 2002 from a merger of the Keidanren (Japan Federation of Economic Organizations) and the Nikkeiren (Japan Federation of Employers' Associations).[33] The amalgamation of these two groups reflected the view that economic and employment issues had become even more closely intertwined than in the past and the hope that a unified business association would contribute more effectively to the adoption of policies needed to overcome Japan's economic stagnation. Like the Federation of German Industry, the Japan Business Federation is primarily a peak association, but it has a more comprehensive membership than the German association and may be even more prestigious.[34] The group is made up of 129 associations representing service firms, industrial corporations, and distribution businesses, 47 regional employers associations, and 1,300 individual companies. One study notes, "The system approximates a hierarchy in which each level aggregates and reconciles the interests represented at that level."[35] The top executives of the country's largest private enterprises provide the leadership for the Japan Business

Federation. It is so highly regarded that its president has been described as the "prime minister of business."

The Japanese Chamber of Commerce and Industry also represents smaller businesses and is composed of regional associations.[36] As with the Diet of German Industry and Commerce, its regional associations are often more influential than the national group, and they can be major players in local government decision making. The Japan Association of Corporate Executives is composed of top executives from Japan's largest companies, and it resembles the Committee for Economic Development in the United States. It prepares studies and assembles research on a broad range of political, economic, and social issues, and it pursues an active dialogue with political parties, government officials, and labor unions on solutions to pressing public problems.

Business organizations in Great Britain combine the associational features of German and Japanese groups with the more individualistic characteristics of American associations. The foremost British association is the Confederation of British Industry (CBI), created in 1965 from a merger of three independent groups representing large firms, small businesses, and companies in their role as employers.[37] The membership of the CBI is composed of individual firms, industry groups, employer associations, and a few nationalized companies. The CBI staff numbers more than 360, but the organization today has limited influence on its members.[38] Even with a single, encompassing business association, British business seldom develops a unified position on national policy issues, and it often fails to develop any position at all. The CBI has traditionally represented the opinions of large firms in heavy industries, but these firms now contact government directly whenever priority issues arise. One contemporary study concludes, "the CBI has had relatively limited impact on the major issues which have dominated British politics since its formation."[39]

Recent years have witnessed the emergence of competitors to the CBI. The Institute of Directors was founded in 1903 as a social club, but it expanded its staff and transformed itself in the 1970s into an effective lobbying organization. With 55,000 members, the group represents the entrepreneurial attitudes of individual managers rather than the established, institutional positions of large corporations. The Institute of Directors broke with the CBI to support cuts by the Thatcher government in subsidies to declining industries. The British Chambers of Commerce has gained an expanded national role as the representative of small business.[40] Although the national association is a weak federation, many local chambers have energetic memberships who are quite influential on regional issues.

Approximately one thousand business organizations have been established in Brussels to influence the policies of the European Union.[41] The most prominent of these is the Union of Industrial and Employers' Confederations of Europe (UNICE), founded in 1958. Like most European business groups, UNICE is a federation of national associations. In UNICE's case, it has thirty-four member associations from twenty-seven European countries. UNICE has been recognized by the European Commission as a representative of employer groups, and, thus, it can claim to speak on behalf of European industry to EU institutions. UNICE's mission is to promote the interests of its member associations to the European Union, but its broad range of interests and cumbersome procedures often leave it outmaneuvered by organizations representing individual industries. The European Round Table of Industrialists (ERT) was formed in 1983 and patterned after the Business Roundtable in the United States. It too has an invited membership of the leaders of its continent's most influential companies, and it too focuses on issues affecting prosperity and the future of government-business relations. The ERT is frequently credited with having inspired the European Union's single-market project that revitalized Brussels institutions and helped them capture public support. A third prominent business organization in Brussels is the EU Committee of the American Chamber of Commerce that was established in 1985. Its members are among the largest multinational firms of American parentage that have already established themselves in Europe, and these firms often become allies of EU institutions in advocating European integration and continental solutions to economic problems.

Activities of National Business Associations

Modern business appeared in its present form in Great Britain and the United States before the national governments in these countries became dominant factors in economic life. Enterprise philosophies in both nations encouraged firms to maintain their distance from government and other firms. Business associations in Britain and the United States remain underdeveloped compared with associations in Germany and Japan, and individual companies are likely to break with business associations when group actions displease them. This limits the ability of U.S. and British groups to develop positions on policy issues or to take stands opposed by individual firms.

German and Japanese business associations grew up in an environment where government was already a principal factor in economic decision making. As a consequence, business associations in these countries are less likely to resent government. The legal systems in these countries are supportive of business associations, close communications between government officials and business, and public financial support for business groups.

Business organizations in Germany and Japan are expected to adopt positions that promote societal and industry interests, not just the interests of individual companies. Business groups in both countries have a quasi-public status that has been described by Henry J. Jacek in the following terms:

> As the [business] organization develops from a purely member-dependent voluntary association concerned with urgent, immediate problem-solving to one with a diversified and dependable financial, personnel and status

resource base . . . then the organization staff develops sufficient autonomy to influence both members and potential members. . . . Indeed, by having such resources the association staff should develop the ability to control member behaviour sufficiently, so as to act as a private interest government. . . . In this way the special interests of current association members are replaced by more general public interests.[42]

Japanese companies are permitted to establish product-oriented associations when their industries encounter recession, have excess capacity, or face technological challenge. These associations may limit competition by setting prices or closing unneeded factories.[43] Japanese associations also receive exemptions from antitrust laws to export goods, divide international markets, monitor foreign commercial and technical developments, and undertake collaborative research. American business groups have no institutional basis for taking positions that could promote social or industry objectives at the expense of individual firms.

Recently a minister at the British Department of Trade and Industry highlighted the significance of business associations: "Trade associations are one of the most important mechanisms available to help deliver economic success but too many are under-resourced and ineffective. . . . If we fail to make real progress [in improving British associations] . . . we will lose out badly to competitors like the German and the Japanese whose trade associations play a big part in their economic success."[44] Should American business associations be strengthened so that they can develop unified policy positions and advocate proposals that are independent of the parochial interests of individual members? Some maintain that fragmented business representation in the United States leads individual firms to pursue short-term goals without concern for the long-term interests of their industry or the society.[45] Such commentators contend that American business associations must be better organized if the United States is to meet the challenges of international competition.[46] The individualistic traditions of American and British business mean that these countries lack a potentially valuable vehicle for shaping informed yet dispassionate public policy.

Other scholars disagree strongly. Business organizations, they insist, already dominate the country's political process.[47] The way to improve public policy is to restrict the political activities of individual corporations rather than enhance the influence and effectiveness of business associations.

SUMMARY

The viewpoints of American business on public policy issues are communicated to government officials through corporate government relations offices and an extensive array of business associations. The *individualistic* pattern of interest representation coincides with American political ideology and reflects the country's fear of economic concentration. Because of their organizational character,

U.S. business groups are less able than associations elsewhere to develop unified positions, less frequently endorse policies that harm individual members, and probably have less influence in the policy process.

The political philosophies of Germany and Japan emphasize the positive benefits of collective action. The patterns of interest representation reflect associational and corporatist principles. These countries believe that influential business groups can enhance economic efficiency and improve the conduct of public policy. Policy proposals hammered out in business associations and then presented to government are based on a fuller understanding of economic and technical issues and a greater awareness of the need to advance the nation's broad economic and social interests. Would the strengthening of U.S. industry associations in relation to their member companies be a constructive option for American business in the new century?

FURTHER READINGS

The following business association Web sites provide current information on each group's legislative agenda and policy activities: National Association of Manufacturers: http://www.nam.org; U.S. Chamber of Commerce: http://www.uschamber.com; and the National Association of Broadcasters: http://www.nab.com. The Web sites of the following groups present at least some of their information in English: the Confederation of British Industry, http://www.cbi.org.uk; UNICE, http://www.unice.org; Japan Business Federation, http://www.keidanren.or.jp; and the Federation of German Industry, http://www.bdi-online.de.

Grant, Wyn. *Pressure Groups and British Politics.* New York: St. Martin's, 2000.
Greenwood, Justin, ed. *The Challenge of Change in EU Business Associations.* New York: Palgrave Macmillan, 2003.
Kennedy, Scott. *The Business of Lobbying in China.* Cambridge, Mass.: Harvard University Press, 2005.
Lynn, Leonard H., and Timothy J. McKeown. *Organizing Business: Trade Associations in America and Japan.* Washington, D.C.: American Enterprise Institute for Public Policy Research, 1988.
Procassini, Andrew A. *Competitors in Alliance: Industry Associations, Global Rivalries and Business-Government Relations.* Westport, Conn.: Quorum Books, 1995.

NOTES

1. See Seymour Martin Lipset and William Schneider, *The Confidence Gap: Business, Labor, and Government in the Public Mind* (New York: Free Press, 1983), 372–73; David Vogel, "The Inadequacy of Contemporary Opposition to Business," *Daedalus: Journal of the American Academy of Arts and Sciences,* Summer 1980, 4–58, esp. 48.
2. Charles Wolf, *Markets or Governments: Choosing between Imperfect Alternatives* (Cambridge, Mass.: MIT Press, 1990), 6–7.
3. See Michael Novak, *Spirit of Democratic Capitalism* (New York: Simon and Schuster, 1982); and Albert T. Sommers, ed., *The Free Society and Planning* (New York: Conference Board, 1975).
4. See Edwin M. Epstein, *The Corporation in American Politics* (Englewood Cliffs, N.J.: Prentice Hall, 1969), 324.

5. Charles E. Lindblom, *Politics and Markets: The World's Political-Economic Systems* (New York: Basic Books, 1977), 356; see also Chapters. 13–14 in the present volume.

6. John A. Cray, "Corporate Identity and Corporate Political Activities," *American Business Law Journal* 21 (Winter 1984): 439–61. See also *First National Bank of Boston v. Bellotti*, 435 U.S. 765 (1978) and *Consolidated Edison of New York v. Public Service Commission*, 447 U.S. 530 (1980).

7. Louis Galambos, *Competition and Cooperation: The Emergence of a National Trade Association* (Baltimore: Johns Hopkins University Press, 1966), 11–36; and Louis Galambos, "The American Trade Association Movement Revisited," in *Trade Associations in Business History*, ed. Hiroaki Yamazaki and Matao Miyamoto (Tokyo: University of Tokyo Press, 1988), 121–35.

8. The Webb-Pomerene Act of 1918 exempts cartels engaged in foreign trade from the Sherman Antitrust Act.

9. This section draws upon information from the individual groups and upon Sar A. Levitan and Martha R. Cooper, *Business Lobbies: The Public Good and the Bottom Line* (Baltimore: Johns Hopkins University Press, 1984), chaps. 2–3.

10. Ibid., 16.

11. David Vogel, *Fluctuating Fortunes: The Political Power of Business in America* (New York: Basic Books, 1989), 288.

12. Ibid., 34.

13. Levitan and Cooper, *Business Lobbies*, 41.

14. David Hosansky, "Hill Feels the Big Clout of Small Business," *Congressional Quarterly Weekly Report*, January 10, 1998, 55–60.

15. Kim McQuaid, *Big Business and Presidential Power: From FDR to Reagan* (New York: Morrow, 1982), 285–308.

16. Levitan and Cooper, *Business Lobbies*, 39.

17. Curtis M. Grimm and John M. Holcomb, "Choices among Encompassing Organizations: Business and the Budget Deficit," in *Business Strategy and Public Policy: Perspectives from Industry and Academia*, ed. Alfred A. Marcus, Allen M. Kaufman, and David Beam (New York: Quorum Books, 1987), 105–18.

18. U.S. Bureau of the Census, *Statistical Abstract of the United States, 1990* (Washington, D.C.: GPO, 1990), 786.

19. This discussion is drawn from the source cited for Figure 7-1.

20. National Association of Manufacturers, *Manufacturing Trade Associations: Their Changing Focus and Management*, 1985, 1987, and 1989 eds. (Washington, D.C.: NAM, 1985, 1987, and 1989).

21. NAM, *Manufacturing Trade Associations*, 1985 ed., 36.

22. George Mellon, "What to Do When Your Own Lobby Is Against You," *Wall Street Journal*, February 16, 1988, 37.

23. Patrick McGeehan, "Leading Financial Services Companies Form Lobbying Group," *New York Times*, January 6, 2000, C7.

24. Juergen Hartmann, *Verbaende in der westlichen Industrie-gesellschaft* (Frankfurt: Campus Verlag, 1985), 76–77, 162–87.

25. Leonard H. Lynn and Timothy J. McKeown, *Organizing Business: Trade Associations in America and Japan* (Washington, D.C.: American Enterprise Institute, 1988), 56–57, 67–68, 172–73.

26. For a discussion of comparable terms, see Philippe C. Schmitter, "Still the Century of Corporatism?" in *Trends toward Corporatist Intermediation*, ed. Philippe C. Schmitter and Gerhard Lehmbruch (Beverly Hills, Calif.: Sage Publications, 1979), 7–52; Peter Katzenstein, *Corporatism and Change* (Ithaca, N.Y.: Cornell University Press, 1984); Wolfgang Streeck and Philippe C. Schmitter, "Community, Market, State—and Associations? The Prospective Contribution of Interest Governance to Social Order," in *Private Interest Government: Beyond Market and State*, ed. Streeck and Schmitter (London: Sage Publications, 1985), 1–29; Alan Cawson, "Introduction: Varieties of Corporatism: The Importance of the Meso-level of Interest Intermediation," in *Organized Interests and the State: Studies in Meso-Corporatism*, ed.

Cawson (London: Sage Publications, 1985), 1–21; Franz Traxler, "Patterns of Associative Action," chap. 2, and Henry J. Jacek, "Business Interest Associations as Private Interest Governments," chap. 3, in *Business Interests, Organizational Development and Private Interest Government: An International Comparative Study of the Food Processing Industry,* ed. Wyn Grant (Berlin: Walter de Gruyter, 1987); and Michael G. Huelshoff, "West German Corporatism at Forty," chap. 7, in *The Federal Republic of Germany at Forty,* ed. Peter H. Merkl (New York: New York University Press, 1989).

27. Wolfgang Streeck, "Between Pluralism and Corporatism: German Business Associations and the State," *Journal of Public Policy* 3, no. 3 (1983): 265–84.

28. The name in German is *Bundesverband der Deutschen Industrie* (BDI). For the history of German associations, see Karl Josef Uthmann and Hermann Freiherr von Wolff-Metternich, *Der Bundesverband der Deutschen Industrie* (Dusseldorf: Droste Verlag, 1974); and Walter Simon, *Macht und Herrschaft der Unternehmerverbaende: BDI, BDA und DIHT im oekonomischen und politischen System der BRD* (Cologne: Pahl-Rugenstein Verlag, 1976).

29. See Hartmann, *Verbaende in der westlichen Industrie-gesellschaft,* 81–108.

30. See Ronald F. Bunn, "Employers Associations in the Federal Republic of Germany," 169–201, and Solomon B. Levine, "Employers Associations in Japan," in *Employers Associations and Industrial Relations: A Comparative Study,* 318–56, ed. John P. Windmuller and Alan Gladstone (Oxford: Oxford University Press, Clarendon Press, 1984).

31. See Milton Derber, "Employers Associations in the United States," in Windmuller and Gladstone, *Employers Associations and Industrial Relations,* 79–114.

32. The association is called the *Deutscher Industrie- und Handelstag* (DIHT). See Hartmann, *Verbaende in der westlichen Industrie-gesellschaft,* 96–98, 102.

33. For a history of Japanese associations, see Matao Miyamoto, "The Development of Business Associations in Prewar Japan," 1–45, and Takeo Kikkawa, "Functions of Japanese Trade Associations before World War II," 53–83, in Yamazaki and Miyamoto, *Trade Associations in Business History.*

34. This discussion is drawn from Lynn and McKeown, *Organizing Business,* 78–81; see also Charles J. McMillan, *The Japanese Industrial System,* 2nd ed. (Berlin: Walter de Gruyter, 1989).

35. Lynn and McKeown, *Organizing Business,* 81.

36. *Nippon Shiko Kaigisho* (Nissho).

37. This discussion is based on Wyn Grant and David Marsh, *The Confederation of British Industry* (London: Hodder and Stoughton, 1977); Wyn Grant, with Jane Sargent, *Business and Politics in Britain* (London: Macmillan Education, 1987), chap. 6; Hartmann, *Verbaende in der westlichen Industrie-gesellschaft,* 109–26; and E. G. A. Armstrong, "Employers Associations in Great Britain," in Windmuller and Gladstone, *Employers Associations and Industrial Relations,* 44–78.

38. William Coleman and Wyn Grant, "The Organizational Cohesion and Political Access of Business: A Study of Comprehensive Associations," *European Journal of Political Research* 16 (1988): 467–87.

39. Grant and Marsh, *Confederation of British Industry,* 207; and A. G. Jordan and J. J. Richardson, *Government and Pressure Groups in Britain* (Oxford: Oxford University Press, Clarendon Press, 1987), 167.

40. Grant, *Business and Politics in Britain,* 128–29.

41. This section draws from Justin Greenwood, *Interest Representation in the European Union* (New York: Palgrave Macmillan, 2003), chap. 3; and Werner Teufelsbauer, "Horizontal Business Associations at EU Level," in *The Challenge of Change in EU Business Associations,* ed. Justin Greenwood (New York: Palgrave Macmillan, 2003), 33–41.

42. Henry J. Jacek, "Business Interest Associations as Private Interest Governments," in Grant, *Business Interests, Organizational Development and Private Interest Government,* 48, 52.

43. Lynn and McKeown, *Organizing Business,* 18–45.

44. Michael Cassell, "Trade Groups Often Ineffective, Says Minister," *Financial Times,* January 30, 1996, 9.

45. Ian Maitland, "Collective versus Individual Lobbying: How Business Ends Up the Loser," in Marcus, Kaufman, and Beam, *Business Strategy and Public Policy,* 96–99.

46. William G. Ouchi, *The M-Form Society: How American Teamwork Can Recapture the Competitive Edge* (Reading, Mass.: Addison-Wesley, 1984). For an analysis of the United Kingdom, see Grant, *Business and Politics in Britain.*

47. See, for example, Michael Useem, *The Inner Circle: Large Corporations and the Rise of Business Political Activity in the U.S. and U.K.* (New York: Oxford University Press, 1984); or Mark Green and Andrew Buchsbaum, *The Corporate Lobbies: Political Profiles of the Business Roundtable and the Chamber of Commerce* (Washington, D.C.: Public Citizen, 1980).

CHAPTER 8

Lobbying Connections

ED GILLESPIE IS founder and co-chair of Quinn Gillespie & Associates, one of the dozen top-billing lobbying firms in Washington.[1] Gillespie chaired the Republican National Committee during the 2004 election cycle, participated in numerous campaigns, worked as a congressional staffer, and was a principal drafter of the GOP's Contract with America. Quinn Gillespie was founded in 2000 by Gillespie and Jack Quinn, former White House counsel to President Bill Clinton and chief of staff to Vice President Al Gore, and now the firm has offices up Connecticut Avenue from the White House. Gillespie, Quinn, and fifteen other lobbyists market their substantive insights, understanding of Washington's quirks and customs, and contacts with the current generation of Washington policymakers. Their clients have included Coca-Cola, DaimlerChrysler, Microsoft, Qualcomm, and Sony.

Business lobbyists seek to influence decisions wherever they are made, and the doctrine of the separation of powers means that government authority in the United States is broadly dispersed. Quinn Gillespie stresses its ability to reach out to decision makers wherever they are located. In a survey of corporate and trade association lobbyists, more than 90 percent agreed that congressional decisions were "very important" for their objectives.[2] Other lobbying targets, however, are not ignored. Fully 75 percent of business representatives report that executive agencies are very important to their issues, 63 percent regard the White House as critical, and 20 percent say that lobbying the courts also is significant.

This chapter begins with an examination of the types of activities Ed Gillespie and other business lobbyists pursue when they attempt to influence congressional decisions. The next section contains a review of the relationships between industry and administrative agencies and an exploration of the tactics businesses use to influence agency decisions. An assessment of the significance of judicial actions for business policy and a review of the legal opportunities available to organizations to gain commercial advantage make up the third section. The final section covers surveys of government structures in other countries and lobbying practices in the European Union.

WHAT DO BUSINESS LOBBYISTS DO?

When corporations seek to influence congressional decisions, several approaches are open to them. They can retain Quinn Gillespie & Associates or one of Washington's 12,500 other contract lobbyists. They can also call on business associations, rely on their own public affairs offices, or create an ad hoc issue coalition to deal with the problem. The form of lobbying they select usually depends on the nature of the issue and the frequency with which similar issues occur. Figure 8-1 relates four forms of lobbying to the characteristics of the issues.

When policy problems arise, businesses think first of established business associations. They pay dues to these organizations, and they want something in return. If an issue recurs frequently and affects all firms in an industry in a uniform way, a company will probably turn to a business association, such as the American Bankers Association or the Beer Institute. These organizations are eager to defend their members and prove their worth. When an issue pits one member against another, however, firms cannot depend on their trade associations for help.

A corporation's own public affairs department is well suited to lobby on issues that occur frequently but affect the firm in a particular way. Corporate lobbyists are experts in their own operations, and they can speak authoritatively about the impact of an issue on employees and customers. They are loyal to the firm and can take a long-term perspective on its problems.

When an issue affects a company in a unique way but comes along only rarely, companies often retain contract, for-hire lobbyists, such as Ed Gillespie. Contract lobbyists are extremely knowledgeable about the government process, adept at working with people from diverse institutions, and familiar with the pressures of public controversy, and many now specialize in specific areas. Anheuser-Busch,

Figure 8-1   Patterns of Business Lobbying

| | | IMPACT OF ISSUE | |
		Specific to Firm	Uniform among Firms
FREQUENCY OF ISSUE	Recurring	Public Affairs Office	Business Association
	Rare	Contract Lobbyist	Ad hoc Coalition

Source: Adapted from Allen M. Kaufman, Ernest J. Englander, and Alfred A. Marcus, "Structure and Implementation in Issues Management: Transaction Costs and Agency Theory," in *Research in Corporate Social Performance and Policy: A Research Annual, vol. 2*, ed. James E. Post (Greenwich, Conn.: JAI Press, 1989), 257–71.

Merrill Lynch, and General Electric all turn to Washington Counsel, dubbed "the Tiffany's of tax lobbying shops," when they want help with tax issues. Other lobbyists specialize in expenditure items, health policy, telecommunications, appointments, and the like. These firms charge huge fees, but they provide the expertise needed for specific situations.

Some policy proposals affect an array of business and nonbusiness interests in an unusual way, and, thus, no existing organization fits the contours of the issue. In these circumstances, group representatives come together to form ad hoc issue coalitions. When legislators sought to restrict the production of big cars to save energy, for example, representatives of senior citizens' groups whose members have trouble getting in and out of small cars, volunteer organizations that transport the handicapped, and police associations who like powerful cruisers joined with business lobbyists to delay the measure.[3]

Business lobbyists have both advantages and handicaps in their lobbying efforts. In a world of elected officials, businesses are not membership groups and, thus, cast few votes. They also embody an objective, corporate profitability, that has little popular appeal. Still, business lobbyists generally have significant expertise, broad networks of contacts, and adequate funding.[4] Furthermore, their firms provide jobs and products the society wants. Business lobbyists draft legislation, find sponsors for bills, develop arguments, shape coalitions, and steer proposals through the legislative process, and they follow a common set of rules. What are the rules for successful lobbying?[5]

Cultivation of Key Figures

Three decades ago, the tone of business representation in Washington was set by a small group of elite lobbyists from such firms as Procter & Gamble, U.S. Steel, and General Motors, and lobbying activities were based on personal access to a few powerholders.[6] Lobbyists from this era knew where to buy good cigars, find the best restaurants, and obtain tickets to Redskins games.

Today, the lobbying process has changed. The circles of influence in Washington in the 2000s are wider than in the past. Congressional subcommittee chairs, individual members, and even senior staff aides now share influence with congressional leaders. Furthermore, the ability of a few corporate lobbyists to set the political strategy of business has waned. New corporations and industries from the South and the West have gained prominence, and they do not follow the lead of a few established figures. Private contact with top public officials is not all there is to lobbying today, even though lobbyists still play golf at prestigious clubs and cultivate personal relationships.

Helping to Shape the Policy Agenda

Not every issue wins attention. The selection of issues to be addressed goes a long way toward determining the impact of a country's policies. In the 1960s, issues of social equity were at the center of the legislative stage, whereas in the 1980s and 1990s questions of economic competitiveness attracted concern.

Corporations, unions, and other interests seek to shape the public attitudes that give rise to policy issues.[7] In 1906 AT&T conducted a print campaign to convince the public, then troubled by the emergence of giant corporations, of the benefits of an integrated, monopolistic telephone system.[8] In the 1960s and 1970s business groups believed that the public did not appreciate the benefits of a market economy, so they developed programs to promote economic education among employees, students, and shareholders.[9] More recently, the Mobil Oil Corporation sponsored newspaper advertisements expressing the company's position on issues affecting the oil industry and the broader society, and these ads stood out because of their aggressiveness.[10]

Another corporate effort to alter policy debates was evident in business support for policy research centers.[11] Through the 1970s, organizations such as the Ford Foundation, the Brookings Institution, and the Institute for Policy Studies achieved quasi-monopoly status in "think-tank" policy development. They usually advocated expanding the role of government in society and restricting the autonomy of private organizations.

In the 1970s, companies and private foundations funded research organizations that stressed nongovernmental approaches to public problems. Recipients of support were the American Enterprise Institute, the Heritage Foundation, and the prestigious National Bureau of Economic Research in Cambridge, Massachusetts. Scholars were encouraged to amplify views that had been undeveloped and disseminate research findings that had been unnoticed. As a result, think tanks proliferated, and a wider spectrum of ideological perspectives shaped legislation.

Development of a Sound Argument

Lobbying has become an analytic and substantive process in recent years. As Congress responds to a growing array of social problems, and government involvement in business operations grows more pervasive, policy assessments have become more sophisticated. Elected officials are not experts in substantive matters, but they want publicly defensible reasons for supporting a proposal. To satisfy the need for a good argument, supposedly objective studies are commissioned by Washington lobbyists as part of lobbying campaigns.

Consulting firms insist that their work is unbiased, but they are not hired to contradict their sponsors.[12] An account of tax legislation revealed that opponents had funded dozens of studies of the allegedly disastrous effects of measures they opposed. According to these studies, the tax proposals would raise apartment rents by 20 to 40 percent, devastate Samoa, displace millions of workers in export industries, and jeopardize "the oral health of the American people." Whatever their shortcomings, these studies provide a measure of the thinking of their sponsors, and they have a meaningful impact on the legislative process.

Nurturing the Grassroots

The aphorism that all politics is local underlines the fact that members are elected from specific districts.[13] Politicians, however, may be less concerned about the opinions of the general public than about the smaller group of attentive citizens who care intensely about an issue and may base future electoral support on that issue.

Washington lobbyists have long relied on grassroots techniques to remind legislators that important constituents are watching what they do. Organizations such as the Chamber of Commerce and corporations such as Schering-Plough and Coca-Cola have built impressive networks of local activists who contact district legislators.[14] Ninety percent of trade association lobbyists and 80 percent of corporate representatives recruit influential constituents to carry their message to legislators.[15]

One famous example of grassroots lobbying occurred when Congress decided to increase revenues by withholding taxes on interest paid on savings accounts.[16] Bankers were angry because the measure would increase paperwork and require them to explain to angry customers why their money had been withheld. In the era of grassroots lobbying, the American Bankers Association hired a market-research firm to hold a series of small-group discussions. When the legislation was explained, citizens were irate. They were unconcerned about the administrative problems of bankers, but they were incensed that government would withhold money from the bank accounts of kids with paper routes, senior citizens, and the poor. To encourage citizens to express their views, the ABA distributed sample letters to be sent to local newspapers, brochures for customers, and special statements for senior citizens.

As a result, bank customers sent 22 million pieces of mail to Congress opposing the withholding scheme, more mail than Congress had ever received on a single issue. Legislation repealing the plan was passed by both houses and enacted into law over the president's objections. The ABA succeeded in winning repeal of the withholding measure because the group's objective coincided with public sentiment and because the ABA was able to mobilize millions of citizens to express their views.

Building Coalitions

Contemporary legislative initiatives frequently lead business representatives to form specialized coalitions. Specific proposals usually affect some corporations in important ways but leave most firms apathetic and unconcerned. As a consequence, business groups often remain silent on such issues while ad hoc coalitions emerge to exchange information and coordinate strategies.[17] Business groups have been most successful in achieving their legislative objectives when they are able to forge coalitions with citizen, labor, and community organizations. These coalitions are a valuable vehicle for coordinating grassroots and other types of lobbying activities.

Understanding PACs

Money has been a prominent tool of business involvement in politics for a century, but the mechanisms of participation have changed. In 1896 the head of the Republican National Committee financed the presidential campaign of William McKinley through assessments on large corporations.[18] In response, the Tillman Act of 1907 made it illegal for businesses to contribute to federal election campaigns. This law was often evaded, however, and after the 1972 election twenty-one companies were found guilty of having made illegal contributions, mostly to the campaign of President Richard M. Nixon.

Political action committees originated in the labor movement in 1943. When Congress barred unions from making direct contributions to political candidates, the CIO set up a committee to receive and disperse voluntary contributions from union members. Campaign reform laws in the 1970s authorized corporations, unions, trade or membership associations, and partnerships to establish PACs and pay their administrative costs. PACs could receive donations, give funds to federal candidates, and use the funds for political purposes that were independent of the campaigns. Corporations and other PAC sponsors, however, were still prohibited from giving organizational funds to federal candidates.

The maximum amount an individual may now contribute to a PAC is $5,000 per year, and PAC contributions are limited to $5,000 per candidate per election. Individuals may contribute no more than $95,000 to federal candidates in each two-year election cycle, directly or through PACs, and no more than $2,000 to an individual candidate's committee. Most contributions to corporate PACs come from the company's executives.

In the 2003–4 election cycle, PACs contributed $310 million to federal campaigns. The PACs that contribute the largest amounts are sponsored by membership associations, such as those for realtors, trial lawyers, or doctors, or by labor unions, such as the Machinists Non Partisan Political League, the International Brotherhood of Teamsters, or the United Automobile Workers, as Table 8-1 indicates. In 2003–4, seven of the fifteen largest PAC contributors were associated with unions, seven were sponsored by trade and membership associations, and one was sponsored by a company.[19] The National Association of Realtors PAC was the largest contributor, with donations of nearly $3.8 million, and the runner-up was the PAC sponsored by the National Automobile Dealers Association, which contributed almost $2.6 million.

Corporate PACs are smaller than labor or association PACs but far more numerous (see Table 8-2). In 2003–4 the largest corporate PAC, sponsored by United Parcel Service (UPS), ranked eighth on the overall list of PAC contributors, and only fourteen of the fifty largest PACs were sponsored by companies. The UPS PAC gave federal candidates $2.1 million in 2003–4, whereas the typical "large" corporate PAC donated $600,000 to $700,000 to federal candidates.

Table 8-1   Largest PACs by Contributions to Federal Candidates, 2003–2004

Rank PAC	Contribution
1 National Association of Realtors PAC	$3,771,083
2 National Automobile Dealers Association	2,584,800
3 International Brotherhood of Electrical Workers COPE	2,304,600
4 National Beer Wholesalers Association PAC	2,289,000
5 Laborers' Political League-Laborers' International Union	2,249,000
6 Build PAC of the National Association of Home Builders	2,221,500
7 Association of Trial Lawyers of America PAC	2,170,499
8 United Parcel Service Inc. PAC	2,139,929
9 American Medical Association PAC	2,077,899
10 United Automobile Workers Voluntary Community Action Program	2,065,200
11 Credit Union Legislative Action Council	2,005,385
12 Service Employees International Union COPE	1,929,000
13 Machinists Non Partisan Political League	1,905,000
14 International Brotherhood of Teamsters PAC	1,890,441
15 United Brotherhood of Carpenters and Joiners	1,890,000

Source: Federal Election Commission, "PAC Activity Increases for 2004 Elections," press release, April 13, 2005.

Despite the moderate size of individual corporate PACs, contributions from corporate PACs in the aggregate are still quite significant. In 2003–4 corporate PACs contributed $116 million to federal candidates, or 37 percent of the $310 million federal candidates received from all PAC sources. Membership and trade association PACs contributed $83 million to federal candidates in that election cycle, and labor-sponsored PACs gave $52 million.

Table 8-2   Contributions of PACs to Federal Candidates, 2003–2004

Type of PAC	Number of PACs	Total donated (in millions)	Status of recipient			Party of recipient	
			Incumbent	Challenger	Open	Democrat	Republican
All PACs	3,258	$310	80%	7%	13%	43%	57%
Corporate	1,402	116	87	3	10	32	68
Membership	722	83	85	4	11	36	64
Trade Association							
Labor	206	52	74	12	13	87	13
Other	928	59	62	15	23	36	64

Source: Federal Election Commission, "PAC Activity Increases for 2004 Elections," press release, April 13, 2005.

PACs favor incumbents. Four out of every five PAC dollars were directed to incumbents in 2003–4, as seen in Table 8-2, and this has traditionally been the case. In 2003–4 the majority of PAC dollars went to Republicans, reflecting the Republican majorities in Congress.[20] In 1987–88, in comparison, when Democrats commanded majorities in both houses, 62 percent of PAC dollars had supported Democratic candidates, and only 38 percent went to Republicans. Not all PACs behave in the same ways. Labor PACs directed 87 percent of their contributions to Democratic candidates in 2003–4 and were more likely to support challengers than the average PAC. In contrast, nonlabor PACs contributed 66 percent of their money to Republican candidates and were more likely to support incumbents.

The behavior of corporate PACs changes from election to election. In general, however, they are cautious. They give an even greater share of their funds to incumbents than the average PAC and notably more to Republicans than to Democrats.[21] Corporate PACs give to legislators who are members of committees that concern them, and they also favor candidates who have supportive ideologies, have backed them on important issues, and represent districts where they have facilities.[22] In contrast, membership PACs and labor PACs examine how legislators have voted on a few key issues.

Careful Use of Other Political Money

The top political finance story of 2004 was the dramatic emergence of the 527 committees. According to the Center for Public Integrity, these groups raised and spent $550 million in the 2003–4 election cycle, almost twice as much as was contributed to federal candidates by all PACs combined.[23] Authorized by the 2002 Bipartisan Campaign Reform Act and named after the section of the tax code that regulates them, 527 groups are tax-exempt organizations that were to raise money for voter mobilization and issue advocacy. Disputes about Federal Election Commission rules, however, allowed the groups to move beyond their original purpose and directly support or oppose individual candidates for president and Congress. Groups oriented toward the Democratic Party were reported by PoliticalMoneyLine to have spent almost twice as much as Republican-oriented groups, but ironically the most prominent 527 group was the Swift Boat Veterans for Truth that ran ads questioning accounts of Sen. John Kerry's military service.[24]

In the 2003–4 cycle the 527 committees operated with little accountability, and they raised funds in large amounts from a handful of donors. Three organizations and four individuals each contributed more than $10 million to 527 committees, and, therefore, each of these donors contributed more than four times as much as the largest corporate PAC. All these donors supported Democratic candidates and issues.[25] The Federal Election Commission has formulated tighter rules for the 2006 election cycle, but there is little reason to believe that the new regulations will be enforced any more effectively than the earlier version. It is also likely that

Republican-oriented contributors will mobilize more effectively in the election cycles ahead as the arms race mentality takes hold in campaign circles.

Providing Assistance in Campaigns

In general, businesspeople stay away from electoral politics.[26] A few corporate leaders participate in presidential, gubernatorial, or senatorial campaigns, but they avoid less visible races and shun ongoing party activities. Whereas 88 percent of corporate lobbyists contribute to election campaigns, only 28 percent of business organizations publish information on voting records, 14 percent donate services to campaigns, and 8 percent endorse candidates.[27] Representatives of nonbusiness interests contribute less often to campaigns but participate more frequently in other forms of campaign activity.

Despite the reluctance of business, public officials want all the campaign support they can get, and some lobbying organizations are becoming increasingly involved in campaign activities. The National Federation of Independent Businesses, representing small businesses, has a well-organized grassroots constituency, and it sensitizes candidates to small-business issues in campaigns.[28] The NFIB also publishes a scorecard rating incumbent legislators on roll-call votes affecting small business, and it was a leading group in financing the development of the GOP's Contract with America. When the AFL-CIO announced plans to spend $35 million to defeat newly elected representatives in one election cycle, the NFIB joined a business coalition that counterattacked with $5 million in issue ads supporting the legislators.

Lobbyists participate in campaigns for one of two reasons. They want either to enhance the election chances of officeholders who are sympathetic to their cause or to affect the conduct of officials who are going to win anyway. Campaign activities in one election indicate to politicians that an organization will probably be active in future elections and might throw its support to another candidate if the official is insensitive to the organization's goals. The growing frequency with which campaign consultants become contract lobbyists underlines the effectiveness of assisting in campaigns as a technique for gaining access to elected public officials.[29] One company's initial lobbying experiences are described in Box 8-1.

LOBBYING ADMINISTRATIVE AGENCIES

The U.S. communications industry encompasses about one-seventh of the nation's economy.[30] Even though Congress is the nation's principal policymaking institution, fundamental decisions affecting telecommunications policy have been made not on Capitol Hill or even in the White House but in administrative agencies and courtrooms. By the 1990s, technological innovations had scrambled relations among local phone companies, long-distance firms, television broadcasters, cable companies, and purveyors of newer technologies, such as cellular phones,

Cases in Development
BOX 8-1 COFFEEHOUSE LOBBYING

Google, Monster.com, and Starbucks all hired their first lobbyists in recent years. As innovative companies, their success has come from breaking the corporate mold and charting their own course. As companies expand, however, they discover more and more often that their operations and ambitions take them to Washington.

Starbucks operates 4,300 stores in the United States and 800 more in Canada and Great Britain, and its aggressive growth plans call for a total of 30,000 coffeehouses around the world. Thus, Starbucks is particularly concerned about trade policy and intellectual property rules. As an importer of premium coffees into many countries, it opposes tariffs on coffee that increase its costs, such as the 90 percent tariff imposed by Thailand. Starbucks also advocated stricter enforcement of copyright standards when it discovered a replica of its stores operating in China.

Starbucks prides itself on the health care program it provides its employees, even part-time workers, but like all firms, it finds the double-digit increase in health care costs a burden. Under an old program that granted tax breaks to manufacturers, Starbucks qualified for reduced taxes by claiming that roasting coffee was a form of manufacturing. When this program was invalidated by the World Trade Organization, Starbucks sought to preserve the millions it had saved in taxes by having a provision included in the 2004 congressional tax bill. Starbucks hired Kris Engskov, a former aide to President Clinton, to head its government-affairs program and retained the lobbying firm of Preston Gates, founded by Bill Gates's father, to help it deal with Congress. A former senator, employed by Preston Gates, contacted a senator whose state was home to a Starbucks roasting plant, and a former Democratic staff member of the Senate Finance Committee, also employed by Preston Gates, called his onetime colleagues still working on the committee staff. Language was added to the bill clarifying Starbucks' claim to reduced taxes, but the provision came to be known as the "Starbucks footnote." With this name, the provision attracted the attention of editorialists and headline writers throughout the country. Starbucks could claim victory in its first notable government relations enterprise, but it came at the price of being identified as a profit-driven special interest rather than an idealistic company concerned only about its employee-partners and coffee growers in poor countries.

Sources: Jeanne Cummings, "Cautiously, Starbucks Puts Lobbying on Corporate Menu," *Wall Street Journal,* April 12, 2005; and Eli Sanders, "A Champ in the City of Coffees," *New York Times,* April 16, 2005, http://www.nytimes.com.

electronic mail, and the Internet. After half a decade of debate, Congress finally passed the Telecommunications Act of 1996 that claimed to promote competition among the various industries, but key provisions in the legislation were ambiguous, and participants disagreed about what they had enacted.[31] What the statute, in fact, did was to place an administrative agency, the Federal Communications Commission (FCC), in a vortex of competing interests and instruct it to resolve the conflicts.

Lobbyists are intensely concerned about policy details, and it was no surprise that the FCC's proceedings attracted platoons of high-priced lobbyists championing the interests of their clients. Indeed, Eric M. Uslaner writes, "Cabinet departments and all manner of independent agencies . . . are gold mines for lobbyists."[32]

Administrative agencies such as the FCC do three things in the policy process that are important to lobbyists.[33] Agencies are one of society's repositories of expertise on policy matters, and their views help shape major legislation. Second, agencies are the institutions that translate statutory generalities into concrete rules. They fill in the gaps in statutes and reconcile conflicting provisions. Finally, agencies determine how administrative rules are applied to individual cases. Thus, industries and corporations have a substantial stake in the decisions agencies make. The FCC had to decide, for example, when the local telephone markets served by Verizon were sufficiently competitive to allow Verizon to offer long-distance service.[34]

Limitations on popular participation and the technical nature of administrative actions suggest that firms may receive a fuller hearing in a bureaucratic setting than in the political arena. Since businesses are a continuing factor in an agency's political environment, administrators may even come to share business perspectives on the issues before them.[35] Business groups may support agency positions in Congress, agencies may shape programs that accommodate group preferences, and both sides will thrive if policies are successful. This harmony of interests has led many theorists to fear that businesses may become so influential in administrative decision making that they could "capture" the relevant agencies.[36]

"Capture" theorists emphasize that business groups have the greatest financial stake in an agency's decision making.[37] Although other groups appear occasionally to express their views, like morning glories they soon fade from the scene. Furthermore, top administrators usually serve in government for limited periods and then move to posts in the private sector. They may plan to seek employment in the industry they regulated, and this may lead them to avoid anti-industry decisions when they are in office.

The warnings of the capture theorists were quite influential. As a result, four principles have emerged to guard against the misuse of administrative discretion.[38] Various *restrictions on agency decision makers* limit contacts between administrators and representatives of business. Legislation requires lobbyists to disclose contacts with executive branch officials, and administrators and business representatives may not discuss pending cases in informal discussions.[39] In addition, for a period after they leave government, key administrators may not work for companies that appeared before them.

Another technique for ensuring impartiality is to identify the *administrative procedures* used to reach decisions. Agencies must hold hearings so that all groups have an opportunity to register their views, and agencies must demonstrate that there is "substantial support" in the record for their judgments. A third principle limiting administrative discretion is bureaucratic *professionalism*. Civil servants are expected to rest their decisions on the norms of neutrality and objectivity, and this should then insulate them from political pressures. *Oversight* of agency decisions by Congress is the fourth technique for ensuring that administrators do not give in to business pressures.[40] When Congress doubts the appropriateness of administrative actions, it can pass new laws, amend existing statutes, reduce agency funds, hold public hearings, or conduct investigations.[41]

A recent trend that affects lobbying of executive agencies is the increased control over administrative decisions by the White House. The White House is now involved in the selection of officials at lower levels, and contemporary presidents practice, according to Uslaner, a "politics of exclusion."[42] Presidents present an ideological agenda and allow access only to groups in sync with the program.

Despite the restraints and restrictions, lobbyists have developed a catalog of techniques to influence administrative decisions:

- *Influence administrative decisions through political channels.* Administrative agencies are sensitive to the opinions of elected officials. White House officials and members of Congress are contacted to encourage agencies to be more responsive to specific viewpoints than would otherwise be the case.

- *Participate in the appointment process for agency officials.* Industries and interest groups often seek to promote candidates responsive to them for top administrative posts in critical agencies and, perhaps more important, to block the appointment of individuals who are hostile to their positions.

- *Mobilize public support.* Administrative agencies are responsive to organizational and individual opinion in the society. To influence agency decisions, lobbyists frequently form coalitions of like-minded groups and mobilize grassroots supporters.[43]

- *Shape the context of administrative decisions through bureaucratic reorganization.* Interest groups seek to have decisions made in an atmosphere that is supportive of their objectives. Computer companies would rather have trade policy determined by the Commerce Department, which they regard as supportive of international sales, than by the State Department, which they view as unconcerned about trade issues.

- *Serve on departmental advisory committees.* Most administrative agencies have advisory committees that allow them to gather the views, expertise, and support of influential figures in their areas of responsibility. Service on these groups allows businesspeople to maintain contacts with top administrators, gather intelligence about shifts in agency perspectives, and promote their views at key points in the policy process.

- *Participate in rule making.* When agencies draft the rules that govern program implementation, the rules are published in draft form so that citizens and groups may comment. A recent study reported that 90 percent of trade associations and 88 percent of businesses took advantage of the rule-making process.[44]
- *Maintain staff contacts.* Business representatives maintain relations with key agency staffers so that they can better understand policy developments and ensure a sympathetic hearing when emergencies arise.

Administrative agencies are often arenas for conflict over major public policies. One environmental analyst describes the process in these terms: "When legislation is passed [by Congress] the contestants shift to the administrative agency, and when that goes the wrong way then to the courts."[45] Policy disputes occur in a succession of venues, and interest groups seek to gain advantage wherever they can.

LITIGATION AS A BUSINESS TACTIC

The significance of judicial involvement in business issues is growing. Although the judicial process is often used to restrain or penalize business, litigation has also become a nonmarket tactic used by corporate management to gain competitive advantage. As one analyst has commented, "The litigation game is yet another form of nonmarket tactic ever more frequently relied upon by management to assure corporate profitability or simple survival."[46]

The United States has the most politicized system of judicial selection of any major industrial country.[47] Most state judges are elected to office rather than appointed, and the typical career experience of top federal judgeships includes involvement in managing policy conflicts. Thus, the American judiciary is also more policy oriented and more deeply involved in administrative issues than are the judicial systems in other major countries.[48] Whereas courts once presumed that administrative actions were proper, judges now accept much of the capture theorists' indictment: bureaucracies are self-serving, excessively beholden to business, unresponsive to citizens, and uninformed about scientific advances. In recent decades, courts have relaxed the requirements to file cases, entertained challenges to administrative procedures, and questioned the substance of agency judgments.[49] As a consequence, the impact of judicial action on administrative issues is pervasive. By one estimate, 80 percent of administrative rules issued by the Environmental Protection Agency are challenged in court.[50]

Probably the most frequent corporate litigation situation with public significance involves suits in which one company argues that another has violated a law.
When computer makers started dropping Netscape's Navigator browser in favor
of Microsoft's Internet Explorer, Netscape's general counsel investigated Microsoft's
business practices.[51] Roberta Katz had been an undergraduate at Stanford in the
1960s, earned a doctorate in anthropology in the 1970s, and then decided to go to
law school. As the head of Netscape's legal department, Katz met with Justice
Department officials who were investigating whether the Microsoft Network would
permit Microsoft to monopolize online services. Katz was more concerned about
the browser industry than about online services, and she instructed Netscape's
outside counsel, the Silicon Valley law firm of Wilson, Sonsini, Goodrich and
Rosati, to complain to the Justice Department about Microsoft's conduct in the
browser business. Although the Microsoft Network failed to live up to expectations,
and America Online became the nation's online standard, Netscape's complaint to
the Justice Department went to the official who would later spearhead the prosecution of Microsoft for violating antitrust laws in the browser business.

The second type of business litigation situation with political relevance involves
corporate challenges to the legality of government action. Such challenges are not
new. Southern textile manufacturers mounted a successful challenge to the constitutionality of national child-labor laws in the early decades of this century.[52]
Recently, both labor unions and an industry group sued the Labor Department to
invalidate the department's rules covering the exposure of workers to formaldehyde,
and, a federal court agreed with SBC Communications that the FCC rules preventing local phone companies from offering long-distance service were unlawful.[53]

Corporate litigation may also seek to redefine the terms of marketplace competition. In product-liability cases, plaintiffs contend that they have been harmed by
products whose makers were negligent, and they seek compensation. The first
successful product-liability suit on behalf of a large group of plaintiffs was filed
against asbestos manufacturers in 1973,[54] and the asbestos companies have paid
more than $1 billion in damages. The manufacturers of silicone breast implants
were defendants in suits arguing that silicone had leaked out of implants, harmed
women's autoimmune processes, and caused tissue disease. The companies agreed
to pay more than $4 billion to settle the litigation.[55] State governments sued ciga-
rette companies to recover the costs of health care for people made ill by smok-
ing, and the tobacco companies agreed to pay $368 billion to end the controversy.[56]

The impact of the liability litigation system in the United States has become
a partisan issue. Major liability suits today resemble lobbying campaigns, with
PACs, soft-money contributions, media advisers, polling experts, focus groups,
and sponsored research, all aimed at swaying judges and juries. Corporations may
win almost all liability suits, but even one or two courtroom losses can cascade into
a movement that devastates a company or industry. Its critics say the process is inefficient and inequitable and rarely delivers the greatest benefits to those who have

suffered the greatest harm. Decisions inflict punishments that seldom fit the crime, and they impose burdens on people who have had nothing to do with the original litigation. Defenders insist that liability litigation is one of the few ways society has of holding wealthy corporations accountable for their actions, and they point out that liability judgments are almost the only means to help the victims of corporate misconduct achieve some measure of justice.

Business and other interest groups have established centers to move legal doctrine in directions they regard as favorable.[57] The Litigation Center of the U.S. Chamber of Commerce was founded in 1977 to shape public policy by participating in lawsuits and supporting companies that were involved in significant litigation.[58] The Chamber's Institute for Legal Reform was established in 1998 to play a more activist role by lobbying legislatures to change policy and working in campaigns to elect friendly judges. The institute was one of the forces behind the 2005 legislation that facilitates the shift of large class action lawsuits from state to federal courts. All parties recognize, however, that legal reform is a costly undertaking that might produce unfavorable publicity and undesirable precedents.

GOVERNMENT RELATIONS IN COMPARATIVE PERSPECTIVE

Lobbying practices reflect a country's governing institutions and political traditions. The U.S. Congress is the world's most assertive national legislature. Like legislatures elsewhere, it receives policy recommendations from the chief executive, but, unlike those of other countries, it then develops its own responses to the problems at hand. In contrast, a handbook for business lobbyists in Great Britain describes the role of Parliament in these terms: "Parliament is no longer—except in a few defined circumstances—a decision-maker in the public policy process. Its place in the power structure is that of an institution through which the Executive operates. . . . Unlike Congress in the United States, it does not lie at the centre of power . . . real power rests far further down the Civil Service hierarchy than is often believed."[59] U.S. administrative behavior also contrasts with the British practice.[60] The British administrative style stresses informality, flexibility, and accommodation, whereas American procedures are adversarial and legalistic. Private consultations with business are built into the British process, whereas the American approach restricts business contacts with agencies. Whereas British administrators make extensive use of self-regulation and negotiated compliance, U.S. firms are often prosecuted for violating administrative rules.

The European Union is a political system often said to suffer from a democratic deficit.[61] The popularly elected European Parliament (EP) has limited lawmaking authority, the members of the European Commission are appointed by the national governments, and the Council of Ministers is an assembly of national officials. To compensate for the European Union's weak electoral base and to build a constituency for its policies, the Commission has encouraged the creation of groups representing an array of economic and social interests.[62] In fact, Gigi Graziano describes the European Union as "a polity which greatly depends on interest groups for governance."[63]

Business dominates the Brussels interest group universe, and its causes are championed by individual companies, trade associations, national business organizations, and the European employers' federation, UNICE.[64] The limited role of the EP in the EU policy process minimizes the effectiveness of election-oriented lobbying techniques, such as campaign contributions and grassroots lobbying. Since the Council of Ministers represents national governments, it is usually susceptible to lobbying through national networks rather than through Brussels activism.

As the EU executive branch, the Commission and its Directorates General need the expertise and political support that interest groups can provide in order to administer programs and prevail in struggles with the Council of Ministers and the EP. The Commission is authorized to assemble expert groups to gather substantive and political information and contact any other organized communities it thinks might be helpful. Thus, groups that are best informed and most influential are afforded the fullest opportunity by the Commission to secure their lobbying objectives.

CORPORATE LOBBYING: PLURALISM OR HEGEMONY?

The fear that corporate lobbying gives moneyed groups excessive influence in the political process is an abiding concern of American voters. Whereas supporters see business involvement in politics as a legitimate reaction to complex problems, critics regard the linkage of economic power and political authority as ominous. Every year corporations and other groups spend billions to influence government decisions because they think these expenditures are effective. Surprisingly, political scientists have had little success in proving that corporate lobbying makes much difference.[65] To provide an understanding of the inconsistency between popular and academic views, in this section I explore the argument that business lobbying has little impact on policy decisions.

The Theory That Business Lobbying Has Little Impact

Four rationales are offered for the view that business lobbying has limited influence on public decisions: poor use of resources, countervailing pressures, primacy of public opinion, and routine interest group support.

Commentators recognize that business is a resourceful participant in the political process, but some maintain that business lobbyists do not use their resources effectively. They note that business has poor political intelligence and is forever seeking to catch up with events after they occur.[66] Business lobbyists often misread situations, become inflexible when they should compromise, and abandon their goals when victory is at hand. Business also fails to coordinate its efforts or develop coalitions. A recent study of proposals to increase corporate taxes concluded that the firepower of business "was potentially fatal to any piece of legislation," but it also noted that business groups "never managed to form an effective 'killer' coalition."[67]

Second, analysts believe that the lobbying power of business can be formidable when the business community is mobilized and united, but they maintain that this almost never occurs.[68] When business advocates take a public position on an issue, they are usually met by a chorus of lobbyists from other business groups championing a contradictory policy.[69] One liberal House member assessed the lobbying of the financial community in these terms: "Business PACs invest in incumbents. It's the banks against the thrifts, the insurance companies against the banks, the Wall Street investment banks against the money center commercial banks. There's money any way you vote."[70] In such conditions, the efforts of business lobbyists cancel each other out.

Third, studies of congressional lobbying question whether business is as influential as is usually thought under any circumstances. On the basis of their review of regulatory issues, Martha Derthick and Paul J. Quirk write: "We suspect that . . . interest group regimes today derive much of their apparent power merely from the absence of challenges . . . and not from any reliable ability to defeat such challenges when they occur. . . . [B]ehind their bloodless victories . . . lies far more vulnerability than has generally been supposed."[71]

These authors maintain that narrow political pressures are less influential than broad public sentiments. A study of environmental legislation and a cross-national review of business lobbying also conclude that business success in influencing legislative decisions depends less on lobbying tactics than on public opinion.[72] Finally, some studies do find a modest relationship between business lobbying, particularly PAC contributions, and the actions of legislators, but these cases still do not demonstrate any causal relationship.[73] Legislators receive campaign support from a group because they are disposed to support that group. The coincidence of lobbying and favorable member action could be a coincidence that would have occurred without any inducements.

Synthesis: The Context of Lobbying

The case for the limited impact of business lobbying has some appeal, but the argument fails to explain why journalists attribute such importance to lobbying activities and why business spends so much to support lobbying programs. In "What Corporations Really Want from Government," R. Kenneth Godwin and Barry J. Seldon begin to address these concerns by distinguishing between collective goods and private goods.[74] Collective goods are government benefits generally available to companies in an industry. Private goods, in turn, are government benefits that are available only to an individual firm. Collective goods characteristically result from broad policy decisions championed by business groups or coalitions and delivered through major legislation. The delivery of such benefits usually occurs only if sanctioned by broad public sentiment. In contrast, private goods are usually obtained through direct, personal contact with key legislators and administrators, and public officials are said to be responsive in these circumstances because they can provide benefits to one organization without facing opposition from others.

Most political science research on lobbying investigates highly visible issues that are framed by media coverage, public preferences, and interest group conflicts. These analyses usually examine roll-call votes in legislatures. They are an attempt to determine if various lobbying techniques, particularly PAC contributions, affect the way a legislator votes on particular issues. This concentration assumes that investigations of roll-call voting are the best way to assess the impact of lobbying. This may not be true. Roll-call voting, in fact, is a formal activity, wherein lobbying may be least influential. Lobbying may have more impact in the sponsorship of legislation, in negotiations over draft legislation, and in the diligence with which a legislator promotes a measure with colleagues, the administration, and agencies.

Godwin and Seldon suggest that most important lobbying issues are specialized questions that involve a single industry or firm, attract little public scrutiny, and inspire no countervailing lobbying activity. Although conceding that lobbyists probably have little impact on high-profile issues for which the patterns of public opinion are already well defined, Godwin and Seldon maintain that more far-reaching analyses of lobbying behaviors in legislative, administrative, and judicial arenas will probably conclude that lobbying is more influential than traditional analyses of roll-call voting have indicated. More persuasive assessments of the impact of lobbying can be done when more attention is devoted to describing the context in which lobbying occurs.

Summary

Corporations communicate their views to officeholders through business associations, their public affairs offices, contract lobbyists, or ad hoc coalitions. The selection of the particular form of lobbying depends on the frequency of the issue and its impact on specific firms. Common targets of business lobbying are Congress, the White House, executive agencies, and the judiciary.

Corporate lobbyists have distinct advantages and disadvantages in the political process, but they follow a common set of rules when they lobby Congress. They cultivate key figures, help shape the policy agenda, develop a sound argument, nurture the grassroots, build coalitions, understand PACs, use other political money carefully, and assist in campaigns. Business lobbyists turn to executive agencies because they help shape legislation, translate statutory generalities into specific rules, and apply administrative rules to individual cases. Since the U.S. judiciary is more policy oriented than judicial systems in other major countries, it too is a lobbying target of business and other business groups.

Suspicions that businesses have excessive political influence are widely held, but academics have had little success in demonstrating the impact of lobbying on political decisions. To assess the significance of lobbying, analysts should examine various types of political behavior and pay more attention to the context in which lobbying occurs.

FURTHER READINGS

For current information about federal campaign finance laws and donations to federal candidates, go to the Federal Election Commission Web site, http://www.fec.gov. See also the Common Cause analysis of the impact of special interest political contributions at http://www.commoncause.org, the Center for Responsive Politics political finance data at http://www.opensecrets.org, PoliticalMoneyLine at http://www.tray.com/cgi-win, and the Center for Public Integrity at http://publicintegrity.org.

Derthick, Martha A. *Up in Smoke: From Legislation to Litigation in Tobacco Politics,* 2nd ed. Washington, D.C.: CQ Press, 2005.

Hunt, Reed E. *You Say You Want a Revolution.* New Haven: Yale University Press, 2000.

Pedler, Robin, ed. *European Union Lobbying: Changes in the Arena.* New York: Palgrave, 2002).

Rozell, Mark J., and Clyde Wilcox. *Interest Groups in American Campaigns: The New Face of Electioneering.* Washington, D.C.: CQ Press, 1999.

Sifry, Micah L., and Nancy Watzman. *Is That a Politician In Your Pocket? Washington on $2 Million a Day.* Hoboken, N.J.: Wiley, 2004.

NOTES

1. This paragraph is based on Bara Vaida, "Gillespie's 'Kiss-and-Kiss,' " *National Journal,* February 19, 2005; Bara Vaida and Lisa Caruso, "Lobbying—Billable Hours," *National Journal,* March 26, 2005; and the Quinn Gillespie Web site, http://www.quinngillespie.com.
2. Kay Lehman Schlozman and John T. Tierney, *Organized Interests and American Democracy* (New York: Harper and Row, 1986), 272.
3. Robert E. Norton, "Can Business Win in Washington?" *Fortune,* December 3, 1990, 80.
4. Edwin M. Epstein, *The Corporation in American Politics* (Englewood Cliffs, N.J.: Prentice Hall, 1969), 67–69.
5. The following discussion is drawn from Raymond H. Bateman, "How to Be a Successful Lobbyist" (paper presented at Rutgers University Political Science Department, New Brunswick, N.J., March 26, 1988).
6. Thomas Byrne Edsall, *The New Politics of Inequality* (New York: Norton, 1984), 113–15.
7. Herbert Waltzer, "Advocacy Advertising and Political Influence: The Campaigns of Corporations to Cue the Public and Tether the Press" (paper presented at the annual meeting of the American Political Science Association, August 28–31, 1986. See also S. Parkash Sethi, *Advocacy Advertising and Large Corporations: Social Conflict, Big Business Image, the News Media, and Public Policy* (Lexington, Mass.: D. C. Heath, 1977); and S. Parkash Sethi, *Handbook of Advocacy Advertising: Concepts, Strategies, and Applications* (Cambridge, Mass.: Ballinger, 1987).
8. Robert L. Heath and Richard Alan Nelson, *Issues Management: Corporate Public Policymaking in an Information Age* (Beverly Hills, Calif.: Sage Publications, 1986), 57.
9. Myron Emanuel, Curtis L. Snodgrass, Joyce Gildea, and Karn Rosenberg, *Corporate Economic Education Programs: An Evaluation and Appraisal* (New York: Financial Executives Research Foundation, 1979).

10. Herbert Schmertz and William Novak, *Good-bye to the Low Profile: The Art of Creative Confrontation* (Boston: Little, Brown, 1986).

11. Andrew Rich and R. Kent Weaver, "Advocates and Analysts: Think Tanks and the Politicization of Expertise," *Interest Group Politics,* 5th ed., ed. Allan J. Cigler and Burdett A. Loomis (Washington, D.C.: CQ Press, 1998), 235–54; Sidney Blumenthal, *The Rise of the Counter-Establishment: From Conservative Ideology to Political Power* (New York: Harper and Row, 1988), 51–58; John S. Saloma, *Ominous Politics: The New Conservative Labyrinth* (New York: Hill and Wang, 1984), chaps. 2–3; Edsall, *New Politics of Inequality,* 117–20; Thomas Ferguson and Joel Rogers, *Right Turn: The Decline of the Democrats and the Future of American Politics* (New York: Hill and Wang, 1986), 103–5; and Jerome L. Himmelstein, *To the Right: The Transformation of American Conservatism* (Berkeley: University of California Press, 1990), 143–45.

12. This example is drawn from Jeffrey H. Birnbaum and Alan S. Murray, *Showdown at Gucci Gulch: Lawmakers, Lobbyists, and the Unlikely Triumph of Tax Reform* (New York: Random House, 1987), 111–12.

13. This section is based on Schlozman and Tierney, *Organized Interests and American Democracy,* 184–98.

14. See Schering-Plough, "Grassroots Network: A Program of Political Development," *Voice,* Fall 1989 and subsequent issues.

15. Ibid., 173.

16. Heath and Nelson, *Issues Management,* 101–3.

17. Sar A. Levitan and Martha R. Cooper, *Business Lobbies: The Public Good and the Bottom Line* (Baltimore: Johns Hopkins University Press, 1984), 140–42.

18. George Thayer, *Who Shakes the Money Tree? American Campaign Financing Practices from 1789 to the Present* (New York: Simon and Schuster, 1973), 48–50; and Michael J. Malbin, "Looking Back at the Future of Campaign Finance Reform: Interest Groups and American Elections," in *Money and Politics in the United States: Financing Elections in the 1980s,* ed. Malbin (Chatham, N.J.: Chatham House, 1984), 232–76, esp. 243–47.

19. See Federal Election Commission, "PAC Activity Increases for 2004 Elections," press release, April 13, 2005.

20. Candice J. Nelson, "The Money Chase: Partisanship, Committee Leadership Change, and PAC Contributions in the House of Representatives," in *The Interest Group Connection: Electioneering, Lobbying, and Policymaking in Washington,* ed. Paul S. Herrnson, Ronald G. Shaiko, and Clyde Wilcox (Chatham, N.J.: Chatham House, 1998), 52–64.

21. Theodore J. Eismeier and Philip H. Pollock, *Business, Money, and the Rise of Corporate PACs in American Elections* (New York: Quorum Books, 1988); and Edward Handler and John R. Mulkern, *Business in Politics: Campaign Strategies of Corporate Political Action Committees* (Lexington, Mass.: Lexington Books, 1982).

22. See J. David Gopoian, "What Makes PACs Tick? An Analysis of the Allocation Patterns of Economic Interest Groups," *American Journal of Political Science* 28 (May 1984): 259–81; and Schlozman and Tierney, *Organized Interests and American Democracy,* 240.

23. Michael Janofsky, "Advocacy Groups Spent Record Amount on 2004 Election," *New York Times,* December 17, 2004, A31.

24. PoliticalMoneyLine, http://www.tray.com/cgi-win/irs_ef_527.exe?DoFn=&sYR=2004, accessed April 6, 2004.

25. The large contributors were the Service Employees International Union; the American Federation of State, County and Municipal Employees; and the AFL-CIO. The individuals contributing $10 million were George Soros of Soros Fund Management, Peter Lewis of Progressive Corporation, Herbert and Marion Sandler of Golden West Financial, and Stephen Bing of Shangri-La Entertainment. In addition to the Web site in the previous note, see the Center for Responsive Politics, http://www.opensecrets.org/527s/527contribs.asp?cycle=2004 and http://www.opensecrets.org/527s/527indivs.asp?cycle=2004, and the Center for Public Integrity, http://publicintegrity.org/527/search.aspx?act=con&sec=indiv&sub=topindiv and http://publicintegrity.org/527/search.aspx?act=con&sec=org, all accessed April 8, 2004.

26. There are, of course, exceptions. See Ronald Brownstein, "So You Want to Go into Politics?" *Inc.,* November 1985, 98–107; and Nicholas Lemann, "New Tycoons Reshape Politics," *New York Times Magazine,* June 8, 1986, 51, 94, 101, 102.
27. Schlozman and Tierney, *Organized Interests and American Democracy,* 211.
28. Mark J. Rozell and Clyde Wilcox, *Interest Groups in American Campaigns: The New Face of Electioneering* (Washington, D.C.: CQ Press, 1999), 40, 108, 126, 140.
29. Monica Langley, "Black, Manafort and Stone Cuts Controversial Path between Campaign Consulting and Lobbying," *Wall Street Journal,* December 23, 1985, 38; and Thomas B. Edsall, "The Power Is Inside, but the Money Is Outside," *Washington Post National Weekly Edition,* December 5, 1985, 11–12.
30. See Darrell M. West and Burdett A. Loomis, *The Sound of Money: How Political Interests Get What They Want* (New York: Norton, 1998), chap. 6.
31. Ibid., chap. 5.
32. Eric M. Uslaner, "Lobbying the President and the Bureaucracy," in Herrnson, Shaiko, and Wilcox, *Interest Group Connection,* 206.
33. Cornelius M. Kerwin, *Rulemaking: How Government Agencies Write Law and Make Policy* (Washington, D.C.: CQ Press, 1994).
34. See Gary Bryner, *Bureaucratic Discretion: Law and Policy in Federal Regulatory Agencies* (New York: Pergamon Press, 1987), chap. 1; and Martin Shapiro, "Administrative Discretion: The Next Stage," *Yale Law Journal* 92 (1983): 1487–1522.
35. Epstein, *Corporation in American Politics,* 69.
36. A fine review of capture theories is found in Barry M. Mitnick, *The Political Economy of Regulation: Creating, Designing, and Removing Regulatory Forms* (New York: Columbia University Press, 1980), chaps. 2–3.
37. Paul J. Quirk, *Industry Influence in Federal Regulatory Agencies* (Princeton: Princeton University, 1981).
38. Bryner, *Bureaucratic Discretion.*
39. For this and the following sentence, see William T. Gormley Jr., "Interest Group Interventions in the Administrative Process: Conspirators and Co-Conspirators," in Herrnson, Shaiko, and Wilcox, *Interest Group Connection,* 217.
40. Bryner, *Bureaucratic Discretion,* 73–78, 85–87; Lawrence C. Dodd and Richard L. Schott, *Congress and the Administrative State* (New York: Wiley, 1979); and R. Douglas Arnold, *Congress and the Bureaucracy: A Theory of Influence* (New Haven: Yale University Press, 1979).
41. *Immigration and Naturalization Service v. Chadha,* 103 S.C. 2764 (1983); and R. Shep Melnick, "The Politics of Partnership," *Public Administration Review,* November 1985, 653–80.
42. Uslaner, "Lobbying the President and the Bureaucracy," 212.
43. Kerwin, *Rulemaking,* 200–203.
44. Ibid., 196–97.
45. Samuel P. Hayes, "The Politics of Environmental Administration," in *The New American State: Bureaucracies since World War II,* ed. Louis Galambos (Baltimore: Johns Hopkins University Press, 1987), 39–40.
46. David Chadwick-Brown, "Litigation as Private Formulation of Public Policy," *Journal of Contemporary Business* 10, no. 3 (1981): 121.
47. Mauro Cappelletti, *The Judicial Process in Comparative Perspective* (Oxford: Oxford University Press, Clarendon Press, 1989); and Mary L. Volcansek and Jacqueline Lucienne Lafon, *Judicial Selection: The Cross-Evolution of French and American Practices* (New York: Greenwood Press, 1988).
48. Jerold L. Waltman and Kenneth M. Holland, eds., *The Political Role of Law Courts in Modern Democracies* (New York: St. Martin's, 1988); see chapters on the Federal Republic of Germany, Japan, England, and the United States. See also Bryner, *Bureaucratic Discretion,* 210–12.
49. R. Shep Melnick, *Regulation and the Courts: The Case of the Clean Air Act* (Washington, D.C.: Brookings Institution, 1983), chap. 10.
50. Bryner, *Bureaucratic Discretion,* 117; and Joseph L. Badaracco, *Loading the Dice* (Boston: Harvard Business School Press, 1985), 128–31.

51. Joshua Quittner and Michelle Slatalla, *Speeding the Net: The Inside Story of Netscape and How It Challenged Microsoft* (New York: Atlantic Monthly Press, 1998), 268–73. For a different perspective, see Wendy Goldman Rohm, *The Microsoft File: The Secret Case against Bill Gates* (New York: Times Business Books, 1998).

52. Stephen B. Wood, *Constitutional Politics in the Progressive Era: Child Labor and the Law* (Chicago: University of Chicago Press, 1968).

53. Albert R. Karr, "Suits Aim to Alter OSHA's New Rules on Formaldehyde," *Wall Street Journal,* December 3, 1987, 12; Dick W. Olufs, *Making of Telecommunications Policy,* (Lynne Rienner, 1999), 152.

54. Marcia Angell, *Science on Trial: The Clash of Medical Evidence and the Law in the Breast Implant Case* (New York: Norton, 1997), 75–77.

55. In addition to Angell, *Science on Trial,* see Gina Kolata, "Panel Calls for Study of Some Implant Risks," *New York Times,* June 22, 1999, F8; and Ronald Bayer, ed., "Public Health Policy Forum," *American Journal of Public Health* 89 (April 1999): 483–96.

56. Carrick Mollenkamp, Adam Levy, Joseph Menn, and Jeffrey Rothfeder, *The People vs. Big Tobacco: How the States Took on the Cigarette Giants* (Princeton, N.J.: Bloomberg Press, 1998); Peter Pringle, *Cornered: Big Tobacco at the Bar of Justice* (New York: Holt, 1998); and Richard Kluger, *Ashes to Ashes: America's Hundred-Year Cigarette War, the Public Health, and the Unabashed Triumph of Philip Morris* (New York: Knopf, 1996).

57. Lee Epstein, *Conservatives in Court* (Knoxville: University of Tennessee Press, 1985); Waltman and Holland, *Political Role of Law Courts.*

58. This information is based on the U.S. Chamber of Commerce Web sites. See http://www.uschamber.com/nclc/ and http://www.instituteforlegalreform.org., accessed March 27, 2005; and Peter H. Stone, "Chamber Target: Securities Lawyers," *National Journal,* February 19, 2005.

59. Charles Miller, *Lobbying Government: Understanding and Influencing the Corridors of Power* (Oxford: Basil Blackwell, 1987), 36, 53. See also Wyn Grant and David Marsh, *The Confederation of British Industry* (London: Hodder and Stoughton, 1977), 129.

60. This discussion is based on David Vogel, *National Styles of Regulation: Environmental Policy in Great Britain and the United States* (Ithaca, N.Y.: Cornell University Press, 1986), esp. 22, 146, 194–95, 267, 282; Alan Peacock, ed., *The Regulation Game: How British and West German Companies Bargain with Government* (Oxford: Basil Blackwell, 1984), 101, 108, 129–30; and Badaracco, *Loading the Dice,* 131.

61. S. S. Andersen and K. A. Eliassen, eds., *The European Union: How Democratic Is It?* (London: Sage Publications, 1996).

62. See Jack L. Walker, *Mobilizing Interest Groups in America: Patrons, Professions, and Social Movements* (Ann Arbor: University of Michigan Press, 1991).

63. Gigi Graziano, "Lobbying and Interest Representation in Brussels" (paper presented at the annual meeting of the American Political Science Association, Boston, September 3–6, 1998), 25.

64. European Commission, *Directory of Interest Groups* (Luxembourg: Office of Official Publications of the European Communities, 1996).

65. See the excellent analysis in Frank R. Baumgartner and Beth L. Leech, *Basic Interests: The Importance of Groups in Politics and Political Science* (Princeton: Princeton University Press, 1998), esp. 128–36.

66. Levitan and Cooper, *Business Lobbies,* 68–82; and David Vogel, *Fluctuating Fortunes: The Political Power of Business in America* (New York: Basic Books, 1989), 11.

67. Birnbaum and Murray, *Showdown at Gucci Gulch,* 287.

68. For a classic statement of this position, see Raymond A. Bauer, Ithiel de Sola Pool, and Lewis Anthony Dexter, *American Business and Public Policy,* rev. ed. (Chicago: Aldine, 1972), pts. 4–6.

69. Dickinson McGaw and Richard McCleary, "PAC Spending, Electioneering and Lobbying: A Vector ARIMA Time Series Analysis," *Polity* 17 (Spring 1985): 574–85.

70. Quoted in Robert Kuttner, "Ass Backward," *New Republic,* April 22, 1985, 22.

71. Martha Derthick and Paul J. Quirk, *The Politics of Deregulation* (Washington, D.C.: Brookings Institution, 1985), 258.

72. Ronald Brownstein, "Trench Warfare," *National Journal,* September 14, 1985, 2047–53; and Alan Gladstone, "Employers Associations in Comparative Perspective: Functions and Activities," in *Employers Associations and Industrial Relations: A Comparative Study,* ed. John P. Windmuller and Alan Gladstone (Oxford: Oxford University Press, Clarendon Press, 1984), 27.

73. The classic statement of this view is found in Alexander Heard, *The Costs of Democracy* (Chapel Hill: University of North Carolina Press, 1960). See also W. P. Welch, "Campaign Contributions and Congressional Voting: Milk Money and Dairy Price Supports," *Western Political Quarterly* 35 (December 1982): 478–95; John R. Wright, "PACs, Contributions, and Roll Calls: An Organizational Perspective," *American Political Science Review* 79 (June 1985): 400–414; and Janet M. Grenzke, "Shopping in the Congressional Supermarket: The Currency Is Complex," *American Journal of Political Science* 33 (February 1989): 1–24.

74. R. Kenneth Godwin and Barry J. Seldon, "What Corporations Really Want from Government: The Public Provision of Private Goods," in *Interest Group Politics,* 6th ed., ed. Allan J. Cigler and Burdett A. Loomis (Washington, D.C.: CQ Press, 2002), 205–24.

CHAPTER 9

Why Does Business Win and Lose in Politics?

SCHOLARS WHO STUDY relations between government and business do not agree on everything they find. Driven by varied ideologies, they have devised the four models discussed in Chapter 2 to describe their understanding of how political systems operate: the business dominance model, the pluralist model, the market capitalism model, and the stakeholder model.

At the same time, most studies of business involvement in politics do agree on one point. Researchers are unanimous in recognizing that business organizations have substantial resources to deploy in the political process. In Charles E. Lindblom's formulation, business forces shape public attitudes, guide economic activity, and participate aggressively in the political process.[1] Lindblom insists that these advantages give business a "privileged position" from which it actually dominates politics; other scholars conclude that business is the single "most powerful interest group sector," and still other experts find simply that businesses "wield significant political power."[2] Since most researchers agree that businesses make up a resourceful group whose efforts usually influence public policy, we should explore both the circumstances in which businesses succeed in achieving their objectives and the conditions under which they fail.[3]

In this chapter I first explore why business wins or loses political contests by considering the relationship between business and political parties. In some countries, businesses' support for particular parties is their most effective strategy for influencing government policy. I then investigate business success and failure by reviewing studies of the context in which policy conflicts occur and by examining AT&T's remarkable experiences with government relations. I conclude the chapter by stepping back from specific events to consider how the characteristics of business systems in the United States affect business success in the political arena.

BUSINESS AND POLITICAL PARTIES: A COMPARATIVE PERSPECTIVE

Political parties represent societal interests to government and shape public policy. Formal affiliations between business groups and political parties are rare.[4] Businesses typically maintain working relations with all parties that might participate in government. Despite this, it is clear that business leaders prefer some parties to others. They have an affinity for parties whose programs promote the economy, particularly their industry, and an aversion to parties that restrict enterprise. The centrist or center-right parties favored by business advocate policies intended to spur economic growth. Left-center or leftist parties usually define themselves in regard to employees' economic and social rights.

Party divisions in Germany, Great Britain, Japan, and the United States are shown in Table 9-1 according to the orientation of the parties toward economic growth or employee rights. Parties in all countries have broader concerns than implied in this table, and the differences among parties are more pronounced in some nations than in others. Still, a review of the heritage and structure of party systems sheds valuable light on relationships between government and business in each country.

Germany

German political parties dominate the policy process.[5] In large measure, the party system is a product of the post–World War II era and reflects a break from earlier antidemocratic traditions.[6] German electoral laws limit representation in the national parliament to parties that receive at least 5 percent of the popular vote. In recent decades, two major and three smaller parties have entered parliament.

German parties are rooted in the country's historic social and economic divisions.[7] The German Social Democratic Party (SPD) has the strongest ties with past eras and remains the favored party of industrial workers and union families. It has abandoned its historic advocacy of the nationalization of industry, sought to expand worker participation in corporate decision making, and begun to entertain measures welcomed by the business community. The Christian Democratic Union (CDU) and its Bavarian affiliate, the Christian Social Union (CSU), attract support from Catholics, practicing Protestants, white-collar workers, farmers, and the traditional middle class; they present a nonsectarian appeal,

Table 9-1 Political Party Orientations

Country	Economic growth	Employee rights
Germany	Christian Democratic Union/ Christian Social Union Free Democratic Party	German Social Democratic Party
Great Britain	Conservative Party	Labour Party
Japan	Liberal Democratic Party	Democratic Party of Japan
United States	Republican Party	Democratic Party

Source: Author.

maintain ties to labor and social groups, and are sensitive to the interests of civil servants.

The Free Democratic Party (FDP) is a small, middle-class party that has played a key role in governing coalitions with both the CDU/CSU and the SPD. The party has supported market-based economic policies, civil liberties, and government assistance to small business. Its centrist position has checked the more extreme tendencies of the two larger parties.

In 1983 the Green Party became the first new party to be represented in the national legislature in thirty years. It gained support by emphasizing pro-environmental and antiestablishment positions, but internal divisions limited the party's impact, and it lost its national representation in 1990. The party reentered the parliament after reunification of the country in that same year, and in 1998 it became the junior partner in a governing coalition with the Social Democrats, its representative becoming the German foreign minister. After reunification, the Party of Democratic Socialism, the successor to the governing party in the German Democratic Republic, also won enough votes to enter parliament.

German political parties are, by Western standards, "conspicuously rich" institutions with "huge party staffs."[8] Germany began public financing of political parties in 1959, and the system now provides legislative parties, party organizations, and party foundations approximately 75 percent of their income.[9] In addition to public funds, parties receive significant amounts from membership dues and private, usually corporate, contributions. Public financing has sustained the minor parties and reduced, although certainly not ended, the influence of private donors.[10]

The direct participation of business leaders in German party politics today is described as "almost non-existent."[11] Another scholar adds, "Various studies have shown that most members of the present business elite believe that they have neither the time nor the skill to devote themselves very much to party politics."[12] This, of course, does not mean that there are no ties between business and the parties. About 10 percent of the members of the national legislature are middle-level business figures, and the FDP, in particular, has close financial and policy bonds with business groups.[13] Some business representatives develop personal ties to party leaders, occasionally participate in meetings of the CDU/CSU, FDP, and even the SPD, help shape party policy, and contribute to party coffers.

Great Britain

Great Britain has a highly organized party system that reflects its industrial heritage, but the class basis of politics is fading.[14] The British Labour Party emerged from the social dislocation of industrialization and was rooted in the union movement. Major industrial unions are affiliated with the Labour Party and provide much of its financial support.[15] Until the early 1990s the party had been divided between rigid socialists, who demanded nationalization of industry, and social democrats, who advocated increased social-welfare expenditures and more government intervention in the economy. The party had been held together by its commitment to the working class, but its unifying force had been weakened as traditional industries contracted.

By the time the Labour Party took control of government in 1997, the party had a new constitution, new structures, and new positions on issues.[16] Tony Blair was elected to head the party in 1994, and he set out to reverse the string of Conservative Party victories by transforming his party and its ideology.[17] In his speech to the 1995 Labour Party conference, Blair used the word *new* on fifty-nine occasions, sixteen times when he spoke of "New Labour."[18] In contrast, he did not refer to the working class even once. Blair's repositioning of "New Labour" shifted its position on three fundamental issues.[19] Labour's commitment to equality remained intact under Blair, but the party promised not to use progressive income taxes to promote equality. Whereas Labour had traditionally favored state ownership of industry and government intervention in the economy, it now applauded private enterprise and endorsed privatization. In contrast to its once-liberal social policies, Labour now opposed crime, attacked the "unacceptable level of anti-social behavior," and condemned "unduly lenient" judges. When Labour swept into office in 1997 with the largest majority it had ever won, the Conservative Party was wiped out in regions it had once dominated.[20]

Historically, the British Conservative Party had been less ideological than Labour. One British scholar has maintained that the defining characteristic of the Conservative Party is the preeminence of the party leader.[21] In the decades after World War II, Labour and Conservative governments agreed on the extent of government intervention in the economy and on labor-management issues. In the 1980s, however, Prime Minister Margaret Thatcher introduced a strident ideological element into British politics by championing free-market policies to revive the nation's faltering economy. Although achieving a substantial measure of success, Thatcher's policies remained a divisive force in the nation's politics. The electoral system allowed the Conservative Party to dominate the nation's politics for a decade even though it received only 40 percent of the popular vote. The party has benefited from the division of the anti-Conservative vote among Labour and two smaller parties, the Liberals and the Social Democrats.

British business has been sympathetic to the Conservative Party, and its support for Labour has traditionally been "negligible," but Blair's New Labour program has attracted visible support in the business community.[22] Despite this, "senior business leaders do not generally seek public office or play important roles" in party policies.[23]

Election campaigns in Britain are short, and British political parties are modestly funded.[24] They receive free broadcast time during election seasons and some support for legislative staff, but there is no general public financing of parties. At the national level, the Labour and Conservative parties receive about equal funding from unions and corporations, respectively. At the local level, the Conservatives have a financial advantage over Labour supporters because of their active local membership and donations from regional companies. The ideological repositioning of Labour has limited contributions from unions, and financial support of the Conservative Party by business has been declining.[25] Despite opposition to his Iraq policy, Prime Minister Blair led his party to a reelection victory in 2005.

Japan

Japanese politics remains in a state of flux as the country's party system struggles to adapt to new social and economic realities.[26] Until the early 1990s Japan provided the world's foremost example of a political system with free elections dominated by a single party.[27] The Liberal Democratic Party had been Japan's governing party since 1955, having overcome the country's ideological polarization by fashioning a political consensus based on economic growth and higher standards of living. The party's success in retaining power had rested on its ability to adapt to changing social and economic conditions, but the increasingly global economy has aggravated the government's problems and limited its revenues available to address them.[28]

When various LDP leaders broke ranks and founded new political parties in 1993, an anti-LDP coalition captured a legislative majority and gave Japan a non-LDP prime minister. The anti-LDP coalition, however, lacked stability, and it soon collapsed. The LDP first returned to power as a junior member of a coalition headed by the Japan Socialist Party, and it then recreated a single-party government following its success in the 1996 elections.[29]

Japan has had an extremely expensive political system.[30] According to one survey, Japan spent three times as much per person on parties and politics as Germany, four times as much as the United States, and eighteen times as much as Great Britain.[31] The LDP had traditionally been better financed than its campaign opponents, and, until the mid-1990s, the Japan Business Federation had been its principal contributor.[32] Within days of the LDP's 1993 defeat, however, the Federation announced that it would no longer collect donations from its members to support election campaigns.[33] Not long after, Japan adopted a system of public funding for elections.[34] Although contributions by private firms have dropped dramatically under the new system, increases in public funds mean that total campaign spending has declined rather slowly. The public finance scheme directs funds to political parties and bypasses individual candidates; this shift has increased the prominence of party-centered campaigns. Japan also adopted a new election system after the LDP's 1993 defeat. Under the current framework, 300 members of the lower house are elected from single-member districts and another 180 are selected according to a system of proportional representation from party-organized lists.

The continuing turmoil in the Japanese political process is also reflected in the rapid founding and subsequent demise of parties and factions. In the parliamentary elections of 2003 and 2004, the LDP received slightly less than half the total vote, whereas the Democratic Party of Japan captured about 35 percent of the returns. The falling away of the other small parties and the concentration of opposition to the LDP in the Democratic Party of Japan suggests that Japan may be slowly evolving into a two-party political system.[35]

The United States

When American parties were founded, government authority was decentralized, and parties were defined on a state and local base. In recent decades, party reforms have asserted the primacy of national rules over state practices. Campaign technology, communications patterns, and fund-raising practices have contributed to the nationalization of the party system, and the growth and professionalization of party staffs in Congress and at national party committees have furthered the nationalizing trends. Despite these developments, the federal system still sustains state and local party organizations.

American parties are candidate centered compared with the parties in other countries, and the ties between social groups and U.S. political parties are looser. The Republican Party was once made up of northeastern liberals and conservative Midwesterners, but the growth in population in the South and the Southeast has moved the party to a middle-class conservative base.[36] The Democratic Party once functioned as the agent of disadvantaged economic groups, labor union leaders, and conservative southerners, but it has encountered difficulty presenting an attractive national program as it has lost the allegiance of southern groups, industrial union membership has shrunk, and international economic concerns have become more prominent.

Election costs have increased dramatically in the United States in recent decades. American campaign finance is still candidate oriented, and the largest share of funds comes from citizens who support individual candidates, issues, or ideologies. Government funds now help finance presidential campaigns and state election contests, and public funding of legislative staffs constitutes, in part, public funding for legislative parties.

Businesses contribute substantial amounts to parties and campaigns. Corporate political action committees, however, are supported by employee contributions rather than company donations, and most are modestly funded. Corporate funds also assist national conventions, subsidize some legislative and party activities, and finance campaign activities in a few states. The corporate role in political finance was enhanced during the Clinton years by the popularization of soft-money contributions to political parties. Most soft-money contributions come from corporations, and, despite the law, much was used for election purposes.

Business contributions in the United States are less partisan than in other countries. Corporations and business groups in Japan, Great Britain, and even Germany direct the overwhelming share of their donations to parties concerned about economic growth and limit contributions to parties that stress employee rights. Partisan divisions in the United States are less clear, and business goals are more narrowly focused. The Republican Party receives substantial backing within the business community, but prominent business leaders endorse Democratic candidates in every election, and certain industries, such as the entertainment industry, consistently support Democratic candidates.

The political representatives of business in the United States are less ideological and more accommodationist than those in our other three countries. The U.S. Congress and its individual members are more influential than their parliamentary counterparts in the other countries. Congress struggles with the White House to control decision making in administrative agencies, and, thus, administrative decisions are more politicized in the United States. The explosive growth of soft-money contributions during the Clinton years and the proliferation of party fund-raising committees in Congress in previous decades, however, have now involved American businesses with political parties more closely than in earlier eras. Variations in the nature of political parties in our four countries highlight the importance of context in assessing the political prowess of business.

WINNING AND LOSING IN POLITICS

Most studies view lobbying as a contest among lobbyists for a legislator's favor that occurs immediately before a vote is cast. In the analysis of interest group activity, as Robert H. Salisbury points out, however, the "game metaphor is profoundly misleading."[37] Rather than understand lobbying as arm-twisting before a roll-call vote, Salisbury insists that interest group efforts be "seen in their larger historical/developmental context." Lobbying success depends on an array of institutional and issue-related factors. Four examinations of business victories and defeats focus on different aspects of the context in which lobbying occurred, and together they illustrate the importance of incorporating context into assessments of business power.[38]

David Vogel appraises the political influence of business in the United States, Great Britain, Germany, and Japan.[39] As a result of his investigation, Vogel concludes that business was most influential in Japan, followed by Germany, Great Britain, and the United States. Business in Japan occupied a truly privileged position, business and labor in Germany together constituted that nation's most powerful interest group sector, and the business communities in Great Britain and the United States could be seen as interest groups that wielded significant power.

Vogel explains the differences in business influence in the four nations by appraising the forces arrayed against business.[40] In Japan, bureaucratic and industrial elites constituted a cohesive social unit, and they faced few significant nonbusiness opponents. The German business community was exceptionally well organized and enjoyed direct access to government, but it faced a powerful trade union federation and an influential environmental movement. Both union forces in Britain and the public-interest movement in the United States articulated visions of society that implied restrictions on the role of business. Whereas the British business community was better organized than its American counterpart and had better access to government, business in the United States was fragmented and its relations with government agencies were episodic and occasionally adversarial.

The political strength of nonbusiness groups in the four countries, Vogel concludes, reflects the openness of a nation's political institutions to interest group pressures. Political and bureaucratic structures in Japan and Germany restrict the access of noneconomic groups to the political process, and thus business faces fewer opponents than in Great Britain and the United States. Rather than attributing political success or failure to the resources that business organizations bring to a policy battle, Vogel's assessments rest on the nature of the opposition to business. He contends, moreover, that "most of the factors that affect the relative political strength of business are outside the control of business."[41]

In *The Conspicuous Corporation: Business, Public Policy, and Representative Democracy,* Neil J. Mitchell accepts the premise that the political system favors business interests, but he also insists that business does not enjoy a political monopoly.[42] Business sometimes loses political contests, and Mitchell explains why.

At the center of Mitchell's analysis are public officials who have their own policy preferences. They want their ideas to become policy, but they also want to remain in office. Under most circumstances, Mitchell believes, business provides enough campaign resources to lead policymakers to accept business positions on policy issues. Policymakers, however, become disengaged from business interests under specific circumstances.[43] If business practices violate community standards, business positions may lose legitimacy. Facing legitimacy problems, the ability of businesses to support policymakers is impaired, and the attractiveness of business positions to policymakers is diminished. As a result, the likelihood of business reversals in the policy arena grows. Business interests may also suffer defeats when policymakers conclude that the antibusiness opposition's ability to mobilize the public outweighs the contributions business can make to officeholders. The most dangerous policy situation for business interests, according to Mitchell, occurs when political leaders are committed to their own policy goals, popular movements succeed in mobilizing voters, and political leaders and movements join to undermine business legitimacy.

Rather than focus on the legitimacy of business or the opposition to business, Jeffrey M. Berry attributes changes in the political power of business to a transformation in the U.S. issue agenda.[44] In *The New Liberalism: The Rising Power of Citizen Groups,* Berry argues that the agenda of American politics has shifted from economic issues to quality-of-life issues, from materialistic concerns to postmaterialistic topics, from economic development to lifestyle, status, morality, and individual rights. As a consequence, liberal citizen groups acquired resources, established institutional structures, and were embraced by the media. Television journalists, Berry found, were increasingly skeptical of the benefits of economic growth and displayed growing respect for those who sought to limit the freedom of corporations. Berry insists that liberal citizen groups have promoted postmaterialistic issues and that business has lost some of its preeminence as a result.

Berry prepared histories of 205 prominent issues considered by Congress, and these accounts document growing tensions between materialistic and postmaterialistic visions of society. Even though business fervently opposed most citizen group initiatives, they were not able to keep them off the legislative agenda. When these issues were considered by Congress, business organizations encountered growing difficulty in defeating them. In the earliest legislative period, business lost only infrequently, but business interests faced a more hostile environment as citizen groups became more numerous and more active. At the end, Berry reports, "business held only a modest advantage over citizen groups in its win to loss ratio."[45]

Gary Mucciaroni investigated national policymaking in the areas of taxation, business regulation, trade protection, and agriculture over several decades.[46] In the mid-1980s he found that Congress curtailed tax benefits for businesses and dismantled regulations that protected industries from competition while also increasing subsidies to agriculture and aiding producers who sought relief from foreign imports. In *Reversals of Fortune,* Mucciaroni asks why some industries succeeded in capturing new government benefits in these years whereas other producers were unable to defend the benefits they had long enjoyed. As Mucciaroni explores this question, he contends that we can "learn more about the political fortunes of interest groups by looking at the policymaking process in which they operate than by looking at the groups themselves."[47]

Producer group defeats, according to Mucciaroni, did not result from the pushing and hauling of organized interests, and they were not inflicted by the public-interest movement or postmaterialistic organizations. The principal opponents of producer groups were actually government actors, normally assembled in bipartisan coalitions including Republicans and Democrats, liberals and conservatives, and the executive and legislative branches of government. Whenever resistance to producer interests appeared, Mucciaroni found that administrative agencies played a key role in that opposition. The official actors responsible for producer defeats believed that the benefits to producer groups were too great, and these leaders held positions that were insulated from immediate electoral pressures and not subject to abrupt dismissal by unhappy constituents. Producer groups won their battles when their claims were thought to benefit the society rather than simply enrich shareholders and employees, and industries were treated more sympathetically when they were seen to be experiencing economic problems.

The four studies discussed here have examined business prowess in political conflicts. Unlike most accounts of lobbying, they do not explain the outcome of policy contests through scrutiny of group activity or enumeration of the resources that groups bring to a contest. These investigations look instead at the character of the issues being considered and the institutional context in which they are addressed. Each of these studies takes as a given that business has influence in the political process, but the four authors describe circumstances when this influence is not enough. For Vogel, the political aspirations of business can be checked by the nature of the opposition, whereas Berry traces successes and failures to the degree of harmony between business goals and societal values. Mitchell concludes that the political campaigns of business are likely to be futile if the conduct of business is perceived to be illegitimate and antibusiness organizers are seen to be successful in enlisting voter support. Mucciaroni demonstrates that business groups may be victorious when their objectives serve public purposes but are more likely to be defeated if public officials who are insulated from political pressures become convinced that the desires of business are unjustified. Despite its unlimited resources, AT&T's experiences in the political arena illustrate the significance of the political and institutional context in assessing the influence of business in politics. See Box 9-1.

Cases in Development
BOX 9-1 THE RISE AND FALL OF AT&T

AT&T, previously known as American Telephone & Telegraph, was once the largest corporation in the world, employing more than a million workers. The firm traced its heritage to an enterprise co-founded by Alexander Graham Bell, and it once symbolized the achievements and influence of American capitalism. The firm embraced and then embodied the concept of universal telephone service, and for generations the quality of its service was unmatched by any telecom firm in the world arena. AT&T stock became the bluest of blue chips, and its consistent dividends and steady performance made it the quintessential investment for widows and orphans.

Despite generations of success, AT&T failed to master the challenges of the modern communications era. Its stellar businesses lost their glitter, and an acquisition spree failed to produce the assets necessary to reshape its operations for the digital age. In 2002 the *New York Times* reported that

(continued)

investors in AT&T stock had lost nearly two-thirds of their investment in the previous decade, and in 2005, SBC Communications, once a small part of AT&T, sought government permission to take over what was left of AT&T.

How had such a distinguished enterprise lost so much of its grandeur? AT&T's Bell Labs had once been the world's foremost industrial laboratory, but AT&T remained stubbornly focused on long-distance service even though enhanced technologies had given its competitors better networks and lower costs. AT&T's enormous marketing power had once initiated styles, but more recently the firm had so badly underestimated the popularity of cell phones that it freely abandoned the lucrative business. Despite failures in technology and marketing, however, AT&T's downfall can be traced primarily to the fact that the company had lost its vaunted ability to manage government relations.

Competition in the telephone business had intensified at the start of the twentieth century, and the Bell system's ownership of installed telephones fell from 80 percent to below 50 percent. As marketplace challenges became acute, the Progressive Movement argued that the U.S. government should control large companies like AT&T, European countries concluded that telephone systems should be taken over by government, and Congress directed the Interstate Commerce Commission to regulate interstate telephone rates.

Faced with deteriorating economic and political situations, AT&T adopted the ingenious policy of championing government regulation. Telephone companies are public service institutions, the company declared, and they should be compelled to provide the highest standard of service. But AT&T also expected something in return, as it wrote in its 1910 *Annual Report:* "If there is to be State control and regulation, there should also be State protection—protection to a corporation striving to serve the whole community from aggressive competition. . . . That competition should be suppressed which arises out of the promotion of unnecessary duplication." The public should be protected, AT&T proclaimed, by suppressing competition and increasing regulation.

In these years, the Department of Justice (DOJ) had been told that AT&T was abusing its market position, and it launched an investigation of the firm's conduct. After protracted negotiations, an AT&T official promised the attorney general that in the future AT&T would allow non-Bell companies use of its long-distance network, permit these firms to remain independent, and provide the government low-cost communications services. AT&T recognized that appropriate initiatives could transform government regula-

(*continued*)

tors from indefatigable foes into invaluable allies. Before long, AT&T, with government help, had reclaimed 80 percent of the local exchange market, controlled almost all long-distance business, dominated the market for telecommunications equipment, and organized the industry's dominant research organization. Alan Stone's telecom history concludes that AT&T won almost every government relations battle in which it participated before 1968, but he finds that it lost most policy clashes after that.

As the importance of competition as a public policy emerged in the mid-1970s, the DOJ again alleged that AT&T was monopolizing phone service. AT&T replied that it managed telephone operations under government supervision and it provided high-quality service at low prices while making modest profits. Failing to head off the DOJ's investigation, AT&T then called on Congress to preempt the DOJ's suit by enacting legislation that would sanction the firm's conduct, but AT&T failed to assemble the necessary majorities, and the legislation died. No trial had yet begun when Ronald Reagan became president, and AT&T went to work persuading key figures of the administration to oppose the suit. At a meeting of the Cabinet Council on Commerce and Trade, the secretaries of defense and commerce argued to President Reagan that the suit against AT&T should be dismissed because breaking up AT&T would destroy the unified communications system needed for national security and dismember a company that was helping relieve the country's balance-of-payments problems. As the debate died down, the group turned to President Reagan, but the president stood up and left for lunch. The meeting adjourned without any decision on AT&T, and the DOJ's prosecution of AT&T continued.

AT&T's antitrust trial began in 1981, and the trial judge brusquely dismissed AT&T's arguments and ruled that the government had established the presumption that the company had violated the Sherman Act. Although AT&T could still offer its defense, the firm's prospects appeared grim, and settlement negotiations became the center of action. The head of the DOJ's Antitrust Division at this time was an obscure Stanford law professor named William Baxter. Baxter insisted that AT&T give up all its local telephone business, then constituting two-thirds of the company's total assets, in order to retain ownership of its long-distance service, manufacturing, Bell Labs, and the Yellow Pages. Having failed to block the DOJ investigation, mobilize Congress, enlist the aid of the president, or win over the trial judge, AT&T was compelled to accept Baxter's terms.

As AT&T restructured its operations after having surrendered the local telephone service, its record of success in government relations continued

(continued)

to be dismal. Although AT&T had expected to have a free hand to compete in its remaining businesses, the trial judge retained jurisdiction over the DOJ's antitrust case and used his control of the suit to restrict AT&T's operations. When AT&T tried to sell its products and services to local telephone customers, the FCC allowed the local phone companies to frustrate AT&T's efforts to reach the customers. Congress then allowed the local phone companies to enter the long-distance market to compete against AT&T, and another Appeals Court invalidated the regulations under which AT&T had begun to provide local phone service. AT&T was the master of its relations with government when it could credibly argue that its goals also served a public interest, but, despite its enormous resources, AT&T lost its political battle when other companies convinced officials that they would promote the society's interests more effectively than AT&T.

Sources: Richard R. John, "Theodore N. Vail and the Civic Origins of Universal Service," *Business and Economic History* 28 (Winter 1999): 71–81; Floyd Norris, "After Some Hostility, AT&T Shareholders Approve Breakup," *New York Times,* July 11, 2002, http://www.nytimes.com; Reuters, "AT&T Racks Up a $12.7 Billion Loss after Charges," *New York Times,* July 23, 2002, http://www.nytimes.com; Richard Waters, "The Twists and Turns of a Tangled Telecom Strategy," *Financial Times,* October 25, 2001, 22; James B. Murray, *Wireless Nation: The Frenzied Launch of the Cellular Revolution in America* (Cambridge, Mass.: Perseus, 2001), 26; W. Russell Neuman, Lee McKnight, and Richard Jay Solomon, *The Gordian Knot: Political Gridlock on the Information Highway* (Cambridge, Mass.: MIT Press, 1998), 156–58 and 160–65; Roger G. Noll and Bruce M. Owen, "The Anticompetitive Uses of Regulation: *United States v. AT&T,*" in *The Antitrust Revolution,* ed. John E. Kwoka and Lawrence J. White (Glenview, Ill.: Scott, Foresman, 1989), 291; and AT&T, *Annual Report, 1910,* 32, 33, reprinted in Alan Stone, *How America Got On-Line: Politics, Markets, and the Revolution in Telecommunications* (Armonk, N.Y.: M. E. Sharpe, 1997), 31, also 12 and 66. For a discussion of the case, see Steve Coll, *The Deal of the Century: The Breakup of AT&T* (Boston: Atheneum, 1986); Peter Temin with Louis Galambos, *The Fall of the Bell System* (New York: Cambridge University Press, 1987).

HALLMARKS OF BUSINESS IN AMERICAN POLITICS

American business pursues its political goals in a policy environment with unique characteristics. The comparisons between the United States and our other countries in the previous chapters highlight distinctive features of the American context. From the beginning, the United States possessed one policy tradition that emphasized the importance of markets and individual activity and another that stressed the significance of governments and collective political decisions. This dual heritage has allowed policymakers to draw upon both traditions to create a changing mix of policies to respond to the country's dynamic economic circumstances. The nation's business system took shape before government became an everyday force in the society, and business organizations developed into preeminent community institutions that defined their own course when the capacity of government to regulate business was quite limited. The American system of corporate governance accepted the enormous power of the founders of the giant firms and extended this authority to the chief executive officers who succeeded them, whereas, in contrast, boards of directors, banks, business associations, and employee representatives have had a more limited role than in other major industrial nations. Because most American businesses do not have constant contact or automatic access to government decision making, they frequently develop policy perspectives that depart from those of government, and, consequently, they have devised strategies to communicate their views to government officials when they conclude it is needed.

The structure of American government disperses authority widely, minimizes the coordinating role of political parties, exalts individual legislators and legislative bodies, and politicizes the activities of administrative agencies and the judiciary. The fragmentation of government authority complicates the government relations function for business and increases the resources needed to carry out that task. Without a dominant locus of public power, the U.S. system rarely sets clear government priorities, seldom coordinates its diverse policies, and usually creates a process for implementing public policies that is contentious and unreliable.

The American system of government is unusually responsive to changes in public sentiment, and the fragmentation of power encourages the creation of interest groups and their increasing participation in government decisions. As a consequence of this openness, American business faces a catalog of resourceful opponents that find support among the media, foundations, and universities; and corporations, moreover, commonly find themselves under political assaults inspired by competing firms. Public opinion in the United States is fluid and dynamic, and it displays starkly ambivalent attitudes toward business. Big business is regarded by a large majority of citizens as necessary for the country's economic progress, and it is lauded for offering the society good products and services and providing workers gainful employment. At the same time, however, business is distrusted by equally large majorities for being too powerful and for placing the desire for profits above the broader interests of the society. Half the population believes that many of the largest companies ought to be broken up for the nation's good. Furthermore, the increasing globalization of the economy and the growing international exposure of large U.S. firms are undermining the positive qualities commonly associated with American business in the public mind.

In the preceding chapters I have identified the enormous resources that business interests possess to pursue their political goals. Because these vast resources will probably continue to be available in the future, any assessment must conclude that business influence in the political process is certainly powerful. At the same time, the distinctive context of American political activity qualifies the exercise of political power by business. The fragmentation of the American political system, the resources available to business opponents, the significance of public opinion and its ambivalence toward business, divisions within the business community, and the unpredictability of the policy process all increase the vulnerability of business to hostile political action. Although there can be no doubt that business is a powerful force in American politics, the context of interest group activity in the United States leaves business interests with a precarious place in the policymaking process. In the following chapters I investigate public policies in six areas that are critical to the success of the American economy.

SUMMARY

Most scholars agree that businesses are influential political actors, but the extent of their influence varies by country and circumstance. Businesses exercise their political influence through relations with political parties that sometimes seek to promote economic growth and on other occasions strive to improve conditions for workers. Political parties in the United States are more candidate centered than parties in our other countries, have looser ties with social groups, and are less partisan and more accommodationist in their campaign contributions. Various researchers have argued that the circumstances in which political action occurs affect the extent of business influence. Vogel argues that the political strength of business reflects the influence of the opponents of business in the political system. The stronger the opponents of business, the less influence businesses can marshal. Mitchell submits that business forces are more influential when the public regards business conduct as legitimate, but he insists that the power of business tumbles when public confidence in the legitimacy of business behavior falls. Berry maintains that the political influence of business depends on the values that dominate the society at any one time. When economic issues are foremost in people's minds, businesses tend to prevail, but when public concerns shift to lifestyle, morality, and individual rights, citizen groups gain prominence. Mucciaroni contends that administrative agencies play a key role in delivering defeats to the business community because their insulation from the electoral process allows them to determine whether the benefits claimed by businesses are already excessive or are, in fact, inadequate to meet the challenges of the times. The case study of the rise and fall of AT&T provides a basis to evaluate the contentions of the various authors about the factors that determine whether business wins or loses in politics.

FURTHER READINGS

The Web site for the Democratic National Committee is http://www.democrats.org; the Republican National Committee site is http://www.rnc.org; the

House of Representatives Republican Policy Committee Web site is http:// www.policy.house.gov; and the Senate Democratic Policy Committee is found at http://www.dpc.senate.gov.

For the British Conservative Party, see http://www.conservative-party.org.uk; for the Labour Party, see http://www.labour.org.uk; and for the Liberal Party, see http://www.libparty.demon.co.uk. For the German CDU, go to http://www. cdu.de, and click on "Englisch" for information in English; for the SPD, go to http://www.spd.de, and click on "English Pages." The Web sites of the smaller parties offer information only in German: for the FDP, see http://www. liberale.de; for the Greens, see http://www.gruene-fraktion.de; and for the PDS, see http://www.pds-online.de.

Bowman, John R. *Capitalist Collective Action: Competition, Cooperation and Conflict in the Coal Industry.* Cambridge: Cambridge University Press, 1989.

Grant, Wyn. *Pressure Groups in British Politics.* New York: St. Martin's, 2000.

McGillivray, Fiona. *Privileging Industry: The Comparative Politics of Trade and Industrial Policy.* Princeton: Princeton University Press, 2004.

Reed, Steven R., ed. *Japanese Electoral Politics: Creating a New Party System.* New York: Routledge Curzon, 2003.

Vogel, David. *Kindred Strangers: The Uneasy Relationship between Politics and Business in America.* Princeton: Princeton University Press, 1996.

NOTES

1. Charles E. Lindblom, *Politics and Markets: The World's Political-Economic Systems* (New York: Basic Books, 1977), esp. chap. 13.
2. "most powerful interest group sector": Jeffrey M. Berry, *The New Liberalism: The Rising Power of Citizen Groups* (Washington, D.C.: Brookings Institution Press, 1999), 86; "wield significant political power": David Vogel, *Kindred Strangers: The Uneasy Relationship between Politics and Business in America* (Princeton: Princeton University Press, 1996), 265.
3. Frank R. Baumgartner and Beth L. Leech, *Basic Interests: The Importance of Groups in Politics and in Political Science* (Princeton: Princeton University Press, 1998), 146.
4. John Windmuller and Alan Gladstone, eds., *Employers Associations and Industrial Relations: A Comparative Study* (Oxford: Oxford University Press, Clarendon Press, 1984), 27.
5. Peter J. Katzenstein, *Policy and Politics in West Germany: The Growth of a Semisovereign State* (Philadelphia: Temple University Press, 1987), 36. See also Lewis J. Edinger, *West German Politics* (New York: Columbia University Press, 1986), 227.
6. Gerald Braunthal, *Parties and Politics in Modern Germany* (Boulder, Colo.: Westview Press, 1996); William M. Chandler, "Party Transformations in the Federal Republic of Germany," in *Parties and Party Systems in Liberal Democracies,* ed. Steven B. Wolinetz (London: Routledge, 1988), 70; and Gordon Smith, "The 'Model' West German Party System," in *The Federal Republic of Germany at Forty,* ed. Peter H. Merkl (New York: New York University Press, 1989), 249–64.
7. See Merkl, *Federal Republic of Germany at Forty;* H. G. Peter Wallach and George K. Romoser, eds., *West German Politics in the Mid-Eighties: Crisis and Continuity* (New York: Praeger Special Studies, 1985); and Stephen Padgett and Tony Burkett, *Political Parties and Elections in West Germany: The Search for a New Stability* (London: C. Hurst, 1986).
8. William E. Paterson, "West Germany: Between Party Apparatus and Basis Democracy," in *Political Parties: Electoral Change and Structural Response,* ed. Alan Ware (Oxford: Basil Blackwell, 1987), 181; see also Arthur B. Gunlicks, "The Financing of German Political Parties," in Merkl, *Federal Republic of Germany at Forty,* 228–45.

9. Karl-Heinz Nassmacher, "Oeffentliche Parteienfinanzierung in Westeuropa: Implementationsstrategien und Problembestand in der Bundesrepublik Deutschland, Italien, Oesterreich und Schweden," *Politische Vierteljahresschrift* 28, no. 1 (March 1987): 109.

10. Arnold J. Heidenheimer, "Adenauer's Legacies: Party Finance and the Decline of Chancellor Democracy," and Gunlicks, "Financing of German Political Parties," 213–45.

11. B. Wessels, "Federal Republic of Germany: Business Profits from Politics," in *The Politicisation of Business in Western Europe,* ed. M. P. C. M. van Schendelen and R. J. Jackson (London: Croom Helm, 1987), 148.

12. Edinger, *West German Politics,* 200.

13. Katzenstein, *Policy and Politics in West Germany,* 14.

14. See Stephen Ingle, *The British Party System* (Oxford: Basil Blackwell, 1987); Peter Byrd, "Great Britain: Parties in a Changing Party System," in Ware, *Political Parties,* 205–24; and George Breckenridge, "Continuity and Change in Britain," in Wolinetz, *Parties and Party Systems in Liberal Democracies,* 203–21.

15. Byrd, "Great Britain," 212.

16. This paragraph is based on Patrick Seyd, "Tony Blair and New Labour," in Anthony King, David Denver, Iain McLean, Pippa Norris, Philip Norton, David Sanders, and Patrick Seyd, *New Labour Triumphs: Britain at the Polls 1997* (Chatham, N.J.: Chatham House, 1998), 49–50.

17. David Denver, "The Government That Could Do No Right," in King and others, *New Labour Triumphs,* 39.

18. Seyd, "Tony Blair and New Labour," 49.

19. David Sanders, "The New Electoral Battleground," in King and others, *New Labour Triumphs,* 236–37.

20. Anthony King, "The Night Itself," in King and others, *New Labour Triumphs,* 236–37.

21. Ingle, *British Party System,* 67.

22. Wyn Grant, with Jane Sargent, *Business and Politics in Britain* (London: Macmillan Education, 1987), 172.

23. A. G. Jordan and J. J. Richardson, *Government and Pressure Groups in Britain* (Oxford: Oxford University Press, Clarendon Press, 1987), 242.

24. Vernon Bogdanor, "Financing Political Parties in Britain," in *Parties and Democracy in Britain and America,* ed. Bogdanor (New York: Praeger, 1984); Grant, *Business and Politics in Britain,* chap. 8; and Byrd, "Great Britain."

25. Grant, *Business and Politics in Britain,* 184; and Bogdanor, "Financing Political Parties in Britain," 141.

26. T. J. Pempel, *Regime Shift: Comparative Dynamics of the Japanese Political Economy* (Ithaca, N.Y.: Cornell University Press, 1998), 203–16.

27. This section is based on Hans Baerwald, *Party Politics in Japan* (Boston: Allen and Unwin, 1986); Gerald L. Curtis, *The Japanese Way of Politics* (New York: Columbia University Press, 1988); Michio Muramatsu and Ellis S. Krauss, "The Conservative Policy Line and the Development of Patterned Pluralism," in *The Political Economy of Japan,* vol. 1, ed. Kozo Yamamura and Yasukichi Yasuba (Stanford, Calif.: Stanford University Press, 1987), 515–54; J. A. A. Stockwin, "Parties, Politicians and the Political System," in J. A. A. Stockwin, Alan Rix, Aurelia George, James Horne, Daiichi Itō, and Martin Collick, *Dynamic and Immobilist Politics in Japan* (Honolulu: University of Hawaii Press, 1988), 22–53; and J. A. A. Stockwin, "Japan: The Leader-Follower Relationship in Parties," in Ware, *Political Parties,* 96–116.

28. Curtis, *Japanese Way of Politics,* 82; see also Pempel, *Regime Shift,* 205.

29. Curtis, *Japanese Way of Politics,* 127–33.

30. Ronald J. Hrebenar, "The Money Base of Japanese Politics," in *The Japanese Party System,* ed. Hrebenar (Boulder, Colo.: Westview Press, 1992), 54–78.

31. Chalmers Johnson, *Japan: Who Governs? The Rise of the Developmental State* (New York: Norton, 1995), 215.

32. Frank Gibney, "Introduction," and Yasuhiro Nakasone, "Politicians, Bureaucrats, and Policymaking in Japan," in *Unlocking the Bureaucrat's Kingdom,* ed. Gibney (Washington, D.C.: Brookings Institution Press, 1998), 4, 50.

33. Leon Hommerman, "Whither Deregulation? An Epilogue to Japan's Industrial Policy," in Gibney, *Unlocking the Bureaucrat's Kingdom,* 267.

34. Steven R. Reed, ed., *Japanese Electoral Politics: Creating a New Party System* (New York: Routledge Curzon, 2003), 180.

35. Ibid., 186.

36. For a somewhat different interpretation, see Thomas Byrne Edsall, *The New Politics of Inequality* (New York: Norton, 1984), 67–68.

37. This quote and the subsequent one are from Robert H. Salisbury, "Interest Structures and Policy Domains: A Focus for Research," in *Representing Interests and Interest Group Representation,* ed. William Crotty, Mildred A. Schwartz, and John C. Green (Washington, D.C.: University Press of America, 1994), 17–18.

38. For the importance of context in understanding interest groups, see also John Heinz, Edward O. Laumann, Robert L. Nelson, and Robert H. Salisbury, *The Hollow Core: Private Interests in National Policy Making* (Cambridge, Mass.: Harvard University Press, 1993).

39. Vogel, *Kindred Strangers,* chap. 11. Vogel also includes France in his analysis.

40. Ibid., 318.

41. Ibid., 316.

42. Neil J. Mitchell, *The Conspicuous Corporation: Business, Public Policy, and Representative Democracy* (Ann Arbor: University of Michigan Press, 1997), chap. 1 and pp. 7, 59, 167–74, 191, 216–17.

43. Mitchell also says that some "heroic" policymakers may become indifferent to the political consequences of their acts and reject business interests even it costs them political support, in ibid., chap. 10, esp. p. 216.

44. Berry, *The New Liberalism,* 2, 5, 29, 61, 83, 84, 86, 130.

45. Ibid., 75–76.

46. Gary Mucciaroni, *Reversals of Fortune: Public Policy and Private Interests* (Washington, D.C.: Brookings Institution, 1995), 2, 4, 9, 11, 13, 19, 165, 181.

47. Mucciaroni, *Reversals of Fortune,* 26.

PART III

Government Policies and Business

CHAPTER 10

Business and Economic Policy

ECONOMIC POLICIES THAT produce robust growth with high employment and low inflation are cheered on all sides. They are associated with rising personal income and improved living standards for citizens, as well as high popularity ratings and increased reelection chances for incumbent officeholders. Economic policies also help determine corporate profits and prospects. They set the tax rates paid by businesses and affect the quantity of goods and services customers can purchase. Economic policies influence the cost and availability of credit, and this, in turn, guides business decisions to invest in new plants and equipment or delay initiatives until conditions are more favorable. Government policies are also a factor in setting currency exchange rates, which help determine whether a company succeeds at selling its products globally or faces intensified competition in its domestic market.

The single most significant development in U.S. public policy since World War II has been the popular acceptance of government responsibility for maintaining the health of the *macroeconomy*—meaning the economy considered in its totality. Although the American tradition still respects markets, business organizations, and individual choice, government is now expected to ensure economic growth, maintain high employment rates, and prevent excessive inflation. When an economy is in recession, economic activity declines and production falls, the need for workers decreases, incomes drop, consumption is reduced, profits decline, and demand for government services grows. Furthermore, recessions are now political as well as economic events. They are usually laid at the feet of incumbent officeholders, especially presidents, and taken as evidence of an administration's failure to manage policy effectively. Conversely, presidents are quick to claim credit for favorable economic events that occur during their tenure, even if these developments have resulted from the actions of their predecessors, other officials, the opposite party, or the private sector.

Monetary and fiscal policies are government's most prominent tools for guiding the nation's economy. *Fiscal policy* refers to the use of the government's power to tax and spend so as to affect the aggregate or overall level of demand in the economy. An expansionary fiscal policy increases demand by boosting spending and reducing taxes; such a policy stimulates employment and economic growth. A policy of fiscal contraction reduces aggregate demand by lowering expenditures and raising taxes. *Monetary policy* influences the economy by altering the supply of money. An increase in the supply of money is expected to increase spending by reducing interest rates, and a decline in the money supply is believed to increase interest rates and reduce spending. Although fiscal policy is focused on the federal budget, monetary policy is based on the actions of the Federal Reserve System. Even though the Federal Reserve cannot dictate interest rates throughout the economy, its ability to expand the availability of credit and lower its price can increase the money supply and thus stimulate demand. Conversely, the Federal Reserve can restrict credit, reduce the money supply, ease aggregate demand, and slow economic activity.

Businesspeople evaluate public policies according to the same standards most people use: their personal views about what is good for society, and the immediate impact of policies on their individual interests. Businesspeople usually advocate a limited role for government in society and endorse public policies that preserve the autonomy of private organizations, such as businesses. Business representatives, however, also champion policies that benefit their organizations. They routinely abandon their ideology and endorse a more interventionist role for government when considering policies that advance their company's objectives.

In this chapter I examine the institutions that make monetary and fiscal policy in the United States and the recent history of policies in this domain. Surpluses, deficits, debts, and other recent policy issues are explored, with a highlight on the tension between macroeconomic policy and a government structure that emphasizes interest group representation. The subsequent chapters in Part III continue the focus on public policy: Chapter 11 covers regulatory policies; Chapter 12, antitrust issues. Competitiveness and industrial policy form the centerpiece of Chapter 13, and developments in trade policy are considered in Chapter 14. Chapter 15 concludes the book with a survey of the role of business in social policies.

FISCAL POLICY

Fiscal policy involves the use of the national government's taxing and spending authority to influence the country's economy. Prior to the Great Depression of the 1930s, the government's normal response to fluctuations in the economic cycle was to stand back and let them play themselves out—to pursue a laissez-faire policy. Traditional laissez-faire economists believed that an economy would automatically correct its imbalances and move toward a state of equilibrium. They expected the dynamics of supply and demand to help an economy adjust to recessions and inflation without government action. In recessionary times, when demand for goods and services was slack, prices would fall, the revenues of less efficient producers would drop, workers would be laid off, and poorly managed factories would shut down. With productive capacity declining, however, prices would in due course stabilize. After the weaker firms had withdrawn from the market, the stronger companies would supply the society's goods in a more efficient manner that would strengthen the overall economy. Demand would increase, productive capacity would be strained, producers would raise prices, and the economic cycle would begin again. Laissez-faire economists thus regarded layoffs, bankruptcies, and downturns in the economy not as something to be avoided but as elements of a natural process that would eventually improve the economy and restore it to equilibrium. Government action, they believed, was less likely to relieve suffering and revive economic activity than to disrupt the natural recuperative powers of the market system.

The Great Depression of the 1930s, however, rippled throughout the economy in ever-widening circles without creating the equilibrium that laissez-faire economists anticipated. Aggregate spending was low, and unemployment rates remained unacceptably high. John Maynard Keynes was a British economist who altered the way economists understood business cycles and conceptualized the role of government in the economy. Standard economists believed that a given level of demand in an economy would produce a commensurate amount of employment. Keynes agreed, but he also insisted that low employment during the depression resulted from inadequate demand. Aggregate demand in an economy is the sum of consumer spending, private investment spending, and government spending, and Keynes argued that government could remedy recessions by increasing demand. To counter a recession, government could either reduce taxes to spur consumer or investment spending, or it could directly increase its own spending, even if this meant that government would spend more than it took in and incur a deficit. Conversely, government could also tame the ravages of inflation by reducing aggregate demand through tax increases and expenditure reductions.

It was not until John F. Kennedy became president in 1961 that Keynesian fiscal policy received its first significant reality test.[1] Kennedy had campaigned in 1960 on the promise to create a full-employment economy and to get the country "moving again." Nevertheless, he was faced with the lingering effects of the mild 1960 recession and the looming prospect of another economic downturn in 1962. Kennedy's Keynesian advisers convinced him of the need to stimulate the economy to boost employment, and they proposed to do this through a program of federal expenditure increases, even though this would increase the federal deficit. Kennedy, however, was sensitive to criticism in Congress and the business community that a surge in federal spending and an increase in the deficit would trigger a new round of inflation. To overcome political opposition to his economic program, Kennedy decided to increase aggregate demand in the economy by cutting taxes rather than by increasing federal expenditures. Tax cuts would prime the economic pump by giving citizens and businesses the wherewithal to increase spending on goods and services in the private marketplace rather than by relying on government expenditures to do the job through the public sector. Kennedy recognized that tax cuts would reduce federal revenues in the short run, but, anticipating the supply-side debates of the Reagan era, he argued that reductions in taxes might provide enough economic stimulus to offset the loss in revenues and perhaps even produce a surplus.[2]

The result of this debate was the Revenue Act of 1964, adopted after President Kennedy's death, which cut personal income tax rates by 25 percent, lowered the corporate income tax, and reduced the tax burden on investment. The tax-cut stimulus did, in fact, produce the anticipated budgetary results. Aggregate spending rose, the deficit declined, and the unemployment rate fell to less than 4 percent, its lowest level in peacetime history.[3]

The President

Responsibility for fiscal policy is shared by Congress and the president. Even though Congress has the constitutional authority to impose taxes and appropriate funds, it is the president who has become the principal figure in the conduct of fiscal policy. The president's original role was based on the Budget and Accounting Act of 1921, which authorized the president to prepare a single national budget and barred individual agencies from making independent budgetary submissions to Congress. Receiving budget requests from the departments and agencies and revenue estimates from staff, the president determines how much government should tax, spend, and borrow in the coming year and then submits recommendations to Congress.

The Budget and Accounting Act also created the Bureau of the Budget to help the president discharge new budgetary responsibilities. The bureau was placed in the Executive Office of the President in 1939, and it was renamed the Office of Management and Budget (OMB) in 1970 to stress its management functions. The OMB continues to supervise the preparation of the executive budget each year and to guide the departments and agencies in implementing the president's policies after the budget has been enacted. The director of the OMB is now a member of the president's cabinet and is usually an influential policy adviser on a range of economy issues.

The national government began to institutionalize the goals of fiscal policy with the passage of the Full Employment Act of 1946. This act formally declared that it was "the continuing policy and responsibility of the Federal Government to use all practical means . . . to promote maximum employment, production and purchasing power."[4] It then created a three-member Council of Economic Advisers (CEA) in the Executive Office of the President to prepare analyses of economic issues for the president. Council members are appointed by the president and confirmed by the Senate, and they are assisted by a staff of professional economists. The members and senior staff are usually recruited from prestigious university departments on the basis of their economic expertise and the compatibility of their views with those of the president. The council's formal responsibility is to draft an annual report to Congress describing the administration's assessment of the condition of the economy, now known as the *Economic Report of the President*. The chair of the council often emerges as one of the president's most prominent advisers and frequently appears before Congress and in the media to promote administration policies.[5]

The Treasury Department dates to the nation's founding, and the secretary of the treasury has been the cabinet member with the most enduring influence on economic issues. The Treasury Department is responsible for collecting the government's revenues, paying its bills, maintaining the currency, managing government credit, and conducting economic relations with other countries and international organizations. In recent decades, presidents have usually selected treasury secretaries who represent stable, conservative policies and inspire confidence in the business community. Following the lead of the first secretary of the treasury, Alexander Hamilton, some treasury secretaries have become prominent economic advisers, whose policy influence has extended into other domains, such as James Baker under President Reagan and Robert Rubin under President Clinton, but other treasury leaders have failed to win the president's confidence and ended up playing marginal roles.

The Office of Management and Budget, the Council of Economic Advisers, and the Department of the Treasury constitute an "economic subpresidency" that advises the president on economic questions.[6] Presidents, however, are strong-willed individuals who create advisory structures that correspond to their particular needs and styles. Presidents Kennedy and Lyndon Johnson held informal meetings with the treasury secretary, the chair of the CEA, and the director of the OMB.[7] President Nixon centralized macroeconomic policy advice under the secretary of the treasury, whom he also designated assistant to the president for economic affairs. Presidents Reagan and George H. W. Bush expanded participation in economic policy discussions by including the secretaries of commerce, labor, transportation, and state and the U.S. trade representative.

To highlight the importance his administration attached to economic policy issues, President Clinton created the National Economic Council (NEC), patterned after the influential National Security Council. The NEC was an influential forum for economic matters during President Clinton's first term, but its importance waned during his second term when the presidential assistant who had directed the council became secretary of the treasury.[8] Under President George W. Bush, economic policy has been concentrated in the White House with the vice president, chief of staff, and the director of the OMB taking the lead and the secretary of the treasury serving as an advocate for administration policies.[9]

Economics is an inexact discipline, and economists rarely agree on the policies they think an administration should pursue. Presidents must assess the opinions and analyses they receive as they balance the diverse goals their administrations seek to achieve. There is no doubt that future presidents will continue to institutionalize economic policy advice in the manner that corresponds to their particular needs and to the circumstances of the day.

Congress

Congress as an institution is torn between its constitutional responsibility to set national policy and the state and district orientation of a membership divided by party, ideology, region, and interest. Because the work of Congress centers on committees and subcommittees, it has limited ability to manage economic issues from a nationwide perspective. Historically, Congress has made economic policy by aggregating the countless microeconomic decisions made in the committees and subcommittees rather than by focusing on the economy as a whole.

The growing significance of macroeconomic policy has led to gradual changes in the way Congress handles economic and budgetary issues. The Full Employment Act of 1946, in addition to creating the Council of Economic Advisers, established Congress's Joint Economic Committee. Composed of seven members each from the House and the Senate, the committee both symbolized Congress's growing concern about macroeconomic issues and sought to promote congressional involvement in macroeconomic policymaking. The committee is explicitly charged with preparing an analysis of the president's annual economic report and devising ways to advance macroeconomic goals of the Full Employment Act. The Joint Economic Committee, however, lacks legislative powers, is limited to an analytic and advisory role, and has had little actual impact on the conduct of policy.

A more significant step in moving Congress toward a macroeconomic consideration of budgetary issues was the Congressional Budget Reform and Impoundment Control Act of 1974. Although the act resulted from a dispute over President Nixon's refusal to spend funds that Congress had appropriated for purposes he did not support, it also led to fundamental changes in the federal budget process. Members of Congress had become distrustful of the *Economic Report of the President* because they feared that the CEA's estimates and analyses were being doctored to support the president's budgetary strategies. To obtain economic expertise of their own, the members created a new congressional agency called the Congressional Budget Office (CBO).

The CBO is a nonpartisan agency staffed by professional economists and budget examiners who are not aligned with individual legislators. Because its revenue estimates and economic forecasts have often been more accurate than those of the OMB and the CEA, the CBO has grown in size and stature over the years. When the president's budget is presented to Congress, the CBO now provides members its assessment of the state of the economy and its appraisal of the president's budgetary proposals. The CBO's activities allow Congress to initiate budgetary discussions from a macroeconomic perspective rather than beginning deliberations on a microeconomic foundation.

Historically, congressional budgetary decisions were based on the actions of the policy-area committees in the House and the Senate and the two chambers' appropriations committees.[10] The policy-area committees would decide how much money they thought should be authorized for each program, and the appropriations committees would then determine how much of the funds authorized by the policy committees should actually be appropriated. The policy-area committees and the appropriations subcommittees were usually centers of feverish lobbying activity as interest groups and their congressional allies struggled to expand funding for their causes in a process that was biased in favor of ever-increasing government expenditures.

In addition to establishing the CBO, the 1974 Budget Reform Act created budget committees in both the House and the Senate. These committees differ from traditional congressional committees in that the members serve for a maximum of six years and then rotate back to the committees from which they came.[11] When members complete their terms on the budget committees, it is hoped that they will share their broader view of budget issues with colleagues who continued to serve on the policy-area committees.

The Budget Reform Act also defined a new set of congressional procedures for making budgetary decisions. After Congress receives the president's budget recommendations in February, the House and Senate budget committees draft a concurrent resolution that becomes, in effect, a congressional macroeconomic budget specifying total revenues, expenditures, deficits, and surpluses. Once the concurrent resolution is adopted, the Senate and House budget committees allocate spending authority and appropriations limits to twenty different functional areas and to the various committees and subcommittees. The examination of the president's funding requests then occurs in the policy-area committees, the appropriations committees, and the full House and Senate. In theory, the actions of the committees respect the guidelines of the budget committees and adhere to the provisions of the concurrent resolution, but numerous departures from the original resolution usually emerge. A reconciliation bill is then prepared to bring the committee actions into conformity with the requirements of the concurrent resolution.

The reconciliation bill is not simply a procedural device, however. Ever since President Reagan used the 1981 reconciliation bill to reduce entitlement spending, reconciliation bills have provided an opportunity for the president and congressional leaders to negotiate sweeping policy issues. The 1990 Omnibus Reconciliation Act capped discretionary spending and established the principle that increases in spending must be offset by reductions in the same program area, and in 1997 Republican leaders joined President Clinton in using the reconciliation process to ratify a deficit-reduction package that adjusted both taxes and expenditures.

Legislative action on the budget is to be completed by October 1, when the new fiscal year (FY) begins, but Congress has rarely enacted all the appropriations bills by this time. To keep the departments and agencies from closing, Congress passes a continuing resolution, permitting departments to spend funds until the necessary appropriations bills are passed and signed by the president.

The complexity of the budgetary process makes fiscal policy a cumbersome tool for managing the economy. Because fiscal policy is implemented through the revenue and expenditure decisions of the annual budget process, policy decisions must be made long before the dimensions of an economic problem are known. It is also difficult for elected officials to battle influential constituencies, cut appropriations for popular programs, sacrifice noneconomic policy goals, or boost taxes in the present in the interest of stabilizing the economic situation at some period in the future.

Ideological differences also complicate the use of fiscal policy. Fiscal policy involves government intervention in the economy, and Democrats are usually quicker than Republicans to embrace government authority to achieve programmatic objectives. When fiscal policy is to be invoked, divisions persist; Democrats normally advocate increased government spending, whereas Republicans typically campaign for bigger tax cuts.

The fundamental logic of Keynesian demand management was also challenged by the experience of the Carter administration, which endured frighteningly large increases in inflation at a time when unemployment soared and the economy stagnated. For these reasons, the use of fiscal policy as a tool for managing the economy has declined in the past two decades, and far greater emphasis has been placed on the importance of monetary policy.

MONETARY POLICY

Article I, section 8, of the Constitution gives Congress the power to coin money and determine its value, but this simple power has ignited numerous political controversies in the nation's history. The First Bank of the United States was established in 1791 to act as the country's central bank and to help manage the debt incurred during the Revolution.[12] Plagued by partisan discord, the bank was depicted as a symbol of economic power and accused of favoring eastern commercial interests at the expense of western development, and it went out of existence when its charter expired in 1811. The Second Bank became a rancorous issue in Andrew Jackson's 1832 reelection campaign, despite the bank's considerable achievements in managing the debt from the War of 1812, calming financial panics, and restraining state banks; it closed its doors with the expiration of its charter in 1836. William Jennings Bryan's famous denunciation of federal monetary policy in his "cross-of-gold" speech at the 1896 Democratic Convention again expressed the long-standing view of western farmers that they were victimized by eastern financial institutions. The series of bank failures, stock market crashes, and financial crises in 1861, 1873, 1884, 1893, and 1907 finally led Congress to appoint a national commission to address the nation's need for a permanent central bank.

The Federal Reserve System was established in 1913 after years of political deadlock over both the appropriate balance of public authority and private influence in a central bank and the need to fashion a regional banking structure to forestall Wall Street domination.[13] The Federal Reserve Act created a system that is headed by a seven-member board of governors—usually known as the Federal Reserve Board or simply "the Fed"—whose members are appointed by the president for fourteen-year terms and confirmed by the Senate. The president also designates the chair and vice chair of the board, subject to the advice and consent of the Senate. In addition, the legislation provided for twelve Federal Reserve banks in major cities across the country to conduct the system's day-to-day operations. The Federal Reserve Board in Washington appoints the chair and vice chair of the boards of directors of each of the twelve Federal Reserve banks, but the private banks in each region own the Federal Reserve bank there and elect most members of its board. The Federal Reserve banks are private, for-profit corporations, and each bank appoints one of the twelve members to an advisory panel to the Federal Reserve Board in Washington.[14]

When originally established, the Federal Reserve Board functioned as an independent regulatory agency assigned to manage the currency, maintain the stability of the banking system, and facilitate the nation's commercial transactions. Neither the president nor Congress had statutory control over the Fed's daily operations, and the only manner in which this could be changed was for Congress to enact a new statute. The twelve Federal Reserve banks distributed the nation's currency, operated a national payment system to clear checks, helped distribute the Treasury Department's bonds to private investors, and purchased and sold government securities in their own name.[15] The Federal Reserve banks could lend money to member banks, and the Federal Reserve Board regulated the portion of deposits that individual banks were required to hold in reserve to ensure the safety of their customers' deposits and the stability of their own loans.

As the Fed helped manage the government debt incurred in World War II, the nation's understanding of monetary policy grew. In 1951 the Fed signed an accord with the Department of the Treasury that transformed its regulatory assignments into tools for conducting monetary policy.[16] The Fed devised three ways of affecting the supply of money in the national economy—in this context money is not simply coins and currency. The Federal Reserve Board's first definition of money (M_1) includes currency, checking accounts, traveler's checks, and all deposits in checking-type accounts. A broader measure of money (M_2) includes all of M_1 plus small savings accounts, small certificates of deposit (CDs), and money-market mutual fund accounts. M_3 includes M_2 plus time deposits and money-market balances held by large institutions.

The Federal Reserve System possessed three specific powers in 1951 that have emerged as primary monetary policy tools. First, the Federal Reserve Board requires that a certain portion of deposits be held by individual banks to guarantee the overall stability of the banking system. Banks cannot make loans with the money they hold as required reserves. When the Fed raises the *reserve requirements,* banks have less money to lend, the money supply declines, and upward pressure on interest rates grows. When the Fed wants to increase the money supply, it can lower reserve requirements, increase the portion of deposits available for loans, and push interest rates downward.

Private banks subject to the Fed's reserve requirements are permitted to borrow money directly from their regional Federal Reserve banks if their reserves fall below the required level. The rate of interest that these banks must pay to borrow the funds is called the *discount rate.* Although the discount rate is formally determined by the directors of the regional Federal Reserve banks, rate-setting in recent decades has been dominated by the Federal Reserve Board itself. Raising the discount rate discourages the private banks from borrowing to make loans and that in turn increases the cost or reduces the availability of loans the private banks can make to their customers. Lowering the discount rate expands the money supply and encourages the private banks and their clients to borrow additional funds. Overnight loans may also be made from one regional Federal Reserve bank to another, for operational reasons or when one bank has excess reserves. The interest rate charged on these loans is called the *federal funds rate,* and changes in the federal funds rate have become a means of affecting the money supply, since the broader credit markets have come to pay great attention to the federal funds rate and frequently follow its lead in setting their own rates.

The final way the Fed influences the supply of money is by buying or selling the Treasury Department's interest-bearing bonds in the open market. These *open-market operations* are conducted under the authority of the Federal Open Market Committee (FOMC), which is composed of twelve members: all seven members of the Federal Reserve Board, the president of the New York Federal Reserve Bank, and the presidents of four other regional Federal Reserve banks, who each serve for one year on a rotating basis. The Fed chair also chairs the FOMC, and the vice chair is the president of the New York Federal Reserve Bank. When the Domestic Trading Desk of the New York Federal Reserve Bank purchases government securities from major brokers, these brokers deposit the funds they receive in their accounts and thus add additional reserves to the banking system as part of M1. These additional reserves increase the ability of banks to make loans and reduce the rates the banks are likely to charge to their customers. Conversely, when the FOMC directs the selling of government securities, funds are withdrawn from the banking system to pay for the securities, reserves decline, the availability of credit is restricted, and interest rates are pushed up. Because of their flexibility and immediate impact, open-market operations are one of the Fed's favorite tools for affecting the money supply.

Monetary economists believe that the nation's fundamental economic problem is not unemployment but inflation.[17] Monetarists argue that the typical

Keynesian prescriptions of tax cuts or increased government expenditures are of little help to a faltering economy because they come at the expense of lower private spending, leaving aggregate demand essentially unchanged. The monetarists trace the ups and downs of the business cycle to erratic swings in the nation's money supply, and they insist that inflation can best be controlled by slow and stable growth in the money supply. Monetarists believe that the economy moves toward a stable equilibrium and that once inflation has been controlled, the other macroeconomic objectives will be within reach.

Inflation was one of the nation's principal economic problems during the 1970s. With high unemployment, declining productivity, and a particularly virulent round of inflation on the horizon, President Carter appointed Paul Volcker to chair the Federal Reserve Board in fall 1979 in an effort to regain the confidence of the business community. Representing a monetarist approach to economic policy, Volcker announced that the Fed would shift its attention from manipulating interest rates to managing the money supply.[18] The Fed hesitated while the 1980 presidential election contest took its course, but Volcker's board regained its anti-inflationary zeal as both the Reagan campaign and then the Reagan administration stressed the need to win the war against inflation. Committed to wringing inflationary expectations from the economy, the Fed put the brakes on the growth of the money supply after the election and sharply limited the ability of banks to make loans. These actions had an immediate impact. The Fed's restrictive policy succeeded in reducing the rate of inflation in the consumer price index from 11 percent in 1979 to 3 percent in 1983, but at the same time, interest rates topped 21 percent, the level of unemployment grew to more than 10 percent, and the nation's real gross domestic product actually declined.[19] Fearing sizable defeats in the upcoming congressional elections, Reagan appointees complained to the media about the Fed's policies, but Volcker held his course. After the dramatic actions of the Fed and the expansionary policies of the Reagan administration, the inflation rate averaged only 2.5 percent per year between 1983 and 1989, unemployment declined to 5.3 percent in 1989, and the nation began an unprecedented period of peacetime economic growth.

Monetary policy is now widely regarded as a more effective tool for managing the economy than fiscal policy because it is more flexible and easier to deploy, has a more immediate impact, and disrupts fewer decisions in individual sectors of the economy. Furthermore, the effectiveness of monetary policy is not dependent on high federal expenditures and a large government presence in the society, as is the case with fiscal policy. The Federal Reserve Board now dominates the conduct of monetary policy, and Paul Volcker (the Fed's immediate past chair) and Alan Greenspan (current chair) have achieved an extraordinary level of national prominence. Economic policy, however, remains more an art than a science, and how well the Fed discharges its policy obligations remains a matter of dispute. Through the early 1990s the most important way the Fed influenced the money supply was through its open-market operations, but under Alan Greenspan, the Federal Reserve has relied more on changes in the federal funds rate to achieve its objectives.[20]

Some critics insist that the Fed has a "banker's bias" and is more sensitive to the threat of inflation than to the hardship and inequality that result from recession.[21] Through its willingness to accept slower than optimal growth rates, the Fed has settled for lower levels of employment and fewer benefits of a vibrant economy than might otherwise be obtainable. Other commentators, in contrast, worry that the favorable conditions in the economy are simply not sustainable, and they predict that the current levels of growth will inevitably lead to rampant inflation and soaring unemployment in the not-too-distant future.[22] The European Union remains a developing governing system, and how it is organized to make fiscal and monetary policy is explored in Box 10-1.

Cases in Development
BOX 10-1 EUROPEAN MONETARY AND FISCAL POLICY

The European Central Bank (ECB) is the central bank for the euro currency and the institution that manages monetary policy for the euro area. The euro area was created in January 1999, and it now has twelve members: Belgium, the Netherlands, Luxembourg, France, Germany, Italy, Spain, Portugal, Ireland, Finland, Austria, and Greece. These twelve countries have adopted the euro as their currency and surrendered their monetary authority to the ECB. Great Britain, Denmark, Sweden, and twelve new EU members have retained their national currencies and do not belong to the Eurosystem. The decision-making body of the ECB is a governing council composed of directors of the central banks of the euro-area countries and six members of an executive board, which has been appointed by the heads of the euro countries.

The ECB's main tasks as the central bank for the euro are to defend the purchasing power of the currency and safeguard price stability in the euro area. In managing monetary policy for the euro area, the ECB defines monetary objectives, sets key interest rates, and determines the money supply. After its first meeting each month, the ECB's governing board announces its interest rate decisions at 1:45 p.m. and then holds a press conference at 2:30 p.m. to outline its assessment of economic conditions and explain its interest rate decisions.

The fiscal authority to tax and spend in the EU is still held by the national governments, regardless of whether a country has adopted the

(continued)

euro or not. France, Germany, Italy and the other national governments set their own tax rates and determine how their revenues should be spent. The division of authority with the ECB responsible for monetary policy and the national governments responsible for fiscal policy leads to some tensions. When the national governments face downturns in the business cycle and increasing unemployment rolls, they complain that they cannot depend on the ECB to provide short-term stimulus by cutting interest rates.

The ECB's record in managing monetary policy is a short one, and it is still too early to reach firm conclusions about the bank's performance. In the first years of the euro's existence, the ECB did little to offset the weakness of the new currency, but this policy helped boost exports and promote foreign investment. As the euro strengthened in 2004 and 2005, the ECB adopted a policy of benign moderation that some compared to the strategy of the U.S. Federal Reserve Board, but economic growth in Europe slowed, and the long-term consequences of ECB's policy choices remained unclear.

Sources: See Miriam L. Campanella, "Euro Weakness and the ECB Economic Governance: A Strategic Institutionalist Perspective," in *EU Economic Governance and Globalization,* ed. Miriam L. Campanella and Sylvester C. W. Eijffinger (Northampton, Mass.: Edward Elgar, 2003), 171–203; and the European Central Bank Web site: http://www.ecb.int, accessed May 12, 2005.

REVENUES AND EXPENDITURES

In 2005 the fundamental features of the U.S. economy were moderate unemployment and low inflation, dynamic corporations and impressive productivity increases, and a national fiscal policy that yielded substantial budget deficits. Both President George H. W. Bush in 1990 and President Clinton in 1993 had devised deficit-reduction programs that combined tax increases and expenditure restraint, and popular support for controlling deficit spending had finally begun to coalesce. President George W. Bush, however, championed large tax cuts in 2001, 2002, and 2003 that were comparable in size to the tax cuts enacted during President Reagan's first term, arguing first that the cuts would reduce the temporary budget surpluses and then that they were needed to stimulate a slowing economy.[23] To make matters worse, these Bush tax cuts were accompanied by enormous spending increases passed between 1997 and 2004 that mandated automatic growth in health care and retirement costs, provided for new national security needs, and embraced surging expenditures for farm subsidies and other discretionary items. Pay-as-you-go budgetary rules were cast aside as child tax credits and earned income tax credits were expanded for lower-income groups and reductions in estate taxes were approved for the wealthy. The OMB estimated that 2005 would produce the largest absolute deficit in peacetime history, reaching $426 billion and 3.5 percent of the nation's gross domestic product.[24] See Table 10-1.

In 1970 about 7 percent of federal expenditures had gone to pay the interest on the national debt; by the mid-1990s interest on the debt required 15 percent of all federal spending, and the OMB estimated that in 2006 interest costs would equal 12 percent of federal spending.

The emergence of a seemingly permanent federal deficit has been accompanied by important shifts in federal expenditures and revenues (Figure 10-1). Defense expenditures declined from 42 percent of federal outlays in FY1970 to 17 percent in FY2006. Corresponding growth has occurred in outlays for social purposes. In FY2006, 24 percent of federal spending supports Medicare and health, and 21 percent pays the costs of Social Security.

As far as revenues are concerned, the post–World War II decades witnessed a sharp increase in the proportion of federal revenues that came from payroll taxes, swelling from only 7 percent of total revenues in FY1950 to 38 percent in FY2006. In addition, the share of receipts produced by personal income taxes also grew in these years from 37 percent of total revenues in FY1950 to 44 percent in FY2001.

Perhaps the most dramatic change in federal revenues in this half century was the drop in the share of revenues derived from corporate income taxes, from 37 percent at the beginning of the period to only 10 percent in FY2006. This decline, however, was partially offset by the fact that employers provide half of payroll tax revenues through their Social Security and Medicare payments. Since stockholders pay income tax on the dividends they receive as their share of corporate profits, some activists also insist that corporate income tax rates should be low

Table 10-1   National Government Finances, 1970–2008

Fiscal year	Receipts	Outlays (billions of current dollars)	Surplus/Deficit
1970	192.8	195.6	−2.8
1975	279.1	332.3	−53.2
1980	517.1	590.9	−73.8
1985	734.1	946.4	−212.3
1990	1,032.0	1,253.2	−221.2
1995	1,351.8	1,515.8	−164.0
2000	2,025.2	1,789.1	236.1
2002	1,853.2	2,011.0	−157.8
2004	1,880.1	2,292.2	−412.1
2006 (est.)	2,177.6	2,567.6	−390.0
2008 (est.)	2,507.0	2,757.8	−250.8

Source: U.S. Office of Management and Budget, *The Budget of the United States, Fiscal Year 2006, Historical Tables* (Washington, D.C.: GPO, 2005), table 1.1.

Figure 10-1 Federal Revenues and Expenditures, Fiscal Year 2006

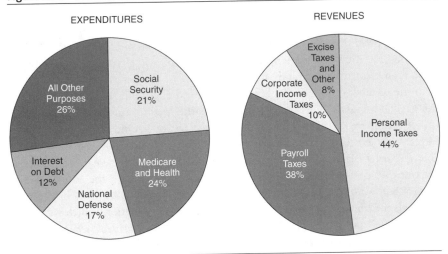

Source: Data are official estimates reported in the U.S. Office of Management and Budget, *Budget of the United States Government, Fiscal Year 2006, Historical Tables*, (Washington, D.C.: GPO, 2005), tables 2.2 and 2.4.

because they constitute double taxation on returns to investors. The level of corporate income tax payments and the profusion of loopholes and exemptions are also testimony to the power of business in the political process.

Systems of taxation are never neutral. They represent a structure of incentives that encourages individuals and organizations to undertake certain types of economic activities and shun others. The provisions of the U.S. tax system have a substantial impact on the choices made by corporate America.[25] Manufacturing firms are capital-intensive companies that benefit from government incentives to invest in plant and equipment, and they favor policies that boost employment, promote prosperity, and stimulate demand for their products. The housing and financial sectors are composed of labor-intensive firms that advocate balanced budgets and stable monetary policies, because inflation, if unchecked, could ravage their markets and erode their profit margins. High-tech start-up firms rely on equity markets to raise capital and on stock options to reward employees, and, consequently, they are intensely concerned about capital gains taxes but rather disinterested in interest rates and the general state of the economy. Small businesses and service companies are labor-intensive enterprises that have been rocked by increases in payroll taxes in recent decades. Although they derive less benefit from investment incentives than do manufacturers, their prosperity does depend on policies that promote the overall economy and generate demand for their products.

EMPLOYMENT

One measure of the success of a country's economic policies is its ability to generate employment opportunities for its citizens. The Bureau of Labor Statistics (BLS) estimates that total employment in the United States will grow to 165.3 million by 2012, an increase of 21.3 million jobs since 2002.[26] This increase is 600,000 larger than the number of jobs added between 1992 and 2002, but the growth will have occurred at a slightly slower rate than in the earlier period, 14.8 percent from 2002 to 2012 compared with 16.8 percent from 1992 to 2002. One of the most significant factors affecting U.S. employment between 1995 and 2002 was the remarkable growth in labor productivity, averaging 2.3 percent per year. Productivity increases are projected to continue between 2002 and 2012 at the annual rate of 2.1 percent. Another factor appearing on the employment horizon in the next decade is the impending retirement of the baby boom generation, which will create job openings and possibly lead to shortages of workers in critical occupations.

The fastest growing major occupational groups between 2002 and 2012, according to the Bureau of Labor Statistics, will be professional occupations and service occupations. These two groups were already the two largest employment classifications in 2002, and they were the highest and lowest groups, respectively, in income and education. The slowest growing occupational groups between 2002 and 2012 will be in farming, maintenance, mining, and construction.

Table 10-2 is a list of some of the specific occupations that the BLS expects to grow most rapidly between 2002 and 2012 and indicates the earnings range and training normally associated with those occupations. The fastest growing career during this period is projected to be medical assistants with an increase of 59 percent; the position of telephone operator is expected to suffer the greatest decline in employment, seeing 56 percent of its jobs being wiped away.[27] Of the thirty fastest growing occupations between 2002 and 2012, fifteen are in the health care area, seven involve the computer industry, three are teachers, and three are based on concern for the environment. Surging health care employment reflects an aging population, advances in technology, and the greater availability of wealth to sustain senior citizens. Increases in computer-related occupations can be traced to the development of new computer technologies and the enhanced applications of existing technologies. Twenty-one of the thirty fastest growing careers require some sort of postsecondary education. Thirteen of the fastest growing occupations fall in the first quartile of earnings, and eight appear in the third earnings quartile. During the 2002–12 period, more job openings are expected to result from the need to replace people leaving their positions than from the growth of the economy as a whole.

SUMMARY

Monetary and fiscal policies have become the government's most prominent tools for guiding the nation's economy. During the twentieth century, both

Table 10-2 Fast-Growing Occupations, 2002–2012
(Numbers in thousands of jobs)

Occupation	Employment		Change		Quartile rank by 2002 median earnings	Postsecondary Education Training
	2002	2012	Number	Percent		
Medical assistants	365	579	215	59	3	Moderate-term on-the-job training
Network systems and data communications analysts	186	292	106	57	1	Bachelor's degree
Physician assistants	63	94	31	49	1	Bachelor's degree
Social and human service assistants	305	454	149	49	3	Moderate-term on-the-job training
Home health aides	580	859	279	48	4	Short-term on-the-job training
Computer software engineers, applications	394	573	179	46	1	Bachelor's degree
Computer software engineers, systems software	281	409	128	45	1	Bachelor's degree
Fitness trainers and aerobics instructors	183	264	81	44	3	Postsecondary vocational award
Database administrators	110	159	49	44	1	Bachelor's degree
Hazardous materials removal workers	38	54	16	43	2	Moderate-term on-the-job training
Dental hygienists	148	212	64	43	1	Associate degree
Self-enrichment education teachers	200	281	80	40	2	Work experience in a related occupation
Environmental engineers	47	65	18	38	1	Bachelor's degree
Postsecondary teachers	1,581	2,184	603	38	1	Doctoral degree
Network and computer systems administrators	251	345	94	37	1	Bachelor's degree

Source: Daniel E. Hecker, "Occupational Employment Projections to 2012," *Monthly Labor Review*, February 2004, table 3.

Note: The quartile rankings of annual earnings data are presented in the following categories. 1 = very high ($41,820 and over), 2 = high ($27,500 to $41,780), 3 = low ($19,710 to $27,380), and 4 = very low (up to $19,600).

Congress and the presidency have developed the institutions and practices needed to take a macroeconomic perspective on fiscal policy issues, but the temptation to sacrifice economic judgments to the demands of short-term political pressures is frequently irresistible. Because of the complexity of the budget process, partisan ideologies, and questions about the logic of Keynesian demand management, fiscal policy tools have received less attention in recent years for the management of the economy, and greater emphasis has been placed on monetary policy.

The Federal Reserve Board manages monetary policy in the United States by altering the supply of money and adjusting interest rates. Monetary policies are more flexible and easier to deploy than fiscal policy, have a more immediate impact, and disrupt less the existing patterns of expenditure and investment.

The consequences of economic policy judgment are seen in the patterns of revenues and expenditures and in the employment prospects for a nation's citizens. The United States now relies on personal income taxes and payroll taxes as its principal sources of revenue and prioritizes Medicare and health policies, Social Security, national defense, and interest on the national debt in its expenditures, but five years into the twenty-first century its economic policy judgments are yielding historically high budget deficits. The economy continues to produce a substantial number of new jobs as it faces the retirement of the baby boom generation, but doubts about the quality of future jobs persist.

FURTHER READINGS

The home page of the Federal Reserve Board's Web site offers the minutes of the Federal Open Market Committee, the Beige Book, explanations of monetary policy, and Alan Greenspan's speeches. See site map: http://www.federalreserve.gov. The *Economic Report of the President* is available through the U.S. Government Printing Office: http://www.access.gpo.gov. Examine "Featured Items." For the OMB's perspective on current fiscal issues, see http://www.whitehouse.gov/omb/budget/fy2006. The Web site of the European Central Bank is found at http://www.ecb.int.

Ferrier, Jasmine. *Passing the Buck: Congress, the Budget, and Deficits.* Lexington: University Press of Kentucky, 2004.

Peterson, Peter G. *Running on Empty: How the Democratic and Republican Parties Are Bankrupting Our Future.* New York: Farrar, Straus and Giroux, 2004.

Steuerle, C. Eugene. *Contemporary U.S. Tax Policy.* Washington, D.C.: Urban Institute Press, 2004.

Thorndike, Joseph J., and Dennis J. Ventry, eds. *Tax Justice: The Ongoing Debate.* Washington, D.C.: Urban Institute Press, 2002.

Tuccille, Jerome. *Alan Shrugged: The Life and Time of Alan Greenspan.* Hoboken, N.J.: Wiley, 2002.

NOTES

1. Herbert Stein, *Presidential Economics,* 3rd ed. (Washington, D.C.: AEI Press, 1996).
2. Council of Economic Advisers, *Economic Report of the President* (Washington, D.C.: GPO, 1963), xxiv.
3. James D. Savage, *Balanced Budgets and American Politics* (Ithaca, N.Y.: Cornell University Press, 1988), 176–79.
4. G. Calvin Mackenzie and Saranna Thornton, *Bucking the Deficit: Economic Policy Making in America* (Boulder, Colo.: Westview Press, 1996), 60, 83, 84.
5. Erwin C. Hargrove and Samuel A. Moorley, eds., *The President and the Council of Economic Advisers: Interviews with CEA Chairmen* (Boulder, Colo.: Westview Press, 1984).
6. This discussion also draws on Jeffrey E. Cohen, *Politics and Economic Policy in the United States,* 2nd ed. (Boston: Houghton Mifflin, 2000), 149–56.
7. The balance of this paragraph is based on James J. Gosling, *Politics and the American Economy* (New York: Longman, 2000), 35.
8. I. M. Destler, *The National Economic Council: A Work in Progress* (Washington, D.C.: Institute for International Economics, 1996).
9. Andrew Balls, "Treasury Feels White House Heat on Policy," *Financial Times,* April 14, 2005, 4.
10. See the classic studies by Richard F. Fenno Jr., *The Power of the Purse* (Boston: Little, Brown, 1966); and John F. Manley, *The Politics of Finance* (Boston: Little, Brown, 1970).
11. This discussion draws from Cohen, *Politics and Economic Policy in the United States,* 158–59.
12. Paul Studenski and Herman E. Krooss, *Financial History of the United States* (New York: McGraw-Hill, 1952); and Forrest MacDonald, *The Presidency of George Washington* (Washington, D.C.: Norton, 1974).
13. Arthur S. Link, *Woodrow Wilson and the Progressive Era, 1910–1917* (New York: Harper and Brothers, 1954).
14. This discussion draws on the impressive work by Marc Allan Eisner, *The State in the American Political Economy* (Englewood Cliffs, N.J.: Prentice Hall, 1995), esp. 118–20, 150–52, 242–44, 299–300, 307.
15. William J. Barber, *From New Era to New Deal: Herbert Hoover, the Economists, and American Economic Policy, 1912–1933* (Cambridge: Cambridge University Press, 1985); and Anna Jacobson Schwartz, *A Monetary History of the United States, 1867–1960* (Princeton: Princeton University Press, 1963).
16. See Cohen, *Politics and Economic Policy in the United States,* 226–27; and William R. Keech, *Economic Politics: The Costs of Democracy* (New York: Cambridge University Press, 1995), 200–202.
17. Mackenzie and Thornton, *Bucking the Deficit,* 32–34.
18. Paul Volcker and Toyoo Gyohten, *Changing Fortunes: The World's Money and the Threat to American Leadership* (New York: Times Books, 1992); John T. Woolley, *Monetary Politics: The Federal Reserve and the Politics of Monetary Policy* (New York: Cambridge University Press, 1984); and William Greider, *Secrets of the Temple: How the Federal Reserve Runs the Country* (New York: Simon and Schuster, 1987).
19. The data here and in the balance of the paragraph come from Mackenzie and Thornton, *Bucking the Deficit,* 34.
20. Glenn Rudebusch, "Interest Rates and Monetary Policy," *FRBSF Economic Letter,* no. 97-18 (June 13, 1997), as quoted in Gosling, *Politics and the American Economy,* 48.
21. See Cohen, *Politics and Economic Policy in the United States,* 228–29; and Lester Thurow, "The Crusade That's Killing Prosperity," *American Prospect,* March–April 1996, 54–59.
22. See Alan Binder, "The Speed Limit: Fact and Fancy in the Growth Debate," *American Prospect,* September–October 1997, 57–62.
23. C. Eugene Steuerle, *Contemporary U.S. Tax Policy* (Washington, D.C.: Urban Institute Press, 2004), chaps. 1 and 11.
24. U.S. Office of Management and Budget, *Budget of the United States Government, Fiscal Year 2006, Historical Tables,* table 1.1 (Washington, D.C.: GPO, 2005).

25. This discussion is based on Cathie J. Martin, *Shifting the Burden: The Struggle over Growth and Corporate Taxation* (Chicago: University of Chicago Press, 1991); and Timothy J. Conlan, Margaret T. Wrightson, and David R. Beam, *Taxing Choices: The Politics of Tax Reform* (Washington, D.C.: CQ Press, 1990).
26. This discussion draws from Daniel E. Hecker, "Occupational Employment Projections to 2012," *Monthly Labor Review,* February 2004, 80–105; and Michael W. Horrigan, "Employment Projections to 2012," *Monthly Labor Review,* February 2004, 3–22.
27. These sentences are based on Hecker, "Occupational Employment Projections to 2012," 100–102.

CHAPTER 11

Regulatory Policy

IT WAS THE best of times and the worst of times for the pharmaceutical industry. In 2004 worldwide sales of brand-name prescription drugs exceeded $500 billion for the first time in history.[1] Eighty-two drugs earned the coveted "blockbuster" status by recording more than $1 billion in annual sales, and revenue growth in developing nations helped the principal pharmaceutical companies offset the gains made by biotech firms and generic-drug competitors. Pfizer maintained its position as the largest pharmaceutical company in the U.S. market with annual sales approaching $31 billion, followed by GlaxoSmithKline, Johnson & Johnson, and Merck.

At the same time, however, troubling aspects of the industry's conduct attracted public concern.[2] Fewer new medications were being developed by the industry, and some regarded this as an industry strategy. In a recent year, only seventeen of the seventy-eight new drugs contained new ingredients, and only seven of these were classified by government as improvements over existing products.[3] The industry appeared to be devoting its resources to copying profitable drugs already on the market and relying on government-funded research to produce the breakthroughs that might lead to important new drugs. Although innovation had slowed, sharp increases in pharmaceutical prices also appeared unstoppable. In the previous twenty years the share of the U.S. gross domestic product that went to prescription drugs had tripled, even though senior citizens traveled to Canada to find cheaper prices, insurers and state governments battled drug companies over high costs, and Congress added a prescription drug benefit to Medicare to reduce total pharmaceutical expenditures.

In addition to high prices and sluggish innovation, public controversy has also enveloped the government agency that regulates drug safety, the Food and Drug Administration (FDA). The pharmaceutical industry has been described as "the most regulated industry in the world," but the FDA's assignment is to balance the benefits of a new medication against the prospect that it might prove lethal for some patients.[4]

The incident that ignited the FDA controversy centered on the class of drugs called cox-2 inhibitors. Cox-2 drugs inhibit an enzyme related to pain but do not cause the gastro-intestinal bleeding produced by similar drugs that is responsible for many deaths.[5] Merck developed a cox-2 inhibitor called Vioxx that relieved pain with less risk of stomach bleeding than aspirin and ibuprofen, and the drug was approved by the FDA in May 1999.[6] Vioxx had one of the most successful drug launches in history, and its use by arthritis patients and other pain sufferers soon yielded almost $2.5 billion in annual sales. Gradually accumulating studies, however, indicated that persistent use of Vioxx was associated with increased risk of heart attack, and in 2002 the FDA instructed Merck to warn patients of this danger on the label. After internal studies and public warnings highlighted the increased risk of heart attacks and stroke, Merck withdrew Vioxx from the market in September 2004. An FDA whistle-blower estimated that Vioxx could have caused 27,785 heart attacks between its approval in 1999 and its withdrawal from the market in 2004, and the company's critics claimed that the pursuit of profits had led Merck to compromise its integrity and leave a dangerous drug on the market.

Politicians and the media put the FDA in their sights and charged that the FDA's treatment of Vioxx and two cox-2 drugs released by Pfizer, Celebrex and Bextra, proved that the "FDA had lost its way when it comes to making sure drugs are safe."[7] Three problems in FDA operations attracted the most attention. First, the FDA is under pressure to bring new drugs to market as soon as possible. In 1992 Congress enacted the Prescription Drug User Fee Act that authorized drug companies to pay the FDA a fee now set at $576,000 to expedite the processing of each new drug application. Critics argue that this procedure has substituted commercial considerations for scientific judgment in the drug approval process. Second, the industry now finances and controls most of the clinical trials on which the FDA rests its scientific judgment, and this allows the sponsors of new drugs to present, organize, and withhold clinical information in the ways that are most favorable to their position. Third, the FDA rarely studies the impact of drugs that have been approved for use. Once a drug has been approved, monitoring usually results from complaints by doctors and independent researchers who encounter ill effects from the product's use. Reforms were proposed to remedy each of these practices.

The eventual outcome of the cox-2 controversy is not yet known, but in February 2005, an FDA regulatory panel of medical experts ruled that the cox-2 inhibitors could remain on the market. Although the committee agreed that the drugs increased the risk of heart attacks and strokes, it concluded that the drugs could still be valuable to some patients. The panel urged that strong warnings about the products be included on the labels and that new research be done to assess their safety. The committee allowed Celebrex to stay on the market by a margin of 31 to 1, it voted to allow the continued sale of Bextra by a vote of 17 to 13, and it approved Vioxx by a 17 to 15 margin. Committee members noted that the safety of previously existing medications had not been tested and if they banned the cox-2 inhibitors they might be driving patients to medicines that could turn out to be even more dangerous.

Does the cox-2 controversy prove that the FDA has "lost its way" in ensuring drug safety? Does it demonstrate that the industry has too much influence in the drug approval process? How should public officials react when medical experts divide rather evenly on a scientific issue? The cox-2 saga is certainly not a typical regulatory event, but it helps us appraise the dynamics of the regulatory process.

In this chapter I outline different theories of regulation and then identify the features of new and old patterns of regulation. The chapter focuses on conduct of regulation and the debates about regulatory reform and concludes with a comparison of the patterns of regulation in the United States with those that appear in other countries.

THEORIES OF REGULATION

Government regulation has been called "a distinctively American approach to balancing public and private interests."[8] Regulation is a mechanism to insist that public purposes be respected by businesses and other nongovernmental institutions in their operations. Two basic theories have dominated our understanding of the place of regulation in the relationship between government and private institutions: the public-interest theory and the private-interest theory.[9]

Public-Interest Theory

Most analyses present regulation as a response to market failure.[10] Regulation seeks to achieve the benefits of marketplace competition for consumers and the society in situations in which competition does not occur.[11] Sometimes the technical factors of an industry's operations prevent competition; such industries are often called *natural monopolies*. Examples include the generation of electrical power and the treatment of sewage, where high capital investment makes competing utility systems too costly, and radio and television broadcasting, where operating rules prevent broadcasters from disrupting each others' signals.

Regulation may also be needed because of a different form of market failure— the failure of the price mechanism. In some industries prices are not an accurate measure of the true social costs of business activity. Some businesses are regulated because their operations pollute the environment, yet marketplace prices do not include the full social costs of pollution. In other instances, a product is more valuable to the society than to the individual consumer, and it is regulated to ensure that enough of that product is provided to meet the society's needs.

Finally, market failure may occur because consumers lack the information needed to make proper judgments about products and producers. Pharmaceutical products are regulated because individual consumers cannot know enough to determine if a particular drug is safe and effective, and health care practitioners are required to meet government standards because individual consumers have little basis on which to appraise medical qualifications.

In each of these instances, regulation emerges as a cure for the failures of the marketplace. According to the public-interest perspective, the regulation of the pharmaceutical industry was intended to provide safe and effective medicines for citizens, and the controversy about cox-2 drugs occurred because regulators lacked the resources to supervise the industry properly.

Private-Interest Theory

According to the private-interest perspective, it is a pretense to maintain that regulation is a public-interest activity.[12] According to this view, people pursue their private interests in the regulatory arena with the same gusto they display in pursuing individual interests in the private sector. Regulation should be understood as nothing more than an effort to use government authority to redistribute income from one group to another. Because numerous studies show that the actual consequences of many regulatory policies are to enrich specific private groups, students of regulation should acknowledge that the actual effects of regulation are, in fact, the intended effects.

Three groups are in the best position to benefit from regulation. First is business. Business does not always act as a class, but as individual companies or industries. When a company's profits are less than optimal, it can cut its prices, improve the quality of its products, increase its advertising budget, or invest in a lobbying effort to secure beneficial regulatory action.[13] When the pharmaceutical industry faced high costs and long delays in securing the approval of new drugs, it launched a campaign to change FDA rules. In response, Congress enacted the Prescription Drug User Fee Act that allowed companies to accelerate the consideration of applications for the approval of new drugs in exchange for a modest fee. When the fate of a blockbuster drug was at stake, the companies were more than willing to make such a bargain.

Members of Congress, too, can benefit by transforming regulation into pork-barrel politics.[14] The creation of the user fee system to expedite the evaluation of new drugs provided the companies a new procedure to communicate their concerns to the FDA officials who were managing the approval process for their application. The process permitted direct, private contact with the relevant officials. Congress had endorsed industry efforts to accelerate the drug approval process, and when difficult issues arose regulators knew that the benefit of the doubt would go to the industry. Members of Congress have influence over regulatory agencies, and the expectation that they will exercise that influence on behalf of reasonable requests from influential organizations helps legislators raise funds in campaign season.

Regulators are also in a position to benefit individually and organizationally from regulation.[15] Extensive regulatory authority can lead to bureaucratic aggrandizement, with surging budgets and growing personnel rosters. Regulation also benefits individual bureaucrats by giving them an opportunity to advance their careers either by garnering professional esteem or by displaying their qualifications for private-sector jobs. When the user fee system increased the revenues of the FDA office that evaluated new drug applications, its prestige and influence increased, and the stature and importance of the office that monitored the use of approved products declined.[16]

From the private-interest perspective, an understanding of regulation is enhanced by acknowledging that regulatory intervention in the marketplace is usually an effort by some group to increase its own wealth and income at the expense of others. According to this theory, the benefits to private groups from regulation are neither a subversion nor an aberration but reflect the fundamental nature of the regulatory process.

Empirical Theory

Regardless of whether regulation is seen to result from efforts to promote public or private interests, regulations inevitably assist some groups at the expense of others.[17] The impact of regulation depends on the details of specific situations, but many regulatory disputes follow normal patterns: consumers versus producers, producers versus other producers, or consumers versus other consumers. Some regulatory issues are disputes between consumers and producers: when a regulated public utility seeks to raise the fees it charges for its product, its opponents are those who must pay the higher costs. Other regulatory disputes are contests between different groups of producers. Research-based pharmaceutical companies battle with generic drug manufacturers for the right to sell individual drugs. The research-based firms employ a small army of lawyers to invoke every possible provision of the patent laws so they can extend their exclusive marketing rights to specific products and block the generic manufacturers from competing.[18] Finally, regulatory questions can place the interests of one group of consumers against the interests of others. Automobile insurance rates, for example, can be higher for the residents of urban areas or safer suburban districts, for careful drivers or the accident-prone, for men or women, for experienced drivers or those who have recently learned to drive. Regardless of the original motivation, every government regulation has a specific impact on various segments of the economy.

DIMENSIONS OF FEDERAL REGULATION

Government regulation is not a complicated topic. Regulations are policy tools—rules that restrict the operations of businesses or other institutions in order to accomplish government-sanctioned purposes. At the end of the nineteenth century, the emergence of an industrial economy and the growing impact of railroads on society led many states to seek to regulate commercial activity. In 1877 the U.S. Supreme Court approved these efforts in the case of *Munn v. Illinois*, wherein the Court enunciated a doctrine that has sustained government regulation ever since: "When private property is devoted to a public use, it is subject to public regulation."[19]

Scores of federal regulatory agencies have been created since the Court handed down its decision, and the number of federal regulations has increased enormously. Regulatory agencies are established by federal statute; they draft rules explaining how they will interpret and implement the laws for which they are responsible. Uniform administrative procedures usually require an agency to publish a proposed rule in the *Federal Register* and allow citizens and organizations an opportunity to comment on the proposal. An agency is required to consider the public comments before it adopts a rule and finally publishes it in the *Code of Federal Regulations*. Once the rules are formulated, agencies apply them to specific cases in a process called *adjudication*. Adjudicatory proceedings can range from the formality of a courtroom trial to the informality of a casual conversation or letter, but the process, nonetheless, results in orders that define the rights and liabilities of individual parties in specific situations.

There are two varieties of regulation: competitive regulation and protective regulation.[20] Although the distinctions are sometimes blurred, governments normally employ *competitive regulation* when they seek to compensate for market failure and create the conditions that should result from perfect competition. This older form of regulation typically concentrates on a single industry and focuses on the industry's operations. Governments generally engage in *protective regulation* when they address the impact of a firm's activities on consumers, employees, or the society. This style of regulation affects a range of industries and emphasizes noneconomic issues. Listed in Table 11-1 are five agencies that stress competitive regulation of industries and five agencies responsible for the protective regulation of specific activities.

Competitive Regulation

The Interstate Commerce Commission (ICC) was created in 1887 as the federal government's first independent regulatory commission (IRC). It served as a prototype for other agencies that were to promote competitive conditions in a particular industry by basing their decisions on expert analyses rather than partisan considerations. It focused originally on a single industry, railroads, and later assumed responsibility for associated industries, trucking and water transport. It exercised its authority over the industry by dealing with three general issues: entry, or which firms were allowed to participate in the industry; the price that firms might charge for their services; and the conditions of service, or the features of the service provided to customers.

When President Clinton signed the Financial Services Modernization Act in 1999, he stressed the historic role of government in maintaining stability and

Table 11-1 Selected Federal Regulatory Agencies

Agency	Year created	Jurisdiction
Competitive Regulation		
Interstate Commerce Commission	1887	Railroads, trucking, some water shipping
Federal Home Loan Bank Board	1932	Savings-and-loan industry; abolished 1990
Federal Communications Commission	1934	Interstate, foreign telephone, television, radio, and cable
Federal Deposit Insurance Corporation	1934	Safety of customer deposits
Federal Energy Regulatory Commission	1977	Replaced Federal Power Commission (1920), natural gas, electricity
Protective Regulation		
Food and Drug Administration	1906	Safety of food and medicine
Equal Employment Opportunity Commission	1964	Enforce 1964 Civil Rights Act banning discrimination
Environmental Protection Agency	1970	Environmental pollution
Occupational Safety and Health Administration	1970	Health and safety standards in the workplace
Consumer Product Safety Commission	1972	Safety and labeling standards for consumer products

Source: Author.

competition within the banking industry.[21] The act repealed parts of the Glass-Steagall Banking Act of 1933 and allowed banks to become affiliated with securities firms and insurance companies.

Sen. Carter Glass, D-Va., and Rep. Henry Steagall, D-Ala., had drafted their legislation to help the nation recover from the Great Depression of the 1930s, the most acute banking crisis the country had ever experienced. Nearly one out of three commercial banks had closed between 1930 and 1933, bank loans had fallen 44 percent, and bank deposits had declined 30 percent.[22] Congress was desperate to restore public confidence in the banking system. As part of its regulatory strategy, Congress raised the minimum amount of capital that national banks must have and created a system of deposit insurance whereby the federal government would guarantee that depositors would recover their money if an insured bank failed. Fearing concentrations of power, drafters of the 1933 statute had also embraced a policy of territorial and functional "segmentation." The act limited a firm's banking operations to a single state and restricted affiliations between banks and securities firms, and subsequent legislation also barred banks from owning insurance companies. By preventing banks from engaging in other types of financial activities, the New Deal legislators sought to safeguard customers' deposits.

The current revolution in information technology has transformed the economics of the financial services industry.[23] Americans purchase approximately fifteen different banking and investment products, such as checking accounts, credit cards, mortgages, life insurance, and mutual funds. Economies of scope now make it cheaper and more effective for one firm to provide an array of services rather than requiring customers to deal with four or five different companies. Citicorp and Travelers Group were so convinced of the profitability of linking a bank and an insurance company that they announced their merger in 1998, fully twenty months before the statute authorizing combinations of banks and insurance companies was enacted.[24]

Changes in government regulation of banks and financial services are always controversial. President Clinton and his congressional allies insisted that the Financial Services Modernization Act of 1999 would spur competition in the industry, reduce prices, enhance the stability of the nation's financial services system, equip financial services firms to compete more effectively in global financial markets, and improve responsiveness to consumer preferences.[25] Under the new law, the Federal Reserve Board and the comptroller of the currency would regulate the new financial conglomerates, the Securities and Exchange Commission would oversee securities operations, and the states would continue to regulate insurance.

In contrast, Sen. Paul Wellstone, D-Minn., commented, "Glass-Steagall was intended to protect our financial system by insulating commercial banks from other forms of risk. . . . Now Congress is about to repeal that economic stabilizer without putting any comparable safeguard in its place."[26] Sen. Byron Dorgan, D-N.D., added, "I was here . . . when it was decided to allow the expansion of savings and loans. We have now decided in the name of modernization to forget the lessons of the past, of safety and soundness."[27] Other opponents, such as Ralph Nader and Robert Kuttner, argued that the new legislation served "mainly to pave the way for more megamergers." The act will not spur competition, they thought, but reduce it: "With these consolidations, senior executives will make even more money and ordinary consumers will have even fewer choices."[28] The legislation weakened privacy and community reinvestment standards, they maintained, and jeopardized the long-term stability of the nation's financial system. Furthermore, industry lobbyists had been the main proponents of the legislation, they said. Clinton's treasury secretary left the administration soon after agreement on the bill and became a top official in Citigroup, the firm that resulted from the Citibank-Travelers merger.

Competitive regulation concentrates on circumstances within an industry. Regulatory agencies that focus on competitive conditions within an industry often regard themselves as defenders of the industry rather than as the watchdog for consumers' interests. In contrast, protective regulation addresses policy goals that cut across industry boundaries and reach beyond the operations of a single industry.

Protective Regulation

Federal protective regulation originated in the Agriculture Department's inspection of meat at the beginning of the twentieth century, and it was enhanced by New Deal efforts to structure labor-management relations, corporate finance, and marketing. Protective regulation is also associated with the expansion of federal regulation in the 1960s and 1970s and is concentrated in the areas of equal employment opportunity, environmental protection, occupational safety and health, and consumer protection.

Part of the justification for protective regulation is that imperfections in the market system create the problems that protective regulation is intended to correct. A perfectly functioning price system, it is argued, would somehow account for the social costs of environmental pollution and occupational disease. More fundamentally, however, protective regulation embodies the nation's values and aspirations, as well as the society's desire to achieve objectives such as pure food, effective drugs, fair labor-management relations, and clean air. Protective regulation reflects the governmental judgment that these goals can best be achieved by restricting the operations of businesses and other nongovernmental institutions.

The Environmental Protection Agency (EPA), created in December 1970, displays the typical features of protective agencies. The structure of these newer agencies reflects disenchantment with classic independent regulatory commissions.[29] The older commissions were often thought to have been "captured" by the businesses they were intended to regulate, unconcerned about consumers, and unable to take the actions needed to solve the industry's long-term problems. The protective agencies are more likely to be located in the executive branch and headed by an administrator rather than a commission. A single administrator is more visible than a commission and is more easily held accountable for an agency's actions or inactions. An administrator is also a presidential appointee, and the president is politically responsible for an administrator's shortcomings. The newer agencies administer rules that cut across most sectors of the economy, and thus these agencies are less likely to be influenced by a single industry or corporation.

The EPA bears symbolic responsibility for the society's anxieties about acid rain, global warming, holes in the ozone layer, toxic wastes, and other environmental nightmares, but its actions are based on specific statutes. The agency's authority is derived from single-purpose statutes covering clean air, clean water, solid wastes, toxic wastes, radon, noise, and other pollutants. Within each area, the EPA first establishes *broad standards.* In air pollution, for example, the EPA has defined national air quality standards for common pollutants, factory emission levels for specific substances, emissions standards for newly constructed factories, motor vehicle emissions standards, and standards for fuels. The EPA then defines *narrow performance and design standards* that restrict how companies operate or mandate how products perform so as to achieve the broad program standards. Protective agencies usually enforce compliance with their standards through a system of permits and certifications that firms must obtain to demonstrate that they are abiding by the agencies' rules.

The design of automobiles in the United States was essentially unregulated until 1966.[30] Safety advocates and environmentalists then argued that the car companies were imposing heavy costs on the society by producing cars that were less safe, less fuel efficient, and more polluting than was necessary. At the same time, auto firms demanded enough regulatory flexibility to take advantage of marketplace opportunities, and, for the employment of their members, labor unions wanted as much domestic production of cars as possible. As protective agencies, the National Highway Traffic Safety Administration and the EPA defined design standards the companies were required to meet to improve safety, increase gasoline mileage, and reduce emissions. The emissions standards specified, for example, how many grams of hydrocarbons, carbon monoxide, and nitrogen oxides cars were permitted to release. Richard Harris and Sidney Milkis describe the controversy that led to the new regulations as a battle between the anti-automobile vanguard and established interests, the outcome of which removed decision-making power from the hands of corporate managers and subjected it to government standards.[31]

Inherent in the standard-setting and enforcement process are specific problems that protective regulatory agencies inevitably face. First, it is often difficult to relate narrow performance and design standards to broad policy objectives.[32] How many grams of nitrogen oxides per mile are permissible? How much health risk is allowable for workers who are employed in factories that use cancer-causing substances like benzene? Second, protective regulation invariably involves compliance costs to business, and these costs generate antagonisms. Theoretically, although not in every instance, the value of the benefits to the society from regulation exceeds the costs, but the parts of the society that pay the costs often differ from those that receive the benefits. Finally, protective regulation can be used to achieve a group's strategic and political goals. Some support for increased regulation of automobiles came from an anti-automotive vanguard that has opposed the influence of automobile and petroleum companies and believes that American society would be better off with fewer cars and more public transit.[33] Table 11-2 is a summary of the key differences between competitive and protective regulation.

Table 11-2   Typical Features of Competitive and Protective Regulation

	Competitive regulation	Protective regulation
Focus of agency	Single industry	Multi-industry activity
Structure	Commission	Executive agency
Focus of rules	Entry, price, service	Standards
Political context	Producers, officials	Diverse interests

Source: Author.

Discussions of regulation sometimes emphasize peculiar historic events or administrative structures and lose sight of the general patterns of government action.[34] Much of government operates by imposing restrictions on business even though the term *regulation* is applied only to specific situations. Criticisms of regulation are motivated both by complaints about competitive and protective regulation and by unhappiness with government's broader goals and activities.

THE CONTEST AMONG REFORM, DEREGULATION, AND REREGULATION

Deregulation was an international trend in the 1980s and 1990s. The movement away from government control of economic decisions took different forms in different countries, but it pervaded domestic policy in Great Britain and the United States and was quite visible in Germany and Japan. Even though deregulation is associated with the Reagan era, its intellectual origins appeared in the 1970s. A review of the criticisms of regulation foreshadows the political conflicts that occurred later.

Criticisms of Regulation

Opposition to government regulation was based on academic criticisms that found widespread support in the 1970s.[35] Again, it is necessary to distinguish between competitive and protective regulation. The mainstream economists who galvanized criticism of competitive regulation had traditionally embraced the goals of government regulation, but they argued in the 1970s that the rules adopted by regulatory officials were sometimes ineffective and often actually blocked the attainment of programmatic objectives.

The Interstate Commerce Commission, for example, was given the additional authority by Congress in 1920 to set railroad rates and oversee the development of the rail industry.[36] During the Great Depression of the 1930s, competition between railroads and lower-cost truckers intensified. The ICC took the side of the railroad industry by requiring truckers to charge the higher rates demanded by the railroads. Without the incentive for innovation, the railroads became even more committed to outdated procedures and technologies, and the financial troubles of the individual railroads multiplied.

In the deregulation era of the late 1970s and early 1980s, Congress determined that the industry's decline had been caused by federal regulation and granted railroads more freedom to set prices and govern their own operations.[37] Federal regulations, it was argued, required railroads, airlines, public utilities, and other regulated industries to incur unnecessary costs, pass up needed efficiencies, neglect promising new technologies, and provide substandard service. The statutory goals of providing safe and efficient services, the critics said, could be more effectively achieved if the regulatory commissions abandoned some of their controls, stressed the basic objectives of the regulatory framework, and insisted that firms actually compete rather than use federal regulations to close the market to more efficient rivals. These same viewpoints were heard again in the debates over the Financial Services Modernization Act of 1999 and in the continuing controversy over the deregulation of electricity markets.[38]

In contrast to the criticisms of competitive regulation, the critics of protective regulation assailed both regulatory procedures and objectives. The statutes authorizing protective regulation in the 1960s and 1970s reflected that era's fear that businesses would have undue influence over regulatory agencies. To prevent producers from dominating the drafting of regulations, legislators often included rigid standards and precise deadlines in the legislation they enacted. Sometimes these provisions were impossible to meet, but they were adopted because their proponents wanted to compel industries to improve their technology.[39] This approach, however, often forced administrators to concentrate on short-term remedies to specific problems that might in turn stand in the way of long-term solutions to basic issues. In addition, these statutes often asserted the primacy of one approach to a statute's goals without recognizing that alternative approaches might turn out to be more effective, and the statutes frequently insisted on the importance of one policy objective without acknowledging the legitimacy of competing purposes. In one observer's words, "the problem is mainly that there are too many instances of regulations that generate large social costs without commensurate social benefits."[40]

Other opponents of protective regulation were less concerned about procedures than about goals. They attacked protective regulation because they opposed the purposes to which it was being put. They believed that the health, safety, environmental, and equity objectives of protective regulations were not worth the increased role of government in society that they entailed. For these critics, regulation symbolized an active, interventionist government, and they were convinced that society was better off relying on the values and choices of individual citizens. Political opposition to some of the goals of regulation combined with evidence that regulatory techniques were sometimes costly and ineffective to produce a deregulation movement in the 1980s and 1990s that ignored the merits of individual programs and sustained a comprehensive attack on regulation itself.

Regulation as a Policy Tool

Regulation is often a difficult policy tool to employ, and it can produce disappointing results. The Federal Communications Commission is required by statute to make its regulatory decisions in accord with the "public interest, convenience, or necessity," but its policy judgments are often contentious. Regulatory standards like the "public interest" are so ambiguous that they can, as Philip M. Napoli concludes, "be utilized on behalf of virtually any policy action taken."[41] They become all-purpose rhetorical justifications that persuade no one who is not already convinced of their legitimacy. Furthermore, the meaning of regulatory standards evolves over time. The public interest standard originally obliged broadcasters to offer programming that would educate listeners and enrich their lives, but stricter judicial interpretations of the First Amendment now restrict the FCC's ability to regulate the content of programming. Recently the FCC has been satisfied that it was serving the public interest if consumers had access to modern communications technologies and a range of competitive services. What is more, regulatory standards are usually designed to fulfill one policy objective but pay scant attention to other considerations. Preserving localism in communications has long been a central principle of communications policy, but the new media environment emphasizes specialized programming that could not be supported by small communities. The public interest standard provides regulators little assistance in making appropriate judgments. The FCC regulates the ownership of various media in the interest of promoting diversity of program content, but its efforts conflict with communications technologies that handsomely reward economies of scale and scope, and there is little evidence that its extensive efforts do anything to produce more diverse program content.

Deregulation

Presidential interest in regulation had been infrequent until the 1970s, when the functioning of the nation's regulatory system came to be seen as a drag on productivity and a factor affecting the country's economic competitiveness. Government regulations were thought to impose unnecessary costs on the economy and to prevent firms from responding effectively to marketplace developments and innovative technologies. Presidents Gerald Ford and Jimmy Carter first spotlighted the importance of regulatory issues, and the period from 1978 to 1982 witnessed a flurry of legislative activity that deregulated many critical industries (see Table 11-3).

Table 11-3   Major Deregulation Statutes, 1978–1982

Year	Name of act	Purpose
1978	Airline Deregulation Act	Ended price, entry, route regulation by 1985
1978	Natural Gas Policy Act	Eliminated intra- and interstate price controls by 1989
1980	Motor Carrier Reform Act	Allowed more flexible pricing in trucking industry
1980	Staggers Rail Act	Allowed railroads flexibility in pricing and ending routes
1980	Depository Institutions Deregulation Act	Eliminated ceiling on S&L interest rates
1982	Bus Regulatory Reform Act	Allowed price, entry competition in the bus industry
1982	Depository Institutions Act	Expanded range of permissible investments for S&Ls

Source: Author.

The statutory initiatives of the years 1978 to 1982 appeared exclusively in the areas of competitive regulation and attracted bipartisan support.[42] During Ronald Reagan's presidency, however, regulation became a more partisan issue. The Reagan administration regarded both competitive and protective regulation as unnecessary burdens that had to be relieved if the country's economy was to be revived. The statutory framework for regulation did not change dramatically after 1982, but the Reagan White House reduced the impact of regulation on the economy by slashing regulatory budgets and appointing officials who were sympathetic to its goals to run agencies. Other presidents also inaugurated administrative reforms that combined efforts to curtail regulation with initiatives to streamline it.

President Ford required agencies to analyze the inflationary impact of proposed regulations, and President Carter created a Regulatory Analysis Review Group to assess the economic impact of major new regulations. President Reagan increased the role of the White House in the development of regulations and named Vice President Bush to lead a Task Force on Regulatory Relief. He also established an Office of Information and Regulatory Affairs to review regulations and required that proposed regulations be subjected to cost-benefit analysis. Its proponents maintain that cost-benefit analyses ensure that the benefits of new regulations exceed their costs before the regulations are imposed, but opponents insist that the quantification of benefits is frequently arbitrary and that the procedure blocks needed restrictions on corporate conduct.

President George H. W. Bush set up a Council on Competitiveness to review proposed regulations, but he also supported the Clean Air Act Amendments of 1990 and the Americans with Disabilities Act of 1990, which imposed substantial new restrictions on private institutions. In 1993 President Clinton commissioned Vice President Gore to conduct a National Performance Review to enhance government effectiveness, and this review recommended that numerous regulations be abolished.[43] President George W. Bush generally favored the deregulation of economic activity, but he also championed the No Child Left Behind legislation that imposed new operational and performance regulations on elementary and secondary institutions.

Regulation Outside the United States

Regulation is an essential mechanism of government control of industry not only in the United States but in other countries as well. Despite the rhetoric of privatization and deregulation, contemporary trends involve both more government regulation and less.[44] Whereas the United States traditionally expressed government interest in the operation of private institutions, such as airlines and telephone companies, through regulation, other nations typically owned these corporations. The United States sometimes deregulated basic industries, but other countries frequently sold them to private investors. Germany, for example, sold stock in Lufthansa, its national airline, and Great

Britain sold its public telephone system. As a result of the sales, both countries created regulatory systems to express the government's continuing interest in the operation of these services. One recent study has concluded that regulatory reform in Great Britain and the United States has generally reduced government control over industry, but it has also found that the recent changes in the regulatory framework in Germany and Japan have reinforced bureaucratic control over firms and markets.[45]

The importance of regulatory policies differs by political system. Although most countries can be defined by their welfare systems and patterns of taxation, S. S. Andersen and T. Burns maintain that the European Union defines itself through its regulatory policies.[46] Facing electoral and interparty competition, the member governments of the Union seek to avoid responsibility for regulatory policies that impose direct costs on their citizens by pointing to the European Union. Without the need to face the electorate, the European Union embraces such policies even though it has a limited budget. The European Commission and the directorates general play the central role in EU operations, and they specialize in administrative politics. Furthermore, support for the European Union has been spearheaded by corporations that find it easier to follow one European regulation than diverse national rules.[47] The interplay of substantive policies, administrative structure, and entrenched interests is also apparent in Indian regulatory policy. See Box 11-1.

SUMMARY

Regulation is a policy tool that ensures that businesses and other institutions respect government objectives in their operations. Regulations require businesses and others to undertake certain actions that government favors and to avoid other actions that government opposes. Sometimes regulations are a device to achieve public purposes, and on other occasions they are manipulated by businesses, other groups, or public officials to advance their private objectives. In either case, regulations deliver benefits to some groups and impose costs on others. Competitive regulations address the conduct of particular industries and are intended to provide the benefits of marketplace competition when such competition does not occur. Protective regulations are used to achieve government objectives in the areas of health and safety. They address the safety of food, the effects of drugs, equal employment opportunity, environmental protection, occupational safety and health, consumer protection, and similar issues.

Debates about the desirability of government regulation are heard on every side. Academic economists galvanized criticisms of competitive regulating in the 1970s when they demonstrated that rules adopted by regulatory officials were sometimes ineffective, often frustrated the policy goals regulators espoused, and were always costly. Opponents of protective regulation believed that the regulatory goals

Cases in Development
BOX 11-1 GETTING INDIA'S INFRASTRUCTURE RIGHT

India's most glaring problem, the nation's finance minister recently declared, is the poor quality of its infrastructure. The infrastructure deficit includes the need for new harbors, power plants, mass transit facilities, and rural road systems. Mumbai, once known as Bombay, is the country's commercial capital and the city that introduces most international investors to India, but it also has one of Asia's worst airports. While India seeks to catch up with China economically, its regulatory system determines the priority given to infrastructure projects by calculating only the direct commercial benefit produced by the specific infrastructure projects. China, in contrast, considers the value of infrastructure proposals on the basis of their comprehensive economic impact. India's shoddy facilities, transportation delays, and infrastructure bottlenecks are reportedly driving international investments to other countries.

In the early 1990s, India increased the market orientation of its economic policy from an older system that had relied heavily on government intervention in making economic decisions. In the years since, various governments have sought to adjust the country's administrative structure to limit the role that government should now play in the nation's economy, but they have had little success. In most circumstances, the administrative reforms were opposed by entrenched groups whose interests would be hurt by the proposals and by public officials who concluded that other issues were more important to their agendas. Recommendations from a reform commission that the size of the state service should be cut 30 percent and that the 350,000 positions should be eliminated immediately were opposed by the powerful civil service groups. India's ethnic and geographic diversity has yielded a federal system of government that divides political authority between the states and the center and an institutional complexity that requires a coalition of parties rather than a single party to organize the government. As a result little has been accomplished in reforming administrative procedures, and prospects for major improvements in the country's infrastructure are limited.

Sources: Edward Luce, "Modest Dream Is Crucial for Future," special report, "India and Globalisation," *Financial Times*, March 22, 2005, 1; and Krishna K. Tummala, "Higher Civil Service in India," in *Comparative Bureaucratic Systems*, ed. Krishna K. Tummala (New York: Lexington Books, 2003), 209–33.

were not worth the intrusion of government in society that the regulations entailed. The ultimate standard for evaluating regulatory initiatives is whether they have positive or negative effects on society. There should be no doubt, however, that as long as citizens want things from government, there will be persistent demands for new government regulations. The appeal of regulation as a policy tool has declined in recent decades, and the advantages of competition as a tool for achieving public purposes has increased. In the next chapter we will examine the competition and the dynamics of antitrust policies.

FURTHER READINGS

The home page of the Office of Management and Budget provides information on regulatory policy and financial management: http://www.whitehouse.gov/omb. The Securities and Exchange Commission is responsible for regulation stock market transactions and administering the disclosure of corporate financial data: http://www.sec.gov.

Angell, Marcia. *The Truth about the Drug Companies: How They Deceive Us and What to Do about It.* New York: Random House: 2004.
Desai, Uday, ed. *Environmental Politics and Policy in Industrialized Countries.* Cambridge, Mass.: MIT Press, 2002.
Dunn, James A., Jr. *Driving Forces: The Automobile, Its Enemies, and the Politics of Mobility.* Washington, D.C.: Brookings Institution Press, 1998.
Hallin, Daniel C., and Paolo Mancini. *Comparing Media Systems: Three Models of Media and Politics.* New York: Cambridge University Press, 2004.
Majone, Giandomenico, ed. *Regulating Europe.* London: Routledge, 1996.

NOTES

1. This and the next two sentences are based on Andrew Jack, "Branded Drugs Sales Top $500bn," *Financial Times,* March 10, 2005, 21.
2. Marcia Angell, *The Truth about the Drug Companies: How They Deceive Us and What to Do about It* (New York: Random House, 2004); and Jerry Avorn, *Powerful Medicines: The Benefits, Risks, and Costs of Prescription Drugs* (New York: Knopf, 2004).
3. Angell, *Truth about the Drug Companies,* chap. 1.
4. Andrew Jack, "No Headache Cure for Costly Drug Regulation," *Financial Times,* April 15, 2005, 11.
5. Andrew Jack, "Master or Servant: The US Drugs Regulator Is Put under Scrutiny," *Financial Times,* January 7, 2005, 9.
6. The balance of this paragraph is based on Christopher Bowe, "Merck's Fall from Grace: After Vioxx, How Can the Drugs Giant Regain Its Reputation," *Financial Times,* November 18, 2004, 13.
7. This quotation from Sen. Charles E. Grassley, R-Iowa, and information in the balance of the paragraph are from Jack, "Master or Servant," 9.
8. Louis Galambos and Joseph Pratt, *The Rise of the Corporate Commonwealth: United States Business and Public Policy in the 20th Century* (New York: Basic Books, 1988), 56.
9. Barry M. Mitnick, *The Political Economy of Regulation: Creating, Designing, and Removing Regulatory Forms* (New York: Columbia University Press, 1980), chap. 3.
10. Marver H. Bernstein, *Regulating Business by Independent Commission* (Princeton: Princeton University Press, 1955).

11. Thomas K. McCraw, *Prophets of Regulation* (Cambridge, Mass.: Harvard University Press, 1984).

12. The private-interest viewpoint is also called the *public choice* perspective. This discussion is based on Sam Peltzman, "Toward a More General Theory of Regulation," *Journal of Law and Economics,* August 1976, 211–40; Robert E. McCormick, "A Review of the Economics of Regulation: The Political Process," in *Regulation and the Reagan Era: Politics, Bureaucracy and the Public Interest,* ed. Roger E. Meiners and Bruce Yandle (New York: Holmes and Meier, 1989), 16–37; William F. Shughart, *Antitrust Policy and Interest Group Politics* (New York: Quorum Books, 1990), chaps. 1–2.

13. Bruce M. Owen and Ronald Braeutigam, *The Regulation Game: Strategic Use of the Administrative Process* (Cambridge, Mass.: Ballinger, 1978).

14. This idea is derived from the concept of the antitrust pork barrel outlined in Richard A. Posner, "The Federal Trade Commission," *University of Chicago Law Review* 37 (1969): 47–89. See also R. Kenneth Godwin and Barry J. Seldon, "What Corporations Really Want from Government," in *Interest Group Politics,* ed. Allan J. Cigler and Burdett A. Loomis (Washington, D.C.: CQ Press, 2002), 205–24.

15. William A. Niskanen, *Bureaucracy and Representative Government* (Chicago: Aldine, 1971); James Q. Wilson, "The Politics of Regulation," in *Social Responsibility and the Business Predicament,* ed. James W. McKie (Washington, D.C.: Brookings Institution, 1974), 135–68.

16. Jack, "Master or Servant," 9.

17. Roger G. Noll and Bruce M. Owen, *The Political Economy of Deregulation: Interest Groups in the Regulatory Process* (Washington, D.C.: American Enterprise Institute, 1983).

18. Angell, *Truth about the Drug Companies,* 9–10.

19. Kermit L. Hall, *The Magic Mirror: Law in American History* (New York: Oxford University Press, 1989), 234–36.

20. This formulation is frequently used; see, for example, Randall B. Ripley and Grace A. Franklin, *Policy Implementation and Bureaucracy,* 2nd ed. (Chicago: Dorsey Press, 1986), 116–76. See also Jeffrey E. Cohen, *Politics and Economic Policy in the United States,* 2nd ed. (Boston: Houghton Mifflin, 2000), 255. (Sometimes this distinction is presented as economic vs. social regulation.)

21. William J. Clinton, "Statement on Signing Legislation to Reform the Financial System," *Weekly Compilation of Presidential Documents* (Washington, D.C.: GPO, November 15, 1999), 2363–66.

22. John D. Hawke, "The New Banking Industry," *Vital Speeches of the Day* 66, no. 3 (November 15, 1999): 66–68.

23. Glenn Coleman, "The Battle for Your Money," *Money,* December 1999, 134–40.

24. Richard W. Stevenson, "Financial Services Heavyweights Try Do-It-Yourself Deregulation," *New York Times,* April 7, 1998, A1.

25. Clinton, "Statement on Signing Legislation to Reform the Financial System"; and Robert Weissman, "Deregulating Finance," *Multinational Monitor,* October–November 1999, 6.

26. Stephen Labaton, "Congress Passes Wide-Ranging Bill Easing Bank Laws," *New York Times,* November 5, 1999, 1.

27. Ibid., 1.

28. Weissman, "Deregulating Finance"; quotations from Robert Kuttner, "A Requiem for Glass-Steagall," *Business Week,* November 15, 1999, 28.

29. Marver Bernstein, "The Regulatory Process: A Framework for Analysis," *Law and Contemporary Problems* 26 (Spring 1961): 329–46; and Roger C. Cramton, "Regulatory Structure and Regulatory Performance: A Critique of the Ash Council Report," *Public Administration Review* 32, no. 4 (July 1972): 284–93.

30. This paragraph draws from James A. Dunn Jr., *Driving Forces: The Automobile, Its Enemies, and the Politics of Mobility* (Washington, D.C.: Brookings Institution Press, 1998), chap. 3, esp. pp. 51, 57.

31. Richard Harris and Sidney Milkis, *The Politics of Regulatory Change: A Tale of Two Agencies* (New York: Oxford University Press, 1989), 80.

32. Eugene Bardach, "Social Regulation as a Generic Policy Instrument," in *Beyond Privatization: The Tools of Government Action,* ed. Lester M. Salamon (Washington, D.C.: Urban Institute Press, 1989), 197–229.

33. For a different example, see Bruce A. Ackerman and William T. Hassler, *Clean Coal/Dirty Air* (New Haven: Yale University Press, 1981).

34. James Q. Wilson, ed., *The Politics of Regulation* (New York: Basic Books, 1980).

35. American Bar Association, Commission on Law and the Economy, *Federal Regulation: Roads to Reform* (Chicago: American Bar Association, 1979); Michael S. Baram, *Alternatives to Regulation: Managing Risks to Health, Safety and the Environment* (Lexington, Mass.: Lexington Books, 1982); Leonard W. Weiss and Michael W. Klass, eds., *Case Studies in Regulation: Revolution and Reform* (Boston: Little, Brown, 1981); and Lawrence J. White, *Reforming Regulation: Processes and Problems* (Englewood Cliffs, N.J.: Prentice Hall, 1981).

36. For a well-presented review of the ICC's development, see Damodar Gujarati, *Government and Business* (New York: McGraw-Hill, 1984), 251–59.

37. This theme was expressed in the Railroad Revitalization and Regulation Act of 1976 and the Staggers Rail Act of 1980. The Motor Carrier Act of 1980 relaxed the ICC's regulation of the trucking industry.

38. Margaret Kriz, "Grounding Out?" *National Journal,* May 22, 1999, 1396; and Margaret Kriz, "Will Electricity Deregulation Fizzle Again?" *National Journal,* February 20, 1999, 472.

39. Larry E. Ruff, "Federal Environmental Regulation," in Weiss and Klass, *Case Studies in Regulation,* 235–61; and Robert E. Litan and William D. Nordhaus, *Reforming Federal Regulation* (New Haven: Yale University Press, 1983), 89–99.

40. White, *Reforming Regulation,* 225.

41. Philip M. Napoli, *Foundations of Communications Policy: Principles and Process in the Regulation of the Electronic Media* (Cresskill, N.J.: Hampton Press, 2001), 94.

42. George C. Eads and Michael Fix, *Relief or Reform? Reagan's Regulatory Dilemma* (Washington, D.C.: Urban Institute Press, 1984).

43. Al Gore, *Creating a Government That Works Better and Costs Less: Report of the National Performance Review* (Washington, D.C.: GPO, 1993).

44. See, for example, Richard B. McKenzie and Dwight R. Lee, *Quicksilver Capital: How the Rapid Movement of Wealth Has Changed the World* (New York: Free Press, 1991).

45. Steven K. Vogel, *Freer Markets, More Rules: Regulatory Reform in Advanced Industrial Countries* (Ithaca, N.Y.: Cornell University Press, 1996).

46. S. S. Andersen and T. Burns, "The European Union and the Erosion of Parliamentary Democracy: A Study of Post-Parliamentary Government," in *The European Union: How Democratic Is It?* ed. S. S. Andersen and K. A. Eliassen (London: Sage Publications, 1996), 227–51. See also Claudio M. Radaelli, *Technocracy in the European Union* (London: Longman, 1999).

47. Giandomenico Majone, ed., *Regulating Europe* (London: Routledge, 1996).

CHAPTER 12

Antitrust and Competition Policy in the New Economy

AT THE END of the 1990s, mergers among giant companies reached an unprecedented level.[1] Behemoth mergers in the banking and petroleum industries, however, were then overshadowed by awesome combinations in the communications sector. America Online, the leading Internet service provider, acquired Time Warner, already the world's largest media company, in what was described as the biggest merger in U.S. history. Eight major telecom deals followed, creating two local telephone empires that each controlled one-third of the nation's phone lines. Verizon resulted from the fusion of Bell Atlantic, Nynex, and GTE, and SBC emerged from combining Ameritech, Pacific Telesis, and SBC Communications. SBC then sought to acquire AT&T's wireline phone business, and Verizon sought to purchase the long-distance and Internet backbone firm, MCI. The wireless telephone landscape was restructured when Sprint merged with Nextel and when Cingular, a joint venture of SBC and Bell South, sought permission to take over AT&T Wireless. Comcast became the nation's premier cable provider by purchasing the assets of two firms that had once been its major rivals, and NewsCorp, owner of the Fox network and cable properties, bought DirecTV, the nation's dominant satellite television enterprise. Finally, GE-NBC acquired Vivendi-Universal Entertainment, making it the last television network to combine forces with a film production company.

These efforts to gain market share and combine old institutions with new technologies took place as a maelstrom of controversy surrounded the country's antitrust laws. A Rip Van Winkle who had slept from the 1970s into the new century would discover that antitrust laws were no longer the looming presence in the country's boardrooms they once were. Antitrust policy is intended to protect consumers by promoting economic competition and discouraging monopolies, mergers, and restraints of trade. For almost a century antitrust rules were one of the most significant features of the nation's business environment. Now antitrust has lost the unqualified allegiance of economists; it has been challenged by trends in domestic and international business and has been defended only intermittently by the federal government.[2]

The purpose of this chapter is to consider whether the antitrust traditions from an industrial era remain a suitable basis for promoting the country's economic and political objectives in a digital age.[3] In it the origins of antitrust laws and the economic assumptions associated with them are explored, and the policy's evolution and the rationale for recent criticisms are examined.

American antitrust laws are unique. No country has tried more consistently to structure economic competition and supervise marketplace behavior than the United States. The uniqueness of the American approach to antitrust is best appreciated by comparing U.S. policies with those of other countries. This chapter includes reviews of the policies of Germany, Japan, and Great Britain. Competition policy has become a global issue, and the chapter covers recent events in international merger and antitrust policy.

AMERICAN ANTITRUST POLICY

Antitrust policy was a passionate issue in the early decades of the twentieth century.[4] It stood at the center of presidential campaigns and reflected a vigorous struggle over the country's future. It is significant that Americans use the phrase "antitrust policy," whereas Europeans speak more soberly of "competition policy." The difference in usage reflects the fact that American laws were inspired more by political fears than by economic theories.

In the decades after the Civil War, U.S. citizens were fearful of railroads, cartels, Standard Oil, large eastern banks, and the plight of farmers. American industry was being reshaped during this period, and mergers took the form of *trusts*, in which the ownership of companies was turned over to the board of trustees of a supercorporation in exchange for a share of the new corporation's earnings. By the end of the century, trusts controlled the production of petroleum, sugar, tobacco, beef, whiskey, harvesting machinery, and other everyday products.

Nineteenth-century legislators did not understand intricate theories of economic competition, but they did recognize that the giant new corporations represented concentrations of economic and political power that jeopardized traditional ways of life.[5] Since trusts had the power to restrict the supply of goods and increase prices, legislators concluded that government should be empowered to regulate the development of trusts and control their practices.

Economic Rationale for Antitrust

Economic analyses of antitrust issues have become more sophisticated in the past century. For antitrust purposes, a monopoly appears when a seller or group of sellers can affect competition by changing the price or conditions at which a product is sold.[6] Trusts and other monopolistic restraints of trade are important in economic terms because they violate the assumptions of a competitive market.

Perfect competition assumes that no buyer or seller has control over prices and that new firms are free to enter the marketplace and join the competition.

Monopolistic restraints of trade are economically inefficient on several grounds. It is necessary first to distinguish allocative from productive efficiency. *Productive efficiency* occurs when a firm is manufacturing its product at the lowest possible cost. *Allocative efficiency* appears when a society distributes resources among economic activities in a manner that provides it the greatest possible benefit.

Monopolistic arrangements are inefficient because monopolists can impose higher prices on the society than are economically warranted. They are allocatively inefficient because the higher prices direct more of society's resources than is appropriate to areas where monopolists are active. Monopolies are also inefficient because monopolists have less incentive to improve products and cut operating costs than producers in competitive markets have.

The most common defense of monopolies is that they can sometimes achieve lower production costs than other firms. The average cost of manufacturing a product often declines as production runs lengthen and the number of units increases. The more items produced, the less it costs to produce each item. Declining average costs, or *economies of scale,* usually result from the specialization of labor and the spreading of fixed costs over a higher level of production. Monopolists who control an entire industry can benefit from economies of scale and from their greater ability to fund extensive research and development programs.

Antitrust Statutes

Antitrust policies have evolved slowly.[7] The Sherman Act of 1890 has been the foundation of the country's antitrust policy for more than a century. Section 1 of the law prohibits agreements among companies that fix prices and restrain trade, and section 2 makes it illegal for firms to "monopolize" particular markets or industries. Table 12-1 summarizes the main provisions of the Sherman Act and subsequent antitrust laws.

The history of the Sherman Act illustrates the problems that have plagued the enforcement of antitrust laws from the start. The original prohibition of agreements between companies to fix prices had the perverse effect of prompting companies to merge with their competitors so they could escape the restrictions of the new law. In addition, the Supreme Court interpreted the ban on actions that "monopolize" a market in section 2 of the Sherman Act to mean that only "unreasonable" or coercive attempts to monopolize a market were prohibited and that monopolies resulting from conventional commercial activities were perfectly legal.[8]

Calls for stronger antitrust laws were a major issue in the 1912 presidential election. The Clayton Act and the Federal Trade Commission Act were part of President Wilson's broad economic package, which also championed creation of

Table 12-1 Major Provisions of Antitrust Laws

Act	Provisions
Sherman Act (1890)	Prohibits agreements to fix prices or restrain trade and bans actions that seek to monopolize a market
Clayton Act (1914)	Prohibits price discrimination, restrictions on retailers, mergers if they lessen competition
Federal Trade Commission Act (1914)	Creates the Federal Trade Commission and prohibits unfair methods of competition
Robinson-Patman Act (1936)	Strengthens Clayton Act rules against price discrimination
Wheeler-Lea Act (1938)	Expands authority of Federal Trade Commission to protect consumers as well as competitors
Celler-Kefauver Act (1950)	Extends Clayton Act's prohibition to encompass various types of mergers
Antitrust Improvement Act (1976)	Requires firms to notify government in advance of pending mergers
International Antitrust Enforcement Assistance Act (1994)	Authorizes cooperation with foreign antitrust authorities

Source: Author.

the Federal Reserve System, the reduction of tariffs, and the adoption of a federal income tax. The Clayton Act sought to guarantee a place for small business, ban corporate mergers accomplished through the acquisition of stock, and prohibit specific actions that lessened competition, such as requirements by manufacturers that retailers purchase all their products from one supplier. The Federal Trade Commission Act created the Federal Trade Commission (FTC) to enforce the Clayton Act, and it also gave the new agency sweeping authority to prevent companies from "using unfair methods of competition."

These two statutes had limited impact when they were enacted because the FTC had little power to enforce its rulings and the Supreme Court interpreted the ban on mergers accomplished through the acquisition of stock to mean that mergers accomplished through purchases of assets were permissible. The Robinson-Patman Act of 1936 strengthened the Clayton Act's rules against price discrimination to help small retailers compete with large chain stores, and the Wheeler-Lea Act of 1938 authorized the FTC to protect consumers as well as companies. In 1950 the Celler-Kefauver Act extended the Clayton Act's antimerger rules to cover asset as well as stock mergers and to ban other forms of mergers. The Antitrust Improvement Act of 1976 required large corporations to notify the government of pending mergers and give the authorities time to investigate proposed mergers for potential violations of law. Acknowledging the growing significance of global economic activity, the International Antitrust Enforcement Assistance Act of 1994 authorizes U.S. officials to make cooperative agreements with foreign antitrust agencies.

Antitrust Litigation

The Antitrust Division of the Justice Department and the FTC are primarily responsible for enforcing antitrust laws, but state governments have also become increasingly active in the antitrust area.[9] In addition, antitrust suits can be brought by private parties who believe they have been harmed by a company's anticompetitive practices. Table 12-2 provides an overview of the implementation of antitrust laws in different eras.

There was little enforcement of antitrust rules between 1890 and 1905, but Supreme Court decisions did establish precedents that helped shape antitrust policy in later periods.[10] *United States v. Trans-Missouri Freight Association,* the first major case involving an agreement among companies to fix prices, was decided in 1897.[11] The defendants acknowledged the existence of a rate-setting association but contended that their rates were fair. They maintained that section 1 of the Sherman Act only prohibited price-fixing agreements that imposed unreasonable rates. By a five-vote majority, the Supreme Court rejected the companies' position and ruled that agreements to fix prices are per se illegal, regardless of the fairness of the prices.

Section 2 of the Sherman Act, banning corporate actions to monopolize a market, was tested in *United States v. Northern Securities Company.*[12] J. P. Morgan and James Hill used the Northern Securities Company to gain control of the only two railroads that served the northern parts of the Midwest and West. The government charged Northern Securities with monopolizing rail transportation in the region in violation of the Sherman Act, and by a 5–4 decision the Supreme Court concurred. More important, the Supreme Court ordered the merger between the two railroads to be dissolved even though the Sherman Act had not authorized this type of remedy. The significance of the divestiture precedent became clear in the period from 1906 to 1920.

United States v. Standard Oil Company of New Jersey is probably the most famous antitrust case in the nation's history.[13] Standard Oil symbolized everything

Table 12-2 Implementation of Antitrust Laws by Time Period

Period	Activities
1890–1905	Little enforcement action, but court decisions establish important legal precedents
1906–20	Spectacular corporate breakups and the creation of the judicial Rule of Reason
1920–38	Little enforcement action
1938–80	Antitrust laws assume modern features and have broad relevance for corporate action
1981–2005	Enforcement concentrates on price-fixing and certain types of merger activities

Source: Adapted from Donald Dewey, *The Antitrust Experiment* (New York: Columbia University Press, 1990), 6–11.

the public disliked about corporate trusts. The government charged that Standard Oil had employed a catalog of illegal and improper practices to gain control of 85 percent of the market for refined oil. In 1911 a unanimous Supreme Court agreed with the government, found that Standard Oil had violated the Sherman Act, and ordered the company dissolved.

The significance of the *Standard Oil* decision was not just the spectacular dissolution of a notorious company, but the rationale for judicial action. Chief Justice Edward D. White defined a two-step process for deciding whether a company had "monopolized" a market. According to White, the court first determines if the company has sufficient market power to be considered a monopoly. If the company has enough market power, the court then decides if the market power has been acquired properly or improperly. A "Rule of Reason," the justice wrote, should help the court distinguish "normal methods of industrial development" from those that were unacceptable. Because there was abundant evidence that Standard Oil had acted illegally, the court ruled that the company had violated the Sherman Act and should be broken up.

The implications of the Rule of Reason's distinction between normal and abusive business practices became clear in *United States v. United States Steel Corporation*.[14] U.S. Steel had been formed in 1901 through the merger of twelve independent companies and was the nation's largest industrial enterprise. It controlled 60 percent of total U.S. iron and steel output when the government alleged that it had violated the Sherman Act. The Supreme Court rejected the government's charge, found that the company's position had been achieved through "normal" rather than abusive tactics, and determined that the firm had never tried to eliminate its competitors. For the Court, U.S. Steel was a "good" rather than a "bad" trust, and it was acquitted.

The Rule of Reason placed an enormous burden on would-be trustbusters. They had to prove that a firm had a dominant market position, had obtained its position through predatory tactics, and had used its power to eliminate its competitors. Because of the burden of proving each of these elements, there was little antitrust enforcement between 1920 and 1938.

The New Deal period of the late 1930s revitalized the antitrust field. Congress enacted the Robinson-Patman and Wheeler-Lea Acts, and the Roosevelt administration stepped up enforcement actions by bringing an indictment against the Aluminum Company of America (ALCOA). The *ALCOA* case dealt a sharp blow to the Rule of Reason standard for interpreting antitrust issues and set the tone for enforcement actions in subsequent decades.[15]

In 1937 the Justice Department charged that ALCOA had monopolized the aluminum market even though there was little evidence that ALCOA had engaged in improper activities. The government relied on the fact that ALCOA controlled the overwhelming share of the market. After lengthy litigation, the Court finally ruled that Congress had not intended to condone good trusts and condemn bad ones. Congress had, the Court insisted, forbade all monopolies. On this basis, the Court rejected the Rule of Reason, declared that market share alone was sufficient evidence of a violation of antitrust laws, and found ALCOA guilty of monopolizing the aluminum industry. The clarity of this ruling led the Justice Department to step up its enforcement activities and prompted Congress to strengthen antitrust standards.

The *ALCOA* era ended sometime in the late 1970s. By this time the Supreme Court had begun to back away from the *ALCOA* principle that market share alone was evidence of wrongdoing. When the government charged that DuPont had monopolized the cellophane industry, the Supreme Court accepted the company's defense that cellophane was only a small part of a larger flexible wrapping materials industry in which DuPont played a limited role.[16] When a competitor argued that Eastman Kodak had used its market power in film to expand the sales of its cameras, the court said that successful marketplace competition should not be an excuse for "legal castigation" and ruled mostly in Kodak's favor.[17]

The start of a new stage in the implementation of antitrust laws was symbolized by the dismissal in January 1982 of a suit the government had launched against International Business Machines (IBM) thirteen years earlier. The Justice Department had charged in 1969 that IBM monopolized the market for general purpose computers by bundling services and requiring customers to purchase entire computer systems, by offering reduced prices in the education market, and by announcing new products in a manner that damaged competitors. After twelve years, 100,000 pages of trial transcripts, and tens of millions of pages of documents, the head of the Justice Department's Antitrust Division concluded in 1982 that the suit was "without merit" and ordered it dismissed. The dismissal of the IBM suit constituted another step away from the *ALCOA* ruling and back toward a Rule of Reason standard for adjudicating monopoly cases.

Enforcement Issues

The antitrust goal of maintaining free and fair competition has emphasized four topics: monopolies, mergers, price-fixing, and anticompetitive practices. Each has presented enforcement problems.

Monopolies. The Sherman Act outlaws efforts to monopolize an industry. This assumes, however, that the boundaries of a market can be clearly delineated. This is often not the case. In the DuPont case, are cellophane and flexible wrapping materials part of one market or do they represent different markets? Does beer constitute its own market or is it part of a larger beverage market? The more broadly the product market is defined, the less monopolistic any company is likely to appear. The same issue arises in determining the relevant geographic market. The more expansive the geographic borders, the less prominent is any single producer.

Analysts also disagree about the appropriate remedy—when a monopoly is discovered, should remedies reward competing firms or safeguard consumers? There is little evidence that consumers benefited from the dissolution of Standard Oil. Furthermore, companies may be monopolies because they are efficient. If the Justice Department had succeeded in breaking up IBM in 1982, the result might well have been a less effective computer industry.

Mergers. The Clayton Act as amended by the Celler-Kefauver Act prohibits mergers that lessen competition. There are three types of mergers. A *horizontal* merger is the union of two or more companies that sell the same product (for example, if Ford Motor were to join with General Motors). A *vertical* merger occurs when companies that operate at different stages of a production-distribution process combine (for example, if Ford were to combine with U.S. Steel because steel is heavily used in manufacturing cars). *Conglomerate* mergers involve companies that sell different but related products, operate in different regions, or are active in completely unrelated product areas (for example, if Ford were to link up with a book publisher).

In 1982 and 1984 the Justice Department issued new Merger Guidelines, defining standards for reviewing proposed mergers that were more lenient than earlier rules.[18] Horizontal mergers are usually motivated by efforts to increase a firm's market share. The guidelines defined the market circumstances in which the department would accept or oppose such mergers. The Justice Department also indicated that its review of proposed mergers would consider the financial condition of the firms, the ease with which new firms could enter the industry, the pace of technological change, and the importance of international competition.

Vertical mergers have no direct effect on the concentration in particular markets, but they attract enforcement attention because they could close markets to independent suppliers and limit opportunities for new firms to enter the market. According to the guidelines, vertical mergers would be examined if there was substantial concentration in the market most affected by the merger. In fact, the Reagan administration sanctioned vertical mergers that would probably have been challenged in earlier periods, and the Justice Department's 1992 Merger Guidelines did not even bother to address vertical mergers.[19]

The courts have approached the issue of conglomerate mergers cautiously. Both the costs and the benefits of conglomerate mergers remain unproven. They have been opposed on the economic grounds that they inhibit potential competition and on the political basis that they constitute undesirable concentrations of wealth and power. Under the Justice Department guidelines, very few conglomerate mergers have been or would be challenged.

Price-fixing. Price-fixing and collusion among firms to restrain trade are prohibited by section 1 of the Sherman Act and by the Federal Trade Commission Act. Explicit price-fixing agreements among firms in the electrical equipment industry were prosecuted in the 1950s. Price-fixing may also occur, although it is more difficult to prove, when firms coordinate their actions even though they have made no agreement to fix prices. Essentially all commentators, scholars, and practitioners oppose collusive activity to fix prices. Active prosecution is usually regarded as an effective deterrent against further collusion.

Anticompetitive Practices. The Clayton, Robinson-Patman, and Sherman Acts outlaw a variety of commercial practices that can limit competition. Price discrimination occurs when a producer sells the same product to different retailers at different prices. The practice occurs when firms seek to boost their sales by favoring high-volume dealers or selling at lower prices in communities where they face strong competition. Price discrimination is illegal when it is intended to harm competitors, but prosecutions are difficult because sellers argue that price differences are justified and are not intended to harm competitors.

Contractual relationships between producers and retailers are also illegal if they have anticompetitive consequences. Among potentially illegal "vertical restrictions" are tying agreements, which occur when a producer allows a retailer to purchase a popular product only if the retailer also agrees to purchase a quantity of a less desirable product. Exclusive dealing agreements that require a retailer to purchase all products from a single producer, and resale-price-maintenance arrangements that allow the manufacturer to set the price of a product charged by the retailer may also be illegal. Administrations at this time were criticized for their lack of enthusiasm in investigating and prosecuting cases involving price discrimination and vertical restrictions.

The enforcement of antitrust statutes rests on the concern that a company would raise prices excessively or that it would drive competitors from the market and then extract higher profits from consumers.[20] In general, enforcement decisions during the Clinton administration continued the lenient trend, but variations were evident. In 1997 the Antitrust Division and the FTC presented their own somewhat more exacting Merger Guidelines. While sanctioning massive consolidation in the aircraft, financial services, petroleum, communications, and automotive sectors, Clinton regulators blocked a merger between Staples and Office Depot, the two office supply chains, even though the two firms together accounted for only 6 percent of the office stationery market.[21] In its final years in office, the Clinton administration prosecuted Microsoft for antitrust violations, filed suit to halt the merger between Sprint and WorldCom, and imposed conditions on mergers resembling those that it had welcomed in its early years. John E. Kwoka Jr. and Lawrence J. White note that the Merger Guidelines released in 1984, 1992, and 1997 had been shaped in large part by economists, and they find that these guidelines have been particularly influential in shaping antitrust doctrines in the years since.[22]

Prominent communications mergers raised troublesome new issues about the structure of product markets and their impact on relationships among sellers, customers, and associated firms.[23] Antitrust officials permitted mergers among local phone companies and cable system operators on the grounds that the markets these firms served were already monopolies and the mergers would not make the situation any worse. These judgments downplayed the fact that an increasing number of firms play multiple roles in the communications sector and offer an array of products and services based on complementary technologies, entrepreneurial expertise, factor costs, and contractual arrangements. The same firms may be rivals in one market and allies in providing other services. Developments in the local phone or cable operations, for example, could delay the deployment of broadband services, and the future of district broadcast satellite systems may be determined by relations among broadcast networks.[24] The integration of complementary markets may not violate traditional prohibitions on tying products or contravene the normal standards for vertical mergers, but it may nonetheless impose costs on consumers and limit opportunities for competing firms.

A review of the evolution of U.S. antitrust policy highlights the ebb and flow of government action, but it understates the American commitment to the principle of marketplace competition. Global policy has been a major focus of antitrust developments in recent years, and this aspect of U.S. antitrust policy is better understood by examining competition policies in Germany, Great Britain, Japan, and the European Union.

COMPARATIVE ANTITRUST POLICIES

U.S. antitrust policy rests on the assumption that competition is politically and economically desirable. Other countries assess competition more equivocally and more instrumentally. They are as likely to fear "excess" competition as they are to applaud full competition. They often use competition policy as a tool to accomplish other government objectives, and if competition standards interfere with other policy objectives, they are not reluctant to set it aside.

Countries develop their competition policies in their own sociopolitical context. U.S. policy was created to deal with domestic conditions in the late nineteenth and early twentieth centuries. The competition policies of Germany, Great Britain, and Japan are a heritage of the post–World War II era, when each country recognized its dependence on the international economy.

The major features of antitrust policies in Germany, Great Britain, Japan, and the United States are outlined in Table 12-3. Noted first is whether a country's approach to antitrust issues is to prohibit any reduction of competition or to regulate the level of competition in the interests of achieving other goals. Then the goals of a country's antitrust policies are indicated—whether to promote competition, to manage the decline or "rationalization" of an industry, or to accomplish other public purposes. Also indicated are whether the countries allow exemptions to

Table 12-3 Comparative Antitrust Traditions

	Germany	Great Britain	Japan	United States
Approach				
Theory	Regulate	Regulate	Prohibit	Prohibit
Practice	Regulate	Regulate	Regulate	Mixed
Goals				
Competition	Yes	Yes	Yes	Yes
Rationalization	Yes	Yes	Yes	No
Public good	Yes	Yes	Yes	No
Exemptions				
Economic	Yes	Yes	Yes	Rare
Technological	Yes	Yes	Yes	Limited
International	Yes	Yes	Yes	Limited
Enforcement				
Government	Mixed	Mixed	Weak	Demanding
Private	Rare	None	Rare	Rigorous

Sources: Based on Report of the President's Commission on Industrial Competitiveness, *Global Competition: The New Reality*, vol. 2 (Washington, D.C.: GPO, 1985), 191; supplemented by David B. Audretsch, *The Market and the State: Government Policy towards Business in Europe, Japan and the United States* (New York: New York University Press, 1989), 77–118.

their antitrust policies and whether antitrust policies are systemically or only occasionally enforced.

Germany

Modern cartels, associations of companies that set prices and limit production, appeared first in Germany in the 1870s.[25] They were organized by industries, banks, and even government to help companies survive recessions, reduce excess production capacity, and sustain prices. The German Law against Restraint of Competition was enacted in 1958 and reflects the government's lukewarm commitment to promoting competition. It states that "competition is not in and of itself the goal, but rather the means for improving efficiency and technical progress."[26] Mergers among competing firms are permitted if they help an ailing industry or serve the broad public interest.

German law emphasizes corporate behavior rather than industry structure. The existence of a monopoly is not illegal in Germany. The government can proceed against a company only if the firm has abused its monopoly position by charging an excessive price, providing inferior goods, or restricting sales. German law exempts from antitrust rules corporate agreements that promote efficiency, advance technical developments, or expand foreign trade. Approximately three hundred cartels have been approved by the German government and continue to function.[27]

The Federal Cartel Office is responsible for administering antitrust laws. Details of proposed mergers must be submitted for review, but the office can block a merger only with the concurrence of other government agencies. Large German companies in core industries rarely face antitrust problems. Daimler-Chrysler, the auto manufacturer, was recently permitted to take over the leading companies in the German defense industry.

Great Britain

Competition policy in Great Britain emerged in the post–World War II period, but it has not been a government priority.[28] It is entwined with other social and economic objectives and is continually balanced against such concerns as public safety, local employment, and regional economic disparities.

Under British law, there is no presumption against monopolies or mergers.[29] Public policy seeks to regulate only those monopolies whose actions harm the public interest. The Thatcher government of the 1980s stressed its view that takeovers and marketplace decisions constituted a superior basis for identifying the public interest. Exemptions from British antitrust rules are permitted for economic, technological, and international purposes.

The British process for enforcing monopoly and merger policies is administrative.[30] It is based on civil rather than criminal law, involves few explicit sanctions, and depends on cooperation between government and industry. The Office of Fair Trading (OFT) identifies possible monopoly situations and refers them for investigation to the Monopolies and Mergers Commission (MMC). If the MMC concludes that action is warranted, the secretary directs the OFT to meet with the dominant firm and seek assurances that the public interest will be protected in the future. Neither competing companies nor consumers who believe that they have been damaged by monopolistic actions may bring legal action to recover damages. Efforts of the South Korean government to deal with the influence of conglomerates are reviewed in Box 12-1.

Japan

Japan had no antitrust policies before the American occupation following World War II.[31] *Zaibatsu* had symbolized the development of the Japanese economy in the early decades of the twentieth century, and the Japanese government opposed Allied efforts to impose antitrust laws. One scholar writes:

> It will be recalled that at the time of the Occupation a wide-spread Japanese interpretation of the antitrust program for Japan was that the United

Cases in Development
BOX 12-1 WRESTLING WITH THE CHAEBOLS

"Chaebols" are large, family-owned conglomerates that have been central to the success of the South Korean economy. Chaebols were originally creatures of the government's development bureaucracies that fashioned close working relations with the firms and provided easy credit to assist them in expanding their export businesses. During the 1970s the size and wealth of the chaebols grew sharply and with it their ability to resist the directions of state planners. By the 1980s the chaebols had developed the capacity to satisfy their own capital needs, and the government found it even more difficult to guide their business decisions. The concentration of economic power in the hands of the chaebols became one of the principal characteristics of the Korean economy in the 1990s, and the government tried to reduce their influence but with little success.

In 2005 the South Korean Fair Trade Commission tried again to limit the influence of the chaebols. The commission believed that the concentration of the economic power in the chaebols limited opportunities for other Korean businesses, and it feared that the bankruptcy of one or two heavily indebted chaebol affiliates might trigger a chain reaction that could lead to the collapse of much of the nation's economy. The Fair Trade Commission sought to allow room for smaller companies and compel the chaebols to focus on their core businesses by ruling that conglomerates with more than $6 billion in assets could invest only 25 percent of their assets in other companies. With ties to the chaebols, all the country's leading newspapers opposed the Fair Trade Commission rules, and chaebol lobbying persuaded the government to restrict and delay the implementation of the commission's plan. Whether the government will be able to create a fairer and more stable corporate system without damaging the country's economy is not yet clear.

Sources: Dong-Myeon Shin, *Social and Economic Policies in Korea* (New York: Routledge Curzon, 2003), 33, 140–41, 177, and 195; and Anna Fifield, "Screws Start to Tighten on the Chaebol" and "Seoul Vows to Press Ahead with Reforms," both in *Financial Times,* March 1, 2005, 1.

States sought to weaken the Japanese economy. . . . It is clear that many Japanese government officials think . . . competition is always "excess competition." Competition (i.e., excessive competition) is considered inefficient, resulting in firms too small, firms unable to cope with cyclical changes, unable to compete effectively in international trade.[32]

Despite the resistance of Japanese officials, Occupation authorities imposed measures dissolving the *zaibatsu,* major corporations, and cartels in what has been described as "the greatest single use of government power in postwar Japan."[33] The Antimonopoly Law enacted in 1947 encouraged reliance on marketplace competition and opposed mergers that lessened competition, but the law was never stringently enforced and was soon relaxed.

The objectives of Japanese competition policy are to increase economic efficiency, stabilize critical industries, and improve the country's position in international trade. The nation's Fair Trade Commission failed to enforce the antimonopoly statutes in the 1950s and 1960s because of pressure from business groups and other government agencies.[34] Exemptions to antitrust laws are permitted to limit competition among small companies, reduce production capacity in declining industries, and gain advantage in import-export transactions.

Some scholars conclude that "few other developed countries have relegated competition policy to such a subservient position" as Japan and contend that Japan's "merger policy at best resembles a sieve."[35] Others, however, insist that the market structure of the Japanese economy has become more competitive in recent years: "The most remarkable change in Japanese industrial organization [in the 1970s and 1980s] has been the decline in cartel-like practices."[36] They point out that the Antimonopoly Law was strengthened in 1977 and maintain that the Fair Trade Commission has moved effectively against price-fixing and collusion by publicizing anticompetitive practices and appealing to Japan's consumer movement even though the agency lacks statutory power to prohibit such practices.

European Union

When six European nations concluded the Treaty of Rome in 1957, European leaders believed that pooling their economic strengths would enhance their economic opportunities and increase their political influence.[37] Because they were determined to eliminate national barriers among the member economies, article 85 of the Rome treaty followed the U.S. practice and explicitly prohibited price-fixing, agreements on production limits, discriminatory treatment of retailers, and other agreements among firms that prevented competition. At the same time, however, article 85 also adhered to the typical European pattern by authorizing the EU Commission to allow corporate agreements that improve production, promote innovation, enhance economic progress, or benefit consumers. The Commission was given considerable latitude for determining when it would oppose efforts to fix prices or carve up markets and when it would grant exemptions. The Commission has had continuing difficulty identifying the standards it uses to evaluate legal monopolies sanctioned by national governments, financial subsidies given by European nations to firms within their jurisdictions, and anticompetitive practices that benefit prominent companies.

The European Union has attempted to guarantee that European firms have sufficient access to markets, technology, capital, and managerial resources to thrive in the global marketplace and also to be sure that they face adequate domestic competition to require them to remain efficient and responsive to consumer preferences. In pursuing its twin lines of policy, the European Union adopted merger regulations in 1989 that allowed the Commission to preempt national governments in approving or rejecting mergers if the worldwide sales of the parties topped 5 billion euros and EU sales in various countries surpassed 250 million euros.[38] Kalypso Nicolaïdis and Raymond Vernon conclude, "Where the internal market may be affected, the [European] Union maintains extensive programs aimed at restraining measures, such as cartel agreements and state subsidies, that imperil market efficiency," but they also find, "when the effect of such measures would be borne largely by outside countries . . . the restraints on such practices are few."[39]

U.S. business leaders welcomed the enactment of the International Antitrust Enforcement Assistance Act in 1994 because they believed their international operations were hurt by foreign cartels and exclusionary international business practices. U.S. antitrust officials concluded bilateral cooperation agreements with Canada, the European Union, Japan, and others and announced that they would give the international enforcement of antitrust laws high priority.

The diverse competition policy traditions discussed here make the enforcement of antitrust laws a problematic effort. What the United States regards as a restraint of trade might be seen in other countries as a measure to promote domestic industry. In the highly competitive global economy, some nations may block merger proposals between companies from other countries in order to improve the competitive position of their own firms. The proposed merger between the aircraft companies Boeing and McDonnell Douglas was the first test of the cooperation agreement between the European Union and the United States. U.S. antitrust agencies approved the proposal, but EU officials blocked the merger until Boeing made concessions that benefited Airbus Industries. Manfred Neumann concludes that merger control in the European Union is "strongly influenced by objectives derived from industrial policy."[40] EU and U.S. officials shared confidential information about Microsoft that facilitated the prosecution of the company, but the European Union continued to prosecute Microsoft long after the U.S. Department of Justice settled the suit. Competition policies emerged in Europe at a time when competition was viewed as only a mixed blessing, and officials' efforts to promote competition enlisted only limited support.[41]

HARMONIZING ANTITRUST TRADITIONS

Competition policy is understood in diverse ways in various countries. Scholars sharing the views associated with the University of Chicago argue that antitrust policies should have no other purpose than maximizing consumer welfare by promoting economic efficiency and minimizing prices.[42] They argue that antitrust policies have been stretched beyond their original purpose to address objectives that are beyond the provisions of the statutes. In general, proponents of the Chicago School believe that corporate mergers and takeovers increase efficiency and seldom reduce competition. According to the Chicago School, antitrust practices should return to their primary goals if U.S. corporations are to meet the challenge of international competition.

The structuralist opponents of the Chicago ideology maintain that existing statutes balance the competing objectives of U.S. antitrust policy quite effectively. They criticize the efficiency orientation of the Chicago School as "minimalist" and regard its marketplace assumptions as "simplistic."[43] They argue that there is no systematic evidence that large corporations enhance long-term economic efficiency, and they point out that U.S. antitrust traditions have opposed concentrations of power for political as well as economic reasons, and they should continue to do that.

Japan and the nations of the European Union have varied understandings of antitrust policy. Whereas British competition policies are somewhat closer to U.S. antitrust policies, German and EU policies reflect a more statist tradition. These entities are more confident that administrative decisions can guide marketplace competition in ways that will enhance their political and economic stature, and they are more skeptical about the ability of the market itself to deliver social and economic benefits to their citizens. Harmonizing various approaches to antitrust law and competition policy is one of the challenges posed by both European unification and the increasing globalization of the world economy.

SUMMARY

U.S. antitrust policies seek to promote economic competition and secure consumer benefits by regulating marketplace competition. They were originally designed to restrain the political and economic power of the giant corporations that appeared during the era of industrialization, and they have evolved slowly. The policies rest today on the Sherman Act of 1890 and the Clayton Act and Federal Trade Commission Act, both of 1914. These pieces of legislation were quite terse, and they have been interpreted by the courts in various ways in different eras. The implementation of antitrust policies has also varied over time, and enforcement efforts now focus on restricting monopolies, anticompetitive mergers, price-fixing, and sales practices that have anticompetitive consequences.

Whereas the United States is usually concerned about too little competition among firms, other nations are likely to fear excess competition. They regard economic competition as a tool to accomplish objectives, such as creating jobs, advancing technological innovation, and promoting the welfare of their economies. This allows other nations to balance competition with other policy goals and to grant exemptions from the normal competition standards to address problems in companies or industries. Competition policy rules may be employed to advance a country's industry policy objectives.

FURTHER READINGS

Merger applications in the communications industry are considered by the Common Carrier Bureau of the Federal Communications Commission: http://www.fcc.gov/ccb/. The FTC Web site is available at http://www.ftc.gov; click on Antitrust/Competition. The Department of Justice's Antitrust Division Web site is found at http://www.usdoj.gov/atr. In addition to an overview of the Antitrust Division and the collection of documents, the Web site offers statements, opinions, and reports about the Microsoft antitrust case. Microsoft's position is available at the company's Web site: http://www.microsoft.com/freedomtoinnovate/.

Ferguson, Charles H. *The Broadband Problem: Anatomy of a Market Failure and a Policy Dilemma*. Washington, D.C.: Brookings Institution Press, 2004.

Hahn, Robert W., ed. *High-Stakes Antitrust: The Last Hurrah?* Washington, D.C.: AEI-Brookings Joint Center for Regulatory Studies, 2003.

Kwoka, John E., Jr., and Lawrence J. White, eds. *The Antitrust Revolution: Economics, Competition, and Policy*. 4th ed. New York: Oxford University Press, 2004.

Neumann, Manfred. *Competition Policy: History, Theory and Practice*. Northampton, Mass.: Edward Elgar, 2001.

Wells, Wyatt. *Antitrust and the Formation of the Postwar World*. New York: Columbia University Press, 2002.

NOTES

1. Richard Waters and Alan Cane, "Making Connections: National Telecoms Monopolies Are Planning Huge Mergers to Head Off Competition and Smaller Rivals Bent on Breaking Up Their Empires," *Financial Times*, April 26, 1999, 15; James Harding, "Consumer Groups Oppose AOL–Time Warner Link," *Financial Times*, April 27, 2000, 4; and Steven A. Holmes, "Huge Bank Mergers Worry Consumer Groups," *New York Times*, April 18, 1998, sec. 1, p. 14.

2. John E. Kwoka Jr. and Lawrence J. White, eds., *The Antitrust Revolution* (Glenview, Ill.: Scott, Foresman, 1989).

3. Steve Lohr, "Smokestack Doctrine, Digital Age," *New York Times*, February 15, 1998, sec. 5, p. 5.

4. Robert A. Katzmann, "The Attenuation of Antitrust," *Brookings Review* 2, no. 4 (Summer 1984): 23–27.

5. These paragraphs on trusts are based on Don E. Waldman, *The Economics of Antitrust: Cases and Analysis* (Boston: Little, Brown, 1986), 2–17.

6. The definition is based on Richard A. Posner, *Antitrust Law: An Economic Perspective* (Chicago: University of Chicago Press, 1976), 8.

7. The account of events in this section is based on A. D. Neale and D. G. Goyder, *The Antitrust Laws of the United States of America: A Study of Competition Enforced by Law*, 3rd ed. (Cambridge: Cambridge University Press, 1980); Dominick T. Armentano, *Antitrust and Monopoly: Anatomy of a Policy Failure*, 2nd ed. (New York: Holmes and Meier, 1990); Martin J. Sklar, *The Corporate Reconstruction of American Capitalism, 1890–1916: The Market, the Law, and Politics* (New York: Cambridge University Press, 1988); and Timothy J. Waters, "Antitrust Law and Policy: Rule of Law or Economic Assumptions," in *Economics and Antitrust Policy*, ed. Robert J. Larner and James W. Meehan (New York: Quorum Books, 1989), 151–77.

8. *Standard Oil of N.J. v. United States,* 221 U.S. 1 (1911).
9. Eleanor M. Fox and Robert Pitofsky, "United States," in *Global Competition Policy,* ed. Edward M. Graham and J. David Richardson (Washington, D.C.: Institute for International Economics, 1997), 243.
10. Unusually helpful reviews of antitrust issues are found in Douglas F. Greer, *Business, Government, and Society* (New York: Macmillan, 1987), chaps. 5–10; Damodar Gujarati, *Government and Business* (New York: McGraw-Hill, 1984), chaps. 6–10; and Martin C. Schnitzer, *Contemporary Government and Business Relations* (Boston: Houghton Mifflin, 1990), chaps. 4–9.
11. 166 U.S. 290 (1897).
12. 192 U.S. 197 (1904).
13. 221 U.S. 1 (1911).
14. 251 U.S. 417 (1920).
15. 148 F.2d 416 (1945).
16. *United States v. E. I. duPont de Nemours,* 351 U.S. 377 (1956).
17. *Berkey Photo v. Eastman Kodak Co.,* 603 F2d 263 (1979).
18. E. Thomas Sullivan, "The Antitrust Division as a Regulatory Agency: An Enforcement Policy in Transition," in *Public Policy Toward Corporate Takeovers,* ed. Murray L. Weidenbaum and Kenneth W. Chilton (New Brunswick, N.J.: Transaction Books, 1988), 106–40.
19. John E. Kwoka Jr. and Lawrence J. White, eds., *The Antitrust Revolution: Economics, Competition, and Policy,* 3rd ed. (New York: Oxford University Press, 1999), 334.
20. Fox and Pitofsky, "United States," 250.
21. Richard Tomkins, "FTC Acts to Block Merger of Stationery Suppliers," *Financial Times,* April 7, 1997.
22. John E. Kwoka Jr. and Lawrence J. White, eds., *The Antitrust Revolution: Economics, Competition, and Policy,* 4th ed. (New York: Oxford University Press, 2004), 15.
23. Kwoka and White, *Antitrust Revolution,* 3rd ed., 328–33.
24. Charles H. Ferguson, *The Broadband Problem: Anatomy of a Market Failure and a Policy Dilemma* (Washington, D.C.: Brookings Institution Press, 2004).
25. Thomas K. McCraw, "Mercantilism," in *The Politics of Industrial Policy,* ed. Claude E. Barfield and William A. Schambra (Washington, D.C.: American Enterprise Institute, 1986), 33–62.
26. Quoted in David B. Audretsch, *The Market and the State: Government Policy Towards Business in Europe, Japan and the United States* (New York: New York University Press, 1989), 66–76.
27. Ibid., 69.
28. Wyn Grant, *Government and Industry: A Comparative Analysis of the US, Canada and the UK* (Hants, England: Edward Elgar, 1989), 96–101.
29. See Tim Frazer, *Monopoly, Competition and the Law: The Regulation of Business Activity in Britain, Europe and America* (New York: St. Martin's, 1988), 24–30.
30. Ibid., 35–38.
31. Audretsch, *Market and the State,* 87–118.
32. Eleanor M. Hadley, *Antitrust In Japan* (Princeton: Princeton University Press, 1970), 447–48.
33. Masu Uekusa, "Industrial Organization: The 1970s to the Present," in *The Political Economy of Japan: The Domestic Transformation,* ed. Kozo Yamamura and Yasuichi Yasuba (Stanford, Calif.: Stanford University Press, 1987), 469–515, esp. 477.
34. Ibid., 477.
35. Audretsch, *Market and the State,* 94, 115.
36. Uekusa, "Industrial Organization," 481.
37. This section is based on Kalypso Nicolaïdis and Raymond Vernon, "Competition Policy and Trade Policy in the European Union," in Graham and Richardson, *Global Competition Policy,* 213, 285, 287, 290, 292, 302, 307.
38. Manfred Neumann, *Competition Policy: History, Theory and Practice* (Northampton, Mass.: Edward Elgar, 2001), 41.

39. Nicolaïdis and Vernon, "Competition Policy and Trade Policy in the European Union," 305.
40. Neumann, *Competition Policy,* 41.
41. David J. Gerber, *Law and Competition in Twentieth Century Europe: Protecting Prometheus* (New York: Oxford University Press, 1998), 436.
42. Robert H. Bork, *The Antitrust Paradox: A Policy at War with Itself* (New York: Basic Books, 1978); and William F. Shughart II, *Antitrust Policy and Interest Group Politics* (New York: Quorum Books, 1990).
43. Frederick M. Rowe, "Antitrust in Transition: A Policy in Search of Itself," *Antitrust Law Journal* 54, no. 1 (1985): 5.

CHAPTER 13

Industrial Policy and High-Tech Industries

IN 2000 THE heads of the European Union states met in Lisbon to adopt a plan to make the Union "the most dynamic and competitive knowledge-based economy in the world" by 2010.[1] They agreed to boost spending for research and innovation, strengthen education, increase infrastructure investments, and improve their regulatory systems. European officials have now traveled most of the way to 2010, and they recognize that their Lisbon strategy has not produced satisfactory results. In 2005 the European Commission and the Council of Ministers developed the Communication on Modern Industrial Policy to re-launch their Lisbon project. The failure of the EU governments to create jobs and increase economic growth has undermined confidence in their institutions and rekindled the debate about the contribution public policy can make to economic success.

Political economists classically assumed that the factors that advanced a nation's economy were fixed and immutable.[2] A country would produce the goods for which it had the greatest natural advantages and then buy the products it needed from other countries. Nations endowed with the advantages needed to produce each era's most highly prized goods would be the most prosperous.

The success of Germany and Japan in reconstructing their economies after World War II and the economic achievements of East Asian nations in the 1970s and 1980s demonstrated that a nation's competitive status was not necessarily fore-ordained. Through the appropriate mix of public policies, some countries were able to fashion the resources needed to produce high-value goods. The belief that comparative advantage was an acquired rather than a predetermined trait led countries to reexamine their policies for revitalizing industries, enhancing economic performance, and improving the standard of living for their citizens.

Together with economic and trade policies, nations typically enact *industrial policies* to promote their economic welfare. When countries seek to improve their international economic position, the phrase *competitiveness policy* is used, and when they seek to enhance the development and commercialization of scientific knowledge, discussion focuses on *technology policy.* Regardless of the particular emphasis, however, industrial policy, competitiveness policy, and technology policy all share the premise that government can and should play an active role in shaping a country's economy. Not everyone agrees with this premise. Authors and officeholders often choose sides and announce whether they support or oppose industrial policy.[3] The effort here is not to stand for or against industrial policy but to distinguish successful industrial policies from policies that have fallen short. By identifying the common features of successful industrial policies, we can assess the likelihood that such policies can help sustain American prosperity in the years ahead.

In this chapter I first examine the idea of industrial policy and then turn to a closer analysis of industrial policies in the United States. I review the history of policies affecting specific industries and outline current arguments for and against industrial policy proposals. An analysis of European and Asian industrial policies provides helpful contrasts to American practice, and it helps explain why industrial policies have succeeded in some circumstances but not others. In the final section of the chapter I concentrate on an area of industrial policy that currently receives special consideration, high-technology policies, and consider whether industrial policies can help the United States sustain its prosperity.

AMERICAN INDUSTRIAL POLICIES AND PROPOSALS

There are two basic definitions of industrial policy—one broad and the other narrow. From the first perspective, the phrase encompasses all government activities that have an impact on the success of a nation's economy.[4] Here *industrial policy* is broadly defined as government "programs that affect the pattern of economic development."[5]

Advocates of this definition identify features of the American economy they believe affect its international competitiveness. They then promote government programs to improve performance in this area. Encompassed within the broad definition of industrial policy are the following topics:

- *Macroeconomic Policies.* Bruce R. Scott and George C. Lodge maintain that the American economy is harmed by an unsound macroeconomic environment.[6] U.S. policies emphasize leisure, consumption, and the redistribution of the economic pie. Improved competitiveness, according to Scott and Lodge, requires the United States to stop responding to short-term consumption desires and adopt economic strategies based on increased savings and investment.

- *Labor-Management Relations.* Lester Thurow traces the problems of American industry to adversarial relations between labor and management.[7] Poor employee motivation, high labor turnover rates, and unstable organizational arrangements are the result of the absence of a sense of equity in major corporations. From Thurow's perspective, the acknowledgment by both labor and management of their interdependence is crucial both for the prosperity of individual firms and the continuing success of the nation's economy.

- *Education and Infrastructure.* Among the factors that Michael E. Porter believes determine the prosperity of nations are advanced educational skills and specialized infrastructure investments.[8] Highly educated personnel and facilities such as university research institutes are essential to design and develop a steady flow of sophisticated products. Without such resources, Porter maintains, a country's prosperity will pass as its natural advantages lose their significance in an increasingly complex world economy.

- *Production Technology.* Stephen S. Cohen and John Zysman argue that competitiveness is determined by the manner in which a nation produces goods and services.[9] They believe that U.S. industry fails to modernize production technologies in critical industries. The failure to promote new production technologies limits the attractiveness of current products and closes off avenues for future economic progress.

- *Cultural Patterns.* Robert B. Reich contends that the United States suffers from a conflict between its business and civic cultures.[10] The cultures embody conflicting notions of freedom, responsibility, citizenship, and community, and tensions between them surface in continuing struggles over the competing claims of economic prosperity and social justice. According to Reich, the failure of the United States to develop a mode of accommodation between these two cultures has hindered the country's economic progress.

Unfortunately, the broad definition of industrial policy is so encompassing as to be unwieldy. When almost everything is seen to be an aspect of industrial policy, the concept loses much of its utility.

According to its narrower definition, industrial policy is government action intended to improve a country's economic well-being through its impact on specific industries.[11] Industrial policies may launch new, high-technology industries, enhance the competitiveness of existing industries, or sustain jobs and firms in declining industries. The phrase *industrial policy* is used in this chapter in this narrow, sector-specific sense.

The United States is often thought to shun special assistance to individual firms and industries. In fact, the country has a long history of stunningly successful efforts to enhance the nation's economic well-being through policies based on particular industries.[12] As noted in Chapter 1, earlier generations accomplished such impressive economic feats as building transcontinental railroads and modernizing the nation's agricultural production and distribution systems. In the past half century, no nation has had a record of more innovative and successful industrial policies than the United States. The chronicle of sector-specific industrial policies reveals impressive triumphs, costly flops, and some cases that are still too close to call.

Industrial Policy Examples

In the two decades after World War II, government policy dramatically improved the quality of private American housing stock, transforming it from adequate to probably the best housing in the world. With political support based on efforts to reward veterans for wartime service, government devised a series of financial arrangements and tax concessions that reduced the risks at each step in the housing construction and sales process. As a result, the housing industry thrived, and a large fraction of the American public obtained better housing than it could afford.

In 1961 the United States pledged to land a person on the moon before the end of the decade and return that person safely to earth. This objective required the rapid development of the nation's space industry and a considerable expenditure of public funds. The first lunar landing occurred in 1969 and was followed by a series of televised landings that symbolized the era's enthusiasm for space exploration. The attainment of the nation's goal was made possible by NASA's flexible administrative structure, new patterns of government-business collaboration, the imaginative cultivation of political support for the space program, and the unusual perseverance of public officials.

Government policies to enhance the nation's telecommunications system have changed from generation to generation, but the result is a telephone system that is unsurpassed in quality, accessibility, and versatility.[13] The original patents awarded Alexander Graham Bell expired at the end of the nineteenth century, and this ushered in an era of competition in the telephone industry. After World War I, state and national regulators allowed AT&T to create a fully integrated telephone system and achieve monopoly status in virtually every aspect of telephone service and equipment. In the 1950s competition began to reappear in the industry, and this development led in 1984 to the breakup of AT&T and the divestiture of the local operating companies. The dismemberment of the phone network permitted the introduction of revolutionary new telecommunications technologies, and the resulting cornucopia of innovations has transformed the nation's economy.

Not every instance of government assistance to specific industries has been successful. Some policy initiatives, in fact, have been expensive failures, resulting either from economic factors or from political calculations. The steel industry turned to government for assistance in the 1970s and 1980s when it encountered severe competitive pressures.[14] Working with steelworker unions, the companies succeeded in obtaining costly tax concessions, procurement preferences, trade protection, and adjustment assistance. The effort expended in gaining these preferences distracted the industry from the need to meet international competition.

As a result, the industry's eventual adjustment was probably more painful and traumatic than it would otherwise have been.

In 1980 Congress created the U.S. Synthetic Fuels Corporation to make the country less dependent on imported oil by developing technologies to obtain oil from domestic shale and coal.[15] The Synthetic Fuels Corporation was authorized to seek $68 billion to meet the goal of producing 2 million barrels of oil a day by 1992. President Carter declared that the synthetic fuels project would dwarf NASA's lunar landing program. In 1985, however, Congress eliminated funding for the Synthetic Fuels Corporation, and the next year the agency went out of business. By then, the project had just one facility in commercial production, yielding only 4,300 barrels of oil per day. However valuable experts thought synthetic fuels might become in the future, officeholders turned their attention to more pressing problems.

Some industrial policies can be labeled successes or failures rather easily, but the country's most celebrated industrial policy initiative, assistance to the Chrysler Corporation, resists easy characterization.[16] As the smallest of the three major American automobile manufacturers, Chrysler had long faced a difficult competitive situation. It had many of the overhead costs of larger companies, but it enjoyed fewer economies of scale and sold fewer cars with which to pay its costs. For half a decade, the firm had sought government aid in the form of development grants, tax credits for car buyers, reductions in its tax obligations, and administrative relief from regulatory requirements. As its situation became more acute, Chrysler worked with its unions, local auto dealers, and professional lobbyists to campaign for government aid. During the presidential primary season, the Carter administration agreed to a package of $1.5 billion in loan guarantees and mandatory concessions to the firm from Chrysler unions, suppliers, and lenders.

Chrysler survived its crisis and was able to repay its loans before the required dates. The company improved its production procedures, but it also reduced its workforce from 122,000 to 84,000.[17] The firm's recovery resulted from plant closings, increases in sales, tax concessions, and import quotas on Japanese cars. The costs to the American public of government assistance to Chrysler and the automobile industry were enormous, but in 1998 Chrysler ended up being acquired by the German industrial giant Mercedes-Benz and American management of the enterprise came to an end.

The review of policies involving housing, the NASA lunar landing, telecommunications, the steel industry, synthetic fuels, and Chrysler confirms that the United States has, indeed, pursued a series of sector-specific industrial policies. Furthermore, these policies are remarkably diverse. They have employed a catalog of policy tools: direct subsidies, credit assistance, government procurement, tax concessions, trade protection, the use of unappropriated funds, and regulatory preferences. In contrast to the ideological antagonisms often provoked by discussions of industrial policy, these policies display a pragmatic willingness to rely on government agencies, corporations, nonprofit institutions, or innovative public-private mechanisms whenever it promises to help achieve a program's objectives. Finally, these policies, especially the successful ones, are unusual in their creativity. They are not cookie-cutter responses to routine problems but imaginative solutions to unique situations. They are episodes in a remarkable and uncommon history of public action to boost economic well-being through policies directed toward specific industries.

Arguments Pro and Con

Industrial policies can provide start-up aid for new industries, offer adjustment assistance to traditional industries, or restructure the marketplace for specific goods. Industrial policy issues have also been raised in debates about proposals to dismantle the Department of Commerce, to eliminate "corporate welfare" expenditures, and to decide the fate of defense conversion and dual-use technology programs in the Department of Defense.[18] One prominent scholar has reviewed the history of industrial policies in the United States and the success of other nations in enhancing their business environment and concluded, "The confidence that we can be competitive without a national strategy . . . no longer accords with present reality."[19] The United States, it is said, must devise a coherent strategy to improve its industrial performance if its firms are to remain successful in the world marketplace.[20]

Industrial policy proposals are commonly supported by policy analysts, liberal officeholders, labor union officials, and representatives of companies and regions that expect to receive aid.[21] These figures argue that markets and macroeconomic policies do not adequately address the problems of specific groups and do not acknowledge the reality of government involvement in international economic competition. They point to the hardships suffered by unemployed workers and abandoned communities through no fault of their own.

Champions of industrial policy applaud successful initiatives from past decades and argue that the country has nothing to fear from an expanded role for government in economic decision making. It is far cheaper, they maintain, for government to rescue troubled companies today than to pay the costs of unemployment assistance, job retraining, and pension bailouts in the future. Moreover, if prominent corporations are allowed to fail, it may panic financial markets and lead to significant disruptions of the economy. If the government stands by and does nothing to halt the collapse of basic industries, the nation's prosperity and its place in the world will inevitably deteriorate.

Opposition to industrial policies is spearheaded by traditional economists and libertarian think tanks, which maintain that the proposals are unfair and simply will not work.[22] They stress that corporations and industries facing hardship do so for fundamental reasons that will not be cured by short-term aid. Programs of temporary assistance provide billions of dollars in "corporate welfare" that distract business, government, and the public from the need to address fundamental problems.

Opponents of industrial policy maintain that government has neither the economic intelligence nor the political fortitude to manage industrial policy programs properly. According to this view, industrial policy measures are likely to produce a series of expensive payoffs to declining but politically influential industries. The result will be increased costs for healthy firms, consumers, and the general economy as government channels scarce resources into inefficient activities. The economist Charles L. Schultze warns, "the surest way to multiply unwarranted subsidies and protectionist measures is to legitimize their existence under the rubric of industry policy."[23]

The review of the industrial policy debate and of past examples of industrial policy underlines the dangers of government support for industry. At the same time, it also demonstrates that industrial policies have been successful in the United States when used to accomplish broadly accepted public goals, when programmatic decisions were shielded from political pressures, and when corporations could be constrained to act responsibly.[24] Further insight into the factors that contribute to the effectiveness of industrial policies is gained by examining experiences in other countries.

INDUSTRIAL POLICY: INTERNATIONAL EXPERIENCES

Traditional European industrial policies relied on public subsidies to producers, and they were to accomplish three goals: to maintain production and employment in existing industries, to promote the growth of new industries and technologies, and to subsidize specific consumer goods.[25] British industrial policies tried to remedy lagging productivity and check the declining British share of world trade by establishing public-private planning procedures, promoting mergers and reorganizations in existing industries, granting British firms procurement preferences, and providing large subsidies for declining and emerging industries.[26] Unfortunately, the aid programs responded more fully to the claims of politically influential groups than to the dynamics of economic growth. A typical assessment of these programs concluded, "the industrial policies . . . involved much waste of public money, and also often had the effect of slowing down the process of industrial adjustment."[27]

The German Ministry of Economic Affairs also provided substantial subsidies to conventional sunset industries such as coal, steel, and shipbuilding, and government authority was invoked to guarantee a market for the industries' products. Although subsidies occasionally helped firms and regions adjust to new economic realities, they usually just delayed the day of reckoning for the declining companies.

The German Ministry of Research and Technology assisted sunrise industries, including biotechnology, computers, aerospace, and nuclear energy, through a system of subsidies, project grants, and tax concessions. The large German contributions to the European Airbus program to manufacture airliners achieved their goal, but the record in other industrial areas was less impressive. The postal, communications, and rail systems in Germany also received massive subsidies. These payments did lower costs to consumers, but the subsidies also reduced the incentives for these systems to modernize their operations. As a result, the total cost of these services remained high, and the quality of service was uneven.

The German economic system achieved an impressive record in the quarter century after World War II and in the cold war era. The country's sector-specific industrial policies, however, made a smaller contribution to this success than did the country's sound macroeconomic policies, consensual policy style, and constructive system of labor-management relations.[28] Policies to sustain older industries, promote new technologies, and reduce the costs of consumer items relied on subsidies and other assistance to producers, but they had only mixed results.

After reunification, Germany made an extraordinary effort in the 1990s to restructure and revitalize the economy of its new eastern states, the former German Democratic Republic. Spending approximately $1 trillion, a new communications and transportation infrastructure for the eastern region was constructed, a modern wholesale and retail network was created, and a complete public administration system, comparable to that found in the West, was installed. The German economic unification program was least successful in sustaining employment in the region's manufacturing industries. Large subsidies were given to German and international firms for taking over existing production facilities, but thousands of companies were eventually closed, and manufacturing employment in the region declined precipitously.

The significance of industrial policy in Japan is a subject of considerable controversy. Some scholars attribute Japan's economic success to the country's institutional arrangements, which have facilitated effective government decision making and allowed close cooperation between firms and government.[29] Others trace Japan's economic success to its macroeconomic policies, which stress personal saving, low interest rates, and limited consumption.[30] Still other analysts maintain that Japan's economic achievements have resulted from sector-specific industrial policies that explicitly targeted individual industries for government assistance.[31]

In Japan's high-growth decades, the Ministry of International Trade and Industry identified a series of industries whose advancement was important to the country's economy. MITI encouraged the reorganization of traditional industries, such as sugar refining, textiles, cement, and chemicals, that had lost their competitiveness. The agency sponsored corporate agreements to restrict output and offered firms subsidies to adopt new practices. MITI also identified sunrise industries, such as computers, biotechnology, financial services, and software. These industries were critical because they would probably expand as national income increased, offered potential economies of scale, would benefit other sectors of the economy, and could become a significant source of future exports.

Japan typically identified a narrow segment of an expanding industry, systematically exploited new techniques, helped achieve economies of scale in production, and offered trade protection to ensure domestic sales.[32] Having targeted key industries, MITI helped firms reach the long-term potential of their markets by providing tax incentives, special depreciation rules, government-funded research assistance, and direct financial subsidies, if they cooperated in increasing economic effectiveness. Favored industries also benefited from below-market interest rates, preferences in public procurement, a domestic market protected from international competition, and incentives to export unneeded production.

A critical feature of Japanese policy was that official action typically supplemented marketplace competition rather than displacing it.[33] Public decisions were intended to establish conditions for investment that promoted corporate productivity and enhanced competition. The Japanese state pervaded the economy, but markets remained fluid, competition among firms and enterprise groups was fierce, and corporate bankruptcies were frequent. Critics point out, however, that Japan's most impressive economic successes occurred in cars, videocassette recorders, robotics, cameras, and video games, areas in which government involvement was minimal.[34]

Japan captured first place in many global industries, and its industrial policies probably contributed to this achievement.[35] Unlike European policies that often countered market trends, Japan's industrial policies typically rewarded firms for improved performance through market incentives. Economic success in Japan, however, depended not on industrial policies alone, but upon a well-educated workforce; effective coordination between industrial and macroeconomic policies; successful industry practices in the areas of personnel, product engineering, and quality control; and corporate discipline that resulted from domestic and international competition.

Sector-specific industrial policies can make only a limited contribution to a country's prosperity. Enough American, German, and Japanese industrial policies have had positive results, however, to warrant an examination of the factors associated with positive results. Successful industrial policies in the United States have characteristically involved the creation of new institutional relationships that offered private companies incentives to cooperate in achieving public goals. Japan's industrial policies altered the structure of marketplace activity to encourage firms to improve their operations in ways that would enhance the nation's economy. In contrast, the conventional European practice of subsidizing the operations of traditional producers has often led companies into more difficult economic straits than they were in before they received the public assistance.

Policy success in both Germany and Japan rested on broad political agreement about the importance of economic growth. Modern governments are composed of semiautonomous agencies with diverse objectives, and industrial societies are based on complicated arrangements among increasingly rigid organizations. Public enthusiasm for industrial policy goals is a critical mechanism for gaining bureaucratic support and achieving administrative coordination. Industrial policies often require that the interests of some groups be sacrificed to achieve economic gains for the broader society. The authoritative role of administrative agencies in Japan and of banks and state ministries in Germany shielded industrial policy judgments from short-term political pressures. Corporations are complex institutions that respond to demands from managers, product organizations, nonmanagement employees, shareholders, and lenders; they sometimes placate these constituencies by sacrificing the resources they need for long-term growth. The export-orientation of the German and Japanese economies forced companies to resist political pressures and emphasize the steps needed to enhance their operations. Industrial policy traditions in Brazil are outlined in Box 13-1.

Contrasting styles of industrial policy in Europe and the United States are illustrated by the different approaches taken to cell phone standards in the two regions. Both regions have addressed three "generations" of mobile phones.[36] The first generation (1G) accommodated traditional analog phone service, the second (2G) provided for digital service, and the third generation of standards (3G) supported higher bandwidth and packet-switched networks. Analog cell phones appeared in Europe in the 1980s, and most countries there developed their own analog standards that were incompatible with the standards of their neighbors. The EU countries decided to establish a uniform 2G standard to promote compatibility among national systems, gain first mover advantages over firms located elsewhere, and capture economies of scale, and the European Union issued a directive instructing member countries to adopt the Global System for Mobile Communications, or GSM.

In the early 1980s, the U.S. Federal Communications Commission approved the Analog Mobile Phone System (AMPS) for 1G service, but the FCC then let operators select any of four standards to support digital, 2G, service. In the United States, two networks adopted the Code Division Multiple Access (CDMA)-One standard, and the others used the GSM standard.

Two standards are now available to support 3G service. One is called Wideband CDMA, or WCDMA, and the other is CDMA2000. CDMA2000 is a simple upgrade of CDMA-One, but WCDMA is essentially incompatible with GSM. If CDMA2000 is successful, and WCDMA is not, the operators that used GSM equipment will face heavy costs and long delays in providing 3G service because they will need to fundamentally reconfigure their networks. The firms that selected CDMA-One as their 2G standard will have an easier and less expensive task in migrating to 3G operations because of the greater compatibility between CDMA-One and the CDMA2000 standards.

Cases in Development
BOX 13-1 INDUSTRIAL POLICY IN BRAZIL

Brazil was said to be the last nation in Latin America to adopt neoliberal economic reforms that trusted the marketplace to promote economic development and advance economic policies. From the emergence of industrialization in the 1940s, the state had been the principal source of the country's economic judgments. The 1988 Constitution envisioned government intervention in the economy, limits on foreign investment, and extensive social welfare rights.

Neoliberal policies began to win supporters in Brazil in the early 1990s when Argentina, Chile, and Mexico registered some success with marketplace reforms, but Brazil's strategy would differ from those found in most other countries. First, Brazil's policies combined an expanded use of the market with extensive social democratic, social welfare principles to fashion policies that provided a safety net to underpin the performance of the market. Second, neoliberalism in Brazil did not imply cutting back the state but using economic policies to rebuild and restructure government to make it more effective. Finally, pro-market policies in Brazil produced foreign exchange by exporting manufactured and processed goods rather than selling off the country's natural resources.

Although business in Brazil has rarely encountered a significant threat from either labor or the government, the preferences of the state have traditionally come first. Business-government relations are usually cordial, but public-private collaborations have yielded few important benefits, and business has exercised little leverage over the decisions of the national legislature. Brazil's statist tradition is underlined by the fact that the country continues to have one of Latin America's largest public sectors.

Sources: Riordan Roett, "Brazil's Protracted Transition to Democracy and Market," in *Post-Stabilization Politics in Latin America: Competition, Transition, Collapse,* ed. Carol Wise and Riordan Roett (Washington, D.C.: Brookings Institution Press, 2003), 199–212; and Nicola Phillips, *The Southern Cone Model: The Political Economy of Regional Capitalist Development in Latin America* (New York: Routledge, 2004), 70–75, 193–98, 235–39.

The EU decision to mandate GSM as Europe's 2G standard improved compatibility among European systems, gave its carriers a headstart over carriers from other regions, and secured economies of scale for its equipment manufacturers. However, EU carriers now face extended delays and substantial costs in delivering 3G service to their customers. The FCC's decision to allow carriers to select among 2G standards enabled some carriers to select the CDMA-One standard, which now appears to have been the best route to provide innovative 3G service. The costs of this approach for U.S. companies were that European carriers were able to offer their service to subscribers before U.S. firms, and European equipment manufacturers could focus their operations on the GSM standard while U.S. companies were still deciding what technical standard would be most popular. Governments making industrial policy decisions often face the issue of mandated versus market-based standards for new products and new technologies.

TECHNOLOGY POLICIES

High-technology industries are a critical aspect of industrial policy.[37] Industries such as communications, computers, and biotechnology have high R&D expenditures and experience rapid technology change. Even though high-tech industries account for only a small share of employment, exports, or value added in manufacturing, they receive special government attention.

Modern economies depend less on raw materials than on technique and know-how. New technologies generate efficiencies that spread throughout an economy and produce strategic advantages for a firm or country over its competitors. Because the benefits to a society from new technologies are greater than the returns received by individual investors, governments often help to finance their country's research and development program. The ability of the United States to maintain the wage levels and living standards of its citizens depends on the development of a stream of new technologies that increase productivity and yield products that can be sold to other countries.

Systems of innovation differ by nation and by era. Before World War II, large corporations provided almost all the resources to fund research and support innovation in the United States. Against the gloomy backdrop of joblessness and economic distress in the 1930s, Robert Teitelman writes, Du Pont created the first synthetic fibers, RCA developed the first television, and the world's first large airliner, the DC-3, was flown by the Douglas Company.[38] Corporations often worked with nearby universities to research new materials, create new products, and develop new procedures to benefit their industry.[39] At this time, national government spending for R&D was less than one-tenth of 1 percent of gross domestic product, and the principal area of R&D expenditures was agriculture.

The U.S. system of innovation was changed dramatically by the events of World War II. With surging expenditures, the federal government emerged as the nation's primary sponsor of R&D activities, and its efforts were concentrated on military technologies. The Department of Defense launched an extraordinary series of successful R&D projects designed to help the military perform its responsibilities, and these projects then provided substantial opportunities for the growth of the civilian economy.[40] Military resources helped launch the country's electronics, computer, communications, and aircraft industries, and military spending sustained these industries until their products developed commercial markets.[41] After the end of the war, the national government continued to be the dominant source of R&D funding, and it became the principal partner of universities in the conduct of basic research.

In the decades after World War II, military agencies continued their close working relationships with corporations and then used the knowledge they gained to invite the most successful industrial laboratories to work on their projects. The Department of Defense arranged preferential loans and tax concessions for helpful firms and offered the prospect of huge procurement contracts. Military procurement shaped production strategies and moved new technologies from the laboratory to the production line. The Defense Department persuaded other government agencies to relax enforcement of antitrust laws for critical industries and to protect domestic markets of essential firms from international competition, and the department itself often aided the sales of products of favored firms to other countries.

The defense record demonstrates that the U.S. government was able to promote targeted industries through a strategy that focused on creating the infrastructure for innovative technologies. This is confirmed by Richard N. Langlois and David C. Mowery's account, "The Federal Government Role in the Development of the U.S. Software Industry."[42] The private sector had taken the initial steps to develop computer science as an academic discipline, but Department of Defense and National Science Foundation contributions to universities had outpaced industry resources by the late 1950s. Federal expenditures supported basic research in computer hardware and software, helped develop research equipment, trained students and researchers, and enhanced the university research infrastructure. Federal policy helped universities become important centers for the cross-fertilization of ideas among industry, the defense community, and academic researchers. The Defense Department supported the establishment of centers of excellence at major research universities, and it was an important source of demand for software products until the market for civilian applications emerged in the early 1980s. Creating the infrastructure and investing in human capital has proved to be an effective U.S. strategy in developing and commercializing new technologies in a variety of industrial areas.[43]

The U.S. system of innovation again began to display new characteristics after the decline in military tensions in the late 1980s and early 1990s. In 2003 the United States spent $284 billion on R&D, but a sharply declining share of these expenditures came from the federal government.[44] As reported in Table 13-1, only an estimated 30 percent of the R&D funds were supplied by the federal government in 2003, in contrast to the 65 percent it had appropriated in 1960. During the corresponding period, the proportion of R&D funds provided by industry almost doubled, from 33 percent in 1960 to an estimated 63 percent in 2003. Unlike the decades before World War II, however, large corporations no longer

Table 13-1   Sources of U.S. Research and Development Funds, 1960–2003

Year	Federal government	Industry	Other institutions
1960	65%	33%	2%
1970	57	40	3
1980	47	49	4
1990	40	55	5
2000	25	69	6
2003(est)	30	63	7

Source: U.S. Department of Commerce, *Statistical Abstract of the United States, 2004–2005* (Washington, D.C.: GPO, *2004*), 764.

monopolized business support for R&D. Start-up companies were now able to secure R&D funds from venture capital firms that invested in new projects and from individual investors and institutions that purchased stock through public offerings. As a result, there were now three distinct sources of funds for scientific research and product development: the federal government, large corporations, and the stock market and venture capital process.[45] Entrepreneurs with new ideas are no longer dependent on government patronage or corporate approval to gain the resources needed to develop their plans but can turn as well to the marketplace. The existence of multiple sources of R&D funding increases the dynamism and flexibility of the U.S. economy.

Approximately 70 percent of R&D activities in the United States are carried out by industry, about 14 percent are performed by universities and colleges, and 9 percent are the direct responsibility of the federal government. Although the industry share of R&D performance has been stable in recent decades, the federal role has been declining, and the proportion of R&D work conducted by universities has increased slightly.[46] Industry activities are concentrated in applied research and product development, whereas universities specialize in basic research. Most university R&D activity is funded by the federal government, but the proportion of university R&D supported by industry has gradually increased.

Another change in the U.S. system of innovation is the declining share of federal funds being appropriated for national defense purposes. In 1990, 72 percent of federal R&D spending went for military and space activities, whereas in 2003 only 62 percent was earmarked for these purposes. The areas that enjoyed the greatest increases in federal R&D support in the past decade are health care—now receiving almost 24 percent of federal R&D funds—and basic research.[47]

Total public and private outlays for R&D are substantially higher in the United States than in other nations because of the larger size of the American economy. In 2000, total R&D expenditures equaled 2.7 percent of GDP in the United States. Total U.S. R&D expenditures as a percentage of GDP are similar to those of Germany and Japan and slightly higher than those of Great Britain, as displayed in Table 13-2. A notable difference in R&D spending among nations is the share that goes to military purposes. Of the four countries, the United States devotes the largest share of its R&D expenditures to defense purposes, and Japan dedicates the smallest share of R&D funds to the military. Military R&D expenditures are falling as a share of GDP in each country; in the United States the share of GDP going to military purposes has fallen from 0.8 percent in 1985 to 0.3 percent in 2003.

Commercial spinoffs from defense expenditures in the past have benefited the general economy. Recent Defense Department statements emphasize the civilian benefits of its R&D program.[48] Some officials have proposed that the Pentagon's high-technology center, the Advanced Research Projects Agency (ARPA), play a direct hand in the development of civilian technologies. Political and industrial leaders oppose the use of a military agency to assist domestic industries, but they favor the creation of a civilian agency to promote the commercial development of new technologies.[49] A national technology office could monitor international competition in key industries, facilitate joint research ventures, designate projects worthy of public support, and safeguard the public interest in publicly supported research areas. The President's Commission on Industrial Competitiveness has proposed the creation of a superagency to preside over government-funded nonmilitary research.[50]

Whatever the case in the past, most economists argue that the benefits to the nation's economy from military R&D expenditures have been declining. Military needs are increasingly divorced from the civilian economy, and military innovations frequently trail rather than lead civilian technologies. Rather than refocus defense resources on civilian activities, opponents of industrial policy insist that the most effective policy to stimulate new technologies would be to increase private research funds by reducing the capital gains tax. Propelling industries to international leadership through the brute force of public appropriations would

Table 13-2 National Research and Development Expenditures as a Percentage of GDP, 1985–2000

	Total R&D				Nondefense R&D			
	U.S.	Germany	Japan	Great Britain	U.S.	Germany	Japan	Great Britain
1985	2.7	2.7	2.6	2.2	1.9	2.3	2.6	1.7
1990	2.6	2.8	2.9	2.2	2.0	2.6	2.8	1.8
1995	2.5	2.3	2.8	2.0	2.0	2.2	2.7	1.8
2000	2.7	2.5	3.0	1.9	2.4	2.4	3.0	1.6

Source: U.S. Department of Commerce, *Statistical Abstract of the United States, 2004–2005*, (Washington, D.C.: GPO, 2004), 766.

require funds that are probably not available, and policies that respond to political pressures by distributing small amounts of money to an array of influential claimants would be futile.

The United States continues to have a vibrant and well-funded scientific community. A larger share of Nobel Prize laureates in the sciences came from the United States in the past decade and in the entire post–World War II period than from all other nations combined.[51] Critics believe that the weaknesses of the U.S. system of innovation lie in the quality of its manufacturing procedures and in its failure to translate scientific breakthroughs into successful commercial products.[52]

PROSPECTS FOR INDUSTRIAL POLICIES

In the year 2005 the U.S. economy certainly looked different from what it had at the end of the 1980s. At that time, evidence of decline in major industries was unmistakable. The consumer electronics industry had virtually disappeared; the semiconductor business appeared to be dominated by Japanese firms; and in cars, steel, and machine tools, imports surged as American companies lost ground to international competitors. By 2005, however, U.S. business firms had responded to the challenge. The service sector had succeeded manufacturing as the engine of economic growth, technological innovations had altered the ways companies conducted their operations, companies had become more efficient in their use of capital, and the global strength of American firms appeared superior to what it had been a dozen years earlier.

How do we explain the transformation? Did the improvements in the U.S. economy result from the government's industrial policies? The key to enhancing the status of a nation's economy is improving the productivity of its firms, and by the year 2005 the U.S. economy had registered a decade of strong growth in productivity. Leading companies had cut costs, improved the quality of products, redesigned production systems, reformed relations with suppliers, and accelerated the deployment of new technologies, and countless smaller firms joined with them. Although there had been a decade of responsible macroeconomic policies, the sea change of the U.S. economy does appear to be more closely associated with management policies than with the government's industrial policies.

Not to be ignored, however, are government projects that did contribute to the nation's economic growth. The Internet is a computer network that was conceived in the early 1960s by visionaries from the Massachusetts Institute of Technology who were associated with the Department of Defense's Advanced Research Projects Agency.[53] ARPA created a computer network that exchanged information among research centers in the 1970s, and in 1985 the National Science Foundation funded a cross-country network that became the backbone of a national system for transmitting messages among smaller computer networks. The Internet is a general architecture on which the World Wide Web system, e-mail, electronic commerce, and a variety of communications modalities are based. The

National Science Foundation spent approximately $200 million on the project, but with this expenditure it deployed a technology that made extraordinary contributions to the nation's economy.

Industrial policies have been successful in the United States and in other countries in promoting economic development, and this can also be the case in the future. The dual challenge, however, is to structure policies that respond to uncertainties of social and technological change and also to create the conditions in which these policies can flourish. If both are not done, procompetitive policies are likely to degenerate into programs that pay off politically influential industries and impede economic growth.

SUMMARY

A broad definition of industrial policy encompasses all government activities that have an impact on the success of a nation's economy. By this definition, industrial policy would encompass macroeconomic policies, labor-management relations, education and infrastructure, production technologies, cultural dynamics, and much more. A narrower definition regards industrial policy as government action intended to improve a country's economy through its impact on specific industries. Although the United States has often shunned assistance to individual industries, government policies have also shaped industrial development and provided the country with significant economic benefits. Proponents of industrial policy argue that government assistance helps firms and industries improve their fortunes and increase economic growth and that this assistance benefits workers, communities, and investors. Without aid, U.S. industries would fall victim to international corporations backed by their home governments and broad changes in economic and technological circumstances. Opponents of industrial policies insist that industries face hardships for fundamental reasons that cannot be cured by short-term aid. Furthermore, governments are more likely to direct assistance to politically influential industries than to industries that are most likely to use the funds effectively. Industrial policies burden taxpayers and other companies, and they are likely to cause more harm than good.

European industrial policies traditionally subsidized producers; policies in Japan were often designed to complement market incentives; and U.S. policies commonly restructured institutional relationships and enhanced the infrastructure of an industry.

Business and industry pays two-thirds of R&D costs in the United States and performs two-thirds of the actual work. The federal government funds 30 percent of research and development expenditures, with 62 percent of this money going to military and space activities and 24 percent earmarked for health care research. Industrial policies have been successful in the United States and other countries, but they can also degenerate into projects that simply reward celebrated industries and impede economic growth.

FURTHER READINGS

The Internet Society provides documents on the history of the Internet at http://www.isoc.org/internet/history/index.shtml. The European Union Web site for the Lisbon strategy is http://www.europa.eu.int/growthandjobs. The White House Office of Science and Technology Web site describes the office: http://www.ostp.gov. The Cato Institute is often critical of industrial policies; search on Industrial Policy on its Web site: http://www.cato.org.

Abbate, Janet. *Inventing the Internet.* Cambridge, Mass.: MIT Press, 1999.

London, Paul A. *The Competition Solution: The Bipartisan Secret behind American Prosperity.* Washington, D.C.: AEI Press, 2005.

Neuman, W. Russell, Lee McKnight, and Richard Jay Solomon. *The Gordian Knot: Political Gridlock on the Information Highway.* Cambridge, Mass.: MIT Press, 1997.

Trumbull, Gunnar. *Silicon and the State: French Innovation Policy in the Internet Age.* Washington, D.C.: Brookings Institution Press, 2004.

Woo-Cumings, Meredith, ed. *The Developmental State.* Ithaca, N.Y.: Cornell University Press, 1999.

NOTES

1. See the EU Web site on the Lisbon Strategy: http://europa.eu.int/growthand jobs/index_en.htm.
2. James A. Brander, "Shaping Comparative Advantage: Trade Policy, Industrial Policy, and Economic Performance," in *Shaping Comparative Advantage,* ed. Richard G. Lipsey and Wendy Dobson (Scarborough, Canada: Prentice Hall Canada, 1987), 1–55.
3. For a review of the arguments and positions, see R. D. Norton, "Industrial Policy and American Renewal," *Journal of Economic Literature* 24, no. 1 (March 1986): 1–40.
4. Aaron Wildavsky, "Squaring the Political Circle: Industrial Policies and the American Dream," in *The Industrial Policy Debate,* ed. Chalmers Johnson (San Francisco: ICS Press, 1984), 28.
5. Ira C. Magaziner and Robert B. Reich, *Minding America's Business: The Decline and Rise of the American Economy* (New York: Harcourt Brace Jovanovich, 1982), 255.
6. Bruce R. Scott and George C. Lodge, "Introduction," in *U.S. Competitiveness in the World Economy,* ed. Scott and Lodge (Boston: Harvard Business School Press, 1985), 1–11.
7. Lester Thurow, *The Zero-Sum Solution: Building a World-Class American Economy* (New York: Simon and Schuster, 1985), 119–25. See also D. Quinn Mills and Malcolm R. Lovell, "Enhancing Competitiveness: The Contribution of Employee Relations," in Scott and Lodge, *U.S. Competitiveness in the World Economy,* 455–78.
8. Michael E. Porter, *The Competitive Advantage of Nations* (New York: Free Press, 1990), 73–85.
9. Stephen S. Cohen and John Zysman, *Manufacturing Matters: The Myth of the Post-Industrial Economy* (New York: Basic Books, 1987), 3–11, 59–65.
10. Robert B. Reich, *The Next American Frontier* (New York: Times Books, 1983), 4–21.
11. See Chalmers Johnson, "Introduction: The Idea of Industrial Policy," in Johnson, *Industrial Policy Debate,* 3–26; and Jeffrey B. Freyman, "Industrial Policy: Patterns of Convergence and Divergence," in *Political Economy: Public Policies in the United States and Britain,* ed. Jerold L. Waltman and Donley T. Studlar (Jackson: University Press of Mississippi, 1987), 44–68.
12. See Ezra F. Vogel, *Comeback: Case by Case, Building the Resurgence of American Business* (New York: Simon and Schuster, 1985).
13. See Gerald W. Brock, *The Telecommunications Industry: The Dynamics of Market Structure* (Cambridge, Mass.: Harvard University Press, 1981); and Steve Coll, *The Deal of the Century: The Breakup of AT&T* (New York: Atheneum, 1986).

14. See, for example, John Strohmeyer, *Crisis in Bethlehem: Big Steel's Struggle to Survive* (New York: Penguin Books, 1986).

15. U.S. Senate Committee on Energy and Natural Resources, *Synfuels from Coal and the National Synfuels Production Program,* 97th Cong., 1st sess., 1981.

16. Robert B. Reich and John D. Donahue, *New Deals: The Chrysler Revival and the American System* (New York: Penguin Books, 1985).

17. Ibid., 243–47, 265.

18. Glenn R. Fong, "Breaking New Ground or Breaking the Rules: Strategic Reorientation in U.S. Industrial Policy" (paper presented at the annual meeting of the American Political Science Association, Boston, September 3–6, 1998).

19. Vogel, *Comeback,* 269–70.

20. Bruce R. Scott, "National Strategies: Key to International Competition," in Scott and Lodge, *U.S. Competitiveness in the World Economy,* 71.

21. Richard E. Foglesong, "The Politics of Industrial Policy in the United States," in *The Politics of Economic Adjustment,* ed. Richard E. Foglesong and Joel D. Wolfe (New York: Greenwood, 1989), 27–64.

22. See Stephen Moore and Dean Stansel, *How Corporate Welfare Won: Clinton and Congress Retreat from Cutting Business Subsidies,* Cato Policy Analysis no. 254 (Washington, D.C.: Cato Institute, 1996). The most prominent statement of opposition came from Charles L. Schultze, "Industrial Policy: A Dissent," *Brookings Review,* Fall 1983, 3–12.

23. Schultze, "Industrial Policy," 11.

24. See Robert B. Reich, "Why the U.S. Needs an Industrial Policy," *Harvard Business Review* 60, no. 1 (January 1982): 74–81.

25. This section benefits from Andrew Black, "Industrial Policy in W. Germany: Policy in Search of a Goal?" in *European Industrial Policy,* ed. Graham Hall (London: Croom Helm, 1986), 84–127.

26. Michael Utton, "Developments in British Industrial and Competition Policies," in Hall, *European Industrial Policy,* 59–83; Freyman, "Industrial Policy," 44–68; and François Duchêne, "Policies for a Wider World," in *Managing Industrial Change in Western Europe,* ed. François Duchêne and Geoffrey Shepherd (London: F. Pinter, 1987), 220–24.

27. Wyn Grant, *Government and Industry: A Comparative Analysis of the US, Canada and the UK* (Hants, England: Edward Elgar, 1989), 112.

28. See Duchêne, "Policies for a Wider World," 213, 228.

29. Chalmers Johnson, "The Institutional Foundation of Japanese Industrial Policy," in *The Politics of Industrial Policy,* ed. Claude E. Barfield and William A. Schambra (Washington, D.C.: American Enterprise Institute, 1986), 187–205.

30. Philip H. Trezise, "Industrial Policy Is Not the Major Reason for Japan's Success," *Brookings Review,* Spring 1983, 13–18.

31. Clyde V. Prestowitz, *Trading Places: How We Are Giving Our Future to Japan and How to Reclaim It* (New York: Basic Books, 1988), chap. 5.

32. See Harvey Brooks, "Technology as a Factor in U.S. Competitiveness," in Scott and Lodge, *U.S. Competitiveness in the World Economy,* 330–33.

33. Robert S. Ozaki, "How Japanese Industrial Policy Works," in Johnson, *Industrial Policy Debate,* 47–70; and John Zysman, *Governments, Markets, and Growth: Financial Systems and the Politics of Industrial Change* (Ithaca, N.Y.: Cornell University Press, 1983), 237.

34. Michael Porter, "Japan's Twin Demons," *Financial Times,* July 5, 2000, 12.

35. Prestowitz, *Trading Places.*

36. This discussion is derived from Neil Gandal, David Salant, and Leonard Waverman, "Standards in Wireless Telephone Networks," *Telecommunications Policy* 27 (2003), 325–32.

37. This section is drawn from Richard R. Nelson, *High-Technology Policies: A Five-Nation Comparison* (Washington, D.C.: American Enterprise Institute, 1984).

38. This section owes much to the formulation and information contained in Robert Teitelman, *Profits of Science: The American Marriage of Business and Technology* (New York: Basic Books, 1994), esp. 4.

39. Bruce L. R. Smith, *American Science Policy since World War II* (Washington, D.C.: Brookings Institution, 1990).

40. Brooks, "Technology as a Factor in U.S. Competitiveness," 333.

41. Ann R. Markusen, "Defense Spending as Industrial Policy," in *Industrial Policy: Business and Politics in the United States and France,* ed. Sharon Zukin (New York: Praeger, 1985), 70–84.

42. Richard N. Langlois and David C. Mowery, "The Federal Government Role in the Development of the U.S. Software Industry," in *The International Computer Software Industry: A Comparative Study of Industry Evolution and Structure,* ed. David C. Mowery (New York: Oxford University Press, 1996), 53–85.

43. Lewis M. Branscomb, ed., *Empowering Technology: Implementing a U.S. Strategy* (Cambridge, Mass.: MIT Press, 1995).

44. U.S. Department of Commerce, *Statistical Abstract of the United States, 2004–2005* (Washington, D.C.: GPO, 2004), 764.

45. Teitelman, *Profits of Science.*

46. U.S. Department of Commerce, *Statistical Abstract of the United States, 2004–2005,* 765.

47. Ibid.

48. Fong, "Breaking New Ground."

49. See Kenneth Flamm, *Targeting the Computer: Government Support and International Competition* (Washington, D.C.: Brookings Institution, 1987), chap. 6.

50. President's Commission on Industrial Competitiveness, *Global Competition: The New Reality,* vol. 1 (Washington, D.C.: GPO, 1985), 22–24, 50–51.

51. U.S. Department of Commerce, *Statistical Abstract of the United States, 1999* (Washington, D.C.: GPO, 1999), 628.

52. Richard Florida and Martin Kenney, *The Breakthrough Illusion: Corporate America's Failure to Move from Innovation to Mass Production* (New York: Basic Books, 1990).

53. See Barry M. Leiner and others, "A Brief History of the Internet," revised February 20, 1998, and Walt How, "A Brief History of the Internet," updated January 27, 2000, both available at the Internet Society's Web site: www.isoc.org/internet/history/index.shtml. See also Katie Hafner and Matthew Lyon, *Where Wizards Stay Up Late* (New York: Simon and Schuster, 1996).

CHAPTER 14

Global Trade Policies

NINETEEN-FOOT-TALL REPLICAS OF the seven dwarfs from *Snow White* support the roof of the Walt Disney Company building in Southern California.[1] Hollywood has long been the ultimate dream factory, but behind the carefully crafted façade of fantasy and illusion is an industry whose history is chronicled not only in scripts and screenplays but also in the reports of MBAs and accounts of the financial press.[2]

In 2004, Disney's revenues exceeded $30 billion. Buena Vista, the firm's domestic film distribution unit, surpassed $1 billion in box office receipts, and the Disney/Pixar release *The Incredibles* grossed $70 million in its opening weekend. Under the Miramax label, *Kill Bill,* volumes 1 and 2, earned more than $300 million, and Disney also released the Martin Scorsese film *The Aviator,* with Leonardo DiCaprio, and *Finding Neverland,* with Johnny Depp and Kate Winslet.

The film industry, however, is changing, and theatrical releases are no longer the industry's principal source of income. Today larger earnings come from television and home video sales, and Disney is active in these areas, too. Disney owns ABC television, ten television stations, ESPN, and various other cable properties. ABC delivered the TV season's biggest sensation, *Desperate Housewives,* and Buena Vista Television syndicated *Live with Regis and Kelly* and the movie review show *Ebert & Roeper. Finding Nemo* became the top-selling DVD of all time for Buena Vista Home Entertainment, and, confirming the value of Disney's film library, *The Lion King,* platinum edition, became the best-selling DVD title ever re-released.

A second change directly involves the topics of this chapter. The motion picture industry has now become a part of international trade and the global economy. Although it was once dependent on the domestic market, one-third of the industry's revenues today come from international sales, and at the Disney Company itself, more than 20 percent of revenues in 2004 came from outside the United States. ESPN produced programming in twelve languages, the Disney theatrical group operated productions of the *Lion King* in six countries, Buena Vista Home Entertainment International broke records in 2004 for international DVD sales, and the Hong Kong Disneyland theme park was to open its gates in 2005.

The success of the U.S. entertainment industry in other countries has made it a significant factor in international trade. As U.S. firms look to international audiences to provide revenues and cover costs, however, they are encountering more and more trade barriers. European television was traditionally fragmented into national markets with government-owned networks dominating programming. In recent years, private broadcasters, satellites, cable technology, and deregulation have eroded local restraints, and European television has grown rapidly. Changes in Eastern Europe, rising per capita income, and the large number of movie theaters have made the European market particularly attractive to the U.S. film industry, but the European Union has limited the impact of American firms by imposing new trade restrictions. The European Union triggered a trade crisis by proposing to restrict television programs produced outside Europe to 49 percent of transmissions. France, Britain, and other countries then followed with even tighter restrictions on the national origin of films and prime-time programming. What Europeans justified as a measure to preserve their cultural heritage was perceived by the American industry as an effort by European producers to gain protection for products they could not otherwise sell.

Since the 1980s the entertainment industry has stepped up its effort to ensure that Hollywood's interests are heard in Washington. The executives of Disney and other prominent studios have increased their contributions to congressional and presidential candidates and become prominent fund-raisers, and their firms have provided the stars who draw additional donors to political fund-raising events.[3] Disney and other firms have opened Washington offices, and trade association leaders, Disney officials, and other industry figures have won places on executive branch trade advisory boards. Its celebrity status allows the film industry direct access to public officials, whereas most corporate officials are relegated to approaching officeholders through their staffs.[4]

U.S. trade representatives complained to the Europeans about the video restrictions, but the issue is complicated by the lack of international rules for dealing with the situation. Traditional trade rules were devised to curtail tariffs, taxes on the import of manufactured goods into a country. The products of the film industry, however, are talent and creative services rather than manufactured items, and the barriers being raised by the Europeans are not tariffs but another form of restriction. How to deal equitably but effectively with nontariff barriers is a challenge the international trading system has not yet resolved.

In this chapter I place the market-access problems of the U.S. film industry in the broader context of international trade. First I examine the rationale for international trade and the basic features of the post–World War II trading system. I then analyze contemporary pressures on the world trade system and political developments that have made those pressures especially troubling. In conclusion I look to the future, questioning how the postwar trading system can be altered to meet the requirements of an increasingly global age.

FEATURES OF THE INTERNATIONAL TRADING SYSTEM

If the world were a single economic unit, nations would specialize in the economic activities they do best. They would make films, manufacture automobiles, produce wine, or design computers. The nations would trade the surplus in their goods for the products coming from other countries. Because each country would concentrate on the goods it produced most efficiently, economic resources would flow to the world's most productive uses, and consumers in every country would gain. "Liberal" or "free trade" policies are policies that reduce restrictions on the movement of products from country to country so that the world acts more like a single economic unit.

The decades immediately following World War II were a period of unprecedented economic growth in the world. Much of this growth is attributed to the liberal trade policies and the stable exchange rates among currencies that then prevailed.

Restrictions on international trade occur because the politics of trade reflect a mismatch between those who benefit from liberal trade policies and those who pay the costs.[5] The losers in international trade are manufacturers and service sector firms, and their workers, that lose domestic sales to imports. These groups often enter the political arena to obtain protection for their products, and their very survival can depend on securing help from the government. The beneficiaries of free trade are consumers who buy international products at lower prices and companies that succeed in expanding their international sales. These groups are usually less diligent in seeking government assistance, even when they encounter trade barriers, because their survival does not depend on government action.

Early Trade Policies

Article I of the U.S. Constitution gives Congress the authority to "regulate commerce with foreign nations" and "lay and collect duties." From the American Revolution through 1820, trade policy was used to support the nation's independence, and imports from European countries were periodically restricted to reinforce international positions and secure American rights.[6] From 1820 to 1934 trade and tariff policy was governed by domestic political considerations, and Congress reigned supreme. Tariff bills were the major item of congressional business; Congress typically responded to industry demands for protection by imposing high duties on imports.

The culmination of congressional activism in trade matters was the Tariff Act of 1930, better known as the Smoot-Hawley Tariff. In formulating this bill, Congress ignored the warnings of experts and allowed industry pleas for protection to dominate the legislative process.[7] The bill raised import duties to record levels, set tariffs for 20,000 different items, and prompted widespread retaliation by other nations in the form of increased tariffs. As a consequence, U.S. imports between 1929 and 1933 plunged from $4.4 billion to $1.5 billion, and exports collapsed from $5.2 billion to $1.6 billion.[8]

The Smoot-Hawley Tariff was the last general trade bill to be enacted by Congress. It was followed by a notably different kind of trade law, the Reciprocal Trade Agreement Act of 1934, which lowered U.S. tariffs in exchange for reduced tariffs from other countries and set the pattern for trade policy that would prevail for the next fifty years. In this historic act, Congress got out of the business of setting tariffs for specific products. Instead, it authorized the president to negotiate lower tariffs with other nations. Congress also insulated itself from the political pressures exerted by the losers in international trade by creating a regulatory agency and directing aggrieved firms to address their complaints there.[9] The delegation of tariff-setting authority to the executive branch did not stop Congress from establishing ground rules for negotiations, but it did relieve Congress of the actual responsibility for setting duties on specific products.

The General Agreement on Tariffs and Trade

The new approach to trade policy emerged slowly, and it was symbolized by the General Agreement on Tariffs and Trade. The GATT system had its origins in an Anglo-American dialog held during World War II on the postwar creation of an agency to be called the International Trade Organization.[10] When it became clear that there would be no consensus on the authority to be given such an organization, a less formal agreement was signed in 1947 endorsing a set of broad commercial principles. Individual countries endorsed the GATT principles as they saw fit. Congress never formally approved the GATT framework, but it was put into effect through an executive agreement issued by President Harry S. Truman.

The GATT was a stopgap measure, made up of guidelines rather than explicit rules. The countries that signed the GATT did not relinquish their sovereignty to a supranational organization.[11] They did not agree to act in ways that might violate their own laws, damage domestic industries, or hurt their national security. What they did was to endorse flexible trading principles that could help contain domestic pressures for protectionism.

The central principles on which the GATT was based were a commitment to trade liberalization, reciprocity in lowering tariffs, and nondiscrimination, or uniformity, in applying tariffs. The GATT envisioned a series of trade conferences at which the parties would seek to reduce tariff levels. One member would agree to lower tariffs on specific products contingent upon a comparable reduction of tariffs by other members. The GATT had no ability to enforce the negotiated tariffs, but a member could apply to the GATT for permission to impose an extra duty on goods that came from a country not complying with the GATT's tariff levels.

The GATT's primary significance over the years was in holding conferences or "rounds" of negotiations on trade issues. The discussions initiated in 1987 were the eighth round of negotiations held since the GATT had been created, and these talks were designated "the Uruguay Round." The U.S. practice is for Congress to delegate to the president authority to conduct negotiations for a specific period and then to accept or reject the outcome of the negotiations as a package rather than engaging in the politically divisive procedure of assessing specific tariff items.

When authorizing particular rounds of negotiations, Congress has focused on various trade topics. The Trade Expansion Act of 1962, authorizing participation in the Kennedy Round of negotiations, considered bureaucratic as well as substantive trade issues.[12] The State Department had been the lead agency on trade issues for three decades, but the Commerce Department charged that the State Department routinely favored foreign firms over American commercial interests. In response to this criticism, Congress created in 1962 a special representative for trade negotiations in the White House to resolve interagency conflicts and coordinate trade policy. The Office of the Special Representative for Trade Negotiations was strengthened in 1974, but executive branch divisions over trade issues persisted. The Commerce and Labor Departments typically favored aggressive actions to defend American commercial interests, whereas the State and Treasury Departments usually sought to preserve harmonious relations with trading partners who might then help to resolve foreign policy and currency issues.

The 1962 Act also authorized aid to firms and employees hurt by international competition. "Trade adjustment assistance" uses tax dollars theoretically generated by international trade to compensate specific groups that can demonstrate that they were the losers in the trade process.[13] Firms can use the assistance to become more competitive in the marketplace, and workers can employ the benefits to learn skills required by modern industries. Trade adjustment assistance was intended to diminish political support for protectionism by demonstrating to aggrieved groups that government would be responsive to their problems.

As a result of the GATT's long-term success in reducing tariffs, tariff barriers on manufactured goods had ceased to be a major issue among major industrial nations by 1970.[14] When Congress authorized U.S. participation in the Toyko Round of negotiations in 1974, attention focused not on tariff levels but on nontariff barriers to trade and the administration of the GATT process. Prominent among the issues were the procedures by which companies obtained relief from actions of international competitors.

The GATT provisions allowed member countries an "escape clause" that authorized them to limit imports of products that injured domestic industries. Article VI of the GATT permitted member countries to take account of "unfair" trade advantages given to foreign competitors by their governments. If a home country subsidized the costs of manufacturing a product for sale in another country, the receiving country was authorized to impose a *countervailing duty* on the import equal to the amount of the subsidy the manufacturer received in the home country. If products from one country were sold in another country for less than their cost of production, the receiving country could impose an *antidumping* levy on the product equal to the difference between the production cost and the sale price.

Responsibility for administering the GATT provisions and the other U.S. trade laws in the United States rests with the International Trade Commission (ITC), an independent regulatory commission. The ITC determines when escape clause, antidumping, and countervailing actions are justified to defend U.S. industry from the improper practices of international competitors. American companies complained that the ITC rarely approved their petitions for relief. In the Trade Act of 1974, Congress made it easier for U.S. firms to obtain relief from unfair trade practices, but companies still complained that their chances of securing positive decisions from the ITC were low.

U.S. Trade Policies

The GATT supplements rather than replaces a country's own trade policies. Despite the GATT, every country has erected barriers to the free flow of trade. Although probably more sinned against than sinning, the United States too has created nontariff policies that restrict imports and support exports.[15]

The United States has established a multitude of specific "Buy American" programs. Many federal statutes require government agencies to purchase American products if they are available at an equal or "reasonable" price. To benefit the merchant marine industry, U.S. ships must be used to transport goods from one U.S. port to another as well as to carry half the commodities sent abroad under the foreign aid program. State laws also mandate the use of U.S. materials by state and local governments, require the purchase of U.S. automobiles, and restrict the use of foreign steel.

Additional rules limit imports of specific products. U.S. agricultural laws authorize import quotas for products included in price-support programs, and in past years quotas were set for sugar, peanuts, cotton, and beef. The U.S. government has also persuaded other countries to accept "voluntary" agreements limiting their exports to the United States. The most prominent voluntary export restraints appeared in the early 1980s, when Japan agreed to limit auto exports to the United States to head off congressional proposals to legislate quotas on Japanese products.

The regulation of the domestic economy is composed of myriad rules that, intentionally or not, also restrict imports. U.S. auto-emissions standards, testing procedures for pharmaceutical products, and product liability requirements all constitute barriers to the free flow of goods from other countries. States and localities have building codes that frequently favor local industry by incorporating specifications for building materials that are met only by products manufactured in the area. International analysts also argue that the litigiousness of

U.S. commercial relationships and the unpredictable administration of U.S. trade laws limit foreign competition.[16]

Like other countries, the United States has adopted policies that promote the export of national goods. The Export-Import Bank (Eximbank) makes loans to foreign buyers to assist them in purchasing products manufactured in the United States, and it guarantees that foreign companies that borrow money from private sources to purchase U.S. goods will repay their loans. The United States has also sought to stimulate exports by linking foreign aid programs to the purchase of U.S. goods. It encourages the formation of export trading companies that are exempt from antitrust laws and offers tax preferences for export activities.

The United States also disrupts free trade through export controls intended to promote economic or foreign policy goals.[17] The Export Administration Act and the International Emergency Economic Powers Act provided the legal basis for embargoes against Cuba, Iran, Libya, North Korea, and Sudan. Although the use of trade controls is a common tool of international relations, the effectiveness of such tactics is a subject of continuing controversy. Sen. Richard G. Lugar, R-Ind., has introduced proposals that would bar the United States from imposing unilateral sanctions on agricultural products and limit the use of sanctions in other circumstances. Although no consensus has emerged, Lugar's measures are favored by human rights organizations convinced that sanctions hurt citizens rather than governments as well as businesses that seek new opportunities to sell their products.[18]

The Uruguay Round of GATT Negotiations

The Uruguay Round of negotiations was launched in 1987, and the results were intended to strengthen and modernize the GATT's rules and procedures.[19] Although the collapse of negotiations had been considered possible, the *Results of the Uruguay Round of Multilateral Trade Negotiations* was formally adopted at a ministerial conference in Marrakesh in April 1994, with the actual agreement made up of twenty-nine individual legal texts and twenty-eight additional declarations, decisions, and understandings.[20] The new accord moved the GATT beyond narrow trade issues and assigned it responsibility for establishing a framework for the conduct of international business.[21] Agreements were reached in many important areas:

- *World Trade Organization.* The agreement established the WTO as a permanent international organization based in Geneva that would promote trade negotiations, administer trade agreements, and resolve trade disputes. Although the WTO is the institutional center of world trade, the GATT still lives as the source of many of the principles that govern international commerce. The WTO is a new organization, but many trade rules can be traced to the GATT's founding in 1947.[22]

- *Agriculture.* Agriculture makes up 10 percent of world trade, but it had never been subject to GATT rules. The new agreement took the first steps to bring agriculture under multilateral discipline, but there were only minor reductions in European agricultural subsidies and only a slight opening in the Japanese and Korean rice markets.[23] Exporting nations sought to limit internal production subsidies for agriculture, eliminate barriers to imports, and reduce the subsidies countries paid to export their products, but to little avail.

- *Services.* The Marrakesh accord included a General Agreement on Trade in Services (GATS). Services in such areas as insurance, banking, tourism, consulting, communications, and film production account for 22 percent of world trade, but there are few rules governing trade in services. The GATS created a broad framework for future negotiations, urged countries not to discriminate among service providers on the basis of their national origin, and presented annexes laying out rules for specific service sectors such as telecommunications, maritime transport, and financial services.

- *Intellectual Property Rights.* Multilateral concern about patents, counterfeiting, and intellectual property has been around for a century, but it was not until the Uruguay Round agreement on Trade-Related Intellectual Property Rights (TRIPS) that explicit intellectual property rules were embedded in the world trading system.[24] Some industrial nations make it illegal to sell counterfeit goods or pirated products, but other countries lack such laws or fail to enforce them. The TRIPS agreement requires WTO members to protect intellectual property rights, but it leaves it to the countries to determine the appropriate method to do this.

- *Investments.* Multinational corporations believe that they face arbitrary actions by host governments. The Trade-Related Investment Measures (TRIMS) agreement outlines standards that recommend that national governments treat international corporations in the same way they treat domestic firms.

- *Sensitive Industries.* Countries frequently protect industries that play an especially sensitive role in their economies such as steel, shipbuilding, and automobiles, and the new agreement sought to phase out these special controls. Since the 1950s, trade in textiles had been limited by bilateral accords and the multilateral Multifiber Arrangement, but the Uruguay Round negotiators abolished textile limits beginning in 2005.

- *Dispute Settlement Procedures.* The GATT's origins as a provisional agreement had left it without reliable mechanisms for settling disputes between governments. The 1994 Dispute Settlement Understanding calls for binding adjudication of disputes by an expert panel followed by an appeals process, but the appeals process can overturn decisions only if all member nations agree.

The political key to the Uruguay Round accord was a deal between the developed and developing nations to trade off import-producing, labor-intensive industries located in developing countries for provisions that would assist expanding, high-tech industries headquartered in developed nations.[25] The abolition of the Multifiber Arrangement, first steps toward the integration of agriculture into the global trading regime, and improvements in market access for developing nations were secured with the acceptance of the TRIPS agreement, the GATS, and TRIMS rules involving international investment that developed nations believed would benefit their industries and their economies.

THE INTERNATIONAL TRADE SYSTEM UNDER STRESS

Trade issues stand today at the center of the political stage for the first time since the 1930s.[26] The agreements described in the previous section as well as innovations in transportation, communications, and information technologies have produced a level of global economic integration that has never been as broad and as deep as it is today. The growing volume of cross-border economic activity and deeper intrusion of the international economy into domestic affairs poses a challenge to the world's governments. At the same time, transformations in the nature of the world trading system have compounded the difficulties in responding effectively to contemporary events.

Changes in the System of World Trade

In the 1950s and 1960s major countries defined the value of their currencies in terms of the dollar, and the United States supported the value of the dollar by guaranteeing its conversion into gold at a fixed rate.[27] This system of fixed exchange rates pegged to the dollar provided great stability for world trade, but it did not survive changes in the value of the dollar itself. In the early 1970s economists concluded that U.S. trade deficits were an indicator that the dollar was overvalued. To solve the problem, the United States devalued the dollar in relation to other major currencies and ended its convertibility into gold. These moves forced the world to shift to the current system of floating exchange rates, in which the value of the dollar is set in the currency markets. Huge pools of international capital have been assembled to speculate in international currencies, and this has increased the risks and uncertainty of global trade.

A second factor increasing instability in world trade was the emergence of new players in the global economy. As noted earlier, the postwar trading system was the product of agreements between governments in Europe and North America. The rise of Japan as an economic power introduced non-Western cultural assumptions into deliberations over trade issues. Concerns about Japanese practices were multiplied when such countries as Korea, Singapore, Taiwan, and even Brazil and Mexico brought their own distinct values and assumptions to the global economy. Twenty-three nations participated in the first round of GATT negotiations in 1947, whereas one hundred and twenty-three countries took part in the Uruguay Round negotiations.[28] The Group of Twenty developing nations, including Brazil, China, India, and South Africa, has won a leadership role in preparing for the new Doha Round of trade talks, with another group of thirty-three countries protecting particular agricultural products, and an assembly of ninety nations advocating the interests of the poorest nations.[29] The growing cultural diversity of nations involved in international trade has complicated the process of reaching agreement on contentious issues. A recent controversy over textile imports from China is described in Box 14-1.

Another change occurring in international trade was growth in the importance of the service sector and the decline of manufacturing.[30] The GATT system was created to reduce tariffs on manufactured goods, but the growing size and complexity of the service sector has posed problems of definition and analysis. Although manufactured goods may be produced at some distant location, services often require direct access to consumers, thus complicating the process of regulation. Many governments now play a more activist role in promoting their nations' economies by offering preferences and subsidies to service industries, but international restrictions on such preferences have proved to be especially difficult to implement.

The fourth development that has increased pressure on the world trade system is the changed position of the United States. In the decades immediately after World War II, the United States provided leadership for the international trade system, but as its postwar dominance ended, it no longer had the ability to insist on free trade principles in the world. The British had defended liberal trade

Cases in Development
BOX 14-1 CHINESE TEXTILE IMPORTS STORM ASHORE

January 2005 brought the end of the Multifiber Arrangement that had limited the exports of textiles to the United States and Europe from developing countries. In preparation for the opening of these markets, Chinese producers reportedly invested billions in retooling their production systems and streamlining their plants. With their improved productivity, Chinese

(continued)

manufacturers hoped to capture fully half of the global market for garments and textiles. U.S and European firms feared the impact of the new rivals, and countries that had benefited from the old quota system, such as Bangladesh and Sri Lanka, did not know how they could compete.

By mid-2005 the U.S. Census Bureau reported that there had been a two-thirds increase in total textile shipments from China, whereas imports into the United States from Mexico and South Korea had declined. U.S. apparel makers warned that the 32,000 Chinese companies would soon dominate the market and erase 650,000 U.S. jobs, and industry associations in Europe expressed similar fears. The United States government and the European Union warned China to restrain its exports or face new quotas. China denounced the threats as "protectionist" and insisted that it was being punished for the weaknesses of the Western textile industry. The United States justified its actions by citing a provision in the agreement by which China joined the WTO that authorized restrictions to "safeguard" an industry being disrupted by imported goods. The United States and the European Union imposed quotas on textile products such as men's shirts and cotton yarn, and China offered to increase its own duties on textile exports. In Congress, U.S. legislators proposed measures that would impose a 28 percent tariff on all Chinese imports unless China revalued the exchange rate between its currency and the dollar.

The controversy has not been resolved, and it promises to be the forerunner of further trade conflicts in other industries as the United States struggles to accommodate Chinese imports. In the 1980s the United States persuaded Japan to voluntarily restrain the number of cars it exported to the United States. As a consequence, Japanese car companies concentrated on the most profitable segments of the auto market and developed the highly successful Lexus in competition with U.S. products. Restrictions on the volume of textile imports might lead Chinese manufacturers to concentrate on profitable high-end products, an area where they could emerge as dangerous competitors to those Western firms that have maintained a significant foothold in that part of the textile industry.

sources: Washingtonpost.com, "China Bristles at Textile Trade Backlash," http://www.washingtonpost.com/wp-dyn/content/article/, accessed June 3, 2005; BBC News, "China Attacks 'Unfair' US Quotas," http://www.newsvote.bbc.co.uk/, accessed June 3, 2005; Alexandra Harney, Alan Beattie, and Raphael Minder, "China Increases Taxes on Textile Exports," *Financial Times.* May 21, 2005, 1; Raphael Minder, "EU Warns China over Textile Exports," *Financial Times,* May 18, 2005, 6; Alexandra Harney, "US Textile Importers Braced for Legal Action," *Financial Times,* April 20, 2005, 4; and Alan Beattie and Alexandra Harney, "China's Textile Rivals Await Outcome of 'Terrible Prophecies,'" *Financial Times,* January 21, 2005, 6.

policies in the nineteenth century, and the Americans had promoted free trade in the years from 1934 to the mid-1980s, but no single nation now has the power to command the world to support free trade. Political changes inside the United States have also complicated the management of the world's trade situation.

Changes in American Politics

Until recently the politics of trade was rather simple. The Smoot-Hawley lesson from 1930 that restrictions on trade harmed the global economy dominated academic and political thinking. Elite groups endorsed liberal trade policies all but unanimously. The executive branch shaped the nation's trade policies, and protectionism was the central trade issue. Few industries were affected by imports, and Congress established institutions such as the International Trade Commission to deflect pressures for legislative action from companies hurt by imports.

By the mid-1980s, however, the situation at home and abroad had changed. The dimensions of international trade had been transformed, and the U.S. economy had been buffeted by transformations. As the U.S. trade deficit exploded, more firms and workers found themselves losers in the trade process. Debates over the North American Free Trade Agreement (NAFTA) and the World Trade Organization increased the visibility of trade issues, and the linkage of trade topics with the environment, working conditions, and human rights complicated already difficult legislative negotiations over trade matters. As the demands for government action in the United States multiplied, other governments around the world became more involved in promoting their economies, and trade disputes became more complicated.

Whereas trade problems have multiplied, congressional ability to resist protectionist pressures has declined. Earlier reforms weakened the House Ways and Means Committee, which once managed trade legislation, and dispersed authority on trade matters to subcommittees that were responsive to specific interests. Furthermore, trade has become an increasingly partisan issue. Democrats once supported international trade by large majorities, but the loss of jobs in traditional industries turned unions into champions of protectionist legislation. As deficits persisted and the elite consensus in favor of liberal trade policies eroded, some Republicans joined Democrats in making trade a basis for congressional criticism of the executive branch, and divisions over trade issues inside both parties became an abiding feature of American politics. Contemporary trade disputes have become more complex than earlier issues, and the political ability to respond effectively to these controversies has declined.

Patterns in U.S. Trade

Every year from 1894 to 1970, the value of U.S. exports exceeded the value of imports. Every year since 1975, in contrast, the United States has had a negative trade balance, usually called a trade deficit. One measure of international trade compares the value of the goods a country imports with the value of the goods a country exports, and the result is the goods, or merchandise, trade balance. Since 1976 the United States has had a merchandise trade deficit. The trade deficit reported each month on the nightly news or in the newspapers is the difference between the value of goods and services exported from the United States and the value of goods and services imported into the U.S. from abroad.[31] A third, even broader measure of international trade transactions is the current account balance, which includes international investment income and unilateral financial transfers as well as goods and services.

Regardless of how it was defined, the size of the U.S. trade deficit surged in the mid-1980s, soared again in the mid-1990s, and has not stopped growing since.[32] As reported in Table 14-1, the trade deficit in goods and services rose from $19 billion in 1980 to $80 billion in 1990, and then reached $378 billion in 2000. In 2004 the deficit in goods and services reached the previously unimaginable figure of $617 billion. In the same period, the U.S. current accounts deficit grew even more rapidly. As indicated in the table, the current accounts deficit increased from $79 billion in 1990, passed $413 billion in 2000, and topped $666 billion in 2004. In 2004 the deficit set a new record, reaching roughly 5.6 percent of gross domestic product, and between 2000 and 2004 the United States added a staggering $2,470 billion, or approximately $2.5 trillion, to its accumulated current account trade deficit.[33]

Table 14-2 is a description of U.S. trading relationships with individual countries and areas for the years 2003 and 2004. The balance of trade in goods between the United States and the six countries and the two areas is given in the table for each of the two years. For both years, the United States had a trade deficit with each country and area. In the final column on the table the percentage increase in the U.S. deficit is shown for each country and area

Table 14-1　U.S. International Transactions, 1970–2004 (billions of dollars)

Year	Export of goods	Import of goods	Balance on goods	Balance on goods+services	Balance on current account
1970	42	40	3	2	2
1980	224	250	−26	−19	2
1990	389	498	−109	−80	−79
2000	772	1224	−452	−378	−413
2004	808	1473	−666	−617	−666

Source: Economic Report of the President, 2005 (Washington, D.C.: GPO, 2004), table B-103; and Christopher L. Bach, "U.S. International Transactions, 2004," table C, *Survey of Current Business*, April 2005.

Table 14-2   U.S. Trade in Goods for Countries and Areas, 2003–2004

Country or area	Balance 2003 (billions of $)	Balance 2004 (billions of $)	Increase 2003 to 2004 (%)
Canada	−54	−68	26
China	−124	−162	31
Germany	−40	−46	17
Great Britain	−9	−11	13
Japan	−68	−77	14
Mexico	−42	−46	11
Europe	−116	−132	14
Latin America	−69	−82	20

Source: Christopher L. Bach, "U.S. International Transactions, 2004," table C, *Survey of Current Business,* April 2005.

between 2003 and 2004. Among the six countries, the United States had the largest trade deficit in both years with China, and the second largest in each year with Japan. Canada and Mexico are the countries with which the United States has the most trade, and both earn substantial trade surpluses as U.S. trading partners. Between 2003 and 2004, the U.S. trade deficit increased most rapidly with China, up $38 billion, or 31 percent; Canada was in the runner-up position.

The popular view is that the U.S. trade deficits result from declining industrial competitiveness or unfair trade barriers erected by other countries. Economists, however, insist that a nation's trade deficit results from the gap between its savings rate and its investments. If a nation invests more than it saves, it must draw in funds from overseas to meet the demand. In the early 1980s huge federal budget deficits and a low personal savings rate saw investments in the United States decline and the national savings rate fall even faster, and this produced the extraordinary increase in the trade deficit. This situation was aggravated by the strong value of the dollar that made imports attractive to American consumers, the revival of the U.S. economy when the rest of the industrial world was in recession, and the debt crisis in the developing world.[34]

During the 1990s the nation's overall savings rate doubled, climbing from 3 percent to more than 6 percent.[35] The trade deficit in those years did not result from low national savings but from a sharp increase in investment as international investors concluded that the United States was an attractive place to put their resources. Increases in both savings and investment then yielded strong gains in U.S. productivity.

What Is the Future of the International Trade System?

The champions of liberal trade policies present a clear case. Over the past half century, openness to international trade and global capital markets has raised living standards and created more affluence for the United States and much of the rest of the world than ever before in history. As argued in the *Economic Report of the President:*

> Through trade, countries can shift resources into those sectors best able to compete in international markets, and so reap the benefits of specialization and scale economies. Opening domestic markets to global capital can improve the efficiency of *investment,* which can promote economic growth. Through firms' *direct investment* in *foreign* affiliates, countries can adopt international best practices in production, including managerial, technical, and marketing know-how.[36]

Although free trade ideology acknowledges that protectionism will always be popular among producer groups losing market share to international competitors, it maintains that the costs of protection to consumers are greater than the benefits to producers. Import restrictions, free trade proponents argue, are like a sales tax whose revenues are used to subsidize protected industries.[37] The Multifiber Arrangement and bilateral accords, for example, limited imports of textiles and clothing. It was estimated that U.S. producers gained slightly more than $4 billion each year in added revenues from these restrictions, but the cost in higher prices to American consumers exceeded $10 billion annually. Protectionism is commonly believed to save jobs, but free trade advocates argue that the price of preserving jobs in the protected industry pushes up costs throughout the economy and sacrifices more jobs than it saves. Restrictions on imports of machine tools, for example, were said to have cost consumers $120,000 in higher prices for each job that was "saved" in the industry.[38]

Although it may be good economic theory, the deck appears to be stacked against the future practice of free trade policies. In a neomercantilist age, government officials champion trade policies that enhance the competitiveness of their national economies and promote the welfare of their strategic industries.[39] Regardless of existing trade rules, most countries are compelled to pursue policies that will yield a national trade surplus, or their economies will be punished by international financial markets. For two decades, the United States has ignored the need for economic discipline and adopted policies that have produced large trade deficits.[40] It has advanced its trade policies without demanding reciprocity from its trading partners, and the result is an enormous annual trade deficit and a nightmarish accumulated trade deficit that cannot be sustained much longer. Somehow the U.S. imports need to be reduced or its exports increased or both.

The WTO Agreements

The World Trade Organization was founded ten years ago. Its creation was accompanied by the adoption of numerous agreements that were, indeed, impressive in scope, but the results of the agreements have been disappointing. Despite its position in the world, the United States has only one vote in the WTO.[41] The European Union negotiates its trade policies as a single unit, but because it has twenty-five members it receives twenty-five votes in the WTO. Like the United Nations General Assembly, each member state in the WTO receives an equal vote. Eighty percent of WTO members are developing nations, and this gives them the majority required to interpret the organization's legal provisions.

The strengthening of the dispute-settlement process was one of the prominent goals of the Uruguay Round, but the new regime has not produced the prompt and decisive resolution of disputes in prominent cases that was promised. Although the United States revised its corporate tax system in response to a WTO ruling and repealed its Anti-Dumping Act, which was determined to violate WTO provisions, some experts conclude that trade "rules are being used not simply to address broadly supported concerns about fairness in international trade but for . . . [political] purposes that are inconsistent with generally accepted notions of fairness."[42] A decade ago the WTO ruled that the European Union did not have sufficient evidence to demonstrate that hormone-treated beef endangered consumers, but the EU prohibition of such beef remains in effect. In the next year, the WTO should finally determine whether EU rules for importing bananas, sugar, and genetically modified foods violate WTO regulations.

The provisions on agriculture left high production subsidies in place, and the chief U.S. trade representative has indicated that little progress was possible in upcoming talks.[43] The General Agreement on Trade in Services has proved to be little more than a framework, and although some positive steps were seen in the agreement on telecommunications, nothing has come from the agreements on maritime transport and financial services.[44] The rules governing intellectual property have run afoul of concerns that poor countries will not be able to afford pharmaceutical products, but little has been done to reduce the massive piracy involving software, films, and other media products. Linkages between trade issues and the environment, investment conditions, labor standards, and human rights have increased uncertainty in the trading system, and prominent nations persist in policies that systematically disadvantage their trading partners.[45] Some free trade advocates now question whether the WTO reforms were adequately conceived and speculate whether they have done more harm than good.[46] Journalists report that the chances of overall progress in the ongoing Doha Round of trade liberalization talks are remote, and there is even less reason to believe that proposed changes could help reduce the U.S. trade imbalance.[47]

Regional and Bilateral Trade Agreements

Regionalism and bilateral agreements have become alternatives to the slowly accumulating concerns about the performance of the GATT and the WTO. The United States designed its Caribbean Basin Initiative to lower tariff barriers among the Caribbean countries and thus improve their economies, and European nations joined together to create a system of preferential trade arrangements to boost their international competitiveness, which now finds expression in the European Union. The United States, Canada, and Mexico expected that they, too, would benefit from increased regional trade, and the three nations agreed on the details of their trade agreement in August 1992.

As it was an election year, the free trade proposal became entwined in presidential politics.[48] Congressional Republicans had supported the NAFTA negotiations, whereas the Democrats in the House and the Senate were split, with the majority probably in opposition. Governor Clinton announced during the presidential campaign that he supported the trade agreement, but he also advocated the negotiation of side agreements dealing with environmental standards, working conditions, and responses to surges in imports. The politically clever response skillfully overcame the division within the Democratic Party during the campaign season. After an uphill battle, the House eventually approved the agreement in November 1993 by a margin of 234 to 200, the Senate followed suit, and NAFTA went into effect on January 1, 1994.

NAFTA would eliminate most tariff and nontariff barriers by 2008, and it liberalized license requirements and established safeguards for cross-border investment. The agreement also stipulated that no nation would be required to lower its environmental or health standards because of NAFTA, and it devised product and domestic-content rules that were intended to help North American firms compete with international competitors in serving the North American market.

In the 1980s the United States also promoted bilateral free trade agreements as a means of obtaining greater balance and reciprocity in its trade relationships. The first agreement was concluded with Israel in 1985, and in 2004 the United States concluded agreements with Australia, Bahrain, and Morocco, and it signed the Central American Free Trade Agreement, which was approved in 2005.[49] A WTO report argues that the proliferation of regional and bilateral trade agreements is undermining the principles of multilateralism and nondiscrimination in trade arrangements on which the WTO rests.

Robert Gilpin argues in *The Challenge of Global Capitalism* that a successful international economy requires a stable political foundation, and he maintains that the political forces that once underpinned an open global economy have been severely weakened.[50] The end of the East-West conflict has given freer reign to parochial interests at the expense of shared concerns and common values. Technological innovation and structural change have challenged established institutions and created anxieties where there was once stability. To ensure the continuation of the benefits of international economic activity, Gilpin insists, political leaders in the United States and other major countries must cooperate in rebuilding the political foundation of an open world economy. They must address the concerns of the poor and the powerless, and they must resist the temptation to ameliorate domestic political tensions by imposing costs on outsiders. The ability of the U.S. entertainment industry to gain access to international markets might be a visible indicator of the future viability of the current trading system.[51]

SUMMARY

The United States was the major world force promoting multilateral free trade in the half century from 1934 to 1984. The Reciprocal Trade Agreement of 1934 and the 1947 General Agreement on Tariffs and Trade restrained protectionism and presented a framework to support increased trade. Despite the limitations on GATT authority and the nationalistic policies pursued by many countries, tariffs were substantially reduced and the volume of international trade grew dramatically.

Since the mid-1980s, however, the international trading system has been subjected to pressures that have eroded the foundations of the earlier arrangements and undermined the tradition of U.S. leadership. During this period, the United States has experienced a dramatically increased trade deficit that has now reached ominous proportions. The Uruguay Round of trade negotiations established the World Trade Organization and created dozens of specialized agreements to sustain future trade relations, but the results of these agreements have been disappointing. The growing volume of regional and bilateral trade agreements underlines the dissatisfaction with the current global regime and constitutes a challenge to the existing system.

FURTHER READINGS

The home page of the U.S. Trade Representative provides information on the history and mission of the office, and the representative's reports, speeches and testimony: http://www.ustr.gov. Data on international trade is available through the Census Bureau at http://www.census.gov/ftp/pub/foreign-trade. The World Trade Organization Web site offers a discussion about the organization and its policies: http://www.wto.org. Information on the Convention on International Trade in Endangered Species is available at the Web site of the United Nations Environment Programme—World Conservation Monitoring Centre: http://www.unep-wcmc.org; click on Species.

Destler, I. M. *American Trade Politics.* 4th ed. Washington, D.C.: Institute for International Economics, 2005.
Hoekman, Bernard M., and Michel M. Kostecki. *The Political Economy of the World Trading System: The WTO and Beyond.* 2nd ed. New York: Oxford University Press, 2001.

Lovett, William A., Alfred E. Eckes, and Richard L. Brinkman. *U.S. Trade Policy: History, Theory and the WTO.* 2nd ed. Armonk, N.Y.: M. E. Sharpe, 2004.

O'Brien, Robert, and Marc Willliams. *Global Political Economy: Evolution and Dynamics.* New York: Palgrave Macmillan, 2004.

Sauve, Pierre, and Robert M. Stern. *GATS 2000: New Directions in Services Trade Liberalization.* Washington, D.C.: Brookings Institution Press, 1999.

NOTES

1. Statements about the Walt Disney Company come from the firm's *1990 Annual Report* and its *2004 Annual Report* (Burbank, Calif.: Disney, 1991 and 2005).
2. Statements about the industry are drawn from Bruce Stokes, "Tinseltown Trade War," *National Journal,* February 23, 1991, 432–38.
3. Ibid., 435.
4. Ronald Brownstein, *The Power and the Glitter: The Hollywood-Washington Connection* (New York: Pantheon, 1990).
5. This chapter relies on the basic text on trade issues, I. M. Destler, *American Trade Politics: System under Stress* (Washington, D.C.: Institute for International Economics, 1986), esp. 3–5.
6. See Richard N. Cooper, "Trade Policy as Foreign Policy," in *U.S. Trade Policies in a Changing World Economy,* ed. Robert M. Stern (Cambridge, Mass.: MIT Press, 1987), 291–322.
7. The classic account is E. E. Schattschneider, *Politics, Pressures and the Tariff: A Study of Free Private Enterprise in Pressure Politics, as Shown in the 1929–1930 Revision of the Tariff* (New York: Prentice Hall, 1935).
8. Destler, *American Trade Politics,* 9.
9. I. M. Destler, "United States Trade Policymaking in the Uruguay Round," in *Domestic Trade Politics and the Uruguay Round,* ed. Henry R. Nau (New York: Columbia University Press, 1989), 191–207.
10. Kenneth W. Dam, *The GATT Law and International Economic Organization* (Chicago: University of Chicago Press, 1970), chaps. 2–3.
11. Stefanie Ann Lenway, *The Politics of U.S. International Trade: Protection, Expansion and Escape* (Boston: Pitman, 1985), 4–7.
12. Claude E. Barfield and John H. Makin, eds., *Trade Policy and U.S. Competitiveness* (Washington, D.C.: American Enterprise Institute, 1987), chaps. 2–5.
13. Ibid., chaps. 22–24; and Robert Z. Lawrence and Robert E. Litan, *Saving Free Trade: A Pragmatic Approach* (Washington, D.C.: Brookings Institution, 1986).
14. Anne O. Krueger, "Introduction," in *The WTO as an International Organization,* ed. Krueger (Chicago: University of Chicago Press, 1998), 6.
15. For an alternative view to the United States being more sinned against than sinning, see Sima Lieberman, *The Economic and Political Roots of the New Protectionism* (Totowa, N.J.: Rowman and Littlefield, 1988).
16. Alan M. Gurman and Andrew D. M. Anderson, *Administered Protection in America* (London: Croom Helm, 1987).
17. William J. Long, *U.S. Export Control Policy: Executive Autonomy vs. Congressional Reform* (New York: Columbia University Press, 1989).
18. Shawn Zeller, "Seeking an End to Sanctions," *National Journal* 32, no. 26 (June 24, 2000): 2002–3.
19. This section is based on *Economic Report of the President, 1991* (Washington, D.C.: GPO, 1991), 243–52.
20. Bruce Stokes, "Apres GATT, le Deluge?" *National Journal,* January 12, 1991, 75–78; Richard Blackhurst, "The Capacity of the WTO to Fulfill Its Mandate," in Krueger, *WTO as an International Organization,* 32.
21. William A. Lovett, Alfred E. Eckes, and Richard L. Brinkman, *U.S. Trade Policy: History, Theory and the WTO,* 2nd ed. (Armonk, N.Y.: M. E. Sharpe, 2004) 83.
22. Thomas Oatley, *International Political Economy: Interests and Institutions in the Global Economy* (New York: Pearson-Longman, 2004), 19.

23. This review is based on Krueger, "Introduction," 3, and Destler, *American Trade Politics,* 231–32.

24. Bernard M. Hoekman and Michel M. Kostecki, *The Political Economy of the World Trading System: The WTO and Beyond,* 2nd ed. (New York: Oxford University Press, 2001), chap. 8.

25. Ibid., 298; and Lovett, Eckes, and Brinkman, *U.S. Trade Policy,* 84.

26. Destler, "United States Trade Policymaking in the Uruguay Round," 192.

27. This section draws from Destler, *American Trade Politics,* 37–55.

28. Robert O'Brien and Marc Willliams, *Global Political Economy: Evolution and Dynamics* (New York: Palgrave Macmillan, 2004), 152.

29. Alan Beattie and Frances Williams, "Who's for the WTO? Trade Is Troubled by Divisions within the Developing World," *Financial Times,* April 5, 2005, 15.

30. See Richard H. Snape, "Reaching Effective Agreements Covering Services," in Krueger, *WTO as an International Organization,* 279–95.

31. The current accounts balance includes trade in both goods and services, such as tourism, transportation, financial services, and film industry services. Nancy Dunne, "US Trade Deficit Soars to a Record $29.2 Bn in February," *Financial Times,* April 20, 2000, 1.

32. Specific data in this section are drawn from *Economic Report of the President, 2004* (Washington, D.C.: GPO, 2004), particularly table B-103.

33. This amount is calculated from the sources identified in Table 14-1.

34. Benjamin Friedman, *Day of Reckoning: The Consequences of American Economic Policy* (New York: Random House, 1988); Destler, *American Trade Politics,* 181–82; and William R. Cline, *United States External Adjustment and the World Economy* (Washington, D.C.: Institute for International Economics, 1989), 51–75.

35. Robert Gilpin, *The Challenge of Global Capitalism: The World Economy in the 21st Century* (Princeton: Princeton University Press, 2000), 345.

36. *Economic Report of the President, 2000* (Washington, D.C.: GPO, 2000), chap. 6.

37. This and the following statements come from the *Economic Report of the President, 1991,* 240–41.

38. Ibid., 241.

39. See Paul K. Krugman, "Strategic Sectors and International Competitiveness," in Stern, *Trade Policies in a Changing World Economy,* 207–32; and Martin Wolf, "Academics Now Advocate Trading Blocs," *Financial Times* (London), October 30, 1989, 19.

40. This argument is developed in Lovett, Eckes, and Brinkman, *U.S. Trade Policy.*

41. Ibid., 85.

42. Robert E. Baldwin, "Imposing Multilateral Discipline on Administered Protection," in Krueger, *WTO as an International Organization,* 297; and Frances Williams, "US Facing Anti-Dumping Investigation," *Financial Times,* April 26, 2000, 7.

43. Mark Suzman, "Barshefsky in Plea for Trade Talks Flexibility," *Financial Times,* February 9, 2000, 5.

44. Snape, "Reaching Effective Agreements Covering Services," 279–95.

45. Edward J. Lincoln, *Troubled Times: U.S.-Japan Trade Relations in the 1990s* (Washington, D.C.: Brookings Institution Press, 1999).

46. Robert Rauch, "Forget About China . . . Can Trade Be Saved from the WTO?" *National Journal* 32 (May 13, 2000): 1495–96.

47. Alan Beattie, "Services Prove to Be the Latest Sticking Point in Doha Trade Negotiations," *Financial Times,* February 10, 2005, 6; Frances Williams, "Doha Global Trade Round 'Close to Crisis,'" *Financial Times,* April 29, 2005, 4; and Lovett, Eckes, and Brinkman, *U.S. Trade Policy,* 176.

48. I. M. Destler, *American Trade Politics,* 3rd ed. (Washington, D.C.: Institute for International Economics and the Twentieth Century Fund, 1995), 219.

49. *Economic Report of the President, 2005* (Washington, D.C.: GPO, 2005), chap. 8.

50. Gilpin, *Challenge of Global Capitalism,* 346–49.

51. Ibid., 231.

CHAPTER 15

Business as Social Actor

CORPORATIONS ARE PROFIT-MAXIMIZING institutions, but social policies affect their operations at every turn. Corporate production decisions, financial judgments, marketing strategies, and human resource choices are all embedded in dense networks of social policies. To what extent should companies be held responsible for achieving equity in the society? Should they be expected to reflect societal standards for equity in their operations, or should they be held to a higher standard? Government programs pursue a multitude of social objectives, and they enlist corporations to carry out an array of tasks. To appraise the various roles of business in social policy, it is necessary to identify the *objectives* government seeks to achieve with such policies and the *assignments* that have been given to business in each policy area. Three basic objectives of business-related social policies are identified in Table 15-1: to accomplish broad societal goals; to protect society from business; and to safeguard workers.

Some social policies use companies to achieve societal objectives that have no necessary relationship to business. Governments need revenues, and businesses maintain continuing relationships with large numbers of workers and have payroll and accounting systems that can be used to collect the funds governments need. Modern governments provide retirement and unemployment insurance programs, and businesses are required to support these projects. The United States has been slow to adopt family policies, but current proposals to provide maternity, parenting, and childcare assistance often rely on business contributions. In the first section of this chapter I explore retirement and health care issues and the role of business in achieving broad societal goals.

Other government policies protect society from injury caused by business. Governments maintain the quality of professional services offered to the public by requiring occupational groups such as doctors, lawyers, plumbers, engineers, and school teachers to secure licenses. Numerous consumer products, foods, medical devices, and drugs may not be sold to the public unless government certifies them to be safe. Government also protects citizens by regulating product labeling and advertising, and it preserves the environment by restricting business products and

Table 15-1   Objectives of Social Policies Affecting Business

Policies to achieve societal goals
    Revenue systems
    Retirement programs
    Health care
    Family policies

Policies to protect society from business
    Occupational licensing
    Consumer protection
    Food and drug quality
    Environmental protection

Policies to protect workers
    Minimum wage and hours
    Labor-management relations
    Equal employment opportunity
    Safe working conditions

practices. To illustrate this type of social policy and appraise the issues it raises, in the second section of this chapter I examine consumer protection policies.

Still other social policies define the relationship between workers and employers. Individual workers are at such a disadvantage dealing with employers that government has established procedures to ensure some measure of equity. Laws prevent the employment of children, establish minimum wage levels, and specify the hours that can be worked. Equal opportunity laws forbid employers from treating workers differently according to gender, race, or ethnicity, and occupational safety measures require firms to protect the health of employees in the workplace. Government also guarantees employees the right to form labor unions and to select representatives to bargain for them with employers. In the final section of this chapter I discuss social policies that affect corporations as employers.

POLICIES TO ACHIEVE SOCIETAL GOALS

The United States is often said to have less developed social welfare policies than comparable nations.[1] Most U.S. social policies, commentators point out, were not inaugurated until late in the game, had only limited significance until the 1930s, and involved relatively low levels of public spending.[2] Although this description contains elements of truth, it also ignores key features of the American historical experience. The United States experienced a broad measure of popular suffrage and the emergence of citizen-based political parties early in the nineteenth century. Industrialization, the advent of corporate hierarchies, and the growth of labor unions occurred in the second half of the century, and large government bureaucracies appeared in the first decades of the twentieth century.

The sequence of historical development saw democracy appear first in the United States, then industrialization, and finally the administrative state. In other countries, government bureaucracies appeared earlier in the process of development, whereas industrialization and democracy came later.

As a consequence of this sequence of development, corporations play a larger role in social policies in the United States than in our other nations.[3] Corporations began to provide health and pension benefits in the United States before the national government had the organizational capacity to administer such programs. Even after national social welfare policies were enacted, government continued to rely on employers to help enforce and administer public programs because of their competence, sophistication, and acceptance. In fact, without a relationship to an employer, an individual cannot receive unemployment compensation or disability insurance. Rather than a single unified national program to provide health care or support retirees, the United States has a series of quasi-public, quasi-private social welfare systems that link together the resources of employers, governments, insurance firms, and private citizens in complex ways.

Employer expenditures for nonsalary personnel costs have grown from one-half of 1 percent of the gross domestic product in 1929 to more than 10 percent in the 1990s.[4] The American Express Company created the nation's first company pension program in 1875 in response to demographic changes then sweeping the country. Urbanization had contributed to the dissolution of the extended family, leaving no one to care for older citizens, and longer life expectancies forced companies to devise a socially acceptable method of replacing less efficient older employees with more vigorous younger ones. In 1916 an amendment to the federal tax code allowed companies to deduct payments to retirees from their income tax base, and after 1919, donations to employee pension funds could also be deducted. By 1930 essentially all railroads had established pension programs for their workers, but only about 15 percent of industrial workers were covered by pension programs, with some plans requiring fifteen to thirty years of service prior to pension eligibility. Most employer pension systems continued to provide benefits during the Great Depression, but 7 percent of the plans were canceled, and others were curtailed or modified.

The passage of the Social Security Act of 1935 did not replace employer pension programs. With people retiring earlier and living longer, and with the federal income tax placing an increasing burden on private savings, retirement expenditures both by companies and through the Social Security system grew rapidly after World War II. Government regulation of employer retirement systems began with the enactment by Congress of the Employee Retirement Income Security Act (ERISA) in 1974. This legislation increased the stability of private plans and the likelihood that retirees would receive their benefits by imposing standards for minimum funding and proper management, and these requirements were tightened by additional legislation in subsequent years. Owing to increased regulation of traditional defined-benefit pension plans, the popularity of defined-contribution retirement plans grew rapidly after 1975. The defined-benefit plans promise to pay retirees a specific amount each year after they stop working, but the defined-contribution systems require employers only to deposit a set amount in each employee's retirement fund at periodic intervals. The employer's liability in defined-contribution plans is limited to making the deposits, and the worker then becomes responsible for managing the funds in the account.

The United States relies more on employers and less on public agencies to provide health insurance than any other major country.[5] The original model for providing national health care was established in Germany in 1883.[6] This program was based on employment: workers and employers in particular industries were required to contribute to an insurance fund that would cover the costs of medical care and pay half the salary of incapacitated workers. Newer health care systems in countries such as Canada have created national insurance programs that cover all residents and pay for medical services on a national or state basis. A third type of scheme is a national health service plan patterned after the program in Great Britain, where a national health service covers all residents and directly provides medical and hospital care free of charge.

U.S. companies began to provide health care to workers after the Civil War. Some firms found that it was in their interest to have a healthy workforce, and other enterprises were located in unsettled areas where medical care was not otherwise available. Although controlling health care and binding workers to companies were sufficient reasons for some firms to provide medical care, most employers did not offer health care at the beginning of the twentieth century. Although insurance was available, medical costs were then low and most workers did not use it.

During the Progressive Era, proposals for government-sponsored universal health insurance were widely debated, but they were opposed by doctors, who feared third parties would gain influence over their practices; by companies, which worried that employees would have more justification to avoid work; and by unions, which concluded that government-sponsored benefits would undermine worker loyalty to unions. During the 1920s medical costs rose, and health insurance became more popular. During the Great Depression, insurance was attractive to workers, who wanted access to care, and it was worthwhile for health care providers, who wanted to ensure that their bills would be paid. The expansion of corporate health insurance plans during World War II resulted from the need of employers to attract qualified workers when they were barred by wartime controls from raising employee salaries, and insurance companies found that contracts with large companies were a good way to hold down administrative costs.

In 1965 two government programs were enacted to provide health care to groups that had difficulty participating in the private insurance market, the aged and the poor. Medicare provides insurance benefits for the aged, and Medicaid offers grants to states to cover part of the cost of medical assistance to the poor. Despite the enactment of these public programs, two-thirds of all nonelderly Americans received health care in the 1990s through voluntary employer-sponsored programs.

Corporations play three distinct roles in social programs.[7] In public programs that require universal participation, such as Social Security and unemployment insurance, government provides benefits directly to recipients, but it requires employers to enforce worker participation in the programs and collect the requisite taxes. In other programmatic areas, government subsidizes employee benefits that are provided by employers. Government provides favorable tax treatment for corporate pension and health care expenditures, and these tax subsidies are adequate legal justification for government to regulate the operation of the programs. Government, for example, limits the amount of compensation that can be paid in tax-free pension benefits, and its "antidiscrimination" rules require that pension and health care plans operate according to its standards of equity and inclusiveness. In addition to the programs that government mandates or supports, corporations also become purchasing agents for social benefits for their employees. Large employers can purchase life insurance and health insurance policies at lower cost than individuals or small groups can, and thus companies can save money and inspire goodwill among employees by offering these benefits at little or no cost to themselves.

Employers play the primary role in helping society achieve its retirement and health care objectives, and they will bear many of the costs as the nation decides that individuals should no longer shoulder the burdens of family life alone. Gregory Acs and Eugene Steuerle point out, however, that this partially public and partially private benefit system has serious shortcomings. Most disturbing are small declines that have occurred in the past two decades in the proportion of workers whose employers pay all or part of their health insurance premiums and in the percentage of workers who participate in employer-sponsored pension plans.[8]

One distinctive feature of the U.S. health care system is its extraordinary cost.[9] In 2001 the United States spent far more on health care than any other major industrial country, more than 14 percent of gross domestic product, in contrast to Switzerland and Germany, the runners-up, which spent 11 percent of GDP.[10] For twenty-five years, business and government have sought "cost containment" strategies for health care expenditures, but the results have been uneven.[11] Companies originally provided health care to employees as a fringe benefit without requiring employees to share the costs. To restrain medical costs, businesses now seek to require employees to pay the first few hundred dollars of medical costs per year and also to pay 10 or 20 percent of subsequent bills.

Businesses have also supported the creation of prepaid group-health programs called health maintenance organizations (HMOs). Proponents argue that HMOs can take a long-term view of the health of a patient, realize economies of scale in providing care, and benefit from more systematic supervision of the provision of care. Because employers receive tax deductions for health care expenditures, government can define the services provided by employer-sponsored health plans, and mandated changes in coverage have continually increased the already high costs employers bear.[12] In addition, federal programs to reduce the government's medical expenditures have limited the rates government pays under Medicare and Medicaid. The subsequent government rates are lower than the rates charged to private health plans and often, critics say, less than the actual costs of providing the services. Doctors and hospitals make up the shortfall by increasing the prices charged to private-sector patients, and an increasing share of these costs are ultimately paid by employers.

Some large companies and insurance carriers have the market power to negotiate their own discounts with health care providers. One consequence of these discounts is that more health care costs are absorbed by small businesses and individuals. Faced with skyrocketing costs, an increasing number of small businesses, whose workers are usually young and healthy, are choosing not to provide health insurance, and this trend adds to the number of workers not covered by health care plans and compounds the difficulties of the millions of Americans who do not receive consistent health care.[13]

Over the past decade, corporate contributions to nonsalary benefits as a percentage of total personnel costs have leveled off, and company involvement in efforts to contain health care expenditures has increased. These efforts could place increased responsibility on individuals, as now appears to be occurring in retirement investment, could expand government mandates for employer social programs, or could assign more direct responsibility to government for the provision of services. Although most policy proposals advocate some combination of these three options, it is likely that the existing corporate role in social welfare policies will be maintained or augmented.

POLICIES TO PROTECT SOCIETY FROM BUSINESS

The consumer protection movement in the United States appeared in three distinct epochs and encompassed an enormous diversity of topics. The first era began at the start of the twentieth century and was embodied in the Pure Food and Drug Act and the Meat Inspection Act of 1906. The second period, which crystallized in the 1930s, found expression in laws designed to protect the consumer against false advertising and misleading labeling. The third period reached its high-water mark in the mid-1970s and was characterized by product-safety legislation and automobile regulation; this era is the focus of our analysis.

The Federal Trade Commission and the Consumer Product Safety Commission (CPSC) are independent regulatory agencies that focus on consumer protection issues.[14] The FTC was created by the Federal Trade Commission Act of 1914 to prevent unfair, deceptive, or fraudulent commercial practices. Although originally empowered to act only when a company was harmed by improper commercial practices, the FTC actually became a consumer protection agency with the enactment of the Wheeler-Lea Act in 1938. In addition to its antitrust responsibilities (discussed in Chapter 12), the FTC, through its Bureau of Consumer Protection, is mandated to protect consumers by means of investigations, cease-and-desist orders, and consent decrees.

In 1969 the FTC was pilloried in one of the earliest Ralph Nader investigations of government agencies as an organization immersed in trivia and neglectful of major issues.[15] When the Nader critique was echoed by the American Bar Association and a range of other groups, the agency's staff was enlarged and professionalized, and the Federal Trade Commission Improvements Act of 1975 was enacted, authorizing the commission to concentrate on industrywide rule making to block unfair commercial practices rather than relying on case-by-case adjudication. The FTC's rule-making process offered extensive opportunities for anyone to appraise and comment on proposed regulations, and the FTC subsidized organizations to advocate viewpoints in its proceedings that it thought were not being adequately represented.

The CPSC was created in 1972 in response to a recommendation by a national study commission appointed by President Lyndon B. Johnson, which had found that 20 million American consumers were injured each year by unsafe products, resulting in 30,000 deaths.[16] Consumer groups carried the day over the opposition of President Nixon and industry lobbyists, and the CPSC was established by the Consumer Product Safety Act, with a mandate to act against the "unreasonable risks of injury" that might result from consumer products. Like the FTC, the CPSC has five commissioners and a small staff. The commission stresses public information and distributes publications on consumer safety, but it also has recourse to the same regulatory tools possessed by the FTC.

Recognizing the opposition of the president, Congress originally maximized citizen participation in the CPSC's rule-making process by authorizing any person to petition the agency to establish a national safety standard for specific products.[17] The CPSC was required to respond to a petition within 120 days, and reasons for the denial of a petition were to be published in the *Federal Register* and were subject to review in a federal district court. When the petitions for rules swamped the commission's capacity to organize a logical regulatory agenda, Congress curtailed the most burdensome participatory procedures, but delays in CPSC actions were common. Enforcement activities focus on information dissemination, education, and industry guidance, but the CPSC can also seek civil penalties and fines.

In the 1970s the FTC chose an adversarial relationship with business and recruited activist attorneys with strong ties to the consumer movement for its staff, whereas the CPSC worked with companies and business associations to devise product standards that would minimize compliance costs. For both commissions Democratic presidents usually selected heads who championed activist regulatory policies and were skeptical of voluntary business compliance; Republican presidents typically nominated commission heads who endorsed self-regulation and advocated administrative procedures that limited their agencies' interventionist initiatives. As was the case with most independent regulatory commissions, Congress maintained close relations with both agencies through the budgetary and oversight processes.

The decade of the 1970s embraced the consumer protection movement, and the FTC responded with investigations into new product areas and rule-making proceedings that promised to impose industrywide regulations on activities that had previously been left to corporate judgment. The FTC became a national symbol for excessive regulation and aggressive bureaucracy, and business responded by mobilizing its resources through the efforts of the U.S. Chamber of Commerce, the National Association of Manufacturers, the American Medical Association, the National Association of Broadcasters, the Association of National Advertisers, the National Automobile Dealers Association, the Grocery Manufacturers of America, and the National Funeral Directors Association.[18] The political assault on the FTC reached into every congressional district, and the Democratic Congress and president moved promptly to restrain the agency.[19] Authorizing a continuation of the previous year's funding rather than passing the agency's budget for the years 1977 to 1980, Congress enacted the Federal Trade Commission Improvements Act of 1980, which required the FTC to submit draft regulations to Congress sixty days before they were to go into effect and exempted certain product areas from FTC regulations altogether.

Faced with White House opposition, the CPSC had difficulty even establishing itself as an organization. President Nixon was slow to make the initial appointments, the officials nominated had little credibility in Congress or among consumer groups, and the agency encountered delays in acquiring resources and assembling a staff. The CPSC was subsequently criticized for its lack of accomplishments, and President Carter considered abolishing the agency. After lobbying by consumer groups, the CPSC's mandate was reauthorized for three years, its performance improved, and it avoided major conflicts with industry.

The Reagan administration believed that the stagnation of the nation's economy was exacerbated by excessive government regulation, and it moved to implement its deregulatory principles. Faced with a Democratic Congress, the Reagan White House did not mount a legislative campaign to amend the nation's regulatory statutes but concentrated instead on administrative action. It sought to accomplish its goals through the appointment to top regulatory posts of supporters who shared its beliefs, reductions in regulatory agency budgets, and the introduction of economic analyses into commission decision-making procedures. Economists and lawyers with economic training were installed in key posts throughout the FTC, and they championed the reliance on markets rather than on the adoption and enforcement of new regulations to punish commercial misconduct. The administration had placed the analytic hurdles that had to be satisfied before regulatory action could begin so high that the regulatory activities of the FTC were drained of whatever vigor they had left.

The CPSC fared no better. It experienced a 24 percent cut in its budget after President Reagan took office, and the reauthorization of its statute by Congress required it to invite industries affected by its rules to provide technical assistance and to suggest voluntary standards to ensure product safety. The CPSC had lost much of its independence during the reauthorization process, and Congress then failed to appropriate funds to replace departing commissioners or staff members. The George H. W. Bush administration halted the efforts to dismantle the nation's regulatory structure, but the agencies were divided up between the Bush moderates and the ideological opponents of regulation, and little progress was made in rebuilding the FTC and the CPSC.

The 1992 Clinton presidential campaign had emphasized the need to reform the regulatory policies of the Reagan-Bush era, and consumer activists hoped that the Clinton administration would create a new golden age for consumer protection, but the results were equivocal. The FTC continued the quest to create an innovative style of regulation based on economic analysis and public participation, but it ended up with little to show for its efforts. It was more active in the new regulatory arenas introduced by the internationalization of economic activity and the Internet. Ann Brown, the new head of the CPSC, was a well-known figure in the consumer protection community, and she rekindled a spirit of activism at the agency, but the centrism of the Clinton administration and the skepticism of a Republican Congress restrained her efforts. The commission emphasized its innovative approaches to protecting consumers, but its actions favored voluntary industry standards and public-private partnerships.

Support for consumer protection policies has normally been impressively broad in the United States but also quite shallow. These policies have delivered small, widely dispersed benefits and imposed heavy, concentrated costs. The fragile consensus in favor of using the broad powers of government to advance the welfare of consumers can be shaken by the mobilization of activists in any quarter. The reformers of the 1970s were frustrated by the failure of the administrative reforms of the New Deal and the Great Society to reshape American values, but, as Richard Harris and Sidney Milkis argue, the organized consumer movement "has not always been in harmony with the public it purports to represent."[20] Consumer groups, they point out, have relied on administrative and legal channels to accomplish their goals and bypassed the country's mass political institutions. Business groups spearheaded a concerted political attack at the end of the 1970s that succeeded in restraining the activists in the FTC and the CPSC, but the industry-directed confrontation was succeeded by an ideological challenge to the existence of the agencies themselves that remains unresolved. There is little evidence of the emergence of a new regulatory regime that can accommodate the interests of the various groups. Deadlock and divisiveness have marginalized the traditional consumer protection agencies, and the resolution of contemporary consumer issues is being increasingly achieved through litigation and product-liability suits.

POLICIES TO PROTECT WORKERS

Each day 100 million Americans go to work, but public policy has not kept pace with the changes that have occurred in their workplace relationships.[21] Employees are potential assets for their employers, but labor-management relations statutes envision a contest over the spoils rather than a process for providing mutual gains for workers and shareholders. Legislation protecting employees assumes a stable workforce treated in uniform ways by a single employer over a considerable period of time, but contemporary corporate practices emphasize the dynamism of global best practices, the networking of Silicon Valley high-tech entrepreneurs, and the contracting-out of an ever-growing array of services. Analyses of corporate hierarchies are now joined by discussions of decentralized decision making, flattened organizational structures, flexible institutional boundaries, and cultural diversity.

Labor Unions

Labor unions were invented to protect their members from workplace abuse, and they grew into powerful bargaining agents for workers between 1930 and 1950. Unions gained effective immunity from prosecution under antitrust laws with the passage of the Norris-LaGuardia Act in 1932, and they prospered with the emergence of the modern system of labor relations, based on the National Labor Relations Act (Wagner-Connery Act) of 1935. This law guaranteed employees the right to bargain collectively with employers, and it required companies to deal with legally constituted labor organizations and prohibited them from engaging in "unfair labor practices" such as firing a worker for being a union member. The Wagner-Connery Act established a permanent National Labor Relations Board to administer the law, investigate complaints, and issue orders to halt actions that violated the law.

As corporations began to emphasize higher-value-added products and put a premium on higher-level skills, unions began to encounter more restrictive legislative action. The Labor-Management Relations Act (Taft-Hartley Act) of 1947 made unions liable for damages resulting from breach of contract, banned a variety of restrictive union practices, and authorized an eighty-day cooling-off period for strikes that might affect the national health or safety. Unions were required to submit annual financial reports, hold fair elections, and conduct their business in accordance with basic democratic rules. The act also created a Federal Mediation and Conciliation Service to reduce the number of strikes by providing federal mediators when labor and management could not agree.

Collective bargaining rather than compulsory arbitration or government decisions has been the preferred choice of American unions to resolve labor-management disputes. Labor contracts usually govern the terms and conditions of employment, including such items as wages, hours, fringe benefits, vacations, and grievance procedures. Contracts can also include specific work rules defining the tasks performed by workers, specifying the number of available employees, restricting the workload to be performed in a given time period, and stipulating the amount of work space required to perform various tasks.

The interpretations of the National Labor Relations Act by the NLRB over the years have determined the precise coverage and requirements of the law. Even though the NLRB's rulings often reflect the policies of incumbent administrations, the nation's collective-bargaining system has remained essentially unchanged since the 1930s.

Although unions usually rely on collective bargaining to advance the interests of their members, they also pursue legislative strategies to secure specific goals. The Davis-Bacon Act, for example, requires contractors to pay high union wage rates on federal construction projects even though equally skilled workers may be available at lower wage rates. Government regulation of labor-management relations spurred the growth of labor unions in the 1930s and 1940s, and it also resulted in the expansion of corporate personnel departments and the hiring of human resource specialists. The years between 1980 and 2005 witnessed a continued decline in union membership and increased managerial discretion in guiding corporate operations. A partisan deadlock over labor-management issues has impeded efforts to adapt New Deal–era statutes to the reality of the new workplace environment.

Government Standards

Safety and equity in the workplace are achieved through government standards as well as through the negotiations of labor unions. The Fair Labor Standards Act of 1938, for example, forbade child labor, guaranteed a minimum wage, and instituted a maximum forty-hour work week for businesses operating in interstate commerce. Other government standards protect workers in the areas of equal employment opportunity and occupational safety.

Equal Employment Opportunity. The 1960s and 1970s witnessed a growing public awareness that the American ideal of equal opportunity was more preached than practiced. The Civil Rights Act of 1964 is the cornerstone of federal policy to prevent discrimination in the workplace. Title VII forbids employers, labor unions, and government agencies from discriminating among employees on the basis of race, color, sex, religion, or national origin in regard to hiring, firing, wages, promotions, fringe benefits, and the like. At the same time, section 703 also states that the title does not require "preferential treatment" to be given to any group or individual because of an "imbalance" in employment patterns. The Civil Rights Act created the Equal Employment Opportunity Commission (EEOC), a five-person board whose members are appointed for five-year terms by the president, and charged it with the responsibility of implementing the law. The powers of the commission were originally limited to investigating complaints and promoting conciliation, and little was accomplished.

The enforcement powers of the EEOC were enhanced by the Equal Employment Opportunity Act of 1972. The new law gave the commission power to initiate court actions and to investigate company records to uncover patterns of discrimination. The EEOC's jurisdiction was also expanded in 1972, and it was given authority over all private employers with more than fifteen workers, including educational institutions, employment agencies, labor unions, and apprenticeship programs.

Another series of laws extended nondiscrimination principles to cover other circumstances. The 1963 Equal Pay Act prohibited wage discrimination among workers because of sex, and the Pregnancy Discrimination Act of 1978 required employers to treat pregnancy and childbirth as a disability under fringe-benefit plans and to guarantee reinstatement of women on leave for pregnancy-related reasons. The Age Discrimination in Employment Act of 1967 outlaws job discrimination on the basis of age; the Vocational Rehabilitation Act of 1973 seeks to ensure equal opportunity for handicapped persons. The Veterans Readjustment Assistance Act of 1974 requires government contractors to take affirmative action to employ and advance veterans of the Vietnam era, and the 1991 Americans with Disabilities Act guarantees the civil rights of the disabled in employment and access to buildings of public accommodation. Mexico's efforts to improve social conditions for its workers are examined in Box 15-1.

More contentious employment, contracting, and admissions disputes arise when consideration shifts from nondiscrimination to more positive forms of affirmative action. The 1964 Civil Rights Act prohibits "preferential treatment" to correct imbalance in employment patterns, but affirmative actions are frequently authorized to compensate for past discrimination. Defining the nature of past discrimination and shaping appropriate remedial programs remain controversial. The U.S. Supreme Court, for example, approved by a 5–4 margin a court order requiring a local sheet metal union to meet a minority hiring target of 29 percent.[22] The majority justified the order by writing that

Cases in Development
BOX 15-1 MEXICAN SOCIAL POLICY OBJECTIVES

Political leaders believe that Mexico should be doing a better job for its workers that it is. The Organisation for Economic Development and Cooperation (OECD) concludes that Mexico's annual rate of economic growth has the potential of exceeding 6 percent, but in 2004 the country's real economic growth was estimated to have reached only 1.3 percent. In the mid-1980s Mexico's political leadership shifted its economic policy from an import substitution strategy that focused on producing goods for the domestic market to a policy that lowered international trade barriers and emphasized manufacturing products for export markets. Unfortunately this policy shift did not yield the economy-wide improvements in productivity, employment, and social well-being that had been anticipated.

In the 1990s high rates of population growth in Mexico produced an annual increase in the working age population of more than 4 percent, or approximately 1.4 million, and labor force participation increased dramatically. The official unemployment rate remained low at 3.3 percent, but this was largely because Mexico considers anyone to be employed who works one hour per week, even if that person works for no pay in a family activity. Although the official unemployment rate appeared low, the rate of underemployment was estimated to top 25 percent. The dominant trend in employment in the last decade has been a decline in the proportion of workers engaged in wage-earning positions at stable companies and a corresponding increase in the proportion of workers in self-employed, low-wage, low-value-added, or unpaid positions.

Recent years have been times of price and monetary stability, but they have also been a period of widening wage gaps among Mexican workers. While wages for less-educated, low-skilled workers have stagnated or fallen in the last decade, the salaries of better-educated, more highly skilled workers have risen, even in the face of the 1994–95 economic crisis. Mexico has scored some successes by increasing exports, but more incentives are needed to encourage firms and workers to operate in the formal sector of the economy, in which productivity, wages, and investment returns are higher. Unless Mexico can extend the social benefits of its export-driven economy to a large share of workers, it is likely to be edged out of its international markets by Chinese goods.

Sources: "Tequila Slammer," www.economist.com/PrinterFriendly.cfm?Story_ID=3524948, accessed February 10, 2005; Carlos Salas and Eduardo Zepeda, "Employment and Wages: Enduring the Costs of Liberalization and Economic Reform," in *Confronting Development: Assessing Mexico's Economic and Social Policy Challenges*, ed. Kevin J. Middlebrook and Eduardo Zepeda (Stanford, Calif.: Stanford University Press, 2003), 523–25, 549–55; Central Intelligence Agency, *The World Factbook—Mexico*, www.cia.gov/cia/publications/factbook/print/mx.htm, accessed January 11, 2005.

the union had practiced "pervasive and egregious" discrimination, but the minority maintained that remedies short of quotas should be used when needed and that such remedies were permissible only when they did not harm innocent nonminority workers.

Occupational Safety and Health. The Occupational Safety and Health Act of 1970 was passed by lopsided votes in both the Senate (83–3) and the House of Representatives (383–5). Its purpose was "to assure so far as possible every working man and woman in the nation safe and healthful working conditions."[23] The Occupational Safety and Health Administration (OSHA) was instructed to reduce hazards in the workplace, improve existing health and safety programs, and to establish mandatory health and safety standards.

OSHA combines executive and judicial functions. It establishes standards for particular substances such as benzene or cotton dust that might harm workers' health and bars workplace practices it regards as unsafe. The enforcement of OSHA standards occurs through inspections of company facilities by OSHA compliance officers, who determine whether the appropriate standards have been met or citations should be issued for probable violations. If an employer contests a citation, the case is sent to the Occupational Safety and Health Review Commission, OSHA's judicial arm, where an administrative law judge hears the case. The judge's decision may then be appealed to the full commission, the U.S. Court of Appeals, and the U.S. Supreme Court.

Workplace health and safety are complex issues, and OSHA's good intentions win wide praise, but OSHA has become one of the most controversial agencies in the federal government. Business groups charge that OSHA has established trivial standards unrelated to health and safety, that enforcement is so inconsistent as to constitute harassment, and that the agency has not produced results that are in any way commensurate with the costs it has imposed. Union representatives insist that the OSHA statute is sound and that the agency has helped defend the health and safety of American workers. They maintain that OSHA would have even greater impact if its standards were tightened up and its enforcement procedures strengthened.

Controversy centers on two issues. The first is whether or not OSHA's standards should emerge from a process that includes an evaluation of the costs and benefits of specific rules. The original legislation does not explicitly recognize the possibility of a trade-off between costs and benefits. OSHA has interpreted the language of the statute to mean that costs should not be considered in establishing most health and safety standards. When business organizations protested that it was unreasonable to ignore costs, the Supreme Court ruled that Congress could have included a cost-benefit test for OSHA standards if it had intended such a standard to be invoked.[24] Cost-benefit tests, the Court wrote, would inevitably lead to less rigorous standards, and Congress had sought more protection for workers, essentially regardless of cost.

The second area of controversy appraises OSHA's record. Academic researchers do not agree on whether OSHA's activities have actually reduced the incidence of workplace injuries. Researchers who focus on aggregate data use statistical analyses that have been unable to link improvements in injury and illness rates with OSHA's efforts. Other studies have examined specific plants or pieces of machinery before and after the inauguration of OSHA standards. These studies have discovered improvements in health and safety, but they have not considered whether these improvements would have occurred without OSHA action.

Labor unions took important steps to protect workers in the era of the 1930s to the 1950s, and government programs enhanced the status of employees in the period between the 1950s and the 1980s. Labor unions, however, are no longer able to move workers with limited skills and education into the middle class, and the ability of statutes to protect workers in the twenty-first century is increasingly circumscribed. To survive and prosper, corporations need to recruit high-quality workers, create conditions that utilize and enhance their skills, devise structures that fulfill their ambitions, and embrace organizational arrangements that sustain diversity, flexibility, and adaptation. There is little evidence that government, unions, or employers have yet identified practices to achieve these goals.

ASSESSMENT AND IMPLICATIONS

Business has played an especially prominent role in the United States in providing social-welfare benefits, shaping consumer protection policies, and defining workplace conditions for millions of Americans. Sometimes companies have been guided by their narrow interests in these endeavors, as in their determined opposition to labor unions and their insistence on paying astonishing, perhaps obscene, salaries to top executives. In general, however, as Lester Thurow has argued, business has reflected the basic values and standards of the public when engaging in its social activities.[25]

In each area we have examined, there is evidence that the social dimensions of business activity are not being conducted as successfully today as in the past. Corporate social benefits are being received by a smaller proportion of workers, and the costs of providing these benefits are escalating. Consumer protection debates have degenerated into contention and division, and the progress necessary to devise new regulatory principles for this critical policy area appears stalled. The professional ambitions and desires of highly trained employees cry out for attention, but corporations and labor unions appear almost oblivious of the need to shape a new workplace environment. The lesson of relations between government and business in past eras and other policy domains is that these challenges are most successfully met when both sides are in a position to contribute to imaginative and innovative responses to national problems.

SUMMARY

Business plays a larger role in social policies in the United States than in our other countries, and the contributions made by business are critical to the effectiveness of the policies. Companies began to provide health and pension benefits for workers before the national government had the resources to support such programs, and now most working age Americans rely on employers to pay most health care costs. As health and pension costs soar, however, efforts by companies to contain their costs jeopardize the current voluntary arrangements. U.S. consumer protection policies have a distinguished history, but the growth of partisanship, litigiousness, and interest group conflict has distracted attention from the important benefits that accrue to the society from these policies. Partisan struggles over labor-management issues have also impaired efforts to adapt New Deal thinking to capture the opportunities of the new workplace environment. Corporations are intended to be profit-making institutions, and disregard of the ways in which businesses sustain social programs places the future of the society in peril.

I have argued in this book that the best way to understand the dynamics of American political economy is to investigate the relationships between government and business. Although both sets of institutions suffer from flaws and imperfections, the success of American capitalism depends on the capacity of each to be an active partner in the revitalization of the other.[26] Under the rules of the U.S. system, government has influenced the country's ultimate economic decisions, and economic groups have participated in the most basic political judgments. When faced with the need for reform and renewal, whether in social policy, corporate governance, regulation, or technology policy, the United States has been able to draw on multiple traditions and so avoid solutions based on a single doctrine or ideology. When systemic challenges have been permitted to fester, such as in the need for reform of political finance, the legitimacy of both sectors has suffered.

The current relationship between government and business in the United States rests on the public conclusion that the relative independence of business provides greater benefits than would be achieved through tighter government controls. Each era, however, must reconsider this judgment in light of its own needs and aspirations. As has been demonstrated in the past, no single alignment of government and business can offer a permanent solution to the nation's problems. Each new era must strive to reform and revitalize both government and business so that each sector can be a source of strength for the other.

FURTHER READINGS

The Web site of the Federal Trade Commission promises that it is "working for consumer protection and a competitive marketplace"; see http://www.ftc.gov/. At its home page, the Consumer Product Safety Commission insists that it is "saving lives and keeping families safe"; see http://www.cpsc.gov/. Both Web sites provide information about their respective organizations, their rules, and regulations. The National Labor Relations Board Web site offers its press releases, public notices, and decisions at http://www.nlrb.gov/. The Occupational Safety and Health Administration Web site is found at http://www.osha.gov.

Adolino, Jessica R., and Charles H. Blake. *Comparing Public Policies: Issues and Choices in Six Industrialized Countries.* Washington, D.C.: CQ Press, 2001.

Glazer, Amihai, and Lawrence S. Rothenberg. *Why Government Succeeds and Why It Fails.* Cambridge, Mass.: Harvard University Press, 2001.

Levy, David L., and Peter J. Newell, eds. *The Business of Global Environmental Governance.* Cambridge, Mass.: MIT Press, 2005.

Rothstein, Bo, and Sven Steinmo, eds. *Restructuring the Welfare State: Political Institutions and Policy Change.* New York: Palgrave Macmillan, 2002.

Wunnava, Phanindra V. *The Changing Role of Unions: New Forms of Representation.* Armonk, N.Y.: M. E. Sharpe, 2004.

NOTES

1. This section relies on Edwin Amenta and Theda Skocpol, "Taking Exception: Explaining the Distinctiveness of American Public Policies in the Last Century," in *The Comparative History of Public Policy,* ed. Francis G. Castles (New York: Oxford University Press, 1989), 292–333.
2. Margaret S. Gordon, *Social Security Policies in Industrial Countries: A Comparative Analysis* (New York: Cambridge University Press, 1988).
3. Mansel G. Blackford, *The Rise of Modern Business in Great Britain, the United States and Japan* (Chapel Hill: University of North Carolina Press, 1988); and Alfred D. Chandler Jr., "Government versus Business: An American Phenomenon," in *Business and Public Policy,* ed. John T. Dunlop (Cambridge, Mass.: Harvard Graduate School of Business Administration, 1980).
4. This section relies heavily on Gregory Acs and Eugene Steuerle, "The Corporation as a Dispenser of Welfare and Security," in *The American Corporation Today,* ed. Carl Kaysen (New York: Oxford University Press, 1996), 360–82, esp. 367.
5. In addition to ibid., see P. Starr, *The Social Transformation of American Medicine* (New York: Basic Books, 1982); and Jamilyn J. Field and Harold T. Shapiro, eds., *Employment and Health Benefits: A Connection at Risk* (Washington, D.C.: National Academy Press, 1993).
6. Gordon, *Social Security Policies,* 198–204.
7. Acs and Steuerle, "The Corporation as a Dispenser of Welfare and Security," 362–67.
8. Ibid., 376–77.
9. Gordon, *Social Security Policies,* 223–24.
10. U.S. Bureau of the Census, *Statistical Abstract of the United States* (Washington, D.C.: GPO, 2004), table 1330.
11. Patricia Munch Danzon, "Health Policy in 1984: The Crisis in Costs," in *To Promote Prosperity: U.S. Domestic Policy in the Mid-1980s,* ed. John H. Moore (Stanford, Calif.: Hoover Institution Press, 1984), 125–36.
12. Julie Kosterlitz, "Softening Resistance," *National Journal,* January 12, 1991, 64–68.
13. Julie Kosterlitz, "Unrisky Business," *National Journal,* April 6, 1991, 794–97.
14. This discussion is based on Richard A. Harris and Sidney M. Milkis, *The Politics of Regulatory Change: A Tale of Two Agencies,* 2nd ed. (New York: Oxford University Press, 1996); and Marc Allen Eisner, Jeff Worsham, and Evan J. Ringquist, *Contemporary Regulatory Policy* (Boulder, Colo.: Lynne Rienner, 2000), esp. chap. 9.
15. Edward F. Cox, Robert C. Fellmeth, and John E. Schultz, *The Nader Report on the Federal Trade Commission* (New York: Baron, 1969).

16. *Final Report of the National Commission on Product Safety* (Washington, D.C.: GPO, 1970).

17. Eisner, Worsham, and Ringquist, *Contemporary Regulatory Policy,* 208.

18. Ibid., 214.

19. Barry R. Weingast and Mark J. Moran, "Bureaucratic Discretion or Congressional Control? Regulatory Policymaking by the Federal Trade Commission," *Journal of Political Economy* 91 (1983): 765–800.

20. This statement and much of the argument in this section is based on Harris and Milkis, *Politics of Regulatory Change,* esp. 388, but also 367, 370, 387, 389.

21. This section is drawn from Thomas A. Kochan, "The American Corporation as an Employer: Past, Present, and Future Possibilities," in Kaysen, *American Corporation Today,* 242–68.

22. *Sheet Metal Workers of N.Y. Local 28 v. EEOC,* 54 U.S. 3596 (1986).

23. Occupational Safety and Health Act, Public Law 91-596.

24. *American Textile Manufacturers Institute, Inc. v. Donovan,* 69 U.S. 185 (1981).

25. Lester Thurow, "Almost Everywhere: Surging Inequality," in Kaysen, *American Corporation Today,* 383–413.

26. Robert Heilbroner, *21st Century Capitalism* (New York: Norton, 1994), 68, 70, 91, 130.

Glossary

Administrative guidance. The practice of Japanese administrative agencies encouraging corporations to act in ways that support the government's economic policies and objectives.

Aggregate demand. The sum of consumer spending, private investment, and government expenditures in an economy.

Alliance capitalism. A term used to emphasize the significance of long-term corporate affiliations in the Japanese economy.

Allocative efficiency. The extent to which the allocation of resources among various uses provides the greatest possible benefit.

Analog communications. A communications technology that uses electrical impulses to reproduce sound waves.

Antitrust policies. Policies that make it illegal to fix prices, restrain trade, or monopolize an industry.

Associationalism. A system of interest representation that stresses the role of industry or trade associations in the conduct of public policy.

Auditor. An impartial financial expert who examines and verifies an organization's accounts and records.

Balance of payments. A measure of the surplus or deficit a nation has in international trade and related financial activities. A country's balance of payments can be calculated on the basis of the value of products that are bought or sold across national borders, the value of goods and services traded cross-nationally, or its "current account" that includes goods and services as well as international investment income and unilateral financial transfers.

Balance sheet. A quantitative statement of a firm's assets, liabilities, and financial operations.

Board of directors. A group of individuals elected by a firm's shareholders to establish the firm's policies and select its senior management.

Bretton Woods Agreements. Post–World War II agreements concluded in 1944 to facilitate economy recovery that structured the World Bank, the International Monetary Fund, and the General Agreement on Tariffs and Trade.

Business cycle. Regular fluctuations in a country's economic well-being reflected in the rise and fall of growth rates, unemployment, income levels, prices, and similar indicators.

Capitalism. A form of economic organization in which there is substantial private ownership of the means of production, significant reliance on markets to allocate resources, and meaningful limits on governmental control of economic activity.

Capture theory. The theory that government regulatory agencies are dominated by industries or other groups that they regulate and that the policies of these agencies reflect the preferences of the regulated businesses or groups.

Cartel. Business association that can regulate production, set prices, and divide markets for the benefit of the firms in an industry.

Commerce clause. The clause of the U.S. Constitution (Article I, Section 8, Clause 3) that gives Congress the power to regulate interstate and foreign commerce, and this authority has become the constitutional justification for national regulation of almost all aspects of economic activity.

Committee on Political Education (COPE). A political organization established by the AFL-CIO to assist election campaigns of labor-backed political candidates.

Communism. An ideology that favors public ownership of the means of production and governmental allocation of economic resources.

Competition policy. A European term for antitrust policy.

Competitive advantage. The ability of one economic actor to produce a good or service at a lower cost than another.

Competitive market. A market in which no single buyer or seller is powerful enough to affect prices or other terms of sale of a product.

Competitive regulation. Competitive regulation focuses on the operations of an industry and seeks to create the conditions in the industry that would exist if perfect competition in the industry were possible. It concentrates on which firms may enter the industry, what prices they may charge, and what conditions in providing service may prevail.

Concurrent resolution. A congressional resolution passed by both the House of Representatives and the Senate that does not need the signature of the president to be valid.

Contract lobbyist. An independent lobbyist hired by a client to work on a specific governmental project.

Contract with America. A 1994 campaign proposal by congressional Republicans to reduce the role of government after which the Republicans unexpectedly won control of the House of Representatives.

Cooperative capitalism. A term usually used to highlight the tendency of the German economic system to encourage negotiated agreements among firms and between union representatives and corporate managers.

Coordinated market economy. A style of capitalism that relies on institutional arrangements to guide economic activity, as found in Germany and Japan.

Corporate governance. A system of government rules and industry practices that specifies who controls a company, how the senior managers are selected, how senior managers are held accountable, and how firms contribute to shareholder and public goals.

Corporation. A legal entity that allows investors to combine resources to go into a business while limiting their financial liability to the amount they have invested in the enterprise.

Corporatism. A governance model that posits that political systems that integrate labor and management organizations into the public policy process will function most successfully.

Derivative. A financial instrument whose value is derived from the value of another financial product or commodity.

Digital communications. A communications technology that translates all forms of messages into binary code of zeros and ones.

Direct investment. Investments in companies, plants, and equipment, usually implying an active role in the management of the assets.

Discount rate. The interest rate private banks must pay to borrow money from their regional Federal Reserve bank when their reserves fall below the required level. Changing the discount rate is one of the techniques used by the Federal Reserve Board to adjust the money supply in the national economy.

Dumping. In international trade, selling a product in one country at a price that is less than the cost of manufacturing the product in the country where it was made.

Economies of scale. The decline in per-unit production costs that normally accompanies increases in the number of units of goods and services provided.

Economies of scope. The cost savings that normally occur when a firm provides multiple goods or services that can benefit from the use of a common development, production, or distribution infrastructure.

Equities. Investments that carry the right to ownership of a small fraction of a company's assets, such as a share of stock.

Euro. The currency of a group of European nations, including Germany, France, Spain, Italy, and some other members of the European Union.

Factory system. A production system based on power-driven machinery, the interchangeability of parts, and continuous processing that replaced production by hand.

Federal funds rate. The interest rate Federal Reserve banks pay when they borrow funds from each other. Changing the federal funds rate is one technique used by the Federal Reserve Board to adjust the money supply in the national economy.

First mover advantages. The competitive benefits that accrue to the company that first brings a product to market.

Fiscal policy. Governmental policy that concerns raising revenues and authorizing expenditures for specific purposes and thus affecting the overall level of demand in the economy.

527 Committee. An entity authorized by the 2002 Bipartisan Campaign Reform Act, intended to raise money to support voter mobilization and issue advocacy, and named after a section of the tax code that regulates committee behavior.

Foreign direct investment. Investments by economic actors from one country in the one companies, plants, or equipment located in another country.

Framework state. A state whose principal task is to create the institutional structures in which its political and economic activity occurs.

Free trade policies. Governmental policies that neither impede or support the movement of goods across national borders.

Fringe benefit. A job benefit provided by an employer in addition to a salary, such as life insurance coverage.

Generic drugs. Drugs that are no longer protected by patents and, thus, may be produced and sold by any manufacturer.

Globalization. As an economic concept, globalization denotes an increase in cross-border commercial activity that today implies a deeper level of economic integration among countries than in past eras. Globalization can also be used to describe cultural, technological, or political conditions.

Grassroot lobbying. A lobbying technique that seeks to mobilize voters in local constituencies to express their view on a specific issue to public officials.

Gross domestic product (GDP). The value of all goods and services produced within a country's borders.

Gross national product (GNP). The value of all goods and services produced in facilities owned by a country's residents.

Home country. The country were a multinational corporation has its headquarters.

Horizontal merger. A merger between firms that make the same product.

Host country. The country where a multinational corporation is active but not headquartered.

Impoundment. The presidential refusal to spend funds appropriated by Congress due to the president's opposition to the purposes of the expenditures.

Industrial policy. Governmental action intended to improve a country's economic well-being through its impact on specific industries.

Infrastructure. Permanent, public facilities that support community and commercial activities.

Inside director. Members of a company's board of directors who are employed as executives by the company.

Interventionist philosophy. The doctrine that economic decisions are made best when government influences the choices of individuals and firms.

Iron triangle. A subgovernment whose stable membership represents congressional subcommittees, administrative agencies, and established interest groups.

Issue management. The process by which firms identify and respond to social and political developments that may affect their operations.

Issue network. A subgovernment with a fluid and inclusive membership including iron triangle participants, policy activities, advocacy groups, and academic specialists.

Keiretsu. Networks of Japanese companies that cooperate to address common problems in their businesses and in making and selling their products.

Keynesian economics. The economic theory that argues that government can manage economic activity by raising or lowering the level of demand for goods and services.

Laissez-faire philosophy. The doctrine that economic decisions are best made by individuals and firms whose actions are free of governmental restraints.

Liberal Democratic Party. The political party that has dominated Japanese government since 1955 and guided the nation's economic growth.

Liberal market economy. A style of capitalism that relies on market-oriented mechanism to structure economic activity, as in the United Kingdom and the United States.

Macroeconomics. The field of economics that seeks to explain the operations of the total economy, including such aspects as income, employment, and production.

Managerial capitalism. The tradition of corporate governance in which the chief executive monopolizes control of policy and operations.

Market. For economists, a forum where a large number of customers and merchants come together to buy and sell goods. For sociologists, the framework of rules and conditions that stabilize the marketplace and make transactions possible.

Market failure. Economists assume that markets function properly when a sufficiently large number of customers and merchants come together to exchange goods so that no one can affect the terms of the exchange, that consumers have full information about the consequences of any choice they might make, and that the pricing mechanism fully captures all the consequences of a purchase for the parties and the balance of society. When any of these conditions are not met, economists say that a market failure has occurred.

Mercantilism. The economy theory that understands wealth to be a fixed amount of treasure and assumes that government should direct economic activities so as to increase the nation's share of the world's treasure.

Microeconomics. The field of economics that seeks to explain the activities of individual households and firms.

Monetary policy. Government policy that adjusts the stock of money to control inflation, increase economic growth, and promote purposes of the national economy.

Money supply. The amount of money available in the national economy at a given time. The Federal Reserve Board defines money in three ways: M1 includes currency, checking accounts, traveler's checks, and deposits in checking-like accounts; the broader M2 definition includes M1 plus small saving accounts, small certificates of deposit, and money-market mutual funds; and the still broader M3 includes M2 plus time deposits and money-market balances held by large institutions.

Monopoly. Originally, a situation in which there is a single seller of a product or service in the marketplace and commonly used today to designate a situation in which a single seller or group of sellers can influence the price or terms at which a product or service is sold.

Multifiber arrangement. A agreement originally begun in 1974 under the auspices of the General Agreement on Tariffs and Trade that established product-by-product quotas for textile exports by developing nations.

Multinational corporation (MNC). A company that conducts operations on an international scale.

Nationalization. The involuntary seizure of private property by government.

Natural monopoly. A monopoly that results from special circumstances in the functioning of a industry rather than the efforts of individual firms to gain marketplace advantage.

New Deal. The political program of President Franklin D. Roosevelt that argued that government should use public resources and powers to cure the depression of the 1930s and promote equal opportunity and social justice.

Non-government organizations (NGO). Private organizations that promote humanitarian objectives in the international arena.

Non-tariff barriers. A policy or practice, other than a tax or duty, that impedes the importation of goods from one country to another.

Open-market operations. The purchase or sale of government debt by the Federal Reserve to influence the money supply or interest rates.

Organisation for Economic Co-operation and Development (OCED). An organization of thirty industrial nations including the United States, Japan, Canada, Mexico, South Korea, Australia, New Zealand, and a number of European nations that conducts research and provides a forum to discuss economic and social policies.

Outside director. Members of a company's board of directors who are not regular employees of the company and often come from law firms, banks, universities, and other community associations. The independence of outside directors is intended to assist them in evaluating impartially the performance of the senior management.

Peak organization. A business association whose members are other business associations rather than individuals or firms.

Personal capitalism. A term used to highlight the importance of family influence in the operation of British companies.

Pluralism. The theory that societies are composed of multiple power centers that compete with each other to shape public policy. This theory implies that no single group dominates the policy process.

Political action committee (PAC). An organization established by companies, unions, membership associations, or other institutions to raise campaign funds from individuals and disperse them under rules established by government.

Portfolio investment. Investments in stocks, bonds, or other equities, usually implying a passive role in the management of the assets.

Positive government. Government that enacts programs and policies to provide social services for the public.

Privatization. A government policy to provide a public service through a non-government agency or to transfer the ownership a formerly public agency to private individuals or organizations.

Procurement. Purchase of products and services usually for government purposes.

Product liability. The legal standard that determines the grounds on which manufacturers of products can be sued by consumers injured by use of products. Traditional liability law permitted suits if the product were defective, but later standards allow suits if a product is intrinsically harmful.

Productive efficiency. The extent to which production processes yield the greatest amount of goods using a fixed quantity of resources.

Productivity. A measure of the amount of good and services produced from a given quantity of resources.

Progressive movement. A political reform movement from the late 1800s to 1920 that favored direct democracy and withdrawing power from government institutions that were regarded as inherently corrupt. Progressives championed the direct election of U.S. senators, primary elections for nominating candidates, and initiative, referendum, and recall.

Property rights. The authority to determine how a specific asset is used in particular situations.

Proportional representation. An election system that allocates seats in a legislature to political parties on the basis of the party's share of the total vote cast.

Protectionism. Government tariffs or other policies that assist domestic firms by limiting the challenges posed by foreign competitors.

Protective regulation. Protective regulation seeks to guarantee that the impact of business operations on consumers, employees, and society satisfies governmental standards.

Reconciliation bill. A step in the congressional budget process that brings the appropriations decisions of committees into conformity with the spending totals established by Congress.

Regulation. Policy approach that seeks to achieve governmental purposes by stipulating how private institutions may behave in specific circumstances.

Reserve requirements. The percentage of deposits the Federal Reserve Board requires a bank to hold to ensure the stability of banking system.

Restraints of trade. Practices that hamper competition in the marketplace such as price fixing, production limits, efforts to eliminate competitors, and discriminatory treatment of retailers.

Rulemaking. Governmental rules drafted by administrative agencies and used to implement policies authorized by statute.

Seniority. The years of unbroken service in an organization such as Congress with preferences usually extended to those members with greater seniority.

Separation of powers. The assignment of government authority in one policy area to different institutions.

Shareholder or stockholder. A shareholder or stockholder is a person or institution that owns shares of a firm's stock and, thus, owns a share of its profits and assets and has a legal right to participate in its governance.

Sherman Antitrust Act. The 1890 law that bans monopolies and prohibits the restraint of trade and has provided the foundation of U.S. antitrust policy.

Social market economy. A term used to describe the combination of marketplace incentives and social benefits that characterize the German economy.

Socialism. An ideology that advocates governmental ownership of major industries and the extensive provision of social services.

Stakeholder. A societal group whose interests are affected by the actions of a corporation, such as employees, customers, local communities, shareholders, and suppliers.

Stock option. The right to purchase a share of company's stock at a designated price at some point in the future, often granted by a firm to its senior executives.

Subgovernments. A network of organizations that influences the conduct of public policy in specific areas. See Iron Triangle and Issue Network.

Supervisory board. The German system of corporate governance provides for both a supervisory board and a management board. The supervisory board is selected by shareholders and employees, and its main responsibility is to appoint the members of the management board.

Tariff. A tax charged on goods imported into one country from another country.

Think tank. A organization whose principal task is to examine policies and propose solutions to problems. Some think tanks are independent entities, and others are sponsored by interest groups or associations as part of a broader lobbying campaign.

Trade association. A membership association that represents businesses in a particular industry.

Treaty of Rome. An agreement signed by six nations in 1957 to establish the predecessor organization of the European Union.

Trust. A form of corporate ownership popular at the end of the nineteenth century in which the stock in companies in the same industry was surrendered to trustees who operated the resulting firm for the benefit of the ownership.

Vertical integration. The linkage within a single firm of different steps in the production and distribution of goods and services.

Vertical merger. A merger between companies that perform different steps in a production and distribution process.

Westminister democracy. Term use to describe British governing arrangements characterized by two strong programmatic parties, a prime minister selected by the parliament, a prominent cabinet, and a influential bureaucracy.

Wholesale price. The price charged by a manufacturer or distributor to a retail business.

Zaibatsu. Groups of companies owned by families in Japan's traditional economy.

Index